Adventuring
in East Africa

THE SIERRA CLUB ADVENTURE TRAVEL GUIDES

Adventuring in East Africa

THE SIERRA CLUB TRAVEL GUIDE

TO THE GREAT SAFARIS OF

KENYA, TANZANIA, RWANDA,

EASTERN ZAIRE, AND UGANDA

Allen Bechky

SIERRA CLUB BOOKS • SAN FRANCISCO

The Sierra Club, founded in 1892 by John Muir, has devoted itself to the study and protection of the earth's scenic and ecological resources — mountains, wetlands, woodlands, wild shores and rivers, deserts and plains. The publishing program of the Sierra Club offers books to the public as a non-profit educational service in the hope that they may enlarge the public's understanding of the Club's basic concerns. The point of view expressed in each book, however, does not necessarily represent that of the Club. The Sierra Club has some sixty chapters coast to coast, in Canada, Hawaii, and Alaska. For information about how you may participate in its programs to preserve wilderness and the quality of life, please address inquiries to Sierra Club, 730 Polk Street, San Francisco, CA 94109.

Library of Congress Cataloging in Publication Data

Bechky, Allen, 1947-
   Adventuring in East Africa: the Sierra Club travel guide to Kenya, Tanzania, Rwanda, Zaire, and Uganda / Allen Bechky.
      p.   cm.
   Bibliography: p. 427
   ISBN 0-87156-747-4
   1. Africa, East—Description and travel—1981- —Guide-books.   2. Zaire—Description and travel—1981- —Guide-books.   3. Safaris—Africa, East—Guide-books.   4. Safaris—Zaire—Guide-books.   5. Wildlife watching—Africa, East—Guide-books.   6. Wildlife watching—Zaire—Guide-books.   7. National parks and reserves—Africa, East—Guide-books.   8. National parks and reserves—Zaire—Guide-books.   9. Natural areas—Africa, East—Guide-books.   10. Natural areas—Zaire—Guide-books.   I. Sierra Club.   II. Title
DT422.B43   1990
916.7604'4—dc20   89-10572
                                                        CIP

Production by Eileen Max

Cover design by Bonnie Smetts

Book design by Laurie Anderson

Maps by Hilda Chen

Printed in the United States of America on acid-free paper containing a minimum of 50% recovered waste paper, of which at least 10% is post-consumer waste

10 9 8 7 6 5 4

Contents

Preface

Like so many Africa buffs, my love affair with the continent can be traced back to childhood, when my greatest treat was to be taken to the zoo. Although elephants and lions were my favorite animals, many of the less-than-cuddly creatures—such as snakes and crocodiles—held an almost equal fascination, and even then, the symbols that marked an animal a "vanishing species" always saddened me. As I went about growing up in the urban environs of New York City, the existence of wildlife and wild places receded from my consciousness; by the time I finished college, for all I knew, Africa's animals might have been as extinct as the dinosaurs. Luckily, a desire to see the world led me abroad, first to Europe and then to India. There I realized that I could indulge my boyhood fantasies about riding elephants through the jungle in search of Bengal tigers. Riding elephants turned out to be great fun, but finding tigers took plenty of time and hard work, and I soon found myself scouring the national parks of India. Ultimately I succeeded in finding my tigers, as well as a horde of exotic creatures previously unknown to me. In the process, I rediscovered my enthusiasm for wildlife and unleashed a boundless curiosity about the natural world. My next destination had to be Africa.

On that first safari, I journeyed on a shoestring budget. Carrying everything I owned on my back, I learned the ropes of African travel the hard way—staying in flea-bitten local guesthouses and riding on crowded pickup trucks or local buses. I spent endless hours hitchiking empty highways and, where transport failed altogether, I walked. To be forced to wait for rides at the entrances of national parks—literally stalled at the gateway to adventure—was pure frustration, but with patience I managed to tour the major wildlife reserves of East Africa.

I was then a total novice in the arts of wilderness camping, and well remember the terror of my first nights in the bush, at Kenya's Tsavo National Park. Sleepless and sensitive to every sound issuing from the darkness, I fretted about the possibility of snakes entering through the zipperless floor of my second-hand tent, or clumsy elephants stepping on me by accident. Most terrifying were the roars of I-knew-not-how-distant lions. It took many nights to feel at home sleeping out in the wilds.

For the Tanzanian portion of the trip, I shared the rental of an old VW bug. My companions and I soon found ourselves lost on the plain in the Serengeti night: the glitter of hundreds of eyes reflecting our headlights convinced us that we were on the rutted track to nowhere. After pitching camp in the darkness, the dawn revealed that we were exactly where we wanted to be—smack in the middle of the great wildebeest migration. Ever since, I have been a devout fan of the Serengeti, and am never happier than when camped within earshot of the big herds.

In 1972 travelers were common enough in the major parks of Uganda, but it took grit to find gorillas. Gorilla viewing was then an almost unknown activity: gorilla family groups "habituated" to tourists simply did not exist, and merely finding where to search for the giant apes was a major challenge. Inspired by George Schaller's account of research among the mountain gorillas, I climbed the misty slopes of the Virunga Volcanos and trekked to the remote Impenetrable Forest. Although my first adventures in those lush environments led only to the most fleeting and imperfect glimpse of a charging silverback, they kindled a passion for gorillas and their habitat that drew me back to the region many times.

At trip's end, I was truly hooked on safari, so I found a niche in the travel industry, organizing and leading African tours. Ever since, I have been able to plan and execute dream adventures to the great wildlife paradises of the continent. I have guided safaris in all the best known game parks, and have mounted expeditions everywhere from the Semien Mountains in Ethiopia to the deserts of Namibia. My preference has always been for camping safaris and getting off the beaten path; a taste for hiking has led me on unusual foot safaris through game country and treks in Africa's highest mountain ranges. I have been very fortunate to see the best the continent has to offer. After a decade and a half of safaris, my passion for Africa's wildlife and its wild places has not diminished one bit. I hope that some of that enthusiasm comes through in the pages of this guidebook.

My object has been to cover the whole range of safari activities in East Africa from the perspective of one devoted to nature and conservation. Naturally, there is a heavy emphasis on exploring the game parks: I have included information about many excellent reserves that are remote and still relatively unknown, as well as the most celebrated national parks. I have also discussed wilderness areas outside park boundaries, and covered those places that can only be explored by the trekker or hiker. Throughout the book, pride of place is given to natural history, which is, after all, the subject of prime interest on most African safaris. My object has been to facilitate a greater understanding of *what* to look for and *how* to find it, as well as to answer the basic questions of *where* to go. Perhaps most importantly, I try to explain what makes each place unique from the naturalist's point of view. In so doing, I address the all-important issue of *why* to go.

This book is meant to be both trip planner and traveling companion. The "Into Africa" chapter focuses on vital pretrip information. An important section is devoted to the relative merits of the various styles of African travel. It will help you decide whether independent or group touring most suits you; included are descriptions of the operations and advantages of the different types of safaris on the market. The same chapter also reviews the preparations necessary for any trip to Africa: considerations of health, safety, etiquette, and equipment are treated with more than ordinary attention to detail. A separate section deals extensively with the specialized requirements of camping, walking, and living in the bush.

Another introductory chapter, "Africa and the Africans," briefly outlines the geography, history, and peoples of the continent with a view to putting an East African safari into its larger context. The "African Realm" chapter is presented as a primer on natural history. In addition to ecological descriptions of the major habitats and animals, it offers practical hints on how to maximize opportunities to find and enjoy African wildlife. A great deal of further information on fauna, flora, and ecology is woven into the body of the text.

In the area chapters, the material devoted to parks and wilderness places is exceptionally thorough. Each park is introduced by an overview of its natural and human history, and a discussion of any relevant conservation issues. Complete access and accommodation information follows, including the locations of many out-of-the-way lodges and special campsites. Finally, a section on "Touring the Park" shows you how to get the most out of your visit: attention is paid to remote and often overlooked sectors, as well as to principal game-viewing circuits. Plants and animals likely to be encountered in each particular area are pointed out; birds, reptiles, and small mammals are discussed as well as the larger animals. Separate sections offer portraits of some of the interesting tribal peoples of East Africa that will be encountered along the way.

Keep in mind that this volume is no starry-eyed account of the safari scene: not everything in Africa is as wonderful as tour advertisements might suggest, and I try to point out the problems as well as the appeal of the various locales.

Material on cities has been kept to a minimum. Although some might wish for a more in-depth treatment of night life, dining, hotels, and urban culture, such information is available elsewhere, and I have preferred to devote more space to the wild places that are the real focus of the book.

In Africa, as elsewhere, nothing changes as fast as prices, and most of the costs quoted in guidebooks are outdated by the time they see print. For that reason, I have not listed prices for hotels or services other than national park fees (which generally have more stability). Nor have I created formal classifications for hotels and lodges. Instead, I have chosen to describe them in everyday language, using such terms as *budget, moderate,* or *luxury.* You will know which facilities will best suit your needs.

My original intention was to include all the countries of safari interest in sub-Saharan Africa. As work progressed, however, it became apparent that such a task would require an encyclopedia, not a single volume. West Africa was the first region to be dropped because its wildlife is secondary to its cultural interest: it is a fascinating place for those interested in African art and a magnet for black Americans seeking their cultural roots. Ultimately, there was no space left for chapters on Zambia, Botswana, Zimbabwe, South Africa, Namibia, or Madagascar—all countries of prime interest for natural history safaris. Probably, I will one day discuss them in a companion guide to southern Africa.

I hope that my book will add to the enjoyment of your African experience and that it will stimulate you to aid the cause of conservation. The beauty of the place makes the best case for its preservation. See it soon, and do what you can to help. *Safari njema!*

Allen Bechky
November 1988

Acknowledgments

My gratitude goes to the many people who made this book possible. Some provided me with assistance or information; others helped in less tangible but equally important ways—lending inspiration, sharing hospitality, and providing moral support.

Many thanks to all the following for their help in marshaling the facts: Brad Goodhart; Ross Battersea of Wilderness Travel; Tom Ripellino; Peter Ourusoff; Maurice and Elaine Baré of Rwanda Travel Service; Shakir and Abbas Moledina of Ranger Safaris; Thad Peterson of Dorobo Safaris; John Elwel of Equatoria; Edwin Sadd of Bushbuck Adventures; Colin Bell, Chris MacIntyre, Margot Healy, and Russel Friedman of Wilderness Safaris; Conrad Averling of the Eastern Zaire Gorilla Society; Craig Sholley of the Mountain Gorilla Project; Tom MacNamee; Mike Nichols; Minny Purinton; Skip Horner; Fred Becky; Dave Buitron; Clive Ward; Dave Risard of Geo Expeditions; D. G. Dixson of Bruce Safaris; Diani Berger; Arlene Blum; Mark Brady at United Touring International; Chris Slevin of Lindblad Travel; Rick Anderson of the African Fund for Endangered Wildlife—Kenya (AFEW—Kenya); Jim Gardiner; Reno Taini; Nancy George and Joanne Mohr of Peace Corps—Kenya; Doug and Gail Cheeseman; Richard McConnell at Adventure Center; Pierre Jaunet of Catalina Safaris; Mark Nolting; Andrew Fentiman of Safari Consultants; Sandy Smith of Sabena Airlines; Dr. Marco Michelson at the Centers for Disease Control; Gary Lemmer of Sobek; and Dr. Howard Backer.

I am especially grateful to Iain Allan of Tropical Ice for his frequent hospitality in Kenya, and for reading over the chapter on that country. Special thanks also to Chiman and Usha Patel of Tanzania Guides for so generously opening their home in Arusha to me, and to my other friends in Tanzania: Rashidi and Mzee Bernard, who taught me so much; Nobbi, Teodosi, Shabani Big John, Marcelli,

xiii

Saidi, and all the gang at Ndutu and Tarangire, who always greeted me with a sincere "*Karibu*"; my friends among the Masai, Samuel Saringe, Ngarusa Lengiteng, Marias Kinge, and their families.

I am greatly indebted to Jim Cohee, my editor at Sierra Club Books, for choosing me to write this guide and for giving me the freedom to put in what needed to be said. Thanks also to Linda Purrington for editing the manuscript; to Hilda Chen for the fine maps; to Pam Shandrick, Dena Bartholomew, Alan Steck, and Raj Khada for their willingness to read and comment; to Hugh Swift and Midge Murphy for shedding much-needed light on the publishing process; to Ed Bernbaum, John Finger, and Chris Rainer for helping with photographic selection and conversions.

Special thanks also to Dick McGowan and Leo LeBon at Mountain Travel, who sent me on so many expeditions and gave me a long-enough leash to get the book done. Thanks also to all the gang at Mountain Travel who picked up the slack at the office while I took time off for writing.

My deepest gratitude goes to those close friends who saw me through good times and bad, yet never lost confidence in my ability to see the project through: Hans Schnelle, Nancy Miyamoto, and Andreas Schnelle for taking a roving adventurer into their home and giving him a place to work; John Rissman and Jennifer Birkett, Mark and Judy Decker and the kids, Wendy Berg, Dave Parker and Judy Hartman, and my old buddy Jay Rasumny. Very special thanks to Bette Nobel for getting me going and keeping me on track. Thanks also to my good neighbor Jean Osborne, and to my friends Marilyn Simons, Sara Steck, Stan and Amolia Mermelstein, Robyn Gray, Pamela Harlow, Volker and Barbara Schnelle, Pete Moacanin, Norine Nomura, Gary Hassan, Frank Edwards, Larry Letofsky, Bob and Thalia Siegal, Mark Freidman, Stephan De Rassy, Gene "Smersh" Rosenthal, Nancy Smith, Nada Pecnik, Howie Stark, Harvey and Kitty Rudman, Shari Basom, and Cathie Yaussy, each of whom gave me needed encouragement at one time or another over the years.

I give very special thanks for all the love and cheerleading that only a family can give: to my mom, Ruth Bechky, my aunts Rose and Ella, my brothers Ron and Stan and sister Gail and their families, to cousins Lisa Teiger (especially for guiding me through the darkest days of computer illiteracy and for her comments on the first draft) and Andy Alexander-Crossan (and my godchild Benjamin), to cousin Carole and cousin Stu and their families. To my deep regret, two loved ones are no longer here to whom I can acknowledge my debt personally, but I'm sure they would be very happy to see this book in print: my father, Irving Bechky, and Grandpa Max Glassman.

I dedicate this book to the wild animals of Africa. May they grace the Earth with their beauty forever!

1

Africa and the Africans

We are haunted by visions of the old Africa. We conjure images wild and beautiful, fascinating yet terrible, a melange of reality and dream. We see a place where wilderness is still the name of limitless landscapes. Where somnolent elephant bulls droop with the weight of their tusks, and beaded Masai elders stand swathed in ochered robes. We have heard the pulsing drums driving masked dancers to ritual frenzy, and entered King Solomon's mines, guarded by the mummies of long-dead chiefs and wizened crones. We have watched Zulu armies overrun red-coated columns, witnessed Stanley meeting Livingstone, and followed shackled slave caravans on their trail of misery. We have marched with intrepid explorers, alternately punished by desert thirst and tortured by malarial mosquitos. We have followed the tracks of the big game hunters, as portrayed in the stories of Ernest Hemingway and Robert Ruark, and grown up watching the adventures of Tarzan and Jane. We have been charmed by the colonial idyll of Isak Dinesen, a world of aristocratic farmers, romantic white hunters, and delightful natives—sometimes dignified, sometimes savage, always baffling. Drawn from history, literature, and film, these images have a magical attraction.

The images of today's Africa have rather less magic. The news media speak daily of war and revolution, bankruptcy and corruption, and a losing struggle for development. On TV we see the agonized specter of famine, witnessed in the taut faces and swollen bellies of starving children, and the amazing films that document the lives of the wild animals even as they warn us of the increasing threats to their survival. We are saddened by the suffering of the new Africa and fearful for the loss of the old.

It is often said, "The time to go to Africa is now, before it is too late." This counsel reflects our fear that the old Africa will soon be swallowed up by the new. A journey there will at once reinforce

1

and allay your fears, for the old and the new Africas are both very much alive. Before you set off, it's useful to reflect on the geography of the continent as a whole, and to understand a little about the history and lives of its people.

The Natural Regions: An Overview of African Geography

Geologically, Africa is a very old continent. Together with South America, Australia, India, and Antarctica, it was once part of a supercontinent, the ancient Gondwanaland. When that huge southern landmass broke up more than 65 million years ago, Africa was left pretty much with the familiar shape it has today. For nearly the entire length of its shores, the land rose to elevations of more than 1,000 feet within a few miles of the sea. The same geologic forces that broke up Gondwanaland fissured eastern Africa, creating the long chain of lakes, escarpments, and volcanos of the Rift Valley system. But for millenia the central African plateau remained relatively undisturbed. Unlike other continents, Africa was neither submerged by ancient seas nor scoured by Ice Age glaciers.

Almost 12 million square miles in area, Africa is the second largest continent. With the equator running through its middle, most of it lies squarely in the tropics. But Africa is not a jungle continent. Aside from a rainy zone of equatorial forest along the Atlantic coast and the Congo basin, most areas receive less than 40 inches of rain a year. Since rainfall is concentrated in distinct wet seasons, many months are entirely dry. Even where annual precipitation is high, a tremendous amount of water is lost immediately in heavy runoff, with later loss through evaporation over the long dry periods. By far the greater part of Africa is covered by zones of vegetation adapted to varying degrees of aridity: savanna and desert.

The Sahara, largest desert in the world, blankets the northern third of the continent from the Atlantic coast to the Red Sea. In that brutal thirstland, less than 5 inches of rain fall per year throughout a 1,000-mile-wide east–west belt. Even that precipitation is extraordinarily variable; interior regions may go years without a drop.

The Sahara is inhospitable, although it is by no means a monotonous sea of sand. There are indeed large expanses of shifting dunes, the great *erg*, but also extensive barren rock plateaus known as *hamada*, and whole regions of *reg*, covered by empty, pebbly plains.

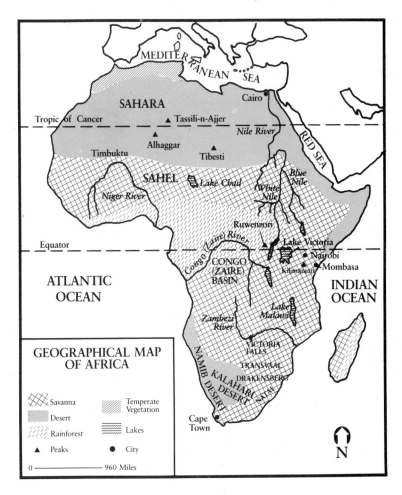

GEOGRAPHICAL MAP
OF AFRICA

- Savanna
- Desert
- Rainforest
- ▲ Peaks
- Temperate Vegetation
- Lakes
- ● City

0 ———— 960 Miles

N

High mountains, notably the Algerian Hoggar (Alhaggar) and the Tibesti Massif of Chad, form an upland backbone in the desert's center. Although the highest Saharan summits, the volcano Emi Koussi (11,023 ft.) and Touside Peak (10,711 ft.), are found in the Tibesti, the grandeur of desert scenery is best seen among the volcanic spires of the Hoggar and the tortured sandstone cliffs of the nearby Tassili-N-Ajjer mountains.

Although some desolate regions are almost sterile, like the Tanezrouft of southern Algeria, the Sahara is not devoid of life. Hardy trees and shrubs manage to cling to various desert niches, while grasses lie dormant until awakened by infrequent storms. Small animals—mostly insects, reptiles and rodents—and even a few species of antelope, have successfully adapted to life without drinking water. In the mountains of the central desert, rock pools and oases provide enough moisture for desert nomads, such as the famous Tuareg of the Hoggar.

Rock paintings tell us that the Sahara has not always been a desert, but has been undergoing a dramatic drying-out process within recent times. Portraits of giraffe and elephant in the waterless heart of the Tassili are sure signs that the region was much wetter only 7,000 years ago. Later paintings show that the Sahara was inhabited by cattle-herding peoples until roughly 1,200 B.C. Generations of gradual desiccation eventually forced most Saharan peoples and animals to emigrate. The desert was left to the few species and tribes that could survive its increasingly harsh conditions.

The Sahara is fringed by areas of higher rainfall and denser human occupation. Although the desert reaches all the way to the sea in parts of Egypt and Libya, most of Africa's northern coast enjoys a delightful Mediterranean climate. Moderate winter rains permit intensive agriculture and a heavy human population. On the southern edge of the Sahara is the Sahel, a semidesert transition zone to the savannas of black Africa. Rainfall is very irregular there, but averages from 10 to 20 inches per year. In some well-watered areas, tribes have settled and are able to raise crops. But most people of the Sahel are pastoral nomads, who must constantly move their herds in search of water and fresh pasturage. In recent years, the Sahel has been hard hit by droughts that have caused devastating famine. Such droughts occur regularly in the Sahel, and are part of the continuing climatic desiccation that created the Sahara. But increased human population, permanent settlement, and overgrazing are quickening the process of desertification: the zone of true desert, the Sahara, advances southward a few miles each year.

The Sahara has played a significant role in African and human history. Its birth concentrated human populations along the river Nile, where agriculture first developed (between 7,000 and 5,000 B.C.) and subsequently required ever greater levels of cooperation. By the time the Pharoahs had built the Great Pyramids (c. 2,500 B.C.), the desert had become a nearly impassable barrier to the lands to the south. Throughout history, caravans of desert traders crossed the vast emptiness, returning with slaves, ivory, gold, and strange tales. But it was a tenuous contact. The Sahara formed an environmental barrier that left Africa isolated from the events of the Mediterranean world. Even today it remains the fundamental boundary between the Arab sphere of North Africa and the equatorial regions of black Africa.

South of the Sahel, rainfall increases markedly, and the country greens up into the lightly wooded grasslands known as tropical savannas. Like the Sahara, the savanna zone stretches across Africa in an unbroken east–west band. In West Africa, the Guinea savanna belt merges into the zone of the equatorial rainforest. In the drier east, savannas dominate the high East African plateau, spreading deep into the South African region. There are many different types of savanna country: some are pure grasslands, while others are dominated by various woodland communities. As a whole, the savannas are the African "bush"—the classic big game country.

The game reserves and national parks of the savanna zone are without doubt the principal draw for visitors to Africa. It is in the celebrated reserves of East and southern Africa that the greatest concentrations of animals remain. West Africa has a much bigger human population. Over time, its wildlife has gone into the cooking pot, and is now seriously reduced in numbers.

The savannas are also home to an incredible variety of peoples. All across the northern savannas and throughout the grasslands of East Africa, pastoral tribes depend on cattle for their livelihoods. Because the savanna zone receives higher rainfall than the drier regions to the north, some 20 to 40 inches a year, it is far richer cattle country. Nevertheless, rain is irregular and seasonal, so cattle-herding tribes have traditionally been nomadic. Nomads tend to cling to their old way of life more fiercely than do agriculturalists. Since they retain their ancestral customs and colorful dress, they are of prime interest to visitors.

Fertile and well-watered savanna regions are inhabited by settled agricultural peoples who have received more stimulus toward westernization and modernization. In farming districts, schools and administrative centers have been in place since colonial times, and most people have abandoned traditional garb in favor of Western clothing. Their tribal religions have largely been supplanted by Christianity or Islam, and native customs have been severely modified by the influence of missionaries. Although much more numerous than their pastoral neighbors, agricultural tribes and regions tend to be overlooked by tourism.

The forest region, the fabled African jungle, is limited to the southern coastal areas of the West African bulge, and the Congo basin of central Africa. Rainfall averages more than 80 inches a year on the coast, and 60 in the interior. Like tropical rainforest all over the world, Africa's equatorial forest is an ancient ecosystem, the product of ages of environmental stability. Rainforests are the most complex of all land habitats, and the most endangered. The West African forests are now heavily settled. Virgin rainforest there has been largely replaced by plantations of cocoa, rubber, oil palms, and subsistence farms. What rainforest remains is threatened by mechanized logging operations and increasing settlement. Its wildlife is under intense pressure, not only from habitat destruction but from its regular use as a source of food. The animals of the rainforest, which include a wide variety of monkeys and birds, are not easily viewed, so the potential for tourism in forest reserves is negligible. The climate—humid and jungle-hot—is also unfavorable. Visitiors go to West Africa mostly for its cultural attributes, particularly the powerful expression of its traditional artwork and dance.

The Tropic of Capricorn marks the edge of the distinctly temperate South African region. The tropical savanna, with its typical baobabs and umbrella-shaped acacia trees, gradually gives way to plant communities that can tolerate a definite period of cool weather. Temperate grasslands appear on the plains of South Africa's Transvaal, and the mountains of Natal and Lesotho are seasonally dusted with snow. The climate gets progressively drier toward the south Atlantic coast, the semidesert Kalahari merging into the true desert conditions of the Namib. The Indian Ocean warms the land on the eastern coast, so semitropical climate persists almost to the Cape of Good Hope. The Cape marks the very southern tip of Africa, where a Mediterranean climate, mild with a cold winter season, produces scrubby vegetation similar to that of the Algerian coast.

Humankind In Africa

Human history in Africa goes back to our very roots. Fossil evidence suggests a line of development stretching from the appearance of the first primate, *Aegyptopithecus* ("the dawn ape"), some 33 million years ago, to the presence of *Homo sapiens*. Current research is focused on the East African Rift Valley, where several discoveries have been made of the earliest hominids (bipedal primates in the human family). Controversy swirls around the exact relationship of the various specimens unearthed, but anthropologists almost universally accept that our ancestors evolved in East Africa. A fully upright hominid left its unmistakable footprints in an ash-filled river-bed near Tanzania's Olduvai Gorge some 3.5 million years ago. It is not certain what species was responsible for the humanlike tracks. A likely candidate is *Australopithecus afarensis,* of which a 3-million-year-old specimen (the celebrated Lucy) has been discovered in Ethiopia. The more recent fossil record goes on to reveal larger-brained species: the first tool user, *Homo habilis* ("able man") and the more refined *Homo erectus* ("erect man"). They lived at least 1.6 million years ago at both Olduvai and at Lake Turkana in Kenya. The earliest *Homo sapiens* are believed to have made their debut no more than half a million years ago. At this point, no one knows where we first appeared, but the betting is heavy that our species was born in Africa.

The most ancient of Africa's present-day ethnic groups are the Pygmies and the Bushmen. The Pygmies still live in the equatorial forests of the Congo basin, while the Bushmen have been exterminated from the high savannas of southeastern Africa and are now found only in the Kalahari desert. Both groups lived as hunter-gatherers, totally adapted to their respective environments. For millenia, they survived in small bands, wandering as the seasons and food sources required.

Of course, blacks are the dominant ethnic group in sub-Saharan Africa today. Their geographic origins are obscure; very possibly they came from North African regions that are now abandoned to the Sahara. The hunters who appear in the Saharan rock paintings of some 5,000 years B.C. were negroid, as were the cattle herders who replaced them. It seems likely that with the great drying out of the Sahara, those black groups moved southward. Iron tools enabled them to penetrate the equatorial forest regions, although their conquest of the forest was limited by the nature of the environment: their cattle succumbed easily to disease spread by the tsetse fly. The black immigrants adapted by cultivating cassavas, yams, and bananas. They built the walled towns of Benin and Ife in the Nigerian forests, where sophisticated artisans created exquisite sculptures in bronze. In the West African savannas, city-states—the ancient, pagan Ghana and the later Muslim Timbuktu—grew into commercial empires that controlled the exchange of the forest's ivory and gold for salt from the desert.

The ancient black tribes of West Africa spoke many languages, but one language group in particular—the Bantu—were spectacularly successful in their expansion throughout sub-Saharan Africa. Bantu-speaking tribes spread through the tropical forest zone, and eventually reached the high plateaus of East Africa, from which they moved southward, almost to the Cape. The Bantu came to dominate the Pygmies of the forest and displaced the Bushman-like hunters from the East African plains. There they encountered other strong tribal groups penetrating from the north. The Bantu herded cattle where they could, but they depended on farming for survival. They introduced agriculture to the forest region and spread the cultivation of millet as they moved into the open savannas of the east.

Two other important tribal groups moved southward with the retreating Saharan savannas. From the upper reaches of the Nile came the Nilotes. Tall, thin-boned pastoralists, they penetrated the grasslands of the Sudan region and the open country of East Africa. Noted for their regal bearing, prowess at war, and aristocratic condescension toward other peoples, the cattle-herding Nilotic nomads are today personified by such well-known tribes as the Masai of Kenya and Tanzania, the Watutsi of Rwanda and Burundi, and the Nuer and Dinka of Sudan. Black Cushitic tribes, speaking languages related to those of their Semitic neighbors in Arabia, occupied the Horn of Africa.

After the collapse of the Roman Empire and the rise of Islam, European contact with Africa was limited by centuries of warfare with the Arabs of the Mediterranean coast. Geographic knowledge was reduced to what could be gleaned from the works of classical Greco-Roman texts. Meanwhile, the Arabs were learning about the continent and peoples to their south: throughout the Middle Ages, they carried on a brisk trade with the tribes of the Horn of Africa, and sent maritime expeditions down the eastern coast. By the tenth century, they had founded a string of towns along the Indian Ocean. These trading outposts eventually developed into the lively city-states in which the Swahili culture of East Africa evolved, and from which the European explorers later set off to "discover" the African hinterland.

The Arabs also succeeded in Islamicizing the tribes of the Sahara. Their camel caravans then carried Islam across the great desert to West Africa, where many of the tribes of the Guinean savannas adopted the faith of Mohammed; the most important of the West African trading empires were Muslim. Arab commercial and cultural influence in black Africa was firmly established centuries before the first European contacts. While Arab geographers had a fairly sophisticated view of the continent, their European counterparts hardly knew that Africa existed. Europeans prized the tale of a great

African king, Prester John, who ruled a Camelot-like Christian kingdom somewhere beyond the realm of the hated Muslims.

The European discovery of Africa began with the voyages of the seafaring Portuguese during the fourteenth and fifteenth centuries. Slowly the Iberian mariners extended their voyages down the Atlantic coast, until Bartholomew Diaz finally rounded the Cape of Good Hope in 1488. He was followed shortly by Vasco de Gama's exploration of the Indian Ocean coast as far north as the Arab towns of Mombasa and Malindi in present-day Kenya. Throughout the "Age of Exploration," while sailors of a dozen European nations were charting the world's oceans and opening up new lands for colonization, European ships also plied the coasts of Africa. Offshore islands were colonized and a few fortified towns founded on the mainland. These posts were meant to supply the fleets cruising to their lucrative East Indian possessions. The African hinterland was deemed too dangerous to explore, and was not thought worth the risk. Its wealth—ivory and especially slaves—was exploited by proxy. Only a few missionaries and explorers bothered to penetrate the interior. With the exception of the establishment of the Dutch colony at Cape Town in 1652, which was to have lasting significance for the history of the continent, no real attempts were made to colonize Africa until the last century.

Yet the Age of Exploration, with its discoveries and exploitation of new lands, had profound effects on the African interior. The colonization of the "New World," particularly the development of plantation agriculture in the American tropics, required the importation of huge numbers of slaves. As the native "Indians" of the Caribbean died off wholesale from epidemics of smallpox and measles, they were replaced by Africans, whose bodies already had some immune resistance to those killers, and blacks soon became the only source of slave labor. Over a period spanning almost four centuries, an estimated 10 million Africans were carried into bondage in the Americas. The social disruption and suffering caused in Africa by the constant depredations of slaving expeditions is incalculable.

Most of the slaving took place in West Africa. White traders preferred to buy slaves at their coastal enclaves, such as Goree Island in Senegal. The business of catching slaves was left primarily to African allies, who received firearms to make their job easier; some coastal tribes grew rich and powerful by transporting the people of the interior to the sea for sale to European buyers. The importance of the savanna empires dwindled as trade shifted from the trans-Saharan caravan routes to the European enclaves on the West Coast. In East Africa, Arab slavers organized their own slave-catching expeditions. They forged a system of inland caravan routes that were later to become the highways of the European explorers. In the beginning of the nineteenth century, Europeans became interested in unraveling the geographical mysteries of Africa. Their maps delineated only the outlines of the continent with any degree of certainty; the interior was left "dark," signifying *terra incognita*. Ironically, it was a new-fledged European passion for suppressing the slave trade that spurred Livingstone's celebrated explorations in southern and eastern Africa. The quest for the sources of the Nile then led to the expeditions of Burton, Speke, and Grant.

As the dark spots on the map filled in, the scramble for colonies began in earnest. King Leopold of Belgium hired Henry Morton Stanley to carve an empire out of the Congo, while Cecil Rhodes pushed his dream of a Cape-to-Cairo British domain. French and British administrators began to exert control over interior regions far from their coastal enclaves. Rivalries among the European nations played no small part in the final division of the continent. When Bismarck suddenly declared German protectorates in Africa, he did so more to obtain bargaining chips against his military rivals than out of genuine interest in empire building. At the Berlin Conference of 1884, Africa was entirely parceled out among the great powers. The colonial era had begun.

The colonial partition of the continent was to have lasting effects on Africa's political and economic development. The lines drawn on the new map of Africa did not reflect any ethnographic or economic rationale for the creation of future nations. Arbitrary borders divided some tribal groups from their closest relatives, while throwing others together with traditionally bitter enemies. Unified regions were sundered, migration and trade routes cut off. Later, these whimsical colonial boundaries were to harden into the inviolable borders of sovereign nations, setting the stage for the political and economic fragmentation that is a major stumbling block to Africa today.

The theory and practice of colonial administration differed under each of the European powers. In some of their protectorates, the British established a system of indirect rule: local rulers were made representatives of the crown, and remained in nominal control as long as they did what they were told. Colonies such as South Africa, Rhodesia, and Kenya, where good land and pleasant climate attract-ed the immigration of white farmers, were given much higher degrees of true self-rule. France and Portugal treated their colonies as overseas parts of the mother country. The French in particular created centralized administrations modeled after their government at home. They also practiced a policy of acculturation toward their African subjects: they encouraged a well-educated African elite to adopt the French way of life and thought.

The European governments that established colonies in Africa did so with economic as well as political motives. They desired minerals, agricultural products, and markets. Naturally, the justification for empire building was more high-minded: the Africans were to be brought out of savagery through economic development and the spread of Christianity. For the supposed beneficiaries of colonialism, the cost proved high. The Africans not only bore the psychological pains of cultural upheaval and racial discrimination, but they also had to endure the physical suffering of forced labor and the horrors of war when they dared to resist. And there was certainly resistance, as is recalled by the glory-filled accounts of colonial military campaigns against the Zulu, Herrero, and Maji Maji. But resistance was futile against the superiority of modern arms.

The Europeans soon turned their sophisticated weaponry on each other. Africa became a battleground during the First World War, and bush fighting raged there until the conflict's bitter end. When the smoke cleared in 1918, Germany had lost all its colonies. Those were parceled out among the victors, to be administered as Mandated Territories under the aegis of the League of Nations. The budding demands of Africans for self-rule were temporarily ignored, and the period of peace that followed was one of quiet colonial development. Roads were built, cash crop economies instituted, public health conditions improved, and, in most areas, educational opportunities for Africans expanded.

The renewal of European fratricide in the Second World War sounded the death knell of colonialism. The seeds of education and development that colonial activities had planted bloomed into national independence movements on all sides. African leaders like Kwame Nkrumah and Jomo Kenyatta voiced the cry of freedom. They were jailed for their efforts, but even from inside they raised the expectations of ordinary Africans that freedom would come. At the war's end, the European countries attempted to resume business as usual in their colonies, but were too exhausted to contest militarily all the national movements that confronted them. Nor was there public support at home to fight to keep the colonies. There was some violence—notably the Mau Mau Emergency in Kenya and, much more bloodily, the Algerian War of Independence—but for most British and French colonies, freedom was granted without protracted bloodshed. In 1957 Ghana became the first black African nation to gain its independence. The next decade saw a flood of new nations, and by 1967 only Portugal's African empire remained intact. In 1975, after protracted guerrilla wars, Portugal granted independence to its possessions, Angola and Mozambique. The white settlers of Rhodesia proclaimed unilateral independence from Britain, while they confronted black independence forces on the battlefield. With the attainment of black majority rule in 1980, Rhodesia became Zimbabwe.

Today the liberation movement in Africa centers on Namibia, the last true colony on the continent, and the question of majority rule in South Africa. Although the whole impetus of African politics in the last three decades has been toward independence and black rule, the unique history of South Africa makes the outcome of the struggle there extremely unpredictable.

Africa's postindependence era has been difficult. The first years were filled with an optimistic idealism that looked toward a bright future of self-determination and economic development. In reaction to the century of foreign domination, a wave of anti-European feeling swept over the African intellectuals who became the leaders of the new nations. The appeal of Marxism, with its call for the rapid development of egalitarian economic systems benefiting the masses, was irresistible on a continent where most people eked out a life of subsistence agriculture. The Soviet and particularly, Chinese socialist models attracted many African leaders. Some countries, notably Ghana and Tanzania, became extremely anti-Western and looked to the communist world for assistance. Most of the new nations, however, while jealously guarding their nationalist prerogatives and often anti-Western in political rhetoric, turned to the West to fund their economic growth.

To the new nations, rapid development meant the creation of large-scale modern industries, and massive projects involving the building of dams and factory complexes were begun. These grand schemes required huge influxes of foreign capital. Many programs looked impressive, but were ill conceived or mismanaged, and did little good for the overall economy. A continual need for further funding started the drift toward permanent debt and dependence on Western aid.

The African elites who became national leaders were idealistic but inexperienced. Although mismanagement of development schemes became commonplace, inexperience had its most disastrous effects in the political sphere. The tendency throughout the New Africa was for the creation of one-party states in which no serious opposition to the government was tolerated. Inept officials or economic managers were protected from criticism or replacement, while poorly planned or mismanaged development projects became institutionalized white elephants. As some economies foundered through stagnation, others were flooded with foreign aid money. The temptation for corruption was often overwhelming; in some countries, bribery became a standard of doing business, and black marketeering a way of life.

One-party rule usually resulted in one-man rule. The leader and his loyal followers often enriched themselves, sending huge sums of money into the safety of Swiss bank accounts. As political power became the road to wealth, and as constitutional change was impossible, the coup d'etat became the principal means of changing the government. Although each coup's leaders could point to the excesses and failures of their predecessors as they announced high-minded goals for reform, too often they fell into the same habits of self-enrichment. The cycle of coup and countercoup became a regular feature of African politics.

Pointing to the mistakes and failures of the recent past, some argue that independence came too soon, that the Africans were not ready for nationhood because they had neither the institutions nor the expertise to govern themselves efficiently. Others excuse every problem by placing all blame on Africa's colonial past. Although neither side has a monopoly on truth, few black Africans would argue that the gains of dignity and self-determination do not overshadow the record of political excess and economic woe. There have been marked advances in public education, and a general increase in services due to the construction of roads, hospitals, water projects, and the like. Overall, the material quality of life for the average African has probably improved over the years of independence. The prospects for a brighter future depend on the willingness of both the African governments and the international community to tackle serious economic and environmental problems.

Today Africa is in a state of chronic underdevelopment. Many of its people are still desperately poor, and the total of the continent's goods and services amounts to less than 5 percent of the world's gross production. The continent remains economically fragmented, with most countries looking to the outside world for trade, rather than developing cooperative markets and meshing economies. The cycle of aid and foreign debt has become a crushing problem. The political horizon is not rosy either: internally, most countries still have no mechanisms for peaceful political transitions. Governments preoccupied with their own security continue to throttle opposition, and the continent remains generally unstable. The intensifying struggle between black and white in South Africa threatens to involve many of the northern nations. Although they do not refuse moral and political support to the black cause in South Africa, those countries can ill afford the drain on their limited financial resources that a military involvement would bring. Furthermore, the theater of east–west power conflict continues to play a lively tune on the African stage, to the general harm of both internal stability and economic development.

Ironically, one major accomplishment of both the colonial and independence eras is fueling a severe environmental crisis. Mass vaccination against disease and the creation of national systems of basic health care have sparked a tremendous population explosion. Africa's population is growing at an astronomical 3.5 percent each year. For cultural and religious reasons, few serious efforts are being made to implement birth control programs. Meanwhile, spiraling populations are compounding the problems of economic underdevelopment. In some places, arable land has absorbed all the human beings it can support. Huge numbers of people are streaming into the capital cities looking for employment that simply does not exist. Many African countries regularly fail to grow enough to feed themselves; when natural disaster strikes, the magnitude of famine is staggering. The extent of the hunger problem goes far beyond the simple solution of putting more land into cultivation. Although untamed wilderness still exists, much of it is fragile land, dry and unsuited to heavy agricultural use, or—like the tropical rainforest— lush only so long as the natural vegetation remains. Agricultural projects and settlement schemes may cause severe and irreparable damage to such environments. Human pressure is already closing in on the lands remaining to African wildlife, while poor agricultural practices and overgrazing are turning whole regions into dust bowls. The population bomb threatens the stability of African governments, which find it increasingly difficult to cope with the demands of additional millions for food, shelter, employment, and a decent life. This explosion may be the biggest problem Africa faces in the postindependence era.

Understanding the Africans

Colonial domination by European civilization had a tremendous impact on Africa's materially primitive societies. From the first contact, Africans started to adopt the technical innovations that were to revolutionize their lives. Fancy trinkets and better tools were the first, irresistible lures. Later, the introduction of monetary economies advanced modern institutions at the expense of traditional values and customs. But the habits of generations were not easily shed, especially among the uneducated. Native culture adapted and endured, synthesizing technological methods with ancient social structures. It is not surprising that the result is a society fraught with contradiction and paradox.

Today, Africans live with this awkward synthesis of old and new cultures. Although leaders strive for rapid technological development and the masses readily accept the material benefits of modernity, African society nevertheless remains essentially conservative and traditional. Within the framework of national identity, Africans are bound by tribal loyalties that determine the social fabric of their lives. The family, extending far beyond Western concepts to include distant relatives within the larger clan and tribe, is the center of the individual's existence. Through family and tribe, a complex web of social obligations gives the individual identity and security from birth to death. While governments struggle to develop modern economies, the vast majority of Africans remain subsistence farmers, tied to tribal homelands that they divide and farm according to the customs of their forebears. A man's wealth is often measured by the number of wives or head of cattle he possesses; a woman's status, by the size of her dowry and the number of her offspring. Although the strength of traditional religions (often condescendingly referred to as "animist") continues to be eroded by Christianity and Islam, the evangelical religions are often grafted onto the old. This fusion allows Africans to retain customary practices (including sorcery and polygyny) that would otherwise be considered unorthodox or heretical.

Africa's contradictions are reflected in the lives of its people. You could meet a modern Kenyan man in Nairobi, and readily learn that he is an educated Christian, holding high degrees and an important government job. But you might fail to discern that he regards himself as a Kikuyu, that he has several wives at his home *shamba,* and that he derives as much status from his tribal landholdings as from

Rural Africans gather at a village market in Rwanda. *Photo by Allen Bechky.*

his modern business enterprises. Although he would not be the "typical" African, his position with roots in two worlds would not be at all unusual.

African women have a much harder time straddling the line between the traditional and the modern. A country woman who goes to the city to find work, but gets pregnant, may no longer be welcome in her former home if her potential to bring in a bride price has evaporated. In addition to native cultural barriers, well-educated women must deal with the same workplace biases and role conflicts experienced by their Western counterparts.

Of course, the pace of social change in Africa is accelerating rapidly. The growth of the state is supplanting tribal identification with national loyalties. Political and state ideologies challenge both ancient customs and modern churches. Most importantly, changing economies threaten the security of the extended family system as Africans migrate by the millions into cities. They trade the boredom of rural life, which offers little but the security of strong family ties in an environment of hard-working poverty, for the excitement of the city and the hope of better economic conditions. Such hopes are more often frustrated than realized, but the life of the village— slow, traditional, and dull—is ridiculed by the growing class of city dwellers.

It would be a mistake to think of Africans as a homogeneous mass. Tribal, religious, and class differences factionalize the population of each country, not to mention that of the continent at large. Nor should we forget that not all Africans are black. The continent's other racial groups are relatively few in number, but have tremendous influence on their societies. Generally higher on the economic ladder and better educated, the nonblack Africans form distinct subcultures that are interesting for both their unique lifestyles and their points of view.

Many whites call Africa home. Known as *mzungu* in Swahili, they are also often referred to generically as "Europeans"—a source of some confusion to Americans. (Asians are not considered white in Africa.) In black-ruled Africa, whites are divided into two distinct groups: the colonial remnants and the expatriates. In most former colonies, some whites stayed on after independence. Those who could not accept black rule immediately packed up for their mother countries or moved "south." In socialist countries, later attrition was caused by the breakup of private landholdings and the strangling restrictions of controlled economies. But in countries such as

Kenya, the whites who remained did very well. Their efficient farms became the mainstays of domestic food production and the chief earners of foreign exchange through export crops. Whites often came to dominate the tourist industry as hoteliers, tour operators, and guides. In parts of western and central Africa, whites from the colonial countries, as well as Greeks and Lebanese, still form the commercial class, keeping small shops that dominate retail trade.

The old colonials and their heirs are an interesting group. They speak the native languages and are often well versed in local customs and lore. Among them are individuals with an extraordinary knowledge of the African wild. Although some colorful characters among them long for the "good old days," most have adjusted themselves to black rule and have deep affection for their countries. They have lost all political power, but have by and large maintained their economic well-being.

The expatriates arrived in the wake of independence. Sponsored by the United Nations and various private or governmental agencies, they continue to flock into Africa to lend technical assistance for development. Where foreign companies are allowed in, they also bring managers and technical experts to see that their subsidiaries are well run. Most expatriates come on two-year contracts, signing on for perhaps one renewal. They are generally well paid, and often receive free housing and cars as well as special privileges. It is not an unattractive life, because the salary and perks allow a standard of living (including servants and child care) that would be beyond their reach in their home countries. Yet most of them remain outsiders, cloistered in a country club existence, well removed from interest in either the local people or the land. The more adaptable among them become permanent residents in their adopted countries, and those with a keen appreciation for the bush often find their way into the safari business.

The community of wildlife researchers comprises another small but distinct subculture that is sometimes encountered in the most out-of-the-way places. Researchers are not generally friendly to tourists, however; some treat all visitors, no matter how well informed, as idiotic interlopers into their private domain. Naturally, they resent interference in their work. Avoid research facilities: they are off limits to all but known financial backers.

Missionaries are still active in Africa, too. It is not rare to find white clerics or missionary doctors working in extremely remote outposts. Although they do not much concern themselves with tourist activities, some missions sponsor crafts shops or rent accommodation to visitors. In East Africa, the large community of Indians—locally dubbed "Asians"—is very influential. They were originally brought over from the teeming Indian subcontinent by the British, to perform coolie labor on the first railroad construction projects. They stayed on after the railways were completed and found their niche as shopkeepers. At that time, the British were primarily interested in the more gentlemanly pursuits of farming and ranching, while the blacks were still too new to the ways of the modern world to compete in business. The Asians prospered and have come to dominate commerce in East Africa. But they have remained factionalized along the ethnic and religious lines of India; the Muslim, Hindu, and Sikh communities do not socialize much or intermarry with each other, and do so much less with the native Africans. Although many are citizens of the various African countries (others hold British or Indian passports), they are nonetheless insecure. Caught between the former white overlords and the African masses, the Asians have never attained any political power, and their economic success has engendered a lot of bitterness on the part of poor blacks, which is easily exploited by demagogic politicians. The Asians are often blamed for black market dealings, while their managerial contributions to the economy are ignored. The various Asian communities, together with the people of Arab descent along the eastern coast, are interesting additions to East Africa's cultural brew. Their colorful costumes, temples and mosques, and excellent cuisine should not be overlooked.

Considering Africa's history, racial prejudice against whites is not the problem it could be. Many white Americans are ill at ease when first arriving; they bring their home-grown fears about visiting poor black ghettos. Yet once in Africa they quickly lose their fear, for though everyone on the street is black, the racial hostility common in American cities is absent. That does not mean that racial tensions never surface. In colonial Africa, and in some circles even today, it was quite common for blacks to be treated as nonpeople: they could be talked about, or even openly disparaged, just as if they were not present. After decades of both overt and subtle abuse, Africans have become sensitive to insult when they perceive that they are not being acknowledged as equals. Few people make an issue of race, but as everywhere, there are thin-skinned types who are quick to take offense, even where none is intended. Attitudes of anger or frustration are easily aroused in visitors who are confronted with apparent inefficiency or bureaucratic delay during such routine transactions as changing money or checking in for airline flights. In those situations, a perfectly innocent remark can cause an unpleasant incident. Africans do not respond positively to anger on the part of whites, and pushiness is despised.

As a rule, black Africans are very friendly, and smiling curiosity about foreigners is more common than not. Country folk are almost invariably polite. Take a walk on any road in East Africa, and a friendly *"Jambo"* will welcome you from every person you pass. Even where met with indifference, you can usually brighten the situation by offering greetings yourself. But incidental rudeness quickly changes the picture: smiling faces turn sullen at the appearance of the intrusive camera. It is wise to remember that friendliness is a two-way street.

Officials can, and occasionally do, like to show off their power for dubious reasons. Activities as innocent as bird watching have been interrupted by abrupt identification checks and arcane interrogations concerning the use of binoculars. A bureaucrat involved in such a petty incident may merely be satisfying his vanity by letting you know who is in charge. But could he be doing his job, as well? In Africa, one never knows, because national governments are so security conscious. Every year film is confiscated and tourists arrested for taking photos of bridges, army bases, presidential palaces, or whatever overzealous officials have seen them snap. And yet, on a continent struggling with white South Africa and on which mercenaries have been involved in coup attempts, can one be too surprised that there are excesses in the interest of security?

Hassles or delays by officials can also be part of the process of angling for bribes. In such situations, a small gift often works wonders; real bribes are rarely needed by travelers who are not up to anything illegal. But remember, on a continent where money is scarce and power absolute, officialdom gets used to accepting inducements to grant permits quickly or to look the other way.

Although officials occasionally create difficulties, the white, Japanese, or black American visitor is likely to receive preferential treatment in most circumstances (but not Indian Asians, or black Americans mistaken for black Africans). There is still a tremendous amount of respect for Europeans, often expressed in a desire to help out, or to make things easier. More often than not, white visitors can breeze through customs lines while resident Africans and Asians are having their baggage pulled to pieces. They are also waved through police checkpoints, while the local people must drudge through a lengthy process of identification. But privilege goes only so far: expect to wait on the same lines as everyone else at banks and post offices, and if you travel on local transport, to be packed like a sardine into the back of a pickup truck.

2

Into Africa: Planning Your Trip

For most of us, an African safari is no light undertaking. But although the continent is distant and unfamiliar, it is not nearly so peril-filled as you might imagine. Good planning can ensure a rewarding journey. Here we consider what preparation you need for a happy and healthy safari, and examine the conditions you'll actually encounter on the road in Africa. Some of the information covered is relevent to areas outside the strict geographical range of this book, but will be useful if you are extending your travels beyond the East African region.

Ways to Travel

To get the most out of your African experience, first think about your objectives. Is your trip to focus on wildlife viewing or on cultural contact? Are you looking for a relaxing holiday, or a real wilderness experience? Do you want your trip to include activities such as hiking or climbing? Getting a clear fix on your goals can be crucial in determining whether you should travel independently or with a group. Whereas that decision usually boils down to simple preference in many parts of the world, in Africa the question is not so clear-cut. Although you may be perfectly at home touring the cities of Europe or trekking the Himalayas on your own, independent travel may not be the best way to satisfy your goals for an African journey. If you want wilderness and wildlife, independent travel can prove frustrating. A good three-week safari tour often provides more deep bush experience than half a year of poking around on your own. For memorable person-to-person contacts

22

with a wide range of people, however, nothing can beat an open-ended, unscheduled journey. Let's consider the varieties of travel available in Africa.

Independent Travel

Even for seasoned travelers, Africa can be a tough place to explore independently. Its size, its poverty, and its political fragmentation make travel more difficult there than on just about any other continent.

Transport is chief among the difficulties. Even international airline travel is fraught with problems. Airline connections among African cities are generally poor; daily flights are more the exception than the rule. Often no service at all is offered between countries you wish to visit. The situation is made worse by government regulations intended to protect national airlines. Sometimes conveniently scheduled flights exist, but government regulations forbid the airline to pick up passengers, even though the national carrier may have service only once a week. The result can be several extra days waiting for a flight, or expensive and time-consuming travel through intermediate countries that you don't even want to visit. Misconnections, extra overnights, and complicated air itineraries are the norm.

International overland travel is also difficult. Roads are poor, distances great. Public transport is distinctly Third World: over-crowded buses compete with trucks carrying loads of packed-in people. Although you'll find the same situation in the Andes or Asia, distances in Africa are often greater, and frequently *nothing* is available to the place you want to go. West African countries trade more with the outside world than with each other, so there are few connecting roads and services. If you are making a transcontinental trip, you may have to wait days, and in some places even weeks, for transport. Also, there is no middle ground: comfortable first-class buses do not exist, for example. You must either have your own vehicle, fly, or struggle for a place on the top of a truck.

International travel is further complicated by border closings, visa problems, and political instability. Of course, there is always a route that bypasses a closed border or a way to obtain a needed visa (or to get border officials to ignore a South African visa, for example). The point is not that travel within Africa is impossible, but that you must be prepared to put up with hassles and delays.

The degree of difficulty varies with the regions and countries that you wish to visit. West and Central Africa are extremely difficult, for the means of transport from one country to the next are very limited. (Your problems in West Africa will be slightly less overwhelming if you can speak French.) South Africa, Zimbabwe, and Kenya stand out as countries that have excellent roads and good systems of local transportation.

Where transport is good, you will have no trouble traveling from one town to another, but you will find limited access to the game reserves or national parks. Almost universally, vehicles are required for entering and touring the wildlife parks. You'll have no choice but to book local tours, rent vehicles, or fly into camps that provide game viewing as well as accommodation. These services can be expensive.

If you have the right spirit, there are tremendous benefits to independent travel. For maximizing personal contact with people, there's no substitute for going on your own. Fending for yourself, you will certainly meet all sorts of people you would miss if you were on a guided tour. Your freedom enables you to take advantage of unexpected opportunities: invitations to stay in people's homes, to team up with new friends for cooperative adventures, or to stay on in places you especially like. You can focus your energies on attaining the objectives you had when you set out, or pursue new interests that develop. You are completely free to do as you wish.

But freedom has its price. Although it is often possible to team up with other fellow voyagers, such liaisons are usually temporary. You travel together for a spell, or accomplish a specific objective, and then go separate ways. You must be prepared to deal with those times when you are really alone: when you are sick, or depressed, and feel really lonely. Constant planning and organization will be required for you to attain your specific travel goals, and you'll be responsible for slews of decisions regarding both travel and your personal security. In short, you must be a very self-reliant person.

The monetary cost of going on your own presents a paradox: sometimes you can do it at a fraction of the price of an organized tour, yet it can also be much more expensive indeed. Costs depend very largely on your objectives, and the amount of money you have to spend. If you want to have the classic safari experience, a catered four-wheel-drive expedition in the company of an expert guide, that will cost you dearly. But if you will be content with a quick peek into the parks on a standard local tour package, or with a bare-bones camping trip, unquestionably you will save money.

THE BUDGET TRAVELER

Not everyone can throw on a backpack and take off on a footloose adventure, living by wit and without schedule. If you have the personality for it, this kind of travel has some great advantages. A little money can be stretched into a long journey. You have maximum flexibility in where you travel and where you concentrate your time. You can expect to meet lots of people, for the world of the budget traveler is exceptionally open and dynamic. Travelers tend to congregate at strategic places where they exchange experiences and information. They generally travel the same routes and, naturally enough, often stay at the same cheap hotels. Faces become familiar, and a tremendous amount of camaraderie develops on the circuit.

As a budget traveler, expect to immerse yourself in Africa. The only cheap way to get around is to do it as the inhabitants do. You'll be squeezing into packed buses or pickup trucks, sharing rides in makeshift taxis, negotiating lifts from lorry drivers, and lugging your pack when all other transport fails. Budget hotels in Africa do not usually win any gold stars, nor do the occasional mission shelters or hostels at which you might stay. Colonial ambience is not their forte. The cheapest hotels are pretty basic: a dingy room, a bed, possibly a sink and private bath. Standards of cleanliness vary considerably: some hotels and missions are meticulously kept, others offer recently used sheets. Fleas, bedbugs, and mosquitos will be at least occasional companions.

Africa has few of the amenities that exist for budget travelers on other continents. Absent are the first-class buses of Mexico or Southeast Asia. The great hotel deals of those regions are also largely missing. Unlike Asia, there is no great volume of middle-class business travelers, so few moderately priced hotels service them. Such hotels are often packed with government officials, and although cheaper than deluxe tourist-class hotels, they may still cost in the range of $20–$30 per night—well above the backpacker's budget.

Also missing is the great food. Although prices in local restaurants are very low, the quality of prepared food is only so-so. With the exception of a few countries, such as Ethiopia, African cuisine is nothing to write home about. In large towns, restaurants serve basic foods—steak, eggs, fried potatos, and a few local dishes. In upcountry villages and bush towns, you will be lucky to have a choice between rice or cornmeal mush with a meat sauce (which can be very good), and a selection of deep-fried snacks—meatballs,

Indian-style munchies, and greasy pastries. You'll probably cook a lot for yourself. In the markets, you'll find good basic foods. Most places you'll be able to feast on a variety of delectable tropical fruits. They will be your salvation. So will the occasional splurge at a fancy big-city restaurant or game lodge.

The toughest problems facing the budget traveler are the logistics of getting into the bush. Without a car of your own, you are limited to traveling the main roads. They can lead you into very remote areas and wonderful cultural experiences, and sometimes they pass through game reserves. But a drive through game country on a main highway is not the ideal way to see Africa's wildlife, and with few exceptions, Africa's national parks are closed to exploration by people without vehicles.

Hitchhiking is possible, but far from ideal. Most parks do not allow hitchhikers to enter, and frown on them soliciting rides at entry gates. Most cars entering the park will belong to groups of people who have paid considerable sums for the privilege and comfort: window space is a premium, so they rarely pick up riders. Other vehicles will be full to capacity with passengers or camping gear. Even when you are lucky, you are at the mercy of the car's owners, a prisoner of their interests—or of their *lack* of interests! After traveling thousands of miles and waiting hours for a ride, you may wind up driving at breakneck speed past exciting animals as you are driven to the lodge. However, you might luck out with a ride with an engaging warden or researcher, and be invited along on an extraordinary safari. That's always the charm of hitchhiking, wonderful things do happen—but don't count on it.

To visit the parks, you'll probably have to find a cheap, locally organized tour or other travelers who want to share a car rental. Budget tours are not always available, and their quality is not always great. Lodges are usually fairly expensive, so most budget operations are camping trips. That's probably more what you want anyway. You can expect to be crowded into a Land Rover or a converted army truck, to share in food preparation and camp chores, and to set up your own tent. These trips often cover a lot of ground fast, so shop around for operators who allow enough time to explore adequately. They may not be the most satisfactory safaris, but they will get you into the parks, where you can't help but see some great things. Car rentals are fairly straightforward, where you can get them. Try to make sure that your personality and goals fit those of your companions: it's rough when you want to be up at 5 every morning to start your game drive and your companions prefer to sleep in.

You won't have to hire a vehicle for some adventures, particularly hiking activitites. National parks that feature hiking, such as Kilimanjaro or Mount Kenya, don't require a car for entry. Access can still be difficult to trekking areas, but the regular modes of transportation, plus determination, will get you to the roadhead. If you are thinking of doing any trekking in game country, better check on commercial walking safaris. They can be found in some countries— notably Kenya, South Africa, and Zambia—but are not generally cheap.

THE AFFLUENT TRAVELER

Travel is often a compromise between time and money: if you have the resources for a dream safari, you probably don't have the time. If you are fortunate enough to have both, traveling on your own may exactly suit your needs.

It is possible to fly to Africa and organize a safari program over there, making arrangements in each locale. Plenty of tour operators are waiting to serve you, and you can realize considerable savings over prebooking with a U.S. tour operator. If you really have time for an extended trip, you'll be able to pick and choose among a whole range of activities of which you were unaware before you left.

The key to a successful safari of this sort is research. You should have a pretty good idea which parks and regions you wish to visit, and a very good knowledge of seasons, both climatic and touristic. Commercial safari seasons tend to coincide with the dry seasons, when it's easier to get around. All camps and safari operators are then quite busy. If you arrive without having made arrangements in advance, you may not be able to book any kind of tour, and certainly won't be able to organize a quality, customized experience. In many areas, particularly in southern Africa, most safari camps shut down completely during the wet months. Those camps that do remain open offer cheaper rates, but the range of activities available is smaller. Seasons are crucially important for specific activities. There is not much point in visiting Tanzania in August if you want to see the Serengeti migration, for it is unlikely that you will see huge herds there at that time of year. It would be even more futile to arrive at Christmas time with the same object. Although the great herds would be accessible in the Serengeti, you wouldn't be able to get out of town: every vehicle would be fully booked. Likewise, don't count on doing a walking safari in Zambia's Luangwa Valley in December: the camps operating them are closed up tight for the rainy season.

Major safari centers such as Nairobi and Johannesburg are the headquarters for numerous outfitters, game lodges, and rental car agencies. A little shopping around there reveals a large selection of bush activities. Easiest to book are seats on regularly departing local tours. These tours are usually short (one week would be long). They include visits to the better-known parks, with accommodation at lodges. They provide the same experience that you'd get on a holiday safari (described in the lodge safari section, later in this chapter). Many luxury safari camps can be reached by plane. Such camps often feature all-inclusive safari services, including game drives.

As a rule, the cost of joining scheduled local safaris is quite reasonable. It is when you are planning to do something off the beaten track that costs really mount up, especially if you are alone or a couple. Throughout Africa, the expense of importing and maintaining vehicles is quite high, and this is reflected in the costs of rentals and charters. In some countries, self-drive car rentals are readily available. In Nairobi or Johannesburg, you can even rent a four-wheel-drive vehicle complete with camping equipment. In other countries, such as Tanzania, self-drive is virtually impossible, because vehicles are too valuable to be entrusted to inexperienced tourists, and you would have to charter a car with driver at prohibitive cost. Where there are many lodges in the parks and good roads, a do-it-yourself safari is relatively easy to organize. Travel to truly remote bush areas, however, should only be undertaken by people used to self-sufficiency in true wilderness country. Careful organization is essential, and a good knowledge of automobile mechanics is highly recommended.

You should also consider hiring a guide. Visiting a national park is not like going to a museum: the things you've come to see are not guaranteed to be there. Game spotting is an acquired skill. If you are a novice and on your own, you are sure to miss lots of things that an experienced guide would notice. Top guides do not come cheap, and are heavily in demand. If you want to have the benefit of an expert guide on a private safari, you must count on expenses well above those of the highest-quality tours, and must arrange your safari well in advance of your arrival. On the tours you are likely to be able to book on short notice in East Africa, an African driver serves as guide. In southern Africa, safari camps tend to send their guests out with professional white safari guides. (See the complete discussion of guides in the group travel section, later in this chapter.)

In the main tourist capitals, you should be able to book some kind of safari arrangements within a few days of arrival (except during peak holiday periods). Keep a flexible schedule, to allow adequate time for checking around. Your task will be much easier if you have done your research (reading this book is a good start). Write to the tourist offices of the countries to be visited for the names and brochures of various local tour operators. A copy of *Swara* magazine, published by the East African Wildlife Society, will contain the advertisements of numerous Kenyan safari outfitters. That will give you a start on who to see, and what kind of trips are available.

Still, it must be emphasized that the safaris available on short notice include only the most standard itineraries. If you want the ultimate safari, custom outfitted for your party, you will have to arrange it in advance. Although you can book such a trip directly with a local safari operator, the vagaries of correspondence make the process difficult. It is probably better to let a good American safari company handle the arrangements for you. It will save you a lot of work, for it is a time-consuming process to explore itineraries, fix workable dates, and negotiate prices. U.S. tour companies represent the various safari outfitters. They have quick access to communication, and a good understanding of the logistics of planning these trips. You will find it much more convenient to pick up the phone to discuss your questions than to wait for answers from a correspondent in Africa. It will certainly cost more, but the convenience and certainty of satisfaction make it worthwhile.

TRAVELING WITH YOUR OWN VEHICLE

Few adventures in Africa are beyond you if you are traveling with your own four-wheel-drive vehicle. You can penetrate the heart of the Sahara, splash through the muddy tracks of the equatorial forest region, and roam game parks at will. It requires a large investment to start, and you'll need to take a big chunk of time to make it worthwhile. The reward is that you will have total freedom of access, even to the most remote areas. For serious projects, wildlife studies, or photographic work, a private vehicle is absolutely essential.

Getting a car into Africa is the first serious problem. Almost all African nations impose very severe customs duties on imported vehicles, often in excess of 100 percent of the value of a new car of that model. In order to enter or pass through African countries without paying these duties, you will have to obtain a *carnet de passage* for your vehicle. A *carnet* is essentially a document issued by a national motoring club (in the United States, AAA—the American Automobile Association), attesting that a bond equal to the value of the duties has been posted by a bank or insurance company. If you bring your car into a country and fail to reexport it, through sale or loss, the bond will be paid to the national customs. Premiums for these bonds are high, and if you lose or sell the car without the bond being properly canceled, you may be responsible for paying back the full amount. This is important, because a common rationale for bringing a car to Africa, particularly for those who are driving across from Europe, is the idea of selling it at the end of the journey. As long as the sale is properly concluded, with all duties paid to the country in which the vehicle is sold, the bond will be properly canceled and you will receive your deposit back, less premiums. If it sounds complicated to sell a car in Africa, it is. It can be done, however, for good vehicles are always in demand.

Although it's possible to have your car shipped to a coastal African country and pick it up there, more commonly travelers buy a vehicle in Europe and drive across the Sahara. The trans-Africa drive is surely the best way to get a sense of the size and ethnic dimension of the continent. Obviously, such an expedition takes a great amount of preparation and planning. You must be an able mechanic, and carry all manner of spare parts with you. Even so, you may be stuck in the depths of the Central African Republic for weeks, waiting for that spare part you *didn't* bring. That's part of the adventure. It is no picnic to negotiate Saharan sands and equatorial mud, or dealing with officialdom in a dozen different countries. For an anecdotal account of a transcontinental journey, read *Overland and Beyond* by Jonathan and Theresa Hewat (London: Lascelles, 1981). Although the *Sahara Handbook* by Simon and Jan Glen (London: Lascelles, 1981) details only the routes across the western desert, it is a goldmine of information on equipment and techniques that would be equally apropos of motor safaris throughout the continent.

Even if you plan to limit your vehicular safari to a single country or region, you will require special equipment and self-reliant mechanical skills in order to undertake backcountry expeditions. Sand ladders, heavy-duty jack, complete puncture repair kit, and a healthy supply of spares are essential. African drivers and mechanics can perform miracles of automative repair—they keep relic vehicles running for years after they would have been condemned to the junkyard elsewhere, and have a flair for substitutions when the needed part is unavailable. They can be counted on to help if you have a problem—assuming that you are in an area where anyone is going to find you. When bringing your car into a shop for repairs, even routine maintenance, however, you must be on your guard. Quality parts are expensive and sometimes rare. It's possible to bring your car in for a tuneup and later to discover that good parts have been taken out of your car and replaced with old ones. Stay in the shop while work is done, and take an active interest in what is going on.

That hazard illustrates the main drawback of having your own car: your life will revolve largely around your vehicle. Care and maintenance, security, red tape—permits, insurance, road taxes—can become major preoccupations. If you are not prepared for a comfortable marriage to your machine, better consider a tour, or a local rental.

Where rentals are possible, they allow you the freedom and fun of complete mobility, while relieving you of many emotional burdens. You still must be prepared to be self-reliant in the bush, but you'll worry less. Some countries, notably Kenya, offer rentals of well-equipped four-wheel-drive safari vehicles. Packages sometimes include camping equipment. Regular two-wheel-drive cars are cheaper. They can be used for safaris to the more popular parks, where you can even find accommodations at permanent camps and lodges.

Group Travel

Tours are a convenient way to adventure in Africa. Not only do they offer security and access to the wild, they also often present the best solution to the time and budget conundrum.

Most visitors to Africa are participants on some sort of group tour. Given the difficulties of individual travel, groups are attractive even to those who would not choose to join a tour when visiting other continents. Groups offer the security of prepared itineraries and companionship, and solve the problems of transport and accessibility to the wildlife parks. They also provide direction and assurance that you will get to the places of particular interest—a big step toward reaching your personal travel goals. Adventure tour itineraries may allow you to take part in activities that would be difficult or impossible on your own.

Not everybody is suited to group travel. Before you join a tour, you should consider, first and foremost, your suitability for participation in a group. On any tour, you will have much less independence than you are used to. If you look on any kind of schedule as a straitjacket, you'll find yourself constantly struggling against the constraints of an itinerary. Group dynamics require some tolerance for personalities or interests different from your own. You may be thrown together with a bird watcher who will want to stop for a look at every winged creature in Africa, and with a barfly intent only on getting to the next lodge selling cold beer. Such mismatches are more likely to occur on general-interest tours, where every member arrives with his or her own idea of what a safari should be, and group goals may be no more clear than seeing the places mentioned in the itinerary. Tours organized around more specialized goals—a mountain climb, birding, or photography—tend to reduce conflict among members, as group goals and personal interests coincide. But personality differences are inevitable. Most people can deal with group dynamics effectively enough to reach their personal goals for the trip, have a good time, and develop good, even lasting, friendships. Occasionally, however, an individual just doesn't fit in—a sad situation for all concerned.

SAFARI GUIDES

One of the chief advantages of any type of tour is the presence of a guide. It's the guide's job to see that your trip runs smoothly, as well as to find wildlife and inform you about the country. The quality of guides varies enormously. Experience, knowledge, and an engaging personality are the necessary ingredients. If they are mixed right, you've got a guide who will ensure that you have a meaningful and pleasant safari.

You can expect to encounter different kinds of guides on the various types of safari tours. A professional guide adds tremendously to the depth of a safari experience. Not only will you see more, but your understanding and appreciation of animals, environment, culture, and history will be heightened. Although not necessarily an expert in all fields, he or she will have special areas of expertise that can really enrich your trip. The quality of a professional guide's knowledge of natural history is usually excellent: some are highly trained naturalists, others work on the strength of years of bush experience as campers or hunters. You will be strongly influenced by your guide's point of view on all African matters. Clients tend to accept their guide's words as written in stone. But keep them in perspective: not all guides are truly expert naturalists, and more than one has been known to pass along mythical wildlife lore as fact. Also, the overwhelming majority of professional guides are white, and their perspective on the country's politics and people differs markedly from that of black Africans. Carry a few healthy grains of salt.

On most tours, an African driver doubles as guide. Many such guides are outstanding. They may possess great knowledge of the animals' habits and the ability to identify creatures great and small, including the more colorful birds. Their skills at spotting animals can be amazing, and they often regale visitors with a fascinating repertoire of bush stories. Other drivers can do little more than dash around the usual spots looking for sleeping lions. Generally, safari drivers are competent enough to show you a full variety of game and a good time. Few can provide you with deep background on natural history or conservation, yet they can be a great resource for learning about the country. For most visitors, their driver is the main cultural link to black Africans. Take advantage of the opportunity to talk with him. Your discussions will reveal much about the lives and attitudes of typical Africans.

CHOOSING A SAFARI

A tremendous number of companies offer group tours to Africa. Destinations, itineraries, and travel styles are as varied as you could want, ranging from standard holiday safaris to the most esoteric adventures. Your satisfaction from any particular tour will depend largely on your expectations for the experience. If you are seeking a total immersion in the wilds of the African bush, don't expect to find it on a brief holiday safari that rambles around to a few game lodges and luxurious country clubs. The same itinerary would prove a wonderful vacation, if your aim is to enjoy African scenery and wildlife on a relaxed schedule, in modern comfort. A review of the various types of safaris available will help you make the right choice for your trip.

OVERLANDING

For the comprehensive trip across Africa, overland tours are by far the most popular. Unless you are prepared to mount your own motor expedition, or are ready to endure a very arduous hitchhiking trip, there is virtually no other way to make the transcontinental journey. The appeal of such a trip is obvious. How better to appreciate Africa's size and ethnic diversity, to experience the subtle shifts of climates and cultures on a continental scale, to get a feel for the whole of Africa? Overland tours make that kind of journey accessible.

Overland expeditions are organized around the use of large four-wheel-drive trucks. These vehicles are tough. They are designed for military uses, then specially converted to carry passengers on the long trip across Africa. They usually carry about eighteen to twenty passengers, sometimes more. Most have one driver-leader, though some companies also provide a second driver or cook. All communal camping equipment is provided: tents, stretcher cots, chairs, and cook gear. Everything is done expedition style. Participants buy and prepare food communally, sharing cleanup and camp chores. The driver takes care of the mechanical side of things, but members should be prepared for digging, pushing, cutting bush, and repairing bridges as required to keep the expedition moving.

Overland tours are organized in two segments: a long leg across the Sahara to Nairobi, and a shorter, easier trip through eastern Africa to Johannesburg. Members may buy into either segment. Naturally, most operators run back-to-back departures, so trips also head north from Joburg (Johannesburg) or Nairobi. Expeditions vary in length. Most companies allow three months for the northern trip, and about a month for the journey to South Africa. A few companies put on special departures taking about twice that time, allowing a lot more stops and side trips. Considering their duration, overland trips are incredibly cheap. This is to some extent due to the operators' penchant for fiddling with the black (illegal) markets along the way. Veteran operators know all the tricks of currency exchange, and can cut costs appreciably.

Overland tours are cheap, not comfortable. Conditions of travel and camping are rough. The trucks are outfitted with a canvas roof over the rear passenger section, which affords much-needed shade. The canvas, fitted with plastic windows, can be unfurled down the sides to provide rain protection, but usually remains rolled up to allow maximum ventilation and visibility to the sides. Forward views are somewhat blocked by the truck cabin, but passengers often ride on top of the cab for a bird's-eye view. Seating configurations on trucks vary considerably, but most are pretty weird. Most commonly, two rows of seats run the length of the vehicle, along the open sides or down a central column. Consequently, passengers sit in lines, either facing inward toward each other or back to back, facing outward in one direction. Very few trucks are outfitted with more sensible forward-facing seats. Trucks are slow; bouncy on wet, mudholed roads, dusty in dry conditions. Distances are great, the country sometimes monotonous. When the landscape assumes a sameness for days on end, and the dust forms choking clouds, participants take on a glazed, shell-shocked look. Cleanup facilities are not always available, so clothes tend to stay dirty. Camps are efficiently organized, but not elegant. The tents are durable, although not generally top-quality, well-ventilated pieces of equipment. It *is* an expedition, and you have to roll with the punches. You must be willing to accept repeated coatings of desert dust and annoying attacks by jungle insects.

As you might expect, overland trips attract a predominantly young crowd. Some operators have an age limit of forty years old. Others have no absolute limit, but screen older applicants for suitability. Still, there are adventurous people in their sixties who have fulfilled a life's dream by taking an overland journey.

It is very hard to judge overland tour itineraries. The brochures usually detail a proposed route, or several alternative routes, but the actual one taken depends on the political and economic situations in the various African countries. Outbreaks of warfare, border closings, or currency crises periodically cause the route to be altered. All overland companies tend to use similar routes and alter their itineraries in the same way. The classic overland route enters Africa in Morocco, crossing the Sahara through Algeria to Niger or Mali. It skirts the northern edge of the West African region, passing through the Sahel in Burkina Faso (formerly Upper Volta) or southern Niger to Lake Chad and the Cameroons, where it breaks into savanna country. After crossing the desert and western savannas, the road enters the equatorial forests of the Central African Republic and Zaire. In former times the route passed into Kenya through Uganda or the southern Sudan, but political upheaval has forced the overlanders further south. Currently they dip down to Rwanda and Tanzania before doubling back to Nairobi. A second major route follows the Nile directly to East Africa via Egypt and the Sudan. It is not currently favored. Due to the civil war in the southern Sudan, it's necessary to complete that journey by air.

The western route encompasses quite an interesting chunk of Africa. It's a long, tough journey through some very fascinating regions. It presents a very good representation of desert, forest, and savanna country, and a fabulous mix of peoples: Arabs and Africans, English-speaking and Francophone, nations formerly English, French, Belgian, and German. From Kenya southward, the journey is easier and faster. Roads are better in East Africa, and after passing through Tanzania and Malawi into Zambia, the trucks are on tarmac all the way to Joburg, unless they detour into Botswana's game country.

Although changes in routing are occasionally abrupt, conditions are usually stable enough for the itinerary's published route to work. But there is another destabilizing factor: breakdown. When mechanical failures occur, as they often do, time is lost in making repairs. A reasonable number of days for maintenance and repair are built into every itinerary, but when major problems pop up, there can be serious delays. If a truck is stuck in Bangui (capital of the Central African Republic) for three weeks waiting for spare parts to be flown in, cleared by customs, and installed, that time has to made up somewhere. All too frequently, many of the interesting sidetrips, the days supposed to be devoted to cultural and wildlife pursuits, have to be passed up in order to make up lost time.

Overland trips, while providing a fascinating view of the continent, do not usually rate highly for wildlife experiences. Although the brochures describe all the game reserves along the way, the drivers often pass them up or visit them only briefly. After enjoying excellent wildlife viewing in one game park, chalking up lions and elephants and all the major species, overland tours commonly rush through other reserves on the route, or avoid them altogether. Major attractions are sometimes ignored. I have known trucks to pass up the opportunity to view the Serengeti migration when they could easily have done so, to fail to descend into Ngorongoro after camping on the crater rim, and to divert from scheduled vists to Botswana's reserves in favor of the shortcut to Johannesburg.

Even more than on other tours, the leader-driver is the crucial determinant in the nature of the overland experience. The leader may be terrific: totally knowledgeable, and enthusiastic to a fault.

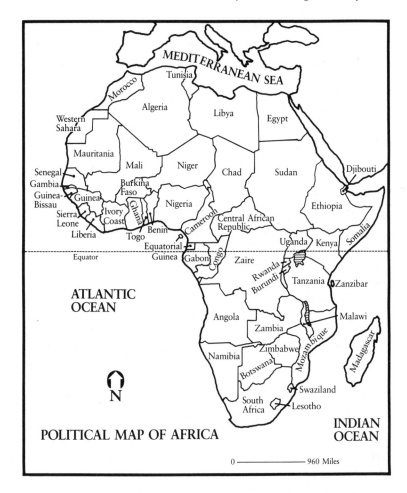

POLITICAL MAP OF AFRICA

Or he may be little more than a skilled mechanic, interested only in reaching the next town where cold beer is available. The leader not only drives the truck and coordinates expedition logistics but also sets the tone for all the group's activities. Although expeditions require teamwork, they are not truly democratic. The leader is paramount. He can manipulate a majority rule situation; his authority generally gets a strong body of support for his decisions even if they undercut major goals for some trip members. Divisive situations are not uncommon.

On trips of such long duration, it should be no surprise that close quarters almost inevitably lead to personality conflicts. Although some lucky expeditions generate terrific camaraderie, other groups degenerate into warring factions whose members are no longer on speaking terms. It is very difficult to live with the same fifteen people for weeks on end. You must carefully consider your adaptability to such a situation before you go. If you are not a "group person," this is the wrong adventure for you.

BUDGET CAMPING SAFARIS

The budget traveler can realize many benefits of group travel by choosing tours to specific regions or countries. Budget-oriented tour operators have sprung up in a number of areas, offering access to the bush at reasonable prices. Trips are generally short, ranging from as little as a week, to minioverland expeditions of up to six weeks duration.

Less geographically ambitious than trans-Africa trips, regional tours have several advantages. Itineraries are more clear-cut, so major attractions are not likely to be missed out. Importantly, the focus of each trip is sharpened. Incidences of group burnout and serious personality conflict are also greatly reduced. Travelers who have the time can take a combination of shorter tours in different areas, focusing their resources on activities of particular interest. Budget operators now run regular departures in Kenya, Tanzania, Botswana, and South Africa. Travelers can shop around locally, although most reputable companies have representatives in the United States or London, so it's possible to plan and book before departure.

Although a few nights in hotels may be included, budget safaris are by nature primarily camping trips. The minioverland operations have the same logistical organization as their lengthier cousins, based on the expedition truck. Many local operators use smaller four-wheel-drive vehicles such as Land Rovers, running groups numbering as few as six passengers. This can be a mixed blessing, as a Land Rover crammed to capacity with gear and campers is neither comfortable nor ideal for game viewing. Solutions to the space problem vary: some Land Rovers carry roof racks for gear, others tow trailers. On the very cheapest tours, the vehicle is inevitably crowded. Staff is limited to the leader-driver. Cooking and camp chores are participatory. A few outfitters specially design their own safari vehicles to accommodate up to eight passengers comfortably, and include the services of a cook. Typically, the higher-priced trips are more comfortable, and more attention is paid to the details of the itinerary.

Since most of these trips emphasize the national parks, game viewing is usually quite good. Some valuable game-viewing time is inevitably eaten up by making camp or cooking meals, but most itineraries allow for a pretty decent look around each park. The question often arises as to whether trucks or Land Rovers are superior for game watching. Trucks are noisier, but I have never seen any evidence that the animals in the well-visited parks are more scared by trucks than smaller vehicles. Land Rovers are superior for negotiating broken, off-road ground, which is useful for following prowling cats or checking into gullies where something interesting may be hiding. Unfortunately, increased traffic volume, with subsequent environmental damage, is resulting in progressively fewer reserves where off-road motoring is allowed. The advantage of a truck's height is balanced by roof hatches on Land Rovers. Clearly, Land Rovers are superior for quick, quiet communications between driver and passengers. That is important for maneuvering into the best photographic position without scaring animals away. Easy communication is also a clear advantage in game spotting. It's difficult for passengers on top of a truck to get the driver to stop if they see an animal he has missed. Some trucks are outfitted with a buzzer system; when the passengers spot something, they signal a stop. On balance, either type of vehicle provides satisfactory game viewing, provided that group members remain quiet, and that the driver switches off the engine when observing game. The noise and fumes of engines really spoil the natural beauty of the bush.

Budget-type camping trips are good value for the experience they provide. They are not ideal from the standpoint of comfort. Like the overland expeditions, some outfitters have age limits and all emphasize that the experience is for the young at heart. But if money is a prime consideration, this is the way to go for the adventurer interested primarily in game viewing.

LODGE SAFARIS

Over the last twenty years, hotel accommodations have been built throughout Africa to accommodate a surge of tourist interest. Today, most game parks have some kind of lodge facility, be it a luxury modern hotel or a permanent tented camp. These facilities have really opened up the African bush to those who wish to enjoy its beauties without sacrificing the habitual comforts of home. That means most of us. Overwhelmingly, the most popular type of African adventure is the lodge safari.

The majority of lodge trips can be classified as "holiday safaris." These are meant to showcase the wonders of the bush in a relaxing style, without the inconveniences of outdoor living. Generally holiday safaris are of short duration—ten days to two weeks in Africa is the norm—and reasonable cost. In fact, by the standard of the daily expense of a weekend in New York, the typical holiday safari is a steal. These trips are truly all-inclusive tours, members have merely to step off the plane to be shuttled through Africa with hardly a moment to fend for themselves. Participants enjoy a round of game drives, relaxation at lodge swimming pools, sumptuous buffets, and more game drives. Such a safari is not everyone's dream of African adventure, but it is a terrific vacation.

Lodges come in many shapes and sizes. Their general quality is very high in terms of comfort, cleanliness, and service. Each facility has its own ambience. The newer safari lodges are modern hotels designed for harmony with the natural setting. Spacious verandahs in bars and dining rooms look out over game-viewing areas. Attractive grounds mix native vegetation with brilliantly flowering tropical plants. Rooms are comfortably cool, pleasantly furnished, and faultlessly clean. For a break from game viewing, guests can relax at the lodge swimming pool. Food is excellent—the buffet tables fairly groan under the weight of platters of delectable fruits, cold-cut meats, hot dishes, and sweets.

Many lodges are famous for their beauty as well as comfort. They are often situated in fantastic locations, overlooking stunning landscapes well visited by game. Some lodges are so well placed, usually at strategic water points, that game can be seen at any time. I have sat on a lodge verandah and watched a herd of 200 elephants feeding in the river valley immediately in front. For those tired of beating the bush, an afternoon spent relaxing at the lodge can be just as productive as a game drive. The modern bush hotel is exemplified by Kilaguni and Samburu lodges in Kenya. Kilaguni is built overlooking a waterhole against a backdrop of the stark cones of extinct volcanos. Samburu is built on the bank of a jungle river, alive with crocodiles and exotic birdlife. To see natural beauty and game, you need only sit at the bar and wait.

Older lodges, particularly those established under colonial administrations, often make up in charm what they lack in modern architecture. At Rwindi Lodge, in Zaire's Parc National des Virunga, accommodations consist of whitewashed stucco rondavals, circular cottages with pointed thatched roofs in imitation of typical African huts. Dinners are al fresco (outdoor) barbecues of steak and local fish, with piles of delicious Belgian-style fried potatos. Ngorongoro's Crater Lodge has much the spirit of an old English hunting lodge—wild game even appears on the menu on occasion. Guests are accommodated in cozy log-hewn cabins.

Another form of lodge accommodation is the permanent tented camp. Tented camps can be superdeluxe or more simple, but they all allow a taste of the camping experience without the expense of organizing a private expedition. They are a great concept in bush hotels, as guests enjoy all the comforts of the hotel-type lodges, including excellent food. Tented camps are romantic, and they are fun. You can have unforgettable animal experiences not possible in the lodges: an elephant may nibble on a tree growing right next to your tent. The night sounds, whether the roars of distant lions or the nearby rustlings of some unknown animal, inspire all kinds of imaginings—philosophical, romantic, or fearful. It's all quite safe as long as you remain inside.

The standard for permanent tented camps is almost universally high. The large "Manyara" tents are really quite elegant, and will fulfill your Hemingway fantasies for safari accommodation. The tents are large canvas pavillions erected on sturdy concrete foundations. They are fully insect-proof: the walls join to a tough plastic floor, while zippered doors and netted windows afford security and good ventilation. Above the tent, a thatched covering provides cooling shade and extra rain protection. Each has its own verandah. A rear door leads to an attached bath area, which includes shower, sink, and toilet. Most (but not all) have clever hot-water systems rigged up: usually water is heated in a 50-gallon drum mounted over a wood-burning furnace. This "Tanganyika boiler" is primitive but provides the same luxurious cleanup you would get in a hotel. Tent furnishings include twin camp beds, tables, and chairs. Some camps run generators to provide electric light, others depend on kerosene lamps.

Transport for most holiday safaris is provided by minibuses. These vans have become almost as ubiquitous in the African scene as the zebra, whose stripes they sometimes imitate. Although often the butt of derisive comment, safari buses are actually excellent, reliable vehicles. They have to be, for the rutted tracks they ply daily take a terrible toll on automobiles. When all is said and done, safari vans carry people in relative comfort, even into very remote country. They are pretty much restricted to roads and game tracks, but not entirely: the old VW vans had surprisingly good off-road capability, and the newer-model vans often have four-wheel drive. They don't have the versatility and go-anywhere ability of Land Rovers, but they are quite capable of getting through on really muddy roads and standing up mechanically to the rigors of long safaris. Although they lack the off-road mystique of Land Rovers, they are probably more comfortable. Late-model vans seat up to eight passengers, though seven should be considered maximum for comfort. Roof hatches permit passengers to pop out the top for game viewing or photo taking. Safari vans are reliable vehicles, perfectly suited for lodge-type holiday safaris.

Holiday safaris allow adequate, not superlative game viewing. Short itineraries are not comprehensive, and several days will be eaten up in towns or country clubs. Game viewing is concentrated in the most celebrated national parks, where the animals tend to get used to vehicles. Lodges are strategically situated in areas where there is an abundance of resident game, ideal for short game drives. The regimen is generally fixed: wake-up coffee and an early morning game drive, with return to the lodge for breakfast. A later morning game drive returns in time for lunch, after which the mid-afternoon is spent relaxing and digesting before another drive from about 4 p.m. to sunset. For most safarists, this is plenty of game viewing, especially if the drives are productive, and such a schedule fits well with the conventional rhythm of safari life.

There are some disadvantages. The safari tracks near lodges are regularly crowded by tour vehicles. The thrill of discovery and the rewards of undisturbed observation get lost in a herd of minibuses jostling for position around a lion pride. Lodge schedules must be met: when the choice is to sit tight with the chance to witness a lion hunt or to go without breakfast, you'll most likely be at the buffet table at the time of the kill. If game concentrations near the lodge are poor, the preset schedule probably won't permit you to travel to other areas. Holiday safaris do not leave much room for flexibility.

Most lodge tours are set up to be short and cheap, so as to appeal to the widest possible market. Driver-guides are the rule, so detailed environmental interpretation cannot be expected. The drivers will show you the animals, and probably a very good time, which is what a holiday safari is all about.

More serious tours also use the lodge safari format. Generally of longer duration and more comprehensive itinerary, they are escorted by expert guides. Guides lend not only expertise but flexibility, as they can decide when conditions warrant a longer drive with a picnic in the bush or arrange a late breakfast at the lodge. Properly organized and led, a lodge trip can be a very satisfying safari experience. Although the bush ambience is somewhat dimmed by the large numbers of tourists at the lodges, where people watching may take precedence over wild animal study, the lodges are a very pleasant base for forays into the wild.

QUALITY CAMPING SAFARIS

Camping safaris in Africa do not have to be rough, participatory affairs. They can be quite luxurious by the standards most of us are used to for camping at home. If you want an authentic bush experience of the sort you've seen in the movies, a quality camping safari is the way to go.

These tours carry you into the bush in Land Rovers or similar small four-wheel-drive vehicles. Your baggage, camping equipment, and camp staff go on a support vehicle, which travels ahead separately. Your party roams the bush at will, and when you pull into the campsite at the end of the day, everything is prepared and waiting: tents up, dinner cooking, hot water ready for a wash. The level of comfort is high. Tents are large and well ventilated. Passengers sleep on either stretcher cots or foam pads laid on the ground; in most cases bedding is supplied, although some operators require participants to bring along a sleeping bag. Members dine in a special mess tent, which also serves as social center when rain forces the group away from the campfire. The staff sees to the setup of toilet and shower tents, and all camp chores. A professional guide is always in attendance. For logistical purposes, and to provide a break from camping, a few nights at lodges are usually included on quality camping tour itineraries.

These safaris have a lot of advantages. You get the real ambience of living in the bush, while doing so comfortably. Your time is not eaten up by camp chores beyond packing up your personal gear on travel days. You will have more time for exploring the bush, and for pursuing your own interests around camp. The efficiency of camp staff and the quality of guides is generally top standard, so you can expect the trip to be both enjoyable and informative. Of course, you can also expect to pay top dollar for all this professional pampering.

It may surprise you that a quality camping trip is more expensive than a lodge safari. Consider that in addition to the costs of transport and accommodation, the expense of the support vehicle, staff, and expert guide must be borne by the group. Also, four-wheel-drive vehicles are more expensive to operate and have less seating capacity than safari vans. Group size is an important cost factor: small groups get prohibitive in price, while groups of ten to fifteen people are more economical, with fifteen being about the logistical limit on this type of trip.

While bearing all this expense, participants must still accept that quality camping safaris may not be as comfortable as lodge trips. They are complicated operations; things can and do go wrong. If a breakdown delays the support vehicle, camp will be far from ready when you arrive. Instead of the expected warm washwater and a cold drink awaiting, you may face the organized chaos of a camp going up in the dark. Camp showers are available, but it takes time for water to be heated on the fire and transferred to the shower bucket for each individual's use: you may have to wait an hour before your turn in the shower tent rolls around. Refrigeration and ice for cold drinks is not always available. At night, the latrine tent will seem an intimidating distance from your zippered tent. No matter how you cut it, you are still camping in the wilderness, and minor inconveniences must be taken with a sense of humor and adventure.

One additional feature of a quality camping safari is too often overlooked by participants. Aside from the guide and drivers, there is the opportunity to get to know the other members of the staff. Talking with them is always interesting and sometimes a revelation. It's a real chance to learn directly about the home lives and concerns of modern Africans.

LUXURY SAFARIS

Luxury safaris are operated on a similar format to quality camping safaris, with all the elegant frills thrown in. Camp accommodation consists of walk-in canvas tents large enough for twin camp beds and a small table. They are similar to the tents used in permanent tented game lodges but do not usually have attached shower and toilet at the rear (though they can if you arrange it beforehand). Canvas mess tents are the rule, sturdy camp furnishings will be of the highest quality, and ice will never be absent. A few extra touches include white cloths on the table, uniformed waiters, and the regular appearance of wine and liquors at meals. The staff is apt to be larger, and the service more polished. Indeed, the entire tone of the safari is more formal. Your guide will fulfill your expectations of the Great White Hunter, as he is likely to be, for many hunters have turned their attentions to this lucrative end of the tourist trade.

The logistics of luxury safaris make these trips available only to small groups. Eight people is the maximum that can be properly looked after. Consequently, luxury trips are usually organized by special request, rather than offered as tours to the general public. Itineraries can be created according to your level of interest and expertise. If you are keen on going to special areas, seeing particular animals or tribes, it can be arranged. But for general-interest trips and first-timers, itineraries are rather standard: you will go to the same parks as the regular lodge tours. You are likely to visit fewer areas, spending more time in each, due to the increased effort needed to move and set up the heavier equipment of a luxury camp.

The quality of every aspect of a luxury safari will be high, and so will the cost. If you want the highest standards possible and also complete control of your own trip, this is the safari for you.

SPECIALTY TOURS

Tours focusing on a special interest, such as bird watching or native arts, have definite advantages. By their nature, group dynamics have a better chance of running smoothly, as everyone's interest is riveted on the same activities. Itineraries are custom-designed to include places that ordinary groups would miss, and special activities are arranged to suit the group interest. In the case of bird groups, microhabitats in little known forest or mountain reserves will be investigated, and there will probably be excursions by boat to search swamps or lakes for hard-to-see species. The well-known parks will also be visited, so the large African mammals will not be missed. Indeed, birders tend to see more varieties of mammals as well as birds, for they tend to be sharp-eyed and constantly alert.

At the same time, specialized groups have too narrow a focus to be enjoyed by all. It is sheer torture for someone who is not interested in birds to spend half an hour swatting flies while the rest of the group attempts to sort out the identity of an undistinguished little brown bird. Make sure your interest is really there before you get involved with such a tour.

Some groups are built around organizational identity rather than special interest. This is especially true of professionals' tours that are designed to give participants a tax writeoff for their vacations. A few technical activities are included, such as visits to clinics or law courts, just to meet the tax requirements. The safari itineraries tend to be poorer for the time lost; unless the technical portions are of genuine interest, these trips are not worthwhile.

A great number of museums and zoos organize their own safaris. Such trips not only build a feeling of participation among members, they help raise money for the institutions. It is standard for a staff member to accompany each group. This can be a real plus, as the escort is often an expert in some African specialty, and may have spent a lifetime doing research in that field. These groups tend toward the lodge safari format. Most itineraries are fairly standardized, but occasionally really terrific specialized tour plans are developed. Quality depends largely on the interest and degree of knowledge of the escort, as he or she may be in charge of planning the tour from the start. These trips are generally quite expensive, for aside from extra charges in the form of a donation to the sponsoring organization, the costs of the escort (and usually his or her spouse) also have to be borne.

FAMILY SAFARIS

It is becoming increasingly popular to take kids to Africa, and many safari operators now offer special trips for people with children. Such tours make great vacations that combine recreation with education, while affording a wonderful opportunity for family bonding. Special family safaris have other advantages as well: discounts are often given to children, and kids will enjoy the presence of peers on tour. Nor will parents feel that their children's behavior is disturbing to other people, as may occur if they are traveling with an ordinary safari group.

Family safari itineraries usually follow the lodge or quality camping formats: kids often crave the amenities more than their parents, even in the depths of the African bush. Small children tend to do very well in the early stages of a safari, when every new type of animal encountered is a major source of fascination. The novelty usually wanes after a few days, however, and young children are then likely to begin getting cranky about being cooped up in vehicles, and to start asking to be left behind in camp.

ADVENTURE SAFARIS

Africa is one area where adventurers who focus on classic outdoor activities—such as hiking, trekking, and rafting—would do well to investigate group travel. Although the group mode may go against the do-it-yourself instincts of many wilderness buffs, the peculiarities of the African outdoors frequently justify group participation.

Indeed, unless you are truly a master of wilderness self-sufficiency and have studiously planned for the trip, some adventures could be foolhardy. Others are simply impossible without great cost. Organized group expeditions allow you to participate on bush adventures without having to tackle a myriad of problems. Although a few trips, such as Kilimanjaro climbs, are relatively easy to organize on your own, foot safaris in big game country or raft trips on African rivers would be next to impossible. They require detailed planning and considerable expense. Where they are to be made in national parks, special permits must be obtained and the participation of professional guides or official personnel may be mandatory. All these arrangements will be worked out in advance when you join an organized adventure tour.

Tours also provide professional guidance, which is essential for any serious African adventure to be attempted safely. The key here is experience. A guide knows the minutiae of the bush: how to handle contacts with potentially dangerous animals, where to find water, which potential swimming holes are crocodile- or bilharzia-free. The African bush is no place to learn the ropes by trial and error.

By their nature, adventure tours are participatory: if you are on a mountain trek, you have no choice but to walk. Still, tours are usually organized on a fully catered basis, so that porters are on hand to carry the heavy loads and a trained staff handles camp cookery. Such tours are never cheap, but are good value considering the costs of doing it on your own.

HUNTING SAFARIS

Until quite recently, safari was synonymous with big game hunting. Although most tourists now do their shooting only with a camera, Africa remains the mecca of the hunting fraternity. After all, the world's largest and most dangerous quarry are found there, as well as a wide variety of other trophy animals. Although banned in Kenya, sport hunting is still permitted in most African countries. The ethics of trophy hunting and its effects on conservation are debatable, but the benefit to the countries involved is clear: cold cash. Many African nations have plenty of wild animals and a desperate shortage of foreign exchange. They readily welcome overseas hunters who, though fewer in number than camera-toting tourists, make a significant additional contribution to national revenues. For today, big game hunting is big business.

A modern hunting safari is a fantastically expensive proposition. In every African country, a nonresident must hire a locally licensed professional hunter to organize and accompany the safari. Their fees tend to be exceptionally high. To the expenses of guiding and outfitting must be added the costs of licenses, guns and ammunition, and taxidermy of trophies. When all these items are tallied, the cost of a hunting safari may total $1,300 a day per person. The typical safari lasts at least three weeks. Hunting companies generally lease blocks of land from the local game department on which they have exclusive rights to hunt. In season, they set up small permanent camps to which they rotate clients. Camps are small but luxurious. Their capacity is usually no more than two hunters, plus their spouses or companions (four hunters would probably be a maximum). Most companies have several camps set up in different regions or reserves. Clients shuttle from one reserve to the next. In one area, the client goes after lion and buffalo; in another, leopard and elephant; in a third, trophy antelopes. Many additional animals are shot for the cookpot.

Hunting safaris are heavily taxed and closely controlled (at least theoretically) by the various African game departments. Licensing rules vary in each country. In some places a hunter pays an expensive flat fee for a particular grade of license that enables him or her to shoot one or two of each animal on a long list of open species. In other countries, the permit is relatively cheap but the hunter pays an additional fee for each animal killed. Either way, the permits provide the game departments with revenues, and clearly limit the numbers and species of animals the hunter may take.

Hunting safaris are specialized affairs, and the details of outfitting such safaris are beyond the scope of this book. They are not casually arranged and generally have to be booked long in advance. The most select of the African hunting companies attend big game hunting shows held annually in the United States, most often in Las Vegas. Many companies have U.S. representatives.

Thoughts Before You Go

No matter what travel style you ultimately choose, you should consider seasonal factors that may affect the timing of your trip, what language difficulties you may encounter, and the types of official documentation that will be required.

SEASONS

In most parts of Africa, the safari season coincides with the dry months; when it is just plain easier to get around. During the rains, roads and tracks dissolve into a series of slippery pools, which even four-wheel-drive vehicles flounder through only with difficulty. Lodges and bush camps may have to close down because neither guests nor supplies can reach them. Game viewing may also be negatively affected by the rains. High grass and thick foliage reduce visibility, enabling game to more easily escape detection. Furthermore, waterholes are then to be found throughout the bush, so animals tend to disperse over wide areas, making them harder to find in large numbers. Many reserves are at their most spectacular at the height of the dry season, when animals concentrate in huge herds around the few remaining sources of water.

Rainy-season safaris do have their virtues. The scenery is at its most glorious: the land is swathed in a riot of fresh greenery, and the cloud-flecked skies seem immense. Although game is more dispersed, many species give birth to their young during the rains. Birdlife is particularly brilliant, as resident birds put on their most colorful mating plumage. Some parks—notably the Serengeti—are at their best in the rainy months, the time when migrating herds swarm over grasslands that are completely waterless in the dry season. Where all-weather roads make park visits practical, rainy-season safaris can be done at some savings, as hotels and tour operators offer lower rates.

Wet seasons vary from one geographic region to another. In East Africa, there are two rainy seasons, although neither is absolutely reliable as to arrival or duration. The heavier "long rains" occur in April and May, while the "short rains" take place around November. Safaris run throughout the rest of the year, although showers may occur during the hot period between December and March. In southern Africa, the weather pattern is quite different. One long wet season lasts throughout the hot summer months: the rains start in November and continue into April. The rest of the year is bone dry. In West Africa, the savanna region has its dry season from November through to April or May, while the rainforest areas have only periods of more or less precipitation.

Temperatures can be a consideration for your visit. Don't plan on crossing the Sahara in the broiling heat of July! Southern Africa has a distinct winter, which runs from June through August. It is cooler in East Africa during that period as well, so those would be the best months to visit if you deal poorly with hot weather.

By and large, East Africa has a delightful climate all year round. The warmest months extend from December through March, with temperatures again peaking in September and October. During those periods, daytime highs run from the 70s to the 90s; nighttime lows are in the 60s and 70s. June and July are relatively cold months; while daytime temperatures hover in the pleasant range of the 70s and 80s, the thermometer may dip into the 50s (or lower) at night. Keep in mind that temperatures vary considerably with altitude, and that you are likely to visit locales of widely differing elevations on a typical East African safari. Low country is always hot at mid-day; nights in mile-high savanna country can be nippy during the cooler months, when "highland" areas (above 7,000 feet) are downright chilly.

LANGUAGES

English is the only language you need for comfortable travel in East Africa and southern Africa. French is essential for West Africa. One or the other will be spoken by all educated people in these regions, and be widely understood by many others.

Although it is fun to be able to converse with local people in their own languages, and certainly worthwhile to learn the native tongue if you will be staying for a long time, it is not necessary for ordinary travel purposes. It is also virtually impossible to prepare yourself to speak even a fraction of the tribal dialects that you could encounter in a single country. It is useful to learn the polite forms of address and expression in the local language of whatever region you will concentrate your visit: it always brightens faces when a foreigner is able to respond to greetings. Phrasebooks in local languages are generally available in capital cities. The only African language dictionaries and phrasebooks widely available in the United States are for Swahili. Swahili is widely spoken only in East Africa and Zaire, where it enjoys official status among the dozens of local languages. Swahili is a charming language; though difficult to master, it is easy to pick up everyday words and expressions. (A small Swahili glossary is included in the appendix, as is a list of useful books for further information on the language.)

DOCUMENTS AND VISAS

You will need a valid passport. Make sure that its validity extends six months beyond the end of your trip, because some nations refuse entry if less time remains till expiration. For entry purposes, you must carry an International Vaccination Certificate showing you've had shots against yellow fever and cholera. (See section on vaccinations and health, later in this chapter.)

Almost all African countries require U.S. citizens to have visas for entry. It is important that you check the visa requirements of each country you plan to visit before you start your trip. For the major tourist-oriented countries of East and southern Africa, the visa process is reasonably straightforward. For many West African countries, the paper shuffling is appalling. If you are going on a tour, the operator will probably obtain the necessary visas for you, or give you detailed instructions on how to get them.

If traveling on your own, you may be asked to provide proof of means or airline tickets that show ongoing transportation. Be sure to request single- or multiple-entry visas as needed, and to find out the *validity* of the visa before you order it. Some countries require that you enter within three months of the date the visa is issued. This is inconvenient for long-term travelers. You'll just have to pick up a few visas at national embassies within Africa—possibly more hassle, but there's no other way to do it.

Nothing complicates the African visa process more than having a South African stamp in your passport. Some countries will not grant you a visa if you already have a South African stamp. Others put on special restrictions, such as requirements that you be a bona fide participant on a prepaid tour. It's also possible that you will be harassed by immigration officials on arrival. Furthermore, regulations concerning holders of South African visas can be changed at any time. The best solution, if you are planning to visit South Africa, is to request a "loose-leaf" visa (which is detachable from your passport) when you apply for your South African visa. Or you can get a second passport from the State Department that is good for entry only to the Republic of South Africa. To visit South Africa, you must have a visa, which is easy to obtain in the United States but difficult once you are in Africa; the only place such visas are available is Lilongwe, the capital of Malawi.

If you are planning an extended independent trip, it is advised to carry a supply of passport-sized photos in case you find it necessary to obtain an unexpected visa.

Equipment and Clothing

Whether you are with a group or touring independently, the first and best rule for travelers is "Go light." Safaris are basically informal; even on luxury trips you can get by with less clothing than you might think. Limit yourself to one piece of luggage and a small bag for carrying those items you will need during the day. It's important to watch size and weight limitations on baggage, especially if your trip includes flights on light aircraft (which may limit the *total weight* of hand *and* checked luggage to as little as 27 pounds). Although international airlines allow two bags of virtually unlimited weight on departure from the United States, the maximum is 44 pounds on return flights or flights within Africa. Overweight charges are expensive. Unless you are planning to bring over specialized equipment (for professional photography, hunting, etc.), there should be no reason for your checked baggage to approach anywhere near the maximum allowance. Leave room for souvenirs you will pick up along the way.

Clothing should be chosen for practicality and versatility. Cotton safari-type clothing, comfortable and subdued in color, is ideal for day wear in the bush. The necessity for khaki colors is dubious, unless you will be on a foot safari. (Avoid camouflage clothing at all costs; it is always regarded with suspicion by military officials and police!) But safari colors are fun, and reinforce the traditional atmosphere. They also lend themselves to color coordination so you can create a varied wardrobe around a few basic pieces. Still, there's no need to buy the latest safari gear; T-shirts and shorts will do just as well.

Be prepared for cool weather as well as warm. Many East African cities and game parks are located in highlands where nights are cold. Dawn and sunset game drives in open vehicles can turn quite chilly. Bring a sweater and windproof parka shell on such drives, and layer your clothes as comfort requires. You may start a game drive in darkness, wearing the whole kit, then gradually peel off until you return for a late breakfast wearing only a T-shirt and shorts.

EQUIPMENT LIST FOR GROUP TRAVELERS

If you are participating on a tour, the operator will send a recommended list of clothing and equipment specific to your trip. For lodge and quality camping trips, the following is a recommended guide, using *maximum* numbers for each item. The actual number of any particular item will vary according to your taste, space available, and weight restrictions that apply to transport on your trip. Keep in mind that you can have laundry done at every lodge where you will be staying for two nights. Camp staff on safaris often do washing as well. (*Note:* African camp staff, who are always male, sometimes decline to wash women's panties or briefs, due to cultural taboos.) It's a great packing idea to arrange your clothes in large self-sealing (e.g., Zip-Lock) plastic bags. Also check the independent traveler's list for items that may be of use to you.

- *Duffle bag or suitcase:* It should be medium-sized (large is okay, if you have to pack a sleeping bag) and rugged. An additional bag or suitcase can usually be left in your gateway city hotel while you are out on safari. If you have any dressy city clothes for ongoing travel, leave them at the hotel.

- *Underwear:* Five or six cotton. In cool seasons it's a good idea to bring along light-weight polypropylene longjohns for nightwear, because lodges and camps may not provide that extra blanket you'd like. A cotton warm-up suit can be used for the same purpose, and doubles nicely as evening wear around the campfire.

- *Shirts:* Five or six short-sleeved, or T-shirts. At least one long-sleeved shirt should be brought for sun protection or cool weather.

- *Pants:* Two pairs of durable cotton or blend; one dressier pair for lodges and the other for use in the bush. Jeans are not recommended, for they are uncomfortable in hot weather and take too long to dry.

- *Shorts:* Two pairs.

- *Sweater:* one light to medium weight, depending on season. Also, a polypropylene jacket or down vest is welcome in the cold months.

- *Skirts:* Optional. Although not needed in the bush, they are appropriate for wear in African cities. Pants are acceptable in Nairobi, but few African women wear them, so you may feel more comfortable in a skirt when you are in town.

- *Jacket:* One windproof parka shell. Goretex is ideal because it is waterproof as well. Classic safari jackets look good but are less practical.

- *Socks:* Five to six pairs, cotton.

- *Footwear:* One pair of comfortable walking shoes with traction soles (an additional pair is useful for walking safaris or rainy-season trips). Runners or tennis shoes will do. Also, bring a pair of rubber sandals to use in the shower, hotel rooms, etc.

- *Hat:* Essential; preferably wide-brimmed. If it doesn't come with a drawstring, you should rig up a system for securing it on your head. If not, you'll be holding your hat or chasing it every time you pop your head out of a moving safari vehicle.

- *Raingear:* A poncho is useful on camping trips, even if you have a waterproof jacket. A small folding umbrella is optional for lodge trips. Check the likelihood of rain during your visit.

- *Bathing suit*

- *Optional clothing:* Bandanas, nightclothes.

- *Day pack or camera bag:* The former is preferable, and *essential* if you are going to participate on any foot safaris. Some type of small bag is needed to tote camera equipment, a sweater, guide-books, water bottle, and miscellany along on game drives.

- *Miscellaneous:* sunglasses, sun screen, insect repellent, medical kit and water purification tablets (see "Staying Healthy" section), water bottle (essential because dehydration is a common problem), toiletries, flashlight (compact but *sturdy,* with extra bulb and batteries), Swiss Army-type knife with scissors (optional but perennially useful).

- *Binoculars:* These are *essential* for good game viewing. Do not plan to share a pair; each safari member should have his or her own.

- *Optional miscellaneous items:* Cameras and photographic equipment, reference books, plastic self-sealing bags, stuff sack for dirty clothes, washup towelettes (useful), a roll of toilet paper, plastic spade, traveler's alarm clock, shoulder pouch, pocket calculator, and a collapsible nylon bag with zipper for packing souvenirs. Check the independent traveler's list for other items.

- *Giveaways:* You are sure to meet people to whom you wish to give small gifts. Clothing, especially T-shirts, is useful, as you can wear it, and then give it to someone (perhaps your driver) at the end of the trip. Many well-meaning people bring candy or balloons to give to children; these items are always a hit, but balloons spread disease from mouth to mouth, and candy is very destructive to teeth. It is far better for the kids to give them pencils or pens. Frisbees and balls are great friend-makers. Postcards of your home town and country are also great items: Africans are keen to learn about your life, too.

- *Sleeping bag:* On some camping tours, you may have to provide your own bag. Unless you are doing a real mountain trip, a lightweight summer bag (usually rated down to 40°F) will do fine in most situations. In fact, you will more often be too warm than too cold. Bring along a cotton *sleeping bag liner* or small *sheet;* it is all you will need on those tropical nights when you would roast inside even the lightest sleeping bag.

EQUIPMENT LIST FOR INDEPENDENT TRAVELERS

The group traveler's equipment just listed would suit the affluent traveler, too. With a little judicious packing and paring, the entire list can be squeezed into a manageable duffle and a day pack. Look over the following list for the odd items you might find useful: I'd particularly recommend the shoulder pouch, money belt, and pocket calculator.

As a budget traveler, you will want to carry far less. You won't have the aid of taxis, porters, or tour leaders. You'll be carrying your own load wherever you go, so every item you bring must be carefully weighed for its overall utility. It would be impossible to carry everything on the list above. The paradox is that you may need even more items, especially if you plan on camping and hiking. You must be ready for varying conditions of hot weather and cold, and even more prepared to be self-sufficient. The only solution is to cut down radically on the amount of clothes items, and every item that is not *absolutely* essential. Also, for ease of carrying (possibly for long distances), you will want to use a backpack instead of a duffle bag.

- *Backpack:* A rugged pack with an internal frame is best. It will take quite a beating on top of buses and trucks (not to mention airplanes). It should be large enough to pack your sleeping bag and all other gear within. Loops and slots for tying things on outside are handy for treks but not so practical for use on public transport. Also take a large flour sack to put the pack in when you are traveling on buses and planes; it hides your gear from prying eyes and helps prevent damage to buckles and straps.

- *Foam pad:* Needed for warmth on cold ground as well as for sleeping comfort.

- *Tent:* See *Camping equipment.*

- *Stove and fuel bottle:* See *Camping equipment.*

- *Cook kit, tableware, scrubbers:* See *Camping equipment.*

- *Skirt:* Recommended, especially a long skirt if you will visit Muslim countries.

- *Rainwear:* A poncho will protect not only you but also your pack.

- *Footwear:* If you are planning on serious mountain walking, you'll want to bring a pair of light-weight, ankle-height hiking boots.

- *Money belt:* Essential, since you will often be exposed to the public situations where pickpockets thrive. Keep your valuable documents (passport, vaccination card, air tickets) as well as money and travelers' checks in it during bus trips and other high-risk situations. Some experienced travelers prefer to sew special secret pockets into their trousers.

- *Shoulder pouch:* A handy item for carrying documents and travelers checks when they will be needed. It should have a tough strap that will resist slashing, and should not be carried conspicuously in dubious situations. Useful to all travelers for taking valuables on game drives or to meals, rather than leaving in hotel rooms.

- *Pocket calculator:* I highly recommend a model that converts to metric measurements automatically.

- *Miscellaneous:* Towel, gloves (see *Camping equipment*), sewing kit, sink stopper (flat), clothesline and pins, safety pins, can opener, various-sized plastic bags, combination lock for hotel rooms.

CAMPING EQUIPMENT LIST

With the exception of plastic jerry cans, lamps, and cleanup items, it's best to purchase quality equipment before you go.

- *Tent:* Bring a good, light-weight model, even if expensive. Good ventilation is important. Sturdiness is critical: before you go, test that it will stay up and dry in a storm. Fully zippable doors and floors will add security against crawlies.

- *Stove:* Kerosene-burning is best because that's the most commonly available fuel in Africa. Such stoves require a flammable starter, such as alcohol paste, which is a hassle, but you will always find fuel. White gas is hard to find, as are butane gas containers (Bluet Camping Gaz cartridges are notably available in Nairobi; Kigali, Rwanda; and Bujumbura, Burundi). Investigate stoves that can burn a variety of fuels, such as the Mountain Safety Research (MSR) stove.

- *Fuel bottle:* Sigg aluminum bottles are ideal. *Note:* It is illegal and dangerous to carry any fuels aboard airplane flights.

- *Cook kit, tableware, utensils:* Get good-quality, light-weight space savers.

- *Leather gloves:* Invaluable for handling thorny wood and campfires.

- *Flashlight:* If you have space, a powerful 6-volt light is best. Its beam will pick up any animals around camp before you step out of your tent at night. I also recommend it to serious game watchers, even on lodge safaris, as one often finds interesting nocturnal animals on the edges of camps and lodges.

- *Lamps:* Again, kerosene is easiest to find.

- *Miscellaneous:* washing basin, dish scrubbers, plastic jerry cans (5-gallon) or collapsible water containers, utility cord.

EQUIPMENT AND CLOTHING NOTES FOR WOMEN

In the most popular safari countries, you can feel free to wear whatever you want. In big cities, lodges, and beach resorts, the local people have been thoroughly exposed to modern Western fashions. In Muslim countries or areas, wear concealing dress to conform to local custom and to avoid sexual harassment. Some countries, such as Tanzania, have official dress codes prohibiting miniskirts and other skimpy attire. Tour group members are never bothered about such matters, but independent travelers may be. An exception is Malawi (in southern Africa), where it is forbidden for women to wear pants, and the regulation is zealously enforced.

Tampons and sanitary pads are hard to find outside major towns such as Nairobi (and then they are expensive), so bring an adequate supply.

CONTACT LENSES

Contact lens wearers always have extra problems when they travel. This is particularly so in Africa, where dust can be a real problem, especially during the popular dry seasons. Bring plenty of lubricant, and a pair of glasses as a backup. You should rely on a chemical system of cleaning contact lenses, rather than on an electrical cooker.

ELECTRICITY

Voltage and socket systems vary around the continent. Hotels in capital cities usually have twenty-four-hour electricity; game lodges run on generators that are turned off at night to conserve fuel. If you will need power, bring a 110–220 volt converter kit that includes a variety of socket plugs. Even then such adapters do not always work properly because African voltages are often inconsistent.

On camping safaris, the only electrical power may be the 12-volt battery of your vehicle. If you are bringing rechargeable battery packs, buy a kit that will permit you to recharge them from a car, and test it before the trip. Some vehicles allow access to the battery through the dashboard (possibly through cigarette lighters), but all are not so equipped. If not, you will have to rely on the driver's ingenuity in cutting and splicing wires directly to the battery.

PHOTOGRAPHY

Bush Africans may consider cameras regular pieces of the tourist's everyday dress, just like their own beaded jewelry. They could be right. Almost every tourist sports a camera. We all want a photographic record of our safari. Here are a few hints on how to make the most of your opportunities.

For the casual photographer, there is no need to run out to buy a complete new camera system. If it's a personal remembrance you are after, any of the new automatic cameras will yield satisfactory results. Scenery, companions, hotels, and people are easy subjects, while satisfactory wildlife shots can be taken in the game parks where animals let you get close. Use print film, in 100 or 200 ASA, for best color results. Faster ASA film is preferable for stop-action shots, but may produce overexposed photos.

Animals are challenging subjects for even the most experienced photographers. Those revealing wildlife shots we see in *National Geographic* are not taken on casual safaris. They are the result of months of patient work by professionals shooting with sophisticated equipment from the privacy of their own vehicles. And the pictures you see are culled from thousands. That's not to say that you can't get great shots on your safari. The opportunities are there— you can come home with lots of good pictures, and a handful of great ones.

Serious photographers will carry a 35-mm SLR (single-lens reflex) camera with interchangeable lenses. A good zoom lens is indispensable for speed and versatility in framing. An 80- to 200-mm zoom can get good wildlife pictures, even portraits, of most of the larger park animals. Lenses of 300 mm or longer are needed for quality bird pictures and for shots of the many small or shy mammals. A wide-angle lens is fun for creative shots and for getting close subjects in the context of their surroundings, while a standard 50-mm lens is used for scenery and portraits. (A zoom in the low 28- to 150-mm range could serve for all those purposes.) A macro lens is recommended for flower and insect subjects. It's obviously helpful to have two camera bodies so that you won't be constantly changing lenses.

For speed and convenient operation from a vehicle, it's best to rely on lenses that can be hand held. Fixed-focal-length telephoto lenses produce great full-frame shots at considerable distances but require the stability of a tripod for good results. Long lenses are also heavy and a major problem to transport. Easier to carry are mirror lenses, which at 500 mm give great magnification. But they have other disadvantages: fixed at F8, they can be used only in high light situations, are difficult to focus, and have an extremely shallow depth of field. In general, it's impossible to get sharp images while hand-holding any lens over 300 mm. Vehicles are unsteady shooting platforms, unless all passengers are motionless and the engine turned off. A small tripod or bean bag that can be quickly set up on the roof of the car is essential for powerful telephoto work. Motor drive is a crucial accessory for game photography because animals are constantly moving and subtly changing their expressions; when the subject is good and the light is right, you will want to be able to fire rapidly.

Be prepared to use a lot of film: good animal shots demand it. The excitement of the first few days will carry you away. You will shoot everything you see, even when the light is poor and the subject far away. Afterward you will become more selective and won't need a shot of every distant giraffe and warthog. The best time to shoot is in the early morning and late afternoon. The sun is then low, bathing every subject in a perfect, soft, golden light. Mid day tends to be too bright; pictures come out with a washed-out, overexposed look. It's useful to routinely stop down a half or even a full stop, except during those brief daily periods when the light is perfect. Travelers on extended trips have the luxury of shooting exclusively at those hours, but if you'll be in the bush for only two weeks, you'll have to shoot at the less favorable times of day, too.

A flash is useful, not only for night shots around the lodge or camp, but for daytime filler. Africans are particularly hard to photograph: their dark skins contrast strongly with the bright sunlight. Daytime flash can often correct this sometimes insurmountable exposure problem.

It is best to shoot slides. It's much cheaper to cull slides and select the good ones for reproduction than to shoot a lot of similar exposures with print film. When the subject matter is there, and especially when the light is good, you should feel free to shoot with abandon, even if you previously have taken pictures of the same animal. You won't regret the multiple exposures when you cull your slides. Often the dream shot you thought you took has been ruined by the flick of an ear or an unnoticed tuft of grass, while others prove spectacularly expressive and well exposed.

Telephoto lenses require fast film in order to permit shooting at speeds high enough to result in sharp images. Africa is rich in color, though, and the faster-speed films do not give good color saturation. 64 ASA produces vivid color shots; many professionals try to shoot with nothing else. You should count on bringing 400 ASA film too, or there will be times when you will be unable to shoot. Bring more film than you think you will need: it may not be available and would be sure to be more expensive in Africa. Do not overworry about your film going bad in the heat. Keep your reserve and exposed rolls buried deep in your luggage, and it will survive nicely.

You do have to worry about your equipment. The bouncing and dust of safari is hard on photo gear, particularly delicate high-tech electronic cameras. Once they have a problem, they are likely to be useless for the rest of the trip. A backup camera, preferably a manual model, can suddenly become more than just a convenience. It's wise to keep your cameras and lenses packed when not in use. Some suggest keeping them inside plastic bags for dust protection. However, keep in mind that if the camera is not easily accessible and ready to use, you are going to miss many of the best shots. It's really common for a perfect shot to disappear while a photographer fumbles to organize gear. Be ready, not overprotective.

More and more visitors are coming equipped with video cameras. Safari really lends itself to video: the immediacy of the experience really comes through. Buy a quality half-inch recorder so that you can edit your work when you get home; unedited videos lose viewers' interest really fast. Video cameras require a rechargeable power pack (see section on electricity).

Whether you are bringing a camera or a video recorder, learn how to use it properly before leaving home. Finally, don't let photography detract from your experience! Some people see Africa exclusively through a lens. They miss a lot.

BINOCULARS

On safari, a good pair of binoculars is more important than a credit card: don't leave home without one. Binoculars yield better views of big game animals, and allow you to see small creatures that would otherwise remain invisible. In the bush you will be using them constantly, so don't count on sharing with companions; every safarist should have his or her own.

Binoculars range from tiny opera glasses to huge military models. They are classified as 7×35^0, 8×30^0, etc. The first number refers to the power of magnification, the second to the width of the field of view. (Field of view is important mostly in low light situations— generally, the greater the arc, the better visibility will be at dawn or dusk, or in deep forest shade.) Choose a model with 7- to 9-power magnification (anything more powerful shakes as you look through them). Many models in this range come in compact sizes, which are light and therefore very convenient. Top of the line brands include Leitz and Zeiss (both very expensive); other reputable brands include Nikon and Bushnell. Each company produces one line of expensive "custom" models, in addition to cheaper types. The more expensive models offer better-quality glass optics that reduce eye strain (which can become a problem with prolonged use).

Health

As a tropical continent, Africa is beset by health problems almost unknown in the West. Here we shall review the vaccinations needed for an African journey, examine the most serious endemic diseases (and properly assess your risk of infection), and discuss insurance and the quality of local medical care. We'll also consider the contents of your personal medical kit, and assess the health risks associated with food and drink, heat and sun, and the bites of insects or snakes.

VACCINATIONS

As noted earlier, all Africa-bound travelers should carry an International Vaccination Certificate detailing a complete record of inoculations received. This is important not only for meeting entry regulations at borders, but for keeping yourself informed on your current status of protection.

Many African nations *require* vaccination against yellow fever and cholera, though these shots are not required for Kenya and Tanzania if the traveler arrives by air directly from Europe. (Even so, they are recommended if you are planning to travel *between* those two countries, if only to avoid immigration problems should official policy change suddenly.) In general though, anyone planning to visit Africa, especially where an itinerary includes more than one country, should have these two vaccinations. Yellow fever is an often fatal disease borne by the *Aedes aegypti* mosquito. It is really only a problem in West Africa and some coastal regions. Vaccination is effective for 10 years. Cholera is a great, epidemic killer that breaks out in the wake of disasters such as famine, floods, or war. Since you won't be tarrying in areas suffering those hardships, you are unlikely to come in contact with it. It is treatable with antibiotics, but since intravenous fluids are needed to keep the patient alive, it's easier to get vaccinated and stay away from epidemic zones. Vaccination requires a series of two shots; boosters are needed every six months.

Other shots are recommended, especially to overland and independent travelers. They should also be recorded in your health certificate:

• *Tetanus:* You should have this one even for outdoor adventures in your own country. Good for five years.

• *Polio:* If you are under 35 years old, get a booster if you haven't had one since childhood.

• *Typhoid:* This disease is spread through contaminated food and water. Although your chances of contracting it are slight (less than 1 in 25,000) and vaccination is only 70–90 percent effective, most physicians recommend it. Initial vaccination requires two shots, one month apart; boosters are needed every three years.

• *Gamma globulin:* This shot increases your protection from hepatitis. Effective for 3 to 6 months, depending on dose received.

Further information can be obtained from the pamphlet *Health Information for International Travelers* (U.S. government publication No. CDC 86-8280), available from the Public Health Service, Centers for Disease Control, Atlanta, Georgia 30333. You can also telephone the CDC for the most up-to-date information on vaccinations (404/639-2572) and malaria prevention (404/639-1610).

MALARIA

Malaria is a parasitic disease spread by anopheles mosquitos. There are several strains, the most common of which is caused by *Plasmodium vivax.* This form is not generally lethal, but recurs repeatedly if not treated. The organism has a dormant stage when it resides in the liver; it erupts periodically to attack red blood corpuscles, causing the classic symptoms of high fever, severe headache, chills, and aching joints. A weekly dose of chloroquine will help prevent the disease, but another form resistant to that drug is now found in many parts of the continent, including East Africa. This *Plasmodium falciparum* type is responsible for most fatalities.

The World Health Organization's (WHO's) current guidelines for malaria prophylaxis suggest that you take the following drugs:

• *Chloroquine,* 500 mg weekly. Start taking it one week before you reach Africa, and continue for four to six weeks after leaving.

• *Paludrine* (proguanil), 200 mg daily. Begin one week prior to arrival; continue for 4 weeks after departure. This drug is effective against the dangerous *falciparum* malaria, but has not yet been approved for sale in the United States. It is available over the counter in Europe (including many airport pharmacies), as well as in Nairobi and other African capitals.

- *Fansidar.* Bring at least one adult dose (three tablets) on safari, to be taken if you come down with severe fever and have no access to medical care. Fansidar provides effective protection against *falciparum* malaria, but is not recommended for prophylactic use because it can cause severe side effects, particularly in those allergic to sulfa drugs. If you are sulfa-sensitive, consult a physician about using doxycycline (100 mg daily) for malaria protection.

Recommendations for malaria prophylaxis change frequently, so be sure to check with the CDC or your local health department for the latest information.

Malaria is responsible for an estimated one million deaths per year in Africa, and millions more suffer from chronic infection. The victims are mostly rural Africans who have no access to prophylactic drugs or medical care. Tourists are not immune, however; every year some visitors come down with it. If you are unlucky, seek medical attention and you will live to tell the tale. You need no longer fear lifelong recurrences, as there are now drugs to cleanse the liver of dormant parasites.

OTHER TROPICAL DISEASES

Parts of Africa, especially the steamy forest regions, used to be known as "the white man's grave." Modern drugs have made travel much more hospitable, although the tropical forests still harbor more than their share of exotic maladies. It is extremely unlikely that you will contract anything as gruesome as river blindness, Guinea worm, elephantiasis, or leprosy. The following African illnesses are of more concern to visitors, if only because they are better known.

Bilharzia. Bilharzia, or schistosomiasis, is contracted by contact with infected waters. The parasite takes many forms during its life cycle, living first in certain specific species of snail, then briefly as a free-floating microorganism, and finally as a blood fluke inside the human body (in the blood vessels of the intestines or bladder). It enters the body directly through the pores of the skin. Human wastes complete the cycle by putting the organism back into the waters they pollute. In this way, it has been widely spread around the continent. It is found in standing and sluggish waters, especially those in inhabited districts.

The oft-heard rule to avoid bilharzia is an injunction *never* to enter any freshwater bodies in Africa, except the few lakes supposed to be free of infection. This is a good rule *if* you are on your own and have no knowledge of the area you are in. But don't let it scare you into missing out on bathing opportunities when conditions are safe. I've had several clients who were suffering from intense heat exhaustion, but refused to take a cooling dip in the waters of a perfectly safe river (in which I've bathed dozens of times), because they were overly paranoid about bilharzia. Rivers in uninhabited areas can be considered safe, or at least low risk. Camping in remote parks in East Africa would be impossible without using river water for washing; even rustic lodges may pump their shower water out of nearby rivers. Obviously all river-running trips (and many walking safaris) would be out of the question if the water injunction were strictly kept. If you are with professional guides, trust their judgment: they don't want to be infected either. Nonetheless, if you are to go on certain trips, particularly river journeys, there is a certain amount of risk. If you are not prepared to deal psychologically with reasonable risks, avoid such expeditions.

Bilharzia was formerly difficult to cure (the side effects of treatment were nearly as unpleasant as the disease), but a new drug—Biltracide (praziquantel)—clears it up with a single dose of oral medication. If symptoms develop—flulike illness, sometimes accompanied by a skin rash, or especially blood in the urine or stool—after your return from Africa, call the CDC and get a test immediately.

Sleeping Sickness. This disease is spread by the celebrated tsetse fly. Although you may visit parks where tsetse flies are amply present, you have little to fear. The worst zones for sleeping sickness are in tropical West Africa (as usual), not the game parks of the east and south. Many tsetse-infested areas are completely free of human sleeping sickness. It has been estimated that only one in 100,000 tsetse in infected zones carries the trypanosome that causes the disease. Risk of exposure is therefore relatively low for the short-term visitor. The disease is fatal if untreated, but is rare among tourists; it is rarer still for them to let it go unattended.

AIDS. Evidence seems to point to tropical Africa as the original home of the AIDS virus. It is estimated that millions of Africans, both men and women, have been exposed to this deadly disease.

AIDS is transmitted through intimate sexual contact or the use of contaminated needles and blood products. You can practically eliminate your risk of catching it by practicing sexual abstinence or "safe sex" techniques (the use of condoms is recommended). If you must receive shots while in Africa, make sure that the needle has been sterilized. If you must have a blood transfusion, you will have to take your chances or hope that someone in your party will be able to donate the needed plasma. You should know your blood group and type, and record it, in case of emergency. Blood supplies are screened in Nairobi, but are not necessarily reliable elsewhere.

INSURANCE AND MEDICAL CARE IN AFRICA

African medical facilities are generally poor by Western standards. Most countries can deliver only rudimentary medical care to their own citizens; many people in remote areas simply do without. Hopefully, you won't have to go unattended if you need a doctor, but be aware of the quality of care to expect.

Capital cities are the best place to seek care, as the governmental and diplomatic communities have to be serviced by the best. A fully modern private hospital, staffed by European professionals, is likely to be found there. Many countries have public hospitals and clinics where care is very low cost or free. Doctors may be highly qualified, but expect long waits and marginal sanitary conditions, and basic medical supplies may be in short supply. They are suitable to visit for minor complaints, but if anything is seriously wrong, seek out a private hospital or physician, if available. There are also many missionary hospitals and clinics in Africa. Conditions are likely to be as crowded and chaotic as in the government-run public hospitals, but they are often staffed by highly qualified foreign doctors.

Virtually all the above-mentioned facilities are capable of handling routine traveler's complaints, including serious bouts of malaria. Except in the direst emergency, avoid hospitalization, especially surgery, in most African countries. From any African capital, you are only a few hours' flying time from Europe.

Be sure to get medical insurance coverage for the length of your trip. Check your regular health insurance company to see what they cover, or if you can get a supplementary policy through them. Various insurance companies sell travelers' medical policies through travel agents. You must expect to pay any medical costs up front in Africa, and be paid back by your insurance company after you present them with documentation of your bills.

You might consider joining the Flying Doctors Society. It provides medical care to Africans living in remote areas and emergency air evacuation to its members. Write to the African Medical and Research Foundation, 68 Upper Richmond Road, London, SW15 2RP, England, or their U.S. office at 420 Lexington Avenue, New York, New York 10170. Some companies operating safaris in East Africa automatically enroll their clients.

WATER AND FOOD

Food and drink are the commonest sources of travelers' illnesses, from serious diseases like hepatitis to that familiar bugaboo, diarrhea. The basic rule for shunning illness is to watch what you eat or drink. Rigidly applied, this means avoiding all uncooked vegetables or unpeeled fruits and drinking only purified water. The problem is that it is difficult to apply these standards rigorously. Tour members, whether at lodges or private camps, will confront a parade of tempting goodies, including fresh salads. Although standards of cleanliness are likely to be high, there are no guarantees. Budget travelers, living on the local economy, will often be exposed to situations where they have no choice but to accept some risk. In fact, all travelers have to decide for themselves what constitutes reasonable risk.

We have to consider our individual differences in tolerance for new foods and resistance to G.I. (gastrointestinal) problems. The most common cause of tourist diarrhea is the *E. coli* bacterium, which is already present in each of our systems. The introduction of local strains may cause one person's intestines to go completely berserk, while another's adapt with ease. If you know you always get sick when you travel, be totally strict about dietary rules. The experienced traveler whose gut has been exposed to every bug in the world is allowed a lot more discretion. If you are on a short tour, it's worth considering whether a tasty treat may cause three or four days of unpleasantness. That caution is not meant to encourage food paranoia—just decide how you will deal with food risks and accept your luck.

No discretion should be allowed with water. Most lodges and camps claim to provide boiled and filtered drinking water, and use it to make their ice. Nonetheless, it does not hurt to be too careful. Every traveler should have a water purification kit of some kind. Halizone or Potable Agua tablets are acceptable; supernatant iodine solutions are better (they kill giardia and amoebic cysts). All discol-

or water and give it an unpleasant taste, so you might bring along a supply of powdered fruit drinks to make it more palatable. Fancy charcoal-chemical systems work too, but are probably too cumbersome for most travelers. Bring your own water bottle and keep a supply of purified water on hand. Use it to brush your teeth as well as for drinking.

Milk products in lodges and most cities are safe; the milk has been boiled, if not pasteurized. In bush places, it's wise to look for the skin floating on top to be sure it has been boiled.

MEDICAL KIT

Every traveler should have a medical kit for minor emergencies (cuts, blisters, etc.), and medications to cover a fairly wide range of problems. The following items are recommended:

- *Tape and sterile gauze pads:* Breathable medical tape is useful not only for dressings but for covering possible blister sites before they develop. It stays on better than moleskin.

- *Band-Aids:* A few assorted sizes.

- *Betadine:* A germicidal solution for cleaning wounds. Available in convenient swabs.

- *Antibiotic ointment*

- *Scissors*

- *Tweezers*

- *Thermometer*

- *Needle:* For splinters.

The following are useful options to include, especially for long-term travelers:

- *Ace bandage*

- *Temporary tooth filling (Cavit):* Oil of clove and a cotton ball will serve the same purpose if you lose a filling.

- *Eyecup:* Very useful for washing foreign objects out of the eye. Dust and tiny flies in the eye are common, painful problems. Washing removes them faster and more safely than rubbing.

- *Cortisone cream:* For bites.

- *Safety pins*

Many recommended medications require a doctor's prescription. Consult your doctor about dosages, side effects, and possible allergic reactions.

- *Antibiotics:* A wide-spectrum antibiotic can do wonders against serious cases of diarrhea. Bactrim and Septra (brand names for sulfamethoxazole) are highly favored. They are a sulfa drug, so they cannot be taken if you are using Fansidar against malaria. Doxycycline is a mild form of the wide-spectrum tetracycline. Taken prophylactically, it can effectively prevent travelers' diarrhea. However, it makes the skin more sensitive to sunburn, a real concern in Africa.

- *Lomotil* (diphenoxylate and atropine) or *Imodium* (loperamide): Either is effective for stopping diarrhea symptoms. They are plugs, not cures. They are very helpful on those sad days when you have the runs but must face hard travel.

- *Tylenol* (acetaminophen) *with codeine:* Codeine can be used as a plug for the runs, or for serious pain.

- *Valium* (diazepam) or *Halcion* (triazolam): Good on those nights when you *must* sleep, and for overnight airplane flights.

- *Benadryl* (diphenlydramine): A life saver if you suffer terrible itching from insect bites.

- *Antihistamine:* For colds and nasal allergies.

- *Aspirin*

- *Contraceptives:* It's best to bring a supply that will last for the duration of your trip. Condoms may be found sporadically in big cities. Birth control pills and spermicides would be more difficult to find, and possibly of dubious quality.

SUN AND HEAT

Africa is generally hot, sometimes ferociously so. It is very important to keep up your fluid intake. Dehydration can lead to serious heat exhaustion, and in combination with antimalarial drugs, may cause painful kidney stones. Carry your water bottle with you on game drives as well as walks, and drink frequently. Avail yourself of the opportunities to quaff soft drinks, coffee, tea, or beers. The last three are diarrhetics, so you'll lose fluid about as quickly as you gain it, but that's okay as long as you keep drinking.

The African sun should not be underestimated—it can be a real killer, especially during the hot seasons. You should worry more about sunstroke than suntan. When in the sun, wear your hat. If it's really hot, follow the animals' example: take advantage of shade at every opportunity. Avoid sunburn: use sun screen or wear long sleeves if you are particularly photosensitive.

INSECTS AND CRAWLIES

Insect fear is a common pretrip paranoia of Africa-bound travelers. These fears are mostly groundless. Except within the steamy tropical zones, insects are no more a problem in safari country than in many parts of the United States, and for the most part even less so. In certain places and seasons, mosquitos are abundant, but they are more likely to be completely absent from most places on your itinerary. African mosquitos are generally active only at night. They never occur in the daytime swarms that plague hikers in Alaska or the Sierra Nevada. Where they are numerous, long sleeves or insect repellant can be worn outdoors, while mosquito nets or a fully netted tent assure comfort while you sleep.

Flies are an occasional nuisance. Tsetses are voracious biters, and many people suffer extreme itchiness as a reaction. In tsetse fly country, long sleeves and strong repellent are the way to go (repellent has variable results: sometimes it's effective, other times seemingly useless). Some safari veterans suggest that tsetses are attracted to dark colors; this is unproven, but it can't hurt to wear light earth-toned fabrics. Fortunately, tsetses are largely absent from the popular game parks of East Africa; where they do occur, their distribution tends to be spotty. Central and southern African parks are more heavily infested. Although tsetses are responsible for the transmission of sleeping sickness, the incidence is so low that it is not worth worrying about for the short-term visitor. Other flies are occasionally abundant, but are annoying for their numbers rather than their bites. Sporadically, local conditions may be just right for ordinary housefly-type insects to be present in massive numbers. They are often attracted to the warmth and moisture of exposed human skin. It's unpleasant to have carpets of flies sitting on you, even though they don't bite. Long sleeves and repellent effectively prevent this uncomfortable circumstance. Flies are more of an esthetic problem. It horrifies us to see African children sitting indifferently while flies crawl around their eyes (yes, this is unhealthy, for it spreads eye disease), but they have tired of the impossible task of shooing away infinite numbers. You will never get accustomed to that, but you may have to accommodate yourself to their presence.

"Killer bees" are the cause of some concern due to hysterical stories in the press chronicling their invasion of the Americas. The African honey bee does occasionally attack in dangerous swarms, but very rarely. Care should be taken not to provoke attack, particularly by inundating nesting holes with fumes. This sometimes inadvertently occurs when safarists happen to top up their gas tank while beneath the wrong tree. Baobabs are favorite nesting trees because of the number of hollow nesting sites they offer. If a swarm attacks, it does so with great fury. Bee toxins are proportionately among the strongest animal poisons known. Massive numbers of stings can be fatal, but most often the result is swelling and extreme discomfort. Those people most at risk are naturally those who are allergic to bee stings. They may suffer severe anaphylactic shock (swelling of the throat that cuts off breathing), from even a few stings, just as they might from bees at home. If you are severely allergic to bees, you may want to carry injectable adrenalin (available as Anakit with a doctor's prescription) just in case. Chances are, you'll never use it. Antihistamines such as Benadryl are effective in reducing the pain and itching of bee stings as well as scorpion stings and insect bites.

Scorpions are common enough, particularly in hot country. Being secretive and largely nocturnal, they are rarely encountered on lodge safaris. Campers sometimes find them underneath tents when packing up camp. Stings may be sickeningly painful, but only the super-allergic are in any danger. It's best to keep door and floor zips shut whenever you enter or leave your tent, and to keep your duffle zipped as well. This is an effective defense against all discomforting visitors.

Ticks climb aboard animals as they move through brush or long grass. Participants on foot safaris should check for them, especially in moist and warm parts of the body. Remove embedded ticks as soon as possible because they are potential carriers of febrile diseases. Tiny "pepper ticks" look like grains of spice. Itchy rather than dangerous, they can be picked up by the dozens as you walk through wet grass.

SNAKEBITE

Snakes are common animals throughout much of Africa. For the most part, they are small and secretive. Many are poisonous, however, and among them are a few notably large and dangerous species. These generate exaggerated fear, but are in fact not much threat to tourists. The burden of exposure to snakebite is once again borne by indigenous Africans who come into accidental contact with the reptiles during the normal course of their lives: cutting bush, gathering firewood, walking in nighttime darkness. Snakes avoid humans when they can, and you will be lucky even to see one during the course of a two-week game-viewing safari. Campers and hikers are more likely to come into the proximity of snakes and should follow a few commonsense rules to stay out of trouble:

- Use a flashlight when walking at night. This is the best protection against the puff adder, the bane of barefooted bush Africans. It is a common but sluggish snake that freezes motionless when approached, in the hopes of going unnoticed. It most often succeeds, but will bite if stepped on.

- Think snake! In cool weather, they are apt to lie in exposed places, warming themselves in the morning sun. At other times, they usually hide themselves in holes and rock crevices, or under logs. Consider where they are likely to be, and take extra care in high-risk areas.

- Be careful in long grass. Most snakes flee when ground vibrations warn them of approaching danger, so tread hard and they'll get off your path. (This procedure is not recommended when stalking game.)

- If you encounter a snake, back off and give it a chance to escape. Do not attempt to kill or annoy it. Once seen, a snake is no longer a danger unless provoked.

The oft-quoted admonition to wear high boots and long pants whenever walking in the bush is pure nonsense. This rule is applicable to herpetologists who go actively searching for snakes. If you are planning on turning over logs and poking into holes, by all means take these extra precautions and more. Although boots and long pants do effectively protect the legs, they are cumbersome and uncomfortable. Few bush walkers will consider the bother worth the extra margin of protection.

In the rare event of an actual snakebite, do not panic. Try to kill the animal for positive identification (but not at the risk of further bites). Do not make incisions to suck poisons (cutting should probably *never* be done, as it substantially increases the risk of limb loss) or apply tourniquets unless the snake is positively identified as a cobra or mamba. Stay calm: sudden death from even the most poisonous snakebites is rare, while shock from nonpoisonous bites is a common reaction. Get to medical attention as soon as possible. Anti-venom serums are available for all the common poisonous snakes. Several species of cobra spit venom at the eyes of perceived attackers. Venom in the eye causes severe burning and temporary blindness. It should be flushed out immediately with any available liquid (water, Coke, urine) to prevent any risk of permanent damage.

Personal Safety

Perhaps more than other continents, Africa seems tinged with an aura of danger. To routine concerns about the incidence of violent crime (which must be considered wherever we travel) are added worries about wars and political upheavals, as well as fears about wild animals. Here we'll examine each of these issues and put them into a proper perspective.

POLITICAL STABILITY

Africa has a reputation for coups and bush wars. Although there is plenty of conflict on the continent, the news media sometimes blow stories out of proportion. The true danger for visitors is often hard to assess; while news pundits discourse on guerrilla wars and diplomatic negotiations, tourists may be visiting peaceful game parks in another part of the same country. True hot-spots—places where full-fledged wars are in progress and society has broken down— should definitely be avoided. These include the southern Sudan, Angola, Mozambique, and parts of Uganda. South Africa, Namibia, and Ethiopia can be visited in safety because you will not be allowed to go into zones where actual combat is taking place. Random acts of terrorism are always possible, but that is the price of travel anywhere these days.

Coups in the East African countries that are the major safari destinations have been rare. Trans-Africa overland travelers face more risk. In the event of a coup, do what everyone else does: stay out of sight. Violence in these upheavals is usually confined to rival factions. Tourists should stay indoors till the smoke clears, then make their presence known to their embassy as soon as possible. During political crises (such as South African raids on neighboring nations), nervous police or army personnel have been known to accuse tourists of being spies. This may be scary, but will come out all right if you observe the usual rules governing unreasonable arrests: keep your cool, be patient, identify yourself, and insist (politely) on seeing higher-ranking officers.

Tourists occasionally find themselves in trouble for breaching local security regulations, usually by taking photos of forbidden places. These may include bridges, railroads, dams, airports, police stations, and army bases. Such cases can result in protracted negotiations, the confiscation of film, or even detention. When "No Photo" signs are posted, take them seriously.

CRIME

Lawlessness is no worse in Africa than other parts of the world, and the same commonsense rules apply. Cities are the highest crime areas, as the urban poor are the most desperate. Petty thievery is the biggest problem. In crowded situations, be extra alert for pickpockets. Use your money belt around town and when using public transport. Walking city streets, keep a good grip on your purse or shoulder bag. Purse snatchers are fast; they sometimes slash the strap from behind. Hustlers, often with very good raps, have various schemes to part you from your money (usually voluntarily). Politely ignore them. Armed robberies and muggings are common in big cities, so avoid walking the streets after dark.

Money, not rape, is the usual object of violent encounters, and tourists are seldom sexually assaulted. Rapes are sometimes reported to occur on the Kenya coast, where women are advised not to stroll or sunbathe alone on deserted beaches. In major cities and tourist resorts, some men are not shy about approaching foreign women, but for the most part, their come-ons are strictly verbal. Single women will find the level of sexual harassment in Africa is not nearly as bad as in some other parts of the world, such as Mexico or Italy.

The independent traveler will have the toughest time with security. Make sure your hotel room doors lock properly, and even check for access through the window. Gear has to be constantly watched. Team up with other travelers to keep an eye out for each other's possessions.

Theft is not unknown even in the finest hotels or while on safari. Camera equipment can safely be left in your room in tourist-class hotels, or inside your safari vehicle during the day (it's part of your driver's job to look after your gear). But don't leave money or traveler's checks. It's a common technique for hotel personnel to remove only a few checks from the back of the book, so that the theft is not discovered immediately. The best rule is to not put temptation in anyone's path. Avail yourself of the hotel safe, or carry your money with you at all times.

ANIMALS

It's partly the old hunter's mystique of the "dangerous game" that draws us to safari. African animals are not only beautiful; many of them are also large and dangerous. How dangerous? What are your chances of being killed or injured?

Many wild animals can potentially harm humans, but in fact the chances of them bothering with you are extremely low. Wildlife has been on the losing end of a very long war with humanity. By the process of natural selection, the animals have learned to fear us as their chief natural enemies. An animal's first inclination is almost inevitably to run away on contact with humans. There are situations where this is not so, but "accidents" involving tourists are rare. As usual, the brunt of wildlife danger falls mostly on indigenous Africans who come into contact and conflict with animals in the course of their normal lives. Elephants raid crop fields, the farmer gets hurt trying to chase them away. A woman, gathering firewood in the forest, meets a testy buffalo. The fisherman's dugout gets overturned by an angry hippo. The herdsman tries to protect his cattle from a hungry lion, but his spear is not aimed true. Poachers wound an animal, and it kills the next hapless person it meets. These are the typical situations where humans run into trouble with animals.

Most visitors come into contact with wildlife only while touring game parks from the safety of vehicles. Although it is not unknown for large animals to attack cars, it is an extremely rare event and takes some extraordinary provocation. Most parks have rules against getting out of vehicles. Although these regulations are sometimes overrigorous, they are designed to protect naive people from themselves. Even with the rules, the occasional person does something stupid, like get out of the car to take a better picture of lions (see Akagera Park section in Chapter 6). People have problems when they forget that the animals are truly wild. If a human gets too close, the instinct to fight overpowers the instinct for flight.

You are most likely to get into trouble with animals at the lodges where certain individuals lose all fear of human beings. Troops of vervet monkeys or baboons often forage on lodge grounds, stealing food from dining verandahs. Occasionally a bull elephant becomes a lodge regular, too. These animals are "cute," the delight of guests, but should not to be taken for granted. Tourists often feed the baboons, and sometimes get bitten for their kindness (if it is kindness, for feeding reinforces pesty habits for which they sometimes "have to be shot"). Guests also routinely ignore warnings not to approach seemingly tame elephants. This is a mistake, for no matter how tame they seem, elephants are irascible, unpredictable, and capable of mayhem.

To a large extent, whether you have animal problems is up to you. As long as you treat them with proper respect for their capabilities, you can enjoy the wildlife without incident. In fact, you are much less likely to be injured or killed by a wild animal in a game park than by an automobile on one of the main highways.

Special precautions govern safety with animals on camping and foot safaris. They are detailed in the "Living in the Bush" section, later.

Traveler's Etiquette

No one consciously wants to play the part of the boorish tourist. Yet some travelers do as they please, without ever giving any thought to local standards of conduct or assessing their own responsibility for things that take place. Here we'll consider some of the thorny issues of personal behavior you are likely to encounter during your trip to Africa.

CULTURAL IMPACT AND EXCHANGE

Whatever style of adventure you embark on, you are guaranteed to come up against the cultural differences between our supermodern, superrich society and that of Africa. Africans think and do things differently from the way we do: by our standards, many things are done inefficiently or at least peculiarly. Attitudes toward time, business, or politics are governed by different traditions and philosophies. Some of those traditions are very old indeed. At the same time, no country or continent is an island now, and Western influences abound. Africans clamor after the trappings of consumer society. Government officials and the nouveau riche have taken readily to the symbols of conspicuous consumption—the Mercedes car and bottles of imported foreign liquors are badges of success. For ordinary people, high status can take the form of a wristwatch or a good pair of shoes.

Approach Africans with an attitude of respect. By and large, they are hospitable people, ready with a smile and a greeting. Most tourists respond with genuine warmth, but some treat Africans as curiosities, not as people. This rudeness naturally provokes distance if not hostility. Africans are extremely sensitive to condescending attitudes. Traditional people are proud of their tribal attire. Poor Africans do not seek to give offense by the raggedness of their clothes. Avoid giving inadvertent offense through thoughtless condescension.

Nothing will try your diplomatic skills more than negotiating the shoals of paperwork and bureaucracy. What might be a simple task in the United States—cashing a traveler's check at a bank, or reconfirming an airline ticket—can turn into a major test of patience. Long waiting lines, consultations with managers (who may be absent), and unexpected problems are routine in some quarters. Handling paperwork becomes a maddeningly slow process, especially if you are under time pressure. Generally, well-mannered patience and perseverance are your only recourse. A raised voice or bullying tone is inevitably met by a stony wall of resistance. All further entreaties and conversation may be ignored. Apologies may save the day, but just as likely your cause is dead unless you can get to a higher official.

There are situations where any traveler's patience would fail. Scenario: you arrive at the airport to find that the record of your confirmed reservation has disappeared, and you are now waitlisted for an obviously overbooked flight. Of course, it's best to keep your cool and remain polite, but in such truly do-or-die situations, dogged perseverance has to be combined with the right combination of humility and bluster. Where entreaty and threat fail, bribes may see you through, but this approach requires great discretion. When bumped from the flight roster, resubmitting your ticket with a U.S. banknote tucked behind the coupon and a polite suggestion that there may have been some mistake, is more effective than flashing a

$100 bill in full view of lookers on. Bribery is always ethically questionable, but sometimes it works. However, you should resist deliberate shakedowns for bribes when possible.

Politics is another area where you must remain a diplomat. African political systems are almost universally one-party states, governed with varying degrees of authoritarian control. Few countries have any strong tradition of a free press, so where outright repression doesn't inhibit political discussion, indifference and ignorance do. Sources of information are basically limited to the national media, which are absorbed in local trivia (sometimes interesting!), official pronouncements, and ideological rhetoric. Consequently, most Africans are not given to an interest in deep political discussions. But while conversations may be short on sophisticated analysis, they reveal a lot about the way the country is run, and the ordinary citizen's attitudes toward the powers that be. There is generally a strong traditional respect for the authority of the presidential figure. Whoever is in charge of the country you are in, his face will smile down at you in countless shops and offices. Africans are often shocked by foreigners' candid criticisms of their own leaders; no matter how readily they may discuss their country's problems, Africans would rarely think to voice disapproval of their president or party.

Shopping is different in Africa, too. Although modern shops tend to set fixed prices for their goods, local marketeers and artisans are ever ready to bargain. Where appropriate, don't be put off by bargaining. It can be fun, and as in so many parts of the world, it is the traditional way to do business. You'll have to sharpen your negotiating skills, or you may wind up paying twice as much as you need to spend. The standard formula is to offer about half what the vendor asks, and settle in between. (Be careful, though—you can as easily start at a quarter the asking price.) It helps to shop around without expressing too much interest. Prices often come tumbling down if you are willing to walk away. At the same time, there is no use beating a vendor down to a giveaway price—they do have to make a living and are entitled to a profit. Don't make offers on items you don't really want. You may find your price accepted and feel obligated to buy. Trading for Western goods—watches, calculators, clothing—is an acceptable part of marketing. Many travelers bring items especially for this purpose. If you do, try to bring decent goods rather than worthless junk.

Most Africans are cash poor but self-sufficient. The extended family system takes care of the sick and elderly, but some unfortunates are always left out. The desperate resort to begging. It doesn't hurt to give something to obviously handicapped or destitute people. But it may be harmful to make random gifts to perfectly healthy children. Many tourists like to give away candy or balloons. The kids love it, and it's certainly fun to watch the children enjoying the treat. But the long-term effect is to encourage them to demand gifts of every tourist they see, which is not a good habit. It's one of travel's moral dilemmas: do we cause more harm than good through our well-intentioned interactions with indigenous peoples? There really is no answer. If you'd like to bring giveaways, I'd suggest pencils or pens over candy. Such school supplies are always in demand, for adults as well as children.

THE BLACK MARKET

Where economies are tightly controlled, black markets thrive. They are nowhere healthier than in Africa where rates are often laughably low when compared to the actual purchasing power of the dollar in the local economy.

The black market is a reflection of the vicious circle of many African economies. Governments try to maximize their imports of foreign exchange ("hard" currencies like the U.S. dollar, British pound, etc.) by arbitrarily setting their own exchange rates for their currencies. In a free market, these currencies would be valued much lower. By controlling the rates, the Africans force Western companies to pay higher prices for exported commodities. That's good for the African countries. But the system goes wrong because the governments are unable, or unwilling, to squelch the free market. Many people—businessmen, expatriate contract workers, and corrupt government officials—have an interest in getting foreign exchange out of the country. They may need the dollars—which they are forbidden to buy or export—to finance business ventures, foreign travel, education for their children, or the purchase of consumer items unavailable in Africa. Many, especially government officials, want to amass assets outside their own country as security against an uncertain future. For an official in a coup-prone nation, a Swiss bank account is a desirable thing. Although the majority of African citizens see little of it, the wealthier classes have plenty of local currency, and frequently nothing to spend it on. They can afford to buy dollars at two, three, five, twenty times—whatever the market will bear—the official exchange rate, creating the black market. None of the dollars exchanged on the black market do the African country any good. They are all smuggled out and do nothing to help the national treasury with its desperate foreign exchange deficit.

The black market presents the traveler with another moral dilemma. It enables you to stretch your travel dollars; often just a little, sometimes enormously. It also does incontestable harm to the African host economy. It is easy to rationalize black market trading: the exchange rate does reflect the real purchasing power of your money, while the official rate may be blatantly ridiculous. And everyone does it, often including the top political leaders of the country. Whether to participate or not is dictated by each traveler's circumstances. Many budget travelers would be hard put to get along in Africa without it. Tourists on prepaid tours usually have little contact with it. (Their tour companies have presumably paid for the arrangements through official bank channels. In this wicked world, however, that is no guarantee that all the money will see its way to the proper African national treasury.) For group travelers, the black market is a lesser temptation, something that can stretch pocket money for souvenirs. For most, it is not worth bothering with.

Needless to say, the black market is illegal. Most countries have supposedly stringent currency control regulations. On entry you make a written declaration of all cash and travelers' checks. All subsequent currency exchanges (made only with officially authorized institutions—banks, hotels, airlines, etc.) should be recorded on your declaration form. On leaving the country, you have to surrender your currency form to customs. If they count your money going out, and the amount doesn't jive with the figures on your currency form, you are theoretically in trouble. However, it is very rare for customs officers to count a traveler's money, or even check the forms closely. And even if the figures don't measure up, the lamest excuses are almost invariably accepted. When travelers do wind up in trouble through black market dealings, it is usually through entrapment by undercover police. It is inadvisable to change money with people on the street: it is high risk for ripoff, shakedown, or arrest. It's safest to exchange with shopkeepers.

PHOTOGRAPHING PEOPLE

Africans are touchy about having their pictures taken. The roots of this sensitivity may or may not lie with superstitions concerning the camera stealing the soul. It is official discouragement and economic considerations that make Africans reluctant to smile for the camera today.

In postindependence Africa, government officials spread the view that tourists took pictures of Africans only to mock them as curiosities, "just like the animals in the game parks." Officials took a particularly dim view of photos of bare-breasted or spear-toting natives. They were anxious to project a modern image for their countries, not to be seen as "primitives." In some places it became illegal to take pictures of colorful tribespeople. Generally, the word was put out that Africans shouldn't allow themselves to be photographed. That view mellowed with the increasing influx of tourists. Once it became clear that tourists were willing to pay for pictures, photo privileges became an economic resource. Now it's standard to pay people if you wish to take their picture. Many visitors take umbrage at having payment demanded for photos, but you can hardly blame the Africans for asking. They know that foreigners are all wealthy by their standards, and can easily afford a small payment. They also know that pictures are potentially valuable—that they can be sold to magazines for a great deal of money, none of which they will see. They have no way of knowing which shots will end up in a private photo album and which on the cover of *National Geographic*. It really is not unreasonable to pay them a modeling fee.

The worst drawback to paying for photos is that the prices must be negotiated before you take them. This makes it hard to get lively shots, as people tend to stiffen up for the camera. But if you shoot first, even with the intention of paying later, there is likely to be an unpleasant scene. The subjects will think that you were "poaching" a picture. This is a bad bargaining position. People often ask for ridiculously large amounts of money. You shouldn't have to pay very much, but of course it depends on the subject. Dandified Masai warriors in full ochered regalia will naturally want a high fee, while young herdboys might settle for a few coins. Be sure to negotiate a complete deal so that one fee covers as many pictures as you want. Otherwise you may take a snap, but wind up in a new negotiation when you try to take a second. The urge to steal candid shots is sometimes irresistible, but be prepared for problems.

ON SAFARI

Numerous national park regulations govern the behavior of visitors. Park rules vary from one country to the next, but they all have two common threads: (1) the protection of plants and animals and (2) the safety of visitors. Although few tourists argue with safety rules, other restrictions are sometimes ignored. These rules warrant some thought.

Protecting the animals entails more than simply preventing poachers from shooting them. It also means habitat conservation. Toward that end, it is increasingly necessary for park authorities to forbid off-road driving. In heavily visited reserves, cross-country driving is seriously degrading fragile grasslands and leaving tire tracks as permanent scars on the landscape. The "no off-road" rule is often resented: it upsets the wilderness "feel" of safari and makes it difficult to photograph animals that are far from the track. So, however good for the long-term health of the parks, off-road prohibitions are regularly disregarded. Safari drivers, and even park rangers, routinely "poach" on the grass in the hopes of pleasing their clients and garnering larger tips.

The most heavily visited parks are usually the most restrictive. They are also the places where game guards are most likely to allow the rules to be bent. Some reserves have a more sensible policy: you have to stay on the tracks until you spot one of the "biggies," after which you are allowed off the road to take pictures. This rule recognizes that almost everyone will go off the road anyway: this way it can be done in a more relaxed manner, slowly and carefully (which does less damage to the land than high-speed maneuvers), and does away with the syndrome in which park personnel are encouraged to break the rules they are supposed to enforce.

Animals are also protected from harassment. It is sad that many safari drivers, overanxious to please their tourists, behave without regard to animal activities. It is common for a driver to spot an animal and immediately drive straight to it for photos. This can disrupt animals in the process of stalking prey or courtship display. Chasing animals is also too common. It's particularly harmful when young animals are involved, for they frequently get separated and made more vulnerable to enemies. The most contemptible action is the use of vehicles to herd prey animals toward predators in the hope of producing an instant kill. This is not only against park rules, but also against the whole spirit of safari. We come to see animals behave naturally. If we are lucky enough to witness the drama of a hunt, it is a privilege, not an entertainment. To see a kill, you need patience and luck. To see an animal butchered, you need only visit a slaughterhouse in your home town.

Visitors are not usually directly responsible for such bad behavior, just the passive accessories of overzealous safari personnel. But you can prevent serious harassment just by exerting your authority. Remember, it's your safari and you are in control. Don't let your driver disturb the animals because he thinks that it will please you! You can also help prevent other parties from indulging in this sort of thing, if you see it happening.

Visitors sometimes "poach" on parks by not paying their fees. This is one area where you should not cut corners, for fees are the lifeblood of the parks. It takes money to patrol against squatters and poachers who threaten the wildlife's survival, as well as to maintain roads and game tracks for the benefit of visitors. Fees are usually two-tiered: a lower rate for residents of the country and a higher one for foreign tourists. Even the higher rates are still quite reasonable: in Kenya entry fees cost less than the admission price to a film in the United States. That's not bad, especially when you consider what the fee goes to protect and the fact that most parks don't even collect enough to cover their operating costs. Members of group tours themselves ordinarily don't pay, as fees are included in the tour price. But sometimes tour operators try to avoid payment, and this should not be tolerated. Budget travelers, who have to watch every penny, are more prone to fudging on fees. They sometimes gripe about paying the higher prices, especially where the fees must be paid in dollars. Another moral dilemma!

Official regulations have to be tempered with common sense and courtesy. Littering is illegal; moreover, it's ridiculous to come into a pristine natural area and leave trash behind. Safari drivers often leave picnic refuse in the bush. Make sure they take it out or bury it properly. Take care not to interrupt other parties' game-viewing pleasure by talking loudly while observing animals, driving in front of their field of vision, or passing without pause for a look around. You may scare away animals that you can't see or don't interest you, but that others are watching.

Many visitors are unfamiliar with toilet procedures in the bush. If necessary, you can ask your driver to stop anywhere he can. If you are in a game park, do not wander any great distance from the car; even just behind the car will do in the utmost emergency, though you can usually find a discreet bush. Please bury, burn, or carry out any toilet paper. People on camping safaris will find a small spade helpful.

Living in the Bush

Even highly experienced outdoorsfolk need to be extra cautious when getting acquainted with the new conditions of the African bush. Animal dangers may be exaggerated by pop traditions in literature and film, but the animals are there, and so is the potential for serious accident. You will have to learn to live with the presence of large wild animals. You may also find yourself adventuring in populated areas, which presents a new set of problems to the camper.

CAMPING

Camping is surely the best way to appreciate the full magic of Africa's outdoor experience. Pristine natural surroundings, balmy summer-type weather, and the proximity of wildlife are surefire ingredients for excitement and pleasure. That said, be aware of the few flies in the ointment.

Within parks, it is often forbidden to camp outside of designated public campgrounds. Facilities vary: in South Africa, campsites may include restaurants and swimming pools; in other places, nothing more than a signpost may be in evidence. Most official campsites at least provide a water source and a latrine. Water is a prime advantage of formal sites, especially where shower facilities are available. Unfortunately, public campsites have disadvantages too, not the least of which is company. Crowding is a growing problem, particularly in the more well-known parks. Although neighbors don't often spoil the fun, they are intrusive on the wilderness experience. More concretely, public campsites tend to get trashed out. Not all campers are circumspect in handling refuse, and park maintenance crews may be entirely absent. In some reserves, special private campsites are available. Considerably higher fees are charged, and they are generally difficult to reserve. The better commercial safaris feature private sites when they can, but even they are sometimes forced into public campgrounds.

Outside the parks, and occasionally within, you can camp wherever you like. In choosing a wilderness site, water is usually key. If you are traveling with your own vehicle, bring plenty along just in case no water supply can be found. Shade is another consideration. Also note animal paths, particularly where located near a river or lakeshore. It's ideal to situate yourself on a rise where animals can be observed in the daytime as they come to drink, rather than in a

Proximity to wildlife makes camping exciting. It is safe—but animals do come around! *Photo by Allen Bechky.*

gully where they pass during the night. Check the availability of firewood, and clear the ground of thorns before setting up your tent.

Collecting firewood is generally easy, for down wood abounds in most types of bushland and it dries out quickly in the tropical sun. Fires are comforting to us humans, but there is some question as to whether they effectively scare off lions and other camp marauders. One school of thought suggests that the light actually attracts curious animals. Try to judge your need for a nightlong bonfire by the local supply of wood, keeping in mind the heavy pressure of camping parties. Also take care to prevent fires from getting away.

The proximity of wildlife is certainly one of the greatest thrills in African camping. Animals can and will come into your campsite, especially at night. Most are incidental visitors—elephants or antelopes seeking browse. Some are purposeful intruders intent on stealing your food. These latter are mostly small—porcupines or civets looking for scraps—but hyenas are frequent camp scavengers, too. Their mournful whooping cries are a typical nighttime sound, and a good flashlight often reveals their eyes in the darkness beyond the campfire. Lions also patrol campsites on occasion. All this activity is pretty disturbing to the newcomer, but there is actually little to fear. Animals tend to ignore tents. Elephants are remarkably conscious of where they place their feet. They don't trip over tent lines or inadvertently crush sleeping campers. A lion's claw can easily slice open a nylon tent, but he won't bother. As scary as the various noises emanating from the night may be—and the imagination works overtime when the rustlings of unknown animals seem to come from next to your tent—you are quite safe as long as you remain inside. It may be that the animals sense that camps are human territory and retain their natural fear, or that they are simply timid about messing around with unfamiliar objects. The fact remains that animal attacks on tents are extremely rare.

There have been reports of attacks on campers who slept with their tents open, however, so it is mandatory to keep the door zipped shut. You will want ventilation, but keep windows zipped to a reasonable level. You will not feel too comfortable if you wake up to see a lion peering into your tent.

In southern Africa it is somewhat the fashion to sleep out in the open, with camp cots circling around a good fire. This technique should only be used by groups that are accompanied by armed professional guides. Hunting parties often bivouac this way, and the practice has given rise to great campfire stories. One can hardly safari in Botswana or Zimbabwe, for example, without hearing about some poor chap who, while sleeping in the open "just the other night," had his arm carried off by a hyena. Either there are a hell of a lot of limbless hunters down there, or this "Farewell to Arms" story must rank as one of the classic safari myths. Tall tales notwithstanding, sleeping under the stars in big game country is risky. Groups of hyenas will not hesitate to attack a sleeping human. Lions are opportunists, too—don't tempt them.

Lions in camp are worrisome, particularly if they include curious youngsters. On a camping tour, your guide will probably use a car to chase intrusive lions away. If you are on your own and want to be prepared, park your car immediately in front of your tent, leaving the car door unlocked for quick access.

Normally, after the camp has quieted and the fire has died to embers, remain in your tent (and sleep like a log). If you must leave the tent at night, first have a good look around with a flashlight. To urinate, don't bother going far. For bowel emergencies, you might want to go nearby rather than wander any distance to the toilet. Be sure to clean up thoroughly in the morning.

Food and dishes should be properly secured for the night, preferably inside a vehicle rather than a tent. Don't leave shoes, towels, or anything portable lying around outside: hyenas are fond of carrying off odd items and chewing them up in the bush.

In true wilderness campsites, you may have to draw your water from a river. Rivers should be approached with care, especially if crocodiles are present. Crocs are usually afraid of people, but large specimens are opportunists. They make their living partly by keeping an eye on places where animals come down to the water regularly to drink, grabbing the occasional unwary victim. Tourists can fall into this category. Don't hang around the water's edge, wash, or bathe unless the water is clear, with a sandy bottom for good visibility. Avoid these activities at dawn and dusk, and don't go near the water at night, when crocs are most active.

During daylight and early evening hours, most animals will stay out of your camp area because they easily sense human activity. The exceptions are monkeys and baboons, the smarties who have learned that tourists don't bite. Without much fear of humans, they regularly forage at camp refuse dumps, and are adept at darting in to pinch untended supplies. They have even learned to unzip and enter unguarded tents in which food has been stored. It is not pleasant to return to camp to find your provisions gone and your possessions a shambles.

Monkeys are not the only hazard to unguarded camps. Theft is an increasing problem too. Campsites are often located on park boundaries, and are regularly visited by local people. Even campsites deep within a park can be reached by knowledgeable thieves. Tour groups will have staff who can guard camp against both monkeys and people, but individual travelers have to consider the risks of leaving their camp untended. Close to villages, it is wise to pack up your gear and bring it with you. Alternatively, you may hire someone to look after your camp, especially if regular park personnel is available for that purpose.

Camp security is even a bigger headache outside parks. When you are visiting remote tribal areas, throngs of curious locals are likely to come around the camp. This is probably just the experience you want, but be wary of sticky fingers. Again, vigilant camp staff are useful, but even members of guided tours have to be responsible for their own goods in these situations. Security can fail: thieves sometimes cut through the rear walls of tents and enter unseen. Don't leave articles of clothing or other possessions lying around camp. Keep your tent closed tight, and keep your most valuable items locked in a car.

In towns and populated areas, you may be allowed to camp in police or church compounds. These offer a little more privacy and security.

TREKKING AND BUSH WALKING

Africa is limited in areas attractive to trekking enthusiasts. Although wilderness bush abounds, its vastness and the hot climate make it inhospitable to all but the most hardy trekkers. Cooler highland regions are usually under intense cultivation; densely populated and cut by roads, these regions, too, are more likely to be traversed by vehicle than on foot. Unlike other parts of the world, walking is prohibited in most African national parks. Where walking is permitted, special permits or the participation of licensed guides is required.

For all their difficulties, walking safaris are highly recommended. Foot safaris offer the excitement of meeting the animals on their own ground, which is a very different perspective than one gets from game drives. One gets a much clearer impression of the animals' senses and a heightened respect for their capabilities. There is also the chance to learn bushcraft: to recognize scats and learn how to stalk or avoid contacts with wildlife. More, there's a feel to the environment that you can only get from hiking. You'll notice tracks and puzzle out which animals live in the many burrows you discover. You'll pay a lot more attention to the vegetation, too. It will certainly have more effect on you: nasty "wait-a-bit" thorn will hold up your progress, while sharp grasses scratch your legs, and riverine trees beckon you to welcome respite from the sun. You can expect to see less game on walking safaris: you will cover a lot less ground on foot, and many of the animals will slip away unnoticed. Those animals you do see will not usually permit you to get as close as you would in a vehicle. Generally, wildlife observation and photography are more rewarding on game drives. But for a genuine feel for the bush, walking safaris are unbeatable. They are an enlightening supplement to the usual game-viewing safaris based on vehicles.

The chief obstacle to walking in the parks is obviously the danger posed by wild animals. How real is this danger? The fact is, although animals are afraid of humans and most often run away at the first hint of their presence, wild animals can and do attack people. Walkers are at the most risk. Where animals will tolerate close human proximity around camps and lodges, they do so by *their* choice. An individual animal learns to feel enough confidence to considerably reduce the approach distance it will tolerate before it feels threatened. In the bush, an animal's security zone is much larger, and its sensitivity to humans as enemies much greater. Still, its instincts will most often lead to flight. But not always. It may stand its ground, concealed, until provoked into a charge by approaching, unsuspecting people. Or it may not sense approaching danger until the humans blunder too close, resulting in a violent display. Obviously, the risk to walkers is greatly heightened in thick bush.

The presence of an experienced guide reduces the likelihood of aggressive incidents. The guide will know which patches of bush need extra caution to negotiate, or be avoided altogether. Experience will have taught him to read spoor, so that he will know from fresh tracks or dung what animals may be up the trail. He will also be sensitive to the wind. But even professionals can be attacked. That's why foot safaris in big game country really do require the accompaniment of an armed guide. On most foot safaris, a gun is not used at all. Bushcraft and the animals' instincts for avoidance see to that. But once initiated, aggressive incidents are highly unpredictable situations. Correct behavior is essential. To run can invite attack. If a firm stand and shouts don't scare a threatening animal off, a shot in the air is usually enough to send it on its way. If an actual charge is made, it may be necessary to shoot to kill.

Although it's obvious that extensive foot safaris require firearms for your security, that does not mean you can never walk in the bush on your own. In many situations, it is reasonably safe. As a camper, you will probably have to do some bush walking, if only to gather firewood. As a mountain hiker, you will likely walk through forest areas lightly inhabited by dangerous game. Experience will make you bolder, but always keep in mind a few commonsense rules:

- Stick to open country when you can. Good visibililty allows you to spot trouble a long way off. Thick bush invites sudden encounters of the dangerous kind.

- To stalk game, it's necessary to proceed quietly. Walk lightly, speaking only in whispers or not at all. Heavy footsteps and loud, laughter-filled conversation practically guarantee that you will see no animal life. Use the noisy method on forest walks: warn animals of your approach so they will avoid you.

- Stay alert. Keep your eyes and ears open. Even aggressive animals tend to warn intruders away before they charge. A growl, a snort, or a shaking in the bushes, is an invitation for you to retreat or look for a tree to climb.

- Pay attention to wind direction. If you are walking into the wind, you are much more likely to encounter animals ahead.

- Stay cool. Discouraging wild animals from attack is not psychologically unlike handling aggressive dogs. They can be bluffed out. Fear emboldens them; running may invite attack. Give an animal plenty of room to escape, while you back off slowly. If you are in a group, stay together.

- In extremis, climb a tree to evade buffalo. A steep embankment is the most effective barrier to an elephant.

Several species are notably dangerous. All are large and should not be approached without respect for their capabilities.

Elephants have no natural enemies except human beings, who persecute them assiduously. As a result, they become extremely nervous when they sense humans in their vicinity. Bulls, which are often found alone or in small groups, are not ordinarily as dangerous as females. The cows live in tight-knit family groups, which defend their calves very energetically. An encounter with an alarmed group of females is a hair-raising experience. The calves run underneath and behind the enraged mothers, who circle the young, trumpeting discontent. With trunks raised to pinpoint the enemy scent, the females present a wall of pachyderm fury.

Although elephants are obviously highly dangerous, they get by mostly on bluster. A charge is frequently only a bluff, and can be turned by shouts or a warning shot. Without firearms, however, it's very tough to escape from a determined charge. An elephant is faster than the average human, and can plow right through thorny vegetation that would be an impenetrable barrier to a person. Climbing trees is obviously problematical: a steep embankment would give a little breathing space, if it were handy. A better strategy is to avoid too close contact; circle wide around elephants or give them your scent at a long distance, so that they run off and out of your way.

The Cape buffalo (*Syncerus caffer*) has a reputation as the bad guy of the bush. In big herds, which include cows, calves, and bulls, they are extremely skittish and no threat. They will stand, staring balefully, until one bolts. Then the entire herd will follow suit in a retreating storm of thundering hooves and dust. Old bulls live solitarily or in groups of two or three. They are extremely wary and aggressive, and quite capable of defending themselves, even against lions. Unlike other dangerous animals, which may be content to let up on the attack once an enemy has been scared off, the buffalo means business. If he charges, he means to kill you and will press his attack with determination. Although a rifle shot may turn his charge, shouting is not terribly effective. A good tree is a handy escape.

Lions are mostly bluff. Even if disturbed on a kill or while courting, they are more likely to run than attack. They may make fearsome aggressive displays, however. Don't run: you don't want to encourage their instinct to chase running prey. Back off slowly, and be prepared to brazen it out with shouts, hand claps, and waved sticks. Like so many other animals, female lions are valiant in defense of their young, so it is bad news if you inadvertently approach one with small cubs.

It is said that a rhino's charge can be escaped by stepping aside just before he hits you: he will continue straight on and disappear, too blind to find you for a second chance. I'm not sure I'd want to test that theory, but it's a moot point, for the endangered rhino is now too rarely encountered to be considered much of a danger. It's certain that your guides would be loath to shoot one if it did charge, so keep an eye out for a tree.

It should be noted that animal attacks are universally described as "accidents." This implies that they are not routine calamities, and that they are to a large extent preventable. When they do occur, the victim inevitably takes the blame from local pundits: the circumstances always reveal that he or she (or the guide) made some "stupid" mistake. This judgment is harsh, for there is room for just plain bad luck. But there is one cardinal "stupid mistake": to take an animal for granted. In dealing with wildlife, judge an animal's capabilities, not its intentions.

MOUNTAIN SAFARIS

As in other parts of the world, mountains are the most attractive regions for trekkers. The highest ranges in Africa have trail or hut systems to encourage mountain walkers. Porters and guides are available too. Mountain habitats support low densities of dangerous game, so walking with armed guards is not required. The dangers of African mountains are the same as those encountered by trekkers in other parts of the world: hypothermia, traumatic injury, and high-altitude diseases. It's obviously important that hikers be prepared for cold and wet weather on any treks at altitudes above 10,000 feet. Subfreezing weather (which you can expect nightly above about 12,000 feet) is not necessary to produce hypothermia:

any exposure to cold and wet for enough time to lower the body's vital core temperature is sufficient. Good equipment, respect for mountain weather, and common sense are the best protection. Falls that result in broken bones or twisted ankles are a risk on any hiking trip. They are more serious in Africa because of the difficulty of rescue. Porters or park rangers will have to carry you down, an uncomfortable process. Africa is still not in the age of helicopter evacuation. Even after you are down from the mountain itself, your transport problems may not be over unless you are traveling with a vehicle. Make sure to inform local park authorities of your route plan, so that they can check up on you if you don't reappear on time. Porters and local guides are useful in such emergencies: they know where to get help as quickly as possible, and can also carry you down in a pinch.

High-altitude problems can begin at even relatively low elevations, well below the icy mountain summits. The shortness of breath, headaches, and nausea of acute mountain sickness (AMS) are familiar discomforts to many who climb too high, too fast. Acclimatization to altitude by slow stages is the best way to avoid the unpleasantness of this not very serious syndrome. Unfortunately, considerations of time and money often lead trekkers in foreign lands to attempt too much, too quickly. They wind up suffering for their haste. The more serious altitude problems are high-altitude pulmonary edema (HAPE) and high-altitude cerebral edema (HACE). Both are life-threatening conditions that can occur in the highest African mountain ranges. In HAPE, a pneumonia-like condition fills the lungs with fluid that can eventually drown the victim. With the much rarer HACE, excessive fluid in the brain causes coma. Members of hiking or trekking parties on Kilimanjaro, Mount Kenya, or the Ruwenzori should be alert for symptoms of these serious disorders: coughing, gurgling lungs, mental disorientation, and stupor. The best medicine is immediate evacuation to lower altitudes. Recovery is frequently rapid and spontaneous on arrival at normal elevations, although treatment with powerful diuretics or steroids may be used in the most severe cases.

Mountain hikers are well advised to carry plenty of water, and drink much more than normally. Dehydration through vapor loss from normal breathing is considerable at high altitudes. Forcing fluids will help prevent the discomforts of AMS. Some experienced hikers recommend taking the drug Diamox (acetazolamide) as a preventive against AMS. It is a mild diuretic that acts to regulate breathing during sleep, permitting a higher intake of oxygen and a better night's rest. It has the side effect of making you urinate quite often. Like all chemical prophylaxis, it is controversial. I think it helps, but you should consult mountaineering literature and your doctor before you opt for it.

All Africa's classic trekking routes are within national parks, so the accompaniment of an official park guide is mandatory. This is a good rule, for aside from considerations of safety, it makes route finding a lot easier. Porters are an optional luxury, but they are hired so cheaply that they should not be passed up. Purists might insist on carrying their own loads to the top, but most trekkers will find it a welcome relief to be free of the drudgery of carrying a full pack at high altitude. Trekking with porters and guides offers cultural contact with the people of the mountain regions. It also provides a margin of safety in case you should have problems requiring evacuation.

RIVER TRIPS

African river trips are risky business. The normal perils of white water are not so much a problem as the less familiar dangers of hippos and crocodiles, and the possibility of infection with bilharzia. Experience is needed to keep these hazards down to the level of acceptable risk: there is little choice but to go with professionals. Commercial trips are operated in very few places, most notably on the Zambezi River between Zambia and Zimbabwe, on Tanzania's Rufiji River, and in Botswana's Okavango Delta.

One wouldn't think it to look at them, but hippos are one of the most dangerous African animals. They can be a threat to humans both in the water and on land. Highly territorial, aggressive bulls can attack rafts or canoes that venture too close. Their huge bulk can overturn boats; the long tusks that they so often reveal in their threatening "yawn" display, are razor-sharp and capable of cutting a person in two. When a boat approaches, a herd of hippos will splash from their resting place, where they have been lying half submerged, into the security of deeper water. Normally, they stay there, snorting and blowing as they break the surface for a quick peek between dives. Occasionally, an aggressive male will make a determined, purposeful attack. Another danger comes from stragglers, cut off from the main herd, who make sudden late dashes to the river: even an accidental collision with a hippo spells disaster. The technique for running past hippos is to alert animals downstream with the noise of paddles tapped on gunwales. This sends them splashing for deep water, and allows you to keep an eye on their positions as you glide by. The boats then hug the bank, keeping to shallow water and letting the hippos have the security of the deep. Real attacks are rare, but in the course of a river trip you may pass hundreds of these high-strung "river horses."

Hippos are also dangerous on land. They emerge from the water at night, walking long distances to graze. They are skittish and, notwithstanding their bulky shape and short legs, can run with remarkable speed. A human who unknowingly cuts a hippo off from its line of retreat to the water may be suddenly confronted with a "fleeing" hippo—coming right at him or her. Whether run down or bitten, the lethal effect is the same. Care must be taken not to camp on the hippo's regular trails. Also stay alert when walking around riverbanks in the early morning: the animals may still be moving about on land.

We are all familiar with the scenes in Tarzan movies where huge crocodiles slide swiftly into the water in pursuit of unlucky adventurers. More than likely those films were taken of reptiles that were actually escaping. And that's the way you are most likely to see crocodiles. They lie basking on sunny banks, until they sense a boat approaching. Then they vanish swiftly into the muddy water, not to be seen again. Although crocodiles attain dinosaur size, deliberate assaults on boats are almost nonexistent, for they fear humans and only attack with the opportunity of surprise. But they are dangerous to swimmers, and a boat overturned by hippos or rapids puts overboard passengers at risk if large crocs are present.

All in all, the chances of hippo or crocodile attack are slim if experienced hands are there to guide you. Aside from the thrills, river trips in Africa are attractive because they offer the peace of unspoiled wilderness: the waterways take you far off the beaten tracks of the heavily visited parks. Like foot safaris, however, they do not provide the best game viewing. Although a good variety of animals may be seen along the water's edge, it is hard to get close enough to photograph and observe them. A moving boat is also an unsteady platform for using binoculars or cameras to maximum advantage.

3

The African Realm: Tips on Watching Wildlife

Africa's wildlife heritage is fittingly celebrated in superlatives. Such familiar wonders as the elephant, rhinoceros, hippo, and giraffe are only the largest of the continents's astonishing assemblage of mammals. With these march a parade of predators, an immense collection of antelopes, a veritable Ark-full of monkeys and mongooses, aardvarks and insectivores, and a host of other animal oddities. A profusion of colorful birds, weird reptiles, and fascinating insects rounds out the show. As amazing as the variety is the spectacle of numbers, for the African plains are the last place on Earth where vast herds still roam in primeval abundance.

Africa's wild creatures do not live in isolation: each species represents a strand in the web forming the community of plants and animals in which it has carved its niche. Even the briefest safari will traverse many such ecological communities and habitats. The eye soon discerns that the African wild is not a singular entity in which animals occur at random, but an ordered realm, where every creature has its appropriate place. Some species are extremely adaptive and survive in a wide spectrum of environments. Others are confined to specific niches or microhabitats. It would take volumes to describe all of Africa's animals, not to mention their relationships and the habitats in which they live. This guide can do no more than present an overview of the various habitats you may encounter and suggest some useful game-viewing techniques.

A small understanding of African ecology will go a long way toward enriching your safari experience, for the wonder of the animals is heightened by an appreciation and awareness of their total environment. Although the famous big game animals naturally com-

95

mand the most attention, people who look only for lions, elephants, and other large mammals tend to get bored after a few days. Those curious about African wildlife in all its varied forms never have that problem, for it is impossible to run out of new and fascinating discoveries.

Savanna Habitats

Africa's most famous wildlife reserves are almost universally located in savanna country. The savanna owes its extraordinary faunal wealth to its patchwork vegetation. Its blend of grassland, woodland, and bush habitats provides the diversity of niches and abundance of food necessary to support a large and varied population of wild animals. In the classic model, the typical savanna is lightly wooded, with trees spaced widely on open grassy landscapes. In some places, pure grasslands dominate; elsewhere, "bush" country, characterized by denser woods and thickets, is more widespread. Gradations of the three vegetation types are the rule, a condition resulting from a seesaw process of natural succession.

A succession scenario might work something like this: elephants move into an area of savanna woodland that has a generous understory of grass. During the dry season, the pachyderms exhaust the nutritious turf and turn their full attention to the trees. To get at canopy foliage, they push over some trees; other trees die when their bark is peeled off and devoured. After several bruising seasons, the woodland takes on the look of an old battlefield: the gray skeletons of big trees stand among a litter of downed limbs, overturned trunks, and high-rise termite mounds. Seedlings and shrubs, taking advantage of the removal of the old trees, grow rapidly into impenetrable thickets among the wreckage. If fires attack the resurgent bush, these woody plants vanish and open grassland appears in its place. Once shrubs and trees get in a few years of undisturbed growth, however, they become more resistant to incursions by fire. Eventually, trees reach a size that shades out the lower bush, an understory of grass flourishes, and mature woodlands again dominate.

Humans have had a profound influence in shaping the savanna landscape through the use of fire. For generations, African pastoralists have set dry-season fires in order to encourage a flush of fresh grass to sprout with the first hint of rain. Farmers, too, annually fire the bush to clear new land or burn stubble off old fields. Once lit, these fires go untended and rapidly get out of hand. In the dry seasons, whole regions are set ablaze, creating a constant pall that mutes the brilliance of the African sky. Over time, such vast seasonal conflagrations have tended to suppress the regeneration of bush and woodland, and have tipped nature's balance toward the spread and maintenance of grassland.

Many African plants have adapted to a regimen of seasonal fires. Some trees actually need it in order to regenerate: their seeds are so hard that the outer layers have to be burnt before they will sprout. Many savanna species have developed fire-resistant bark that enables large trees to withstand repeated "cool" burns. Such burns occur when the grass is fired early in the dry season. Because it then retains considerable moisture, the grass burns incompletely and in patches. Deprived of fuel, such a fire moves on before it gets hot enough to ignite and damage the canopies of tall trees. Late in the season, when the withered grass is tinder dry, fires are much more destructive.

The wild animals also affect the environment. On the one hand, they harm vegetation where they overgraze; on the other, they encourage regeneration by spreading seed and trampling old growth into mulch. Elephants make the most conspicuous modifications. With appetites to match their bulk, they wreak havoc on woodlands in which they linger, destroying trees and contributing to the spread of grassland. Paradoxically, they wander widely and are constantly distributing the seeds of plants on which they feed. Partially digested seeds are often prepared for germination by passing through the gut of an elephant; the protective outer layers are stripped away, just as they would be by fire. Viable seed then winds up nicely planted in a fertilizing ball of elephant manure. In general, the feeding strategies of the various animals contribute to the stability of their habitats because they are keyed to the food and water resources available at any given season. When supplies are low, game migrates or disperses, decreasing the pressure on any particular tract of land. The animals also recyle nutrients rapidly back into the environment: Africa's bushlands are daily fertilized by the droppings of millions of beasts. Although debate rages as to how best to "manage" parks, when left with enough territory the wild animals tend to be good stewards of their land.

Many plants, including most of Africa's acacias, have evolved thorns as a means of discouraging browsing. Although thorns do not completely protect against feeding animals, the prevalence of "thornbush" and "thorn trees" is a testament to their usefulness.

Giraffes, elephants, and rhinos can devour long acacia thorns without apparent discomfort, but the smaller browsing animals must be more selective. And even the megafauna favor new growth on which thorns are soft and green; after spines harden into wooden needles, the large animals tend to leave them alone, preferring to strip foliage (which is less efficient) rather than devour whole limbs, thorns and all.

The acacias are a particularly widespread group of savanna trees. Many species have the flat-topped umbrella shape so characteristic of the most appealing African landscapes. Besides the tall umbrella acacias are numerous shrubby varieties, such as the prickly wait-a-bit thorn (*Acacia mellifera*). In dense stands, these and the spiny seedlings of the larger types form impenetrable thornbush thickets. All acacias are legumes, and their highly nutritious beanlike seed pods are much sought after by animals. Elephants are very fond of them; camps set among acacias routinely attract bulls when the trees are in fruit. Browsing antelopes, rhinos, and baboons also feed avidly on acacia pods, both on the tree and after they have dropped to the ground.

Woodland and bush are habitat for the "browsing" animals that eat the foliage of shrubs, trees, and leafy plants. Counted among the browsers are such notables as giraffe and rhino, and a potpourri of antelopes ranging from the hare-sized dikdik to the giant eland. Most browsers are highly selective feeders that tend to live singly or in small groups, rather than the outsized herds associated with the grass eaters of the open plains. Trees and bush also provide essential refuge for savanna-dwelling primates, such as vervet monkeys (*Cercopithecus aethiops*) and baboons, as well as a tremendous assortment of woodland birds.

Giraffe (*Giraffa camelopardalis*) primarily inhabit wooded country, though they are often seen crossing nearly treeless plains. Gregarious and ever vigilant, their advantage in height makes it difficult for lions to stalk them without detection. Females join nursery herds after the birth of calves; "creche groups" are sometimes left on their own while the mothers wander off to feed. Bulls may be seen testing their strength against each other in slow-motion bouts of "necking," in which contestants stand parallel and intermittently exchange swings of the head. These matches are ordinarily confined to light sparring for place in the dominance hierarchy of local giraffe society. When real fighting does occur, however, true blows are delivered with tremendous force.

The black rhinoceros (*Diceros bicornis*) is a retiring inhabitant of thick bush. Normally a rather solitary animal, a female is often accompanied by one or two subadults in addition to her calf. The rhino is most active at night, and spends its day napping in the sun or visiting mud wallows. Its eyesight is poor, but its swiveling funnel-shaped ears are sharp, and its sense of smell is very keen. Tick birds, also called *oxpeckers*, usually escort rhinos and act as a security alarm to dozing animals; the suspicious birds fly up noisily when they sense intruders. When frightened, the rhino defends itself aggressively with its horn. The black rhino has a prehensile upper lip, beaklike in appearance, that is used for grasping the leaves and shoots on which it feeds. Its lip and feeding habits distinguish it from the white rhino; the two species are not colored differently as their names would imply. The "white" rhino (*Ceratotherium simum*) takes its English name from the Afrikaans word *weit*, which describes its "wide" square-lipped mouth, designed for efficiently cropping grass. The white rhino is also much larger, weighing as much as four and a half tons, as compared to the black's one and a half tons. The white rhino, formerly rare in East Africa, is now virtually extinct there. It can be seen in the game parks of Southern Africa.

By eating different types of grass, or the same plants at different stages of growth, a whole spectrum of grazing animals is able to share the pasturage of the African grasslands. Both zebra and wildebeest (gnu) are very common grazers that feed on identical grasses. Yet wildebeest prefer to eat the moister blades, while zebra readily crop the higher, tougher stems. Gazelles choose only the tenderest young shoots, and buffalo feed on coarse "rank" grasses, too tough to be chewed by smaller herbivores. Because of the efficiency with which the vegetation is used, grasslands support the greatest game populations; they are the home of Africa's legendary herds. Grazing species such as gazelles are often found in groups of hundreds, and may concentrate by the thousands when feeding conditions are right.

Some animals take full advantage of the broken mosaic of savanna vegetation by both browsing and grazing. Impala (*Aepyceros melampus*) are one of the commonest and most widespread antelopes precisely because they exploit leafy plants as well as grass. Their large, tight-knit herds, which are usually divided into distinct male and female clusters, thrive on the "edges" where grass and bushland meet. Elephants, too, do best in mixed bush country. They

Cow elephants form a defensive circle around their young. *Photo by Allen Bechky.*

feed primarily on grass, but also eat immense quantities of leaves, bark, fruits, and pods. Wooded bush also provides elephants with essential cover from their implacable enemies—human hunters.

The backbone of elephant society is the cow-calf family group. Females spend their entire lives within these closely knit sisterhoods, which are composed of a matriarch, her daughters and granddaughters, and their offspring. Such cow-calf herds may number from ten to fifty animals. Elder females often lead their daughters off to form independent groups, but lifelong relationships with the original matriarch and her family are maintained by frequent meetings on a common "home range." Cows are energetic in defense of their young: trumpeting mothers form a daunting circle around their calves, leaving little opportunity for predators to grab a newborn. Baby elephants are really only vulnerable if they become sick or get lost.

Bull elephants are gregarious, but are loners at heart and wander as they please. A male gets booted out of his family group at puberty, when the females begin to find his sexual attentions unwelcome. At thirteen years of age, he is too big to be bothered by predators, but—having been raised in a strong family environment—tends to feel insecure. Newly independent bulls then seek out the company of others, joining loosely organized herds. These associations are constantly breaking up and rearranging themselves according to the whim of individuals; the same bull, found wandering alone one day, may be accompanied by several colleagues the next, and may have joined completely new chums a week later. When a mature bull encounters a group of cows, he tests their scent to determine whether any are receptive to mating. He may stay with them for several days, but eventually male and females go their separate ways. Over the years, the bulls of a particular region get to know one another quite well; from infancy, they indulge in tests of strength that constantly reestablish their places in the dominance hierarchy. Serious fights between bulls are rare, and usually occur when a stranger, without rank in the local fraternity, emigrates into a new area.

Elephant herds grow larger in the dry season, when the animals concentrate around water. At such times, and when the threat of poaching is constant and strong, elephants may gather in herds numbering in the hundreds. Such large groups normally disperse during the rains.

Predators are at the apex of the ecological food pyramid, and are necessarily much less numerous than the herbivores on which they feed: the proportion of hunted to hunters is greater than 100 to 1. Consequently, predators are only really common in those places where huge herds are gathered.

Africa's abundance and diversity of prey animals supports a magnificent collection of predators. The various carnivores specialize in hunting animals of a weight appropriate to their own. Cheetahs go after gazelles and young antelopes, while leopards pursue a somewhat wider range of small to medium-sized animals. Lions take small animals if the opportunity arises. A gazelle, however, will barely satisfy the hunger of a single adult male, so communal hunts naturally focus on larger animals such as wildebeest, topi, or zebra. Lions are quite capable of attacking prey up to the size of giraffe and buffalo, and occasionally take young hippos, rhinos, or even elephants. Hyenas, though conventionally thought of as scavengers, are formidable hunters in their own right. Working in groups, they can take animals as large as zebra, and attack the calves of buffalo and rhino. Wild dogs also hunt communally, concentrating on small to medium-sized antelopes such as impala, gazelle, and wildebeest. Because of considerable overlap in both habitat and prey, competition among the meat eaters is intense. Although we tend to anthropomorphize the hunters, describing the lion as noble and the hyena as a skulking coward, these judgments have little to do with the

In national parks, wild animals become used to vehicles, so the best viewing takes place on game drives. *Photo by Allen Bechky.*

reality of the animals' lives. The stealing of kills, scavenging, territorial fighting, and intraspecies clashes are integral parts of the survival repertoire of all the hunting species. Violence is a daily fact of their existence. After all, they must regularly kill in order to survive. It is not easy to catch their prey, and every chase holds the possibility of a debilitating injury—a leg broken from a misstep, a jaw dislocated by a zebra's kick, a deep wound from an antelope's horn—which spells their own ultimate doom. In general, the prey species don't have much reason to worry about the predators as long as they are healthy. Nature has seen to it that the hunters overwhelmingly succeed in taking only the slow or feeble—the old, the sick, and the very young.

GAME DRIVES

The game drive has come to be the standard mode of wildlife viewing in the African national parks, where both regulations and safety considerations restrict exploration on foot. Conditions are ideal for vehicular safaris; cruising savanna game country from the security and comfort of a car, you will encounter a large number and variety of animals simply by chance. In many parks, the animals have lost all fear of vehicles and permit you to drive right up to them. Game drives in such places are always invigorating: you may go from one species to the next—observing zebra here, giraffe there, a knot of impala on the right, a trio of elephant bulls dead ahead—as though you were in a great outdoor zoo. But there really is no guarantee on what you will see; the animals are free to move around as they please, and may even pass beyond park boundaries. Even in the most prolific game parks, you may get skunked on a particular drive, especially if you feel you *must* see big cats.

The classic safari schedule calls for game drives in the early morning and late afternoon, the hours when animals are most active and photography is at its best. Dawn is a particularly good time for finding predators. Many of the cats hunt at night, and those that have failed to kill are often still on the prowl at first light. Successful hunters may then be found feeding on their prey, while hyenas or jackals may be scavenging abandoned carcasses. Antelope like to feed during cool early morning, then retire to shade to chew their cud. Zebra, buffalo, and elephant also seek shade against full sun. All resume feeding and movement as afternoon shadows begin to lengthen. For your own comfort, pay attention to these daily rhythms of animal life. Aimless driving during the hot midday hours can get tiresome, and you are generally better off conserving your energy for the prime viewing times.

Keep in mind, however, that the "morning and evening" game drive routine can be overdone, and is sometimes employed as much for the convenience of safari operators and hotel managers as anything else. Although the cooler parts of the day are undoubtedly optimum for comfort, it is simply not true that there is "nothing to be seen" outside the standard viewing hours. Much depends on the season and weather. When the weather is cool, predators can be on the prowl even at midday and in hot, dry weather there is a constant traffic of thirsty animals to watering places at which carnivores may lie in ambush. Sometimes you must go out for the entire day to reach some especially worthwhile, but distant, point. On such expeditions, you can take a cooling midday break while on a picnic in the bush.

On game drives in savanna parks, pay special attention to areas of minihabitat, such as wetlands and forests. Marsh fringes and swamps often harbor lurking predators and are among the best places to view an impressive assortment of herons, ibises, storks, and cranes. Pools and lakes are possible refuges for that most improbable creature, the hippopotamus. Rivers also offer the prospect of seeing hippos, as well as crocodiles, and big trees usually flourish along their banks. Where such riparian forests grow particularly lush, they have the feel of tropical jungle. Rare monkeys and birds, and shyer antelopes such as bushbuck and duiker, may be glimpsed there by careful observers. Neither riverine forests nor marshes are easily penetrated by vehicles, but resident species often show themselves on game tracks that skirt their edges.

No game drive should be conducted as a rushed pursuit of animals not yet seen. In the early stages of a safari, excitement at the prospect of meeting the most famous creatures naturally leads to an emphasis on finding and photographing only the "stars." Although there are surely circumstances in which you will want to focus on a particular species, in general you will do better to relax and observe whatever comes up. Obviously, you won't want to spend an entire morning watching a herd of gazelles when you are hoping to locate your first pride of lions. But after you have seen all the celebrities, pay closer attention to the humbler species, which, though easy to find, are often overlooked. Antelopes are a case in point. Too many people are content merely to catalogue each type, get its picture, and go on without taking further notice. Don't make that mistake, for patience and attention to detail will reward you with a deeper appreciation of the unique character of each species, whether it is the tiny dikdik, nervously twitching in response to every sound and smell that drifts its way, or the homely wildebeest, indulging its repertoire of seemingly uncoordinated bucks and kicks. Watch the constant interaction that goes on among the members of herds. Animals groom each other and assert their places in the pecking order; bulls pursue females and fend off rival males; some individuals graze or sleep, while others stand lookout. Always be on the alert for special activity. When you see a zebra rolling on a bald patch of ground, spend a while watching there. The original animal is likely to interrupt its dust bath as soon as you stop, but others may take its place at the same favored spot. Prolonged observation results in the most interesting sightings and best photographs.

Finding the Cats. In heavily visited parks, the tried and true method of finding the big cats is to look for the circle of safari vans that inevitably surrounds them. Finding predators on your own is not so easy. Random driving is not terribly efficient; you will do better to zero in on those places where they are most likely to lie up. Tree lines along water courses are good tracks to follow because cats appreciate shade and take advantage of riverine bush to rest where prey may inadvertently approach. Rocky outcrops and the bases of hills are also promising resting places. There, too, carnivores find shade among boulders or bushes and enjoy the security of concealment. Outcrops also provide fine vantage points from which to watch for potential prey. In late afternoon, or after rain showers, cats like to sun themselves atop large rocks—a particularly photogenic situation. Most of the time, they are not so obvious. Cats are secretive and can stay well concealed in light bush or high grass, even when not making special efforts to hide themselves. They are easy to miss, so you must search the hot-spots *very* slowly and carefully.

No animal is in as much demand for viewing as the lion (*Panthera leo*), for no safari (and, in some quarters, no game drive) is considered a success without a sighting of these big cats. From up close, their huge size and feline grace make an immediate and dramatic impression: adult females weigh more than 250 pounds, and full-sized males as much as 440. Yet interest in *simba* (the Swahili word for lion) can wane quickly for want of action. Lions sleep a lot, especially during the noontime heat, a habit that leads to persistent accusations of laziness. Such charges are unfounded, for the hours of indolence are punctuated with episodes of explosive violence. A lion's life, like that of other predators, rides an uncertain pendulum swinging between feast and famine. Lions do what they must to survive, no more and no less, and they do it mostly under cover of darkness.

Lions are highly social animals. Ordinarily a pride might consist of only half a dozen adults, but in exceptionally rich habitat, it may have more than thirty members of all ages. At the core of the pride are the adult females, who do most of the communal hunting. Males defend the pride's territory against the trespasses of nonmembers and, in so doing, provide a secure environment for raising cubs. Although pride males seem to lead an easy life, letting the females kill and then appropriating the largest share for themselves, it is not true that they never hunt. At some point, every adolescent male gets ejected from the family by the pride's resident males. The exiles usually form small nomadic bands that must fend for themselves: young males either hunt or they starve. Over the years, the nomads grow in size and toughness until such time as they can successfully take possession of a territory and a group of females, setting themselves up as the lords of a pride. Even afterward, big males are needed to help bring down larger prey such as buffalo bulls.

Lions take obvious pleasure in each other's company. They often lie huddled together, bodies touching. When they rouse themselves from midday torpor, they rub sensuously against each other and give warm greetings to pride members returning from other parts of their territory. Cubs are as cute and playful as kittens. They claw and chew as they scramble over the placid adults, and even try to draw the big males into their roughhouse games. A cub may suckle from any lactating lioness, but as its need for meat grows, it must compete for a place at the kill. Among lions, only the strongest get to eat, and starvation is the fate of many cubs—a cruel but efficient way for nature to limit their population. Lions breed often, and you may well see mating couples *in flagrante delicto*.

Because stealth and the leopard (*Panthera pardus*) are synonymous, this solitary, spotted cat is difficult to find and rates as the number one photographic safari trophy. The leopard's innate need for secrecy is a result of pressure from its larger enemies; even an outsized 175-pound cat is no match for a pride of lions or a gang of hyenas. The leopard has adopted an arboreal niche in which neither of its foes can compete. It uses its extreme agility and phenomenal strength to carry its prey (such as a 115-pound antelope) high into the sanctuary of a tree. Among its favorites are *Acacia tortilis* and sausage trees (*Kigelia africana*) both of which have spreading limbs ideal for catnaps. Unfortunately for would-be observers, leopards are secretive even at rest; rather than choose a bare branch to lie on, they prefer one hidden in the foliage of a tree's canopy. Typically, the only clue to a leopard's presence is the sudden twitch of a hanging tail. Searching for one is thus a tedious business, involving careful scrutiny of every suitable tree—a survey likely to prove fruitless unless you know a cat is in the neighborhood. Once a kill has been stashed, however, a leopard will stay with it, or return to its larder, until its prey is devoured. Check back repeatedly if you find a carcass hanging. When you do see a leopard, remain absolutely quiet: few become truly accustomed to vehicles, and the sound of a human voice may cause a beautifully relaxed animal to descend in a blur of speed. Once vanished in the grass, the shy leopard will not be seen again.

Cheetahs (*Acinonyx jubatus*) are much more easily viewed because they live in open country and are active during the day. They are fairly common in East African parks, especially those possessing a good population of gazelles. Cheetahs readily learn to tolerate vehicles and have even been known to climb on top of cars for a vantage point when searching for prey! These sleek spotted cats can be seen singly or in small groups. Such bands are usually composed of a mother and her full-sized, but not yet independent, offspring. Male litter mates sometimes stay together when they reach maturity, but females become solitary and bear the sole responsibility for cub rearing. Cheetahs depend on speed rather than stealth to catch their prey. They are remarkably efficient hunters but lose many of their kills to stronger rivals. The cheetah's spectacular high-speed chases are often witnessed by visitors. Hunts are most likely to take place near dawn or dusk.

Scanning is a useful technique for finding predators that is too seldom employed. It is especially effective in wide, grassy country where great vistas are open to examination with binoculars. Stop periodically to carefully pan the landscape with your lenses, paying special attention to the "hot-spots." In both morning and late afternoon, this is a good way to discover lions or cheetahs on the move. Cheetahs can then often be seen sitting atop termite mounds, themselves taking a look around. Distant animals may be in plain view with binoculars but would almost surely be missed from a moving car.

Quarry animals often give clues to the whereabouts of predators. Monkeys and baboons take to trees as soon as they see a lion, uttering sharp, barking alarm calls. Antelope also have various warning sounds: impala sneeze, wildebeest snort, reedbuck whistle shrilly. A giraffe that does not look at you when you approach, but gazes fixedly in another direction, is very likely keeping an eye on something more threatening. The presence of vultures is often a telling sign, though not when they are on the wing: circling birds are only soaring on rising thermal currents, searching for food. If you see them coming down, one by one, proceed in their direction, for there will certainly be a carcass. Do not be surprised, however, if no killers are on the scene: most animals that die of natural causes are first discovered by vultures. In the early morning hours, trees festooned with vultures merely indicate an overnight perch. But at midday a flock of sitting birds can mean that lions are guarding a kill below. Because the more common types of vultures are ungainly birds that require a good runway to get airborne, they only touch ground after lions have abandoned a carcass. Lions do not tolerate tampering with their food, and will kill scavenging birds that get too impatient.

Hungry lionesses on a kongoni kill, Tarangire National Park, Tanzania. *Photo by Allen Bechky.*

Hunts and Kills. Almost everyone hopes to see a "kill" during a safari. The chase has elements of beauty as well as drama: both predator and prey have been honed by evolution to play their parts in this ultimate test of survival, and it is fascinating to watch the protagonists perform to their utmost physical capabilities. Yet it is terrible too, for it is hard to see an animal die, and the final struggle is not pretty. Lion, cheetah, and leopard ordinarily kill by strangulation, while hyena and wild dog literally rip their victims apart. Either way, it is violent, though the end is often oddly passionless: the killer does its part without emotion and, once caught, the victim accepts its fate with shocked resignation. After the death struggle, you watch the feast, listening to the sound of crunching bones, and inhaling the scent of fresh red meat. It can be strong stuff, and some who see it wish their luck hadn't been quite so good. Others feel privileged to have witnessed a key chapter in the natural cycle of life.

Although viewing a kill is primarily a matter of luck, your chances are improved by a long stay in an area inhabited by several resident prides of lions. On a first reconnaissance, you can search for the various groups and assess their readiness to hunt. Often enough, you will find lions stuffed from their last feed. Such cats show no more energy than is necessary to change the position of their bulging bellies or drag themselves to water for a drink. They will not hunt again for several days. Hungry lions *look* much more alert, though activity may consist of nothing more than staring into the distance. When their bones are showing, an absence of prey is often all too obvious. After your initial survey, you can check up periodically on the most likely candidates.

A lion hunt is a very slow process. The cats usually start out moving single file, stopping often to lie down and rest; some pride members doze off, while others watch for game. As they get closer to potential prey animals, they gradually spread out into a loose arc. With luck, stealthy flankers can envelop their quarry, putting the pride into an ideal position to launch a successful attack. Lions do not seem to take account of wind direction when they hunt, and the wind frequently defeats their purpose.

When you discover lions in the early stages of hunting, follow along. If no game is near and the cats fall asleep, come back now and then to keep tabs on the situation. When a pride shows signs of movement in the dusk, be sure to return to the vicinity early the next morning. Should they fail to kill during the night, you will have a good chance to see the climax of a hunt. Even when watching the final stalk, however, keep in mind that most attempts end in failure. Time and patience are the keys if the observation of a kill is an important safari goal.

On the other hand, some kills are witnessed merely by luck. Even when watching sleeping lions, you may see unwary animals blunder into their vicinity. The lions' demeanor changes immediately. No longer lazy house cats, they become as taut as bowstrings as they flatten themselves to the ground. If the wind is right and the prey does not sense their presence, it may walk right into their midst. It is about as common to see this kind of opportunistic attack as a successful stalk and kill.

Carcasses. Day and night, death stalks the African herds. Whether victim to predation or disease, each dead animal is the source of food to the various carnivores and carrion eaters. Carcasses present golden opportunities for wildlife viewing because they bring the gamut of flesh-eating animals together where they can be easily observed. At a kill, you can watch the hunter feed, interact with others of its own species, and respond to different types of animals that arrive with an interest in joining the feast. Lions jealously guard their kills, keeping circling hyenas at bay with snarls and occasional charges. Jackals and small vultures sometimes manage to dart in to grab a stray morsel, but hyenas and larger birds must keep a respectful distance. Cheetahs are on the other end of the spectrum: they are built to run, not to fight, and will yield a kill to any serious challenger. Even a single hyena can appropriate a cheetah's meal. If an animal has perished from disease, or lions have abandoned a carcass, the scavengers have their turn.

A crowd of vultures at a carcass provides a fascinating spectacle. Vultures constantly patrol the African sky, scouring the countryside for signs of food. When a bird spies a dead animal, it descends rapidly. Its downward spiral is instantly observed by other airborne vultures that immediately come to investigate, see the carcass, and land in turn. A chain reaction soon brings a steady stream of winged scavengers. Competition becomes heated as dozens of lumbering birds, spreading their wings wide and hissing like angry snakes, bluff and fight for a place on the dead animal. Flocks of white-backed and griffon vultures must wait for one of the less common lappet-faced or white-headed varieties to arrive before they can begin to feed: only those giants have beaks powerful enough to rip open a thick hide. If none of the larger birds turns up, the impatient mob eventually breaks into the carcass through the anus or throat. Vultures are regularly joined at these grisly feasts by tawny eagles, jackals, and marabou storks.

Groups of feeding spotted hyenas (*Crocuta crocuta*) also make interesting viewing. Whether they are scavenging a carcass or devouring an animal they have brought down themselves, the scene is often one of near frenzy. Hyenas cackle with nervous excitement, anxious to fill up as fast as possible before being displaced by lions or others of their own kind. It is amazing to see the rapidity with which they can dispose of an animal: a gazelle practically disappears within minutes, while a buffalo can be reduced to a skull overnight.

The skulls and animal remains scattered throughout the bush illustrate the role of death in perpetuating life. Nothing is wasted. Leftover bones are gnawed by hyenas and jackals during lean times; horns are slowly eaten away by fly larvae.

Night Drives. Although occasionally met in the twilight of dawn or dusk, most of Africa's nocturnal animals are rarely seen. Such curiosities as aardvarks and porcupines are actually quite common, but during the day they stay hidden in underground burrows and hollow trees, waiting for the cover of darkness before starting their daily rounds. Where nighttime drives are allowed, you can often find these creatures with the aid of powerful spotlights that pick out the reflection of eyes in the dark. On closer approach, the mysterious orbs materialize into the silhouettes of owls, bushbabies, spring-hares, and civet cats.

Animals familiar from daytime encounters look different at night, too. Herds of impala appear as eerie constellations of moving eyes, while hippos prance about skittishly when caught on dry land, and hyenas look positively ghostly. Few safari experiences compare with the sight of a lion kill at night: a circling ring of hyenas and jackals moves furtively just beyond the spotlight's glare, as angry lionesses turn from the carcass to chase the intruders into the darkness. Their eyes glowing ferociously in the beams, lions look immensely scary. Prowling leopards are also more likely to be picked up on night drives than during the day.

Unfortunately, night drives are not allowed inside either Kenyan or Tanzanian national parks. They are more regularly featured in some of the reserves of southern Africa, particularly in Botswana, Zimbabwe, and Zambia. In East Africa, night drives must be conducted outside parks, usually on private land—a distinct disadvantage, because they are much more exciting where there is plenty of big game. Outside the parks, night drives are still worth trying now and then, although excessive riding in the dark gets boring (and cold) when there is little to see.

Dry-Country Habitats

True desert is rare in East Africa, but parts of northern Kenya are arid enough to be described as semidesert. Such habitat is not a Saharan wasteland; although bare ground shows between patches of sparse grass and bush, plant life is abundant and a good variety of animals have adapted to a nearly waterless environment. Much vaster tracks of savanna country annually suffer severely dry conditions during the rainless months stretching between June and November. Some plants adapt to this periodic drought by dropping their leaves; others store moisture during rainy seasons. The baobab tree uses both strategies, and its bare limbs and swollen trunk are a familiar sight in seasonally parched bushlands. Although its vegetation may look lifeless, dry bush can be extraordinarily rich in wildlife, especially where sources of water remain available. A number of parks are at their best when they serve as dry-season oases in otherwise waterless country.

Finding wildlife in desert or dry bush habitat is made easier by the scarcity of water: although some antelopes never have to drink, most animals like to slake their thirst daily, and a constant procession of creatures will stream to rivers or waterholes. Observation at watering places, whether from blinds or vehicles, is therefore a rewarding game-viewing technique. Because lions often take up residence around such pools, they are risky places for ambush and animals approach them warily. Giraffe are particularly careful: one will stand a long while, making sure that no cats are lurking about, before attempting to drink. When it decides that the coast is clear, it must spread its front legs wide in order to lower its head—a position of utter vulnerability. The giraffe takes only a quick sip and snaps back to attention, then starts the whole process over again. Elephants also take their time: big ones can quaff more than 30 gallons at a session, an amount requiring at least as many trunkloads. After drinking, they throw water or mud onto their heads and backs. A dust bath and a good scratch against a favorite tree or termite mound are the usual finale to this leisurely ritual.

Forests

African forests are a delight to the senses. Moist and cool, perfumed by woodsy fragrance and ringing with bird sound, they seem full of life, and they are. Yet forests are tough places for game viewing because of poor visibility; it's hard to see the animals for the trees. To compound the problem, resident mammals are relatively scarce and tend to be shy or nocturnal. Even the largest are often only glimpsed fleetingly before they vanish into the shadows. Although avian life is both abundant and interesting—for many extraordinary species are relegated to forest habitat—finding birds in the foliage is difficult and time consuming. None of these conditions makes forests conducive to highly productive game drives.

Walking or camping in a forest is the best way to appreciate its environment. Birds and monkeys are easier to observe when you are on foot. The sound of their alarm calls or the swaying of branches calls attention to their presence in the treetops—signals easily missed from a moving vehicle. Walking also allows you to investigate the many trees, shrubs, and flowers that compete for your interest. If a hike or camp is impractical, make a point of pausing in a forest for a rest or picnic. Even such carside explorations can be revealing.

The forest's large terrestrial mammals are most likely to be encountered at the edges of clearings. Resident animals include elephant, buffalo, browsing antelope (notably bushbuck and various types of duiker), several members of the pig family, and a great collection of primates. With the exception of the primates, all are most likely to be active at night, so dawn and dusk are very much the rule for game driving on forest tracks. At those hours, the deep twilight makes photography almost impossible. Yet despite that drawback, forest game drives can be memorable: it is always exciting to encounter elephants blocking a narrow road through dense timber, or to catch sight of a duiker rooting on the forest floor.

Some of the best forest game watching takes place at lodges especially designed for nighttime viewing. Several Kenyan hotels have been built near floodlit saltlicks and waterholes. Animals are attracted to the salt, and most of the larger forest dwellers can be easily observed. So too are a wide variety of small nocturnal mammals, such as genets and mongooses.

Tropical rainforest is rare in East Africa and where it does occur, it has been largely chopped away for human settlement. Highland forest has also been greatly reduced, but has received some protection in the mountain national parks. These montane forests differ from the lowland types in that they are dominated by a few types of trees—particularly African cedar and podocarpus—rather than showing the extreme diversification of species typical of tropical rainforests. The luxuriance of their vegetation is also somewhat reduced by the relative absence of vines, lianas, and tree ferns from the understory. Unlike their South American counterparts, Africa's lowland rainforests (or jungles) contain few palm trees.

Rivers and Lakes

Large bodies of water are dependable places for finding wildlife. In game country, they are bound to attract thirsty animals to their shores and to provide refuge for specialized aquatic species. Even outside parks, water inevitably signals excellent bird watching. Soda lakes are often ringed with masses of pink flamingos, while the lusher littorals of freshwater lakes tend to support a greater variety of species. Wherever fish are abundant, pelicans, cormorants, and fish eagles also abound. In shallow waters, these are joined by herons, storks, and smaller waders. Ducks and geese are plentiful, too, especially when Eurasian migrants flock to Africa during the Northern Hemisphere's winter.

In East African parks, exploration of rivers and lakes usually stops at the water's edge. That's where most of the action is anyway, but it makes a nice change of perspective to get out on the water. River cruises are particularly exciting: as your boat moves upstream, hippos dive and grunt, while crocodiles slip silently from the banks to vanish in the flood. Such an experience is great fun, though the animals are obviously too scared by engine noise to be closely examined. Where boats can be chartered, however, they offer superior opportunities for bird watching: they can take you to island rookeries and nesting areas, or ply channels through otherwise impassable swamps.

Crocodiles belong to an ancient order of reptiles that have been around in their present form since the time of the dinosaurs. The Nile crocodile (*Crocodylus niloticus*) is widespread in African rivers and lakes. Exceptional specimens can reach a length of 18 feet, and may have been even bigger before they were hunted with firearms. Today, a 14-footer is considered large. Such monsters are dangerous, yet remain afraid of humans. In fact, when you approach basking crocodiles, it is the largest that first disappear into the water: only the most wary live to reach great size. Adult crocs have few enemies besides humans, but it is a different story when they are young, or even before they are born. Although female crocs guard their nests, whole clutches are lost to raiding monitor lizards and mongooses. When the eggs hatch, the babies are subject to attack by large birds, as well as cannibal crocodiles. Footlong hatchlings eat insects and frogs, then fish as they grow. When crocs reach a suitable size and weight, they can attempt to catch large mammals. An unwary animal is grabbed as it drinks, then pulled into the water and drowned. The reptiles also scavenge on animals that die during river crossings or floods, and a dead hippo makes a crocodilian banquet. But ordinarily, crocodiles depend on fish for a living. Crocs are commonly seen basking on sandbanks in rivers. They are normally extremely wary, and must be stalked in complete silence for close photographs.

The hippo (*Hippopotamus amphibius*) is a source of constant wonder. For one thing, the "river horse" (as the ancient Greeks named it, *hippo-*, horse, *-potamus*, river) is much larger than one realizes. When you see a hippo resting in a pool with only eyes and ears breaking the surface, it is hard to guess that the average adult weighs about 3,000 pounds; bulls are frightfully large and can reach over three tons (6,000 pounds).

Hippos avoid heat and sun. A pinkish secretion gives their sensitive skin some protection from burning, but the animal's main relief is the water in which it spends the day. It's great fun to stand watch over a hippo pool. Although the beasts prefer to stay submerged as much as possible when humans are near, they snort and blow, and keep up a steady stream of amusing action. Hippos are highly gregarious, and often pack themselves into compact masses: one leans on the other, each resting a behemoth head on a neighbor's heavy haunches or sturdy back. When one animal moves, another is displaced, and a dozing herd soon dissolves in a chain reaction of grunts and squabbles. If the hippo's nasal snorts are mirth provoking, nothing tops their toilet habits for laughs: stubby tails are raised with a noisy flapping motion that distributes strawlike excrement into the faces of any rearward companions. Great toothy yawns are also sure crowd pleasers. Visitors are tempted to pass these exaggerated gestures off as symptoms of drowsiness, but they are really serious threat displays in which bulls advertise their dangerous tusks, up to three feet in length, to maximum effect.

The hippo's diet consists primarily of grass. It leaves the water shortly after dark, spreads some dung against a bush or tree, and proceeds toward grazing on well-marked paths. Since a hippo eats up to 130 pounds nightly, it may have to travel miles from pool to pasture. Its size is its armor: lions and hyenas rarely attack adult hippos, though calves are at risk.

Few visitors see hippos at night, when they are most active. On land, and at ease, the hippo lumbers along on short legs, head down, cropping grass with its wide square mouth. It's skittish and, when sensing danger, is quite fast, running with an almost dainty tiptoe gait. In cool weather, hippos are more likely to be abroad during the day: they then sleep in tight-packed huddles on sunny sandbanks. If disturbed, however, they are quick to awake and slip back to the security of water.

Hippos have a profound effect on the aquatic environment, and many creatures benefit from their presence. Although crocs occasionally take young ones, they profit more in an indirect way: during the day, hippos deposit huge amounts of dung into the water, providing a rich source of food for fish. Humans also reap a piscine bounty from lakes that have large hippo populations; sadly, it has been well documented that catches decline catastrophically when hippos are eliminated.

Mammals and Field Guides

Ranging from the African elephant to elephant shrews, and aard-wolves to zorillas, the variety of East African mammals is truly mindboggling: the antelopes alone total more than thirty-five species, from 11 separate families. Each animal is unique in form and function, and there is simply not enough space here even to mention them all. Although the major species, and many others, are discussed in the text, the information is far from complete. To fully appreciate Africa's mammalian life, carry a field guide along on your trip.

An illustrated field guide is more than an invaluable aide to identification; it is a great reference for information on many aspects of an animal's natural history: the facts of size and weight, habitat and food preferences, reproductive cycles, social behavior, and daily habits are all put at your fingertips. The most comprehensive is *A Field Guide to the Mammals of Africa Including Madagascar*, by Theodor Haltenorth and Helmut Diller (London: Collins, 1980). Jean Dorst's *Field Guide to the Larger Mammals of Africa* (Boston: Houghton Mifflin, 1969) is not as good, but still useful. John William's *Field Guide to the National Parks of East Africa* (London: Collins, 1967) has nice illustrations of most mammals, but descriptions are very brief.

Your pleasure on safari will be increased as the depth of your knowledge about the animals and their habitat deepens. It is highly recommended to do as much study as possible before you leave home. For further reading, consult the bibliography at the end of this book.

Insects

Most visitors to Africa would just as soon not think about insects, but several types are too important to the continent's overall ecology to pass without notice.

A good number of African parks undoubtedly owe their existence not to an animal that humans wanted to preserve, but to one we couldn't get rid of: the tsetse fly. This insect is reviled as the carrier of human sleeping sickness and also transmits the fatal *nagama* disease to cattle. In those areas where tsetses prosper, cattle and people do not; the fly has kept humans out of whole regions of wooded bush country that otherwise would have been settled long ago. Many such tsetse-infested tracts were designated game reserves, and later turned into national parks. Because of that, it has been argued that the tsetse is the greatest conservator of wildlife in Africa. When scientists find the means to eliminate the fly, the last wild gamelands will be in serious danger of human encroachment. Try to keep this in mind when tsetses buzz around you in hungry swarms, even if you get a few bites.

Tsetse are ordinary-sized flies of the genus *Glossina,* recognizable by the peculiar way they fold their wings over the back: the wings rest one over the other, giving the insect a characteristic cylindrical shape rather than the scissor-winged physique common to other types of flies. Tsetse feed on blood. They rest on the shady underside of bushes or trees, and are attracted by movement to passing animals: they consider automobiles to be fair game. Tsetse bites can be subtle or needle sharp, and some people get terribly itchy reactions. Sleeping sickness, however, is rarely contracted in East African game parks. (See more about tsetses in the health and insects sections of Chapter 2.)

As you drive through the bush, the imposing spires of termite mounds are sure to catch your eye, for these castles of clay are one of the most striking features of many African landscapes. Termites are voracious primary consumers of vegetation that harvest grass as well as dead wood. They are extremely plentiful in all savanna habitats and play a key link in the life histories of many animals.

Termite castles are raised during the rains, when the insects use saliva to fix mud into durable cement; fresh construction can rise inches overnight. The tall towers surround ventilation shafts that reach deep into the earth, providing a cooling system for underground fungus gardens. A variety of small animals live in the tunnels: among the squatters are mongooses, birds, lizards, and snakes. Other animals use termites as a source of food: aardvarks, pangolins, and aardwolves depend on the insects for their survival. "Anthills" that have been torn apart by aardvarks often become the homes of burrowing animals such as warthogs and hyenas. During nuptial swarms, when columns of lace-winged insects spew from the mound like a volcano in eruption, a whole array of animals joins in feasting on them. Baboons, hornbills, eagles, jackals, hyenas, and even humans, all relish the fatty abdomens of reproductive termites, the would-be founders of new colonies.

Termite mounds are more commonly seen than the insects themselves. The "white ants" avoid the heat of the sun and are mostly abroad at night; during the day, you may find them beneath pieces of downed wood. Where you see fresh work on a mound, you can break off a small piece and the fierce soldier termites will emerge to confront you. But be very cautious about poking into the holes on anthills: they are a favorite refuge for the deadly black mamba, as well as for other snakes.

Dung beetles are ecologically important because they rapidly recycle tremendous quantities of fresh excrement back into the earth. These large black "scarabs," which were symbols of rebirth to the ancient Egyptians, are very conspicuous as they roll balls of manure across the plain. Each ball contains a single egg; after burial, a fat grub develops, to emerge in the next rainy season as a "resurrected" beetle. Adults have hard shells that make them unpalatable to all but a few large birds. The larvae, however, are eagerly sought by the bat-eared fox. During the lean dry months, this tiny insect-eating canid uses its oversized ears to locate grubs hidden underground.

Birds and Bird Watching

East African bird watching is arguably the best in the world. Although South America can claim more species, most are hard-to-see creatures of the rainforest. In contrast, excellent visibility in Africa's savanna country makes it easy to witness the beauty and diversity of its birdlife. Almost 1,300 species have been recorded in the region, and it is reasonable for an experienced birder to identify more than 200 types during a typical two-week safari; participants on well-led specialty tours can expect to get up to three times that many. But enjoyment of the birds is not restricted to committed listers; birds are so evident a part of the wildlife scene that many people without any previous interest develop a passion for them while on safari.

The brightly colored species are the first to catch the eye. Some of the prettiest are routinely attracted to lodge feeders: iridescent starlings and golden-yellow weavers are among the regular freeloaders. On game drives, the sight of a colorful bee-eater or kingfisher perched on a bare branch is a real car-stopper. The lilac-breasted roller, a tame and multihued bird that obligingly poses for the camera, is everyone's favorite. King-size birds also readily draw attention, whether beautiful, like the elegant crowned crane, or merely strange to our eyes. The marabou stork falls in the latter category: frocked in sober black and white, its prominent bill, balding pate, and stooped posture give it something of the demeanor of the Aya-

The crowned crane, one of Africa's most beautiful birds. *Photo by Allen Bechky.*

tollah Khomeinei. (And in fact, the bird takes its name from a type of Muslim holy men—the *marabout*—found throughout northern Africa.)

Ranging in size from the pygmy falcon to the monkey-eating crowned eagle, Africa's birds of prey are another group that piques universal interest. Eagles and vultures are almost constantly patrolling overhead, along with a squadron of miscellaneous hawks, buzzards, harriers, and falcons. Graceful as they are on the wing, these raptors are at their most impressive when perched. No one can fail to be moved when staring into the face of the martial eagle, its fierce eyes burning with all the haughtiness of a medieval warload.

Among the smaller varieties are many LBJs ("little brown jobs") that pass just as unnoticed as in your own local city park. But tiny jewel-like species abound, and the assortment of birds is almost endless; an array of shrikes and cuckoos, waxbills and whydahs, hoopoes, hornbills, and honeyguides (to name but a few) seem to pop out of the bush at every turn.

Africa's tropical climate is responsible for this avian wealth, for warm temperatures ensure a year-round food supply of plants and insects. Local abundance varies with the season, however, and some species move around the continent, following the rains in search of the insects, frogs, and fish that multiply in their wake. The exuberance of the rainy season sparks many African birds to breed; mating is serious business, and they put on their most brilliant plumage for the occasion. From September through March, the continent's resident birds are joined by species that migrate to Africa to avoid the Eurasian winter. This migration coincides with the period between East Africa's two rainy seasons, and bird watching is probably at its best at that time. It is then possible to see massive flocks of the white stork (the one that brings the babies), now rare in western Europe.

The average person will be charmed by Africa's birds; the ardent lister will be in heaven. But he or she will face stiff challenges; the sheer variety makes identification a bewildering process, and it is not always easy to catch a good view. Tiny sunbirds won't sit still to be identified, and screening foliage ensures that the shyer species remain more often heard than seen. LBJs, such as larks and wheatears, blend into their surroundings so well that they are difficult to pick out even 10 feet from a car. Such obstacles will not deter the enthusiast, who will be busy from dawn to dusk pursuing dun-colored larks just as eagerly as the most colorful specimens.

To sort out the birds, you will need a field guide. Williams's *Field Guide to the National Parks of East Africa* features the most common and noticeable varieties. Serious birders will want the same author's *Field Guide to the Birds of East Africa* (London: Collins, 1981), a more comprehensive volume that is the standard field reference. If your safari takes place during the northern winter, you may want to bring along *The Birds of Britain and Europe,* by Hermann Heinzel, Richard Fitter, and John Parslow (London: Collins, 1979). *Newman's Birds of Southern Africa,* by Kenneth Newman, (Johannesburg: MacMillan South Africa, 1983), is essential if you will be traveling to Zambia, Zimbabwe, Botswana, or South Africa. *Roberts Birds of South Africa,* by G. R. McLachlan and R. Liversidge (Cape Town: Voecker Bird Book Fund, reissued 1980), and C. W. Mackworth-Praed and C. H. B. Grant's two-volume *Birds of Eastern and North Eastern Africa* (London: Longman, reissued 1981) are the Bibles of African bird lore; too heavy to tote, they are for home reference.

Binoculars are *essential* even for casual bird watching (see Chapter 2 for what kind to get). Spotting scopes are great on lakeshores and mud flats, where you can't possibly get near birds that are otherwise in plain view, and for watching birds on nests. They are cumbersome, however, and cannot always be conveniently set up in game parks.

Reptiles

As you might expect, tropical Africa hosts a wide variety of reptilian life. Although most species go unnoticed or unobserved, a few deserve mention.

Monitor lizards are the continent's largest, growing up to 7 feet in length. The Nile monitor lives near water and is frequently seen sunning itself in overhanging trees or on the banks of streams. They feed on eggs, carrion, fish, and any small animals they can catch, including young crocodiles. Less often seen is the savanna monitor, a thicker-bodied lizard that can be found far from water. It is a voracious predator and defends itself by lacerating enemies with its serrated tail.

Many types of smaller lizards are routinely encountered. Agamas are conspicuous because of the bold colors sported by males: various species come in bright combinations of red, yellow, orange, and blue. Geckos are often seen hunting moths around game lodges and buildings. They have the unusual ability to walk on vertical walls, and can even crawl upside down on the ceiling. Do not become alarmed or injure a gecko if you see one in your hotel room: it can do you no harm, and may remove a few mosquitos. Chameleons are more bizarre, though less visible. It is true that they can change their color; equally remarkable, they can move their eyes, which are set in protruding sockets, in opposite directions. One variety is a giant (almost 2 feet long!), others small; Jackson's chameleon has three tricerotops-like horns on its head. All are totally harmless, but Africans traditionally regard them as harbingers of evil or bad luck.

Turtlelike marsh terrapins are common around water but rarely stick around for a close view. This is not true of the leopard tortoise, a land-dwelling animal that is not noted for speed. It is often encountered crossing the road during game drives, and care must be taken not to run it over. Once seen, it is easily captured for an examination of its beautifully patterned shell. Leopard tortoises can be handled without fear, but they eject a foul-smelling black liquid, so beware if you pick one up. They are preyed on by hyenas, honey badgers, and jackals, but their biggest enemy is fire, which destroys any tortoise that cannot find its way underground.

Although common in most warm habitats, snakes manage to stay well out of sight; on the typical safari, you will be lucky to see even one. But that one can loom large in imagination. Perhaps because of fear, the dangerous serpents most grab our fancy. Every time we spot a green snake, we would like to believe it a deadly mamba, ignoring the fact that many varieties of the same color are perfectly harmless. Contrary to popular opinion, most African snakes are completely innocuous except to the frogs, lizards, and rats on which they feed. Many snakes have no fangs whatsoever.

Africa's poisonous snakes fall into three groups. Colubrid snakes are the most common. With the exceptions of the boomslang ("tree snake") and the vine (or twig) snake, these rear-fanged species are completely harmless to humans. The two mentioned have chemically complex poisons that are potentially lethal, but neither is aggressive, and bites are extremely rare.

The most dangerous snakes are the elapids and the vipers. Cobras and mambas belong to the elapid family. These serpents have short fangs, located at the front of the mouth, that inject potent neurotoxic venoms. Such poisons attack the nervous system, leading to paralysis of the lungs and heart. A bite can be extremely serious; elapids are responsible for the most cases of sudden death. Such a fate is not certain, however: the effect of any bite varies, and the rapidity or severity of poisoning depends on many factors, such as the size of the snake, the amount of venom received (none may be injected at all), and the weight of the victim. It takes a massive dose of venom, delivered directly into a vein, to produce immediate death in an adult human. Several cobra species are capable of spitting their venom for distances up to 10 feet. They aim for the eyes—a tactic designed to protect them from large animals that might otherwise trample on them by accident. The black mamba is the largest and most feared venomous snake in Africa; it reaches a maximum length of 12 feet. By reputation, it is fast and aggressive; it is supposed to be especially protective of the termite mound or rocky outcrop it uses as a refuge. It hunts on both the ground and in trees, unlike the green mamba, which is almost exclusively arboreal. Note that the black mamba is actually olive-green in color; only the inside of its mouth is black. This fact becomes obvious only during the terrifying gaping display that the mamba makes just before it strikes—not something you want to see.

Vipers possess hemotoxic venoms that attack tissue and blood. Such poisons are powerful enzymes meant to begin the process of digestion even before prey is swallowed. Most vipers possess wonderfully camouflaged skin that enables them to lie concealed as a means of defense. The puff adder is a common, slow-moving viper. Large specimens are grossly fat. They are active primarily at night, when Africans are prone to step on them in the darkness. The gaboon viper is also a large and beautifully colored snake; its 2-inch-long fangs contain venom with both hemotoxic and neurotoxic agents. It is extremely dangerous, but very rare and difficult to provoke.

Pythons are not poisonous, but fascinate because of their size: they can reach more than 20 feet in length, although such giants are rare. This snake waits in ambush on a game trail, catches its quarry with a firm bite, and quickly coils around the body in an asphyxiating death grip. Prey consists of small to medium-sized animals, such as monkeys, antelopes, and large rodents. Although a human child could be at risk, an attack on an adult would be accidental: a python simply cannot swallow a full-grown man. But accidents can happen, so it is fortunate that pythons are normally shy and retiring.

Although not a genuine field guide, *Reptiles and Amphibians of East Africa,* by Norman Hedges (Nairobi: Kenya Literature Bureau, 1983), is portable, easily understood, and has pictures and descriptions of all the major species. V. F. M. FitzSimons's *A Field Guide to the Snakes of Southern Africa* (London: Collins, 1980) is detailed and covers most of the East African serpents.

Conservation Notes

While on safari, you will constantly be amazed by the superabundance of animals. Yet the question nags as to how long the game will last. As we begin the countdown to the twenty-first century, two storm clouds loom large on the horizon: commercial poaching is the most dramatic and immediate danger; loss of habitat is the ultimate threat. Both perils are exemplified by the plight of the two major species that are already in serious trouble, the elephant and the black rhino.

In many ways, elephants symbolize everything that is wild in Africa. These giants need expansive amounts of space to survive, and even the game reserves are often not big enough to contain them. The African elephant (*Loxodonta africana*) is the largest land animal; a bull can grow to a height of 13 feet and weigh more than 6 tons (12,000 pounds), although most would tip the scales at about 5 tons (10,000 pounds). Females are smaller, but their food requirements are proportionately the same: an elephant eats about 5 percent of its body weight daily. Whereas in the past elephants could migrate at will over vast tracts of countryside, they have been increasingly confined to national parks and game reserves. These parcels have limited carrying capacities, and often go through major habitat modification when their elephant populations get too large. Even though the conversion of woodland to grassland is good for some species, it has dire consequences for others, including elephants themselves: although the pachyderms depend largely on grass for sustenance, they require shade trees to protect their young from fatal heat stress.

Controversy has raged for years over how to prevent elephants from eating themselves out of house and home. One side advocates "culling" as the solution. In a culling scheme, biologists first determine the number of animals a park can support; its elephants are then counted, the excess number is determined, and teams of expert marksmen go to work. A herd is exterminated in a single deadly fusillade: bulls, cows, and calves are all mercilessly shot down. None are permitted to escape. This brutally efficient technique has several rationales. By removing animals of all ages, the demographic distribution of the elephant population at large is not upset. Annihilation of the entire herd also ensures that no terrified survivors are left to roam the park: elephants have long memories, and traumatized animals could be a hazard to visitors. In addition to keeping the number of elephants within set limits, culling allows parks and national treasuries to reap profits from the sale of ivory, skins, and meat. Intensive culling is employed in the parks of South Africa and Zimbabwe, and authorities there defend their methods with volumes of scientific data.

In East Africa, game wardens have preferred to let nature take its course, trusting to the theory that ecosystems adjust naturally to changes in animal populations. For many years this laissez-faire policy seemed to work fairly well—there was no shortage of either elephants or other game—but some park woodlands were damaged, and there were periodic calls for drastic culls. Such appeals invariably sparked acrimonious disputes among wildlife experts. The ivory trade has made the debate moot: since the early 1970s, a tidal wave of poaching has reduced East Africa's elephant population by more than half.* Perhaps three-quarters of a million elephants remain, continent-wide, but the slaughter, though much decried, goes on unabated. The elephant may soon join the ranks of endangered species.

The black rhinoceros has undergone an even more catastrophic decline. Only fifteen years ago, this prehistoric-looking beast was a common animal in almost every African game park. But its venerable line may soon be coming to an end; poachers have now completely exterminated the rhino in most areas, and its numbers have declined overall by more than 90 percent.

Since ancient times, the horns, and other parts of the rhino's body, have been sought-after ingredients in oriental medicines. Rhino horn is made of compacted hairlike tissue, similar to our fingernails. Although its most publicized use is as an aphrodisiac, powdered horn is considered efficacious for any number of disorders, and is more often used to lower blood pressure than to raise it (mainly it is used to reduce fever). Whatever its application, it is still worth its weight in gold throughout Asia. Taiwan is the biggest importer, though much of its stock is reexported to feed mainland China's huge market. Rhino horns are also in demand in Yemen, where they are carved into handles for *jambia*, the dagger worn by every adult male. A rhino horn handle is a highly prized status symbol. Thousands have been sold, and the tiny Arabian nation is one of the world's principal consumers of rhinos.

For many of us, the slaughter of endangered species is an unqualified evil, and a very emotional issue. Yet we should not be too fast to point the finger at others. If certain Arabs have a taste for wearing rhino horn adornments, that fashion is not much different than our own love of ivory jewelry. If Africans poach to make a living, that should be no surprise on a continent on which per capita income is measured in hundreds of dollars a year. (It is true that only a few people at the top get rich off the bloody trade, while most of those doing the actual shooting see little of the profit—but their rewards are still relatively good for Africa.) Above all, we must not forget that the chain of death often ends in the Western world: in 1986, the United States imported more than 5 million pieces of

---

*A 1987 survey by researcher Iain Douglas-Hamilton for the United Nations Environment Program (UNEP) puts the fifteen-year (1973–1987) decrease in elephant populations at 53 percent for Tanzania, 85 percent for Kenya, and 89 percent for Uganda.

carved ivory in the form of jewelry, statues, or other trinkets. That amount—equal to one-third of the world market—required the deaths of an estimated 32,000 elephants!* Just as much as we decry the activities of local hunters and vicious foreign businessmen, we must work to reduce our own demand for ivory products and put pressure on our industrialized trading partners to do the same.

The scale of poaching is clearly appalling, yet it is aimed primarily at only the few species for which there are lucrative markets. For less persecuted animals, the critical issue for survival is the preservation of habitat. Although large territories have already been set aside for parks and reserves, wildlife habitat must inevitably shrink as Africa's human population continues to grow. Even before the latest surge in poaching activity, elephants were thought to be declining at roughly 3 percent every year, which is about the same rate as that of human increase. Already the parks are becoming islands in a sea of human habitation. Very shortly, Africa's larger animals will have been banished from all land that has not been specifically reserved for them. Few parks encompass entire natural ecosystems that meet the year-round requirements of their fauna. In most, wildlife populations change as animals migrate to and from surrounding countryside in accordance with seasonal availability of food and water. As the process of "islandization" advances, the carrying capacity of the parks will almost certainly stabilize at lower levels.

Islandization also spells genetic trouble; as populations are confined, decreases in local gene pools will lead to a weakening of stocks, especially of rarer species such as rhinos. Their reproduction will require scientific management in order to protect genetic diversity. Such programs are not only expensive, they negate the essence of wilderness and wildlife. Distasteful as this may be, in the not-too-distant future many African parks may be managed like drive-through zoos. Others may simply vanish as the tide of humanity washes away the boundaries of reserves that do not produce sufficient tourist revenues.

Technology is also contributing to the destruction of African wildlife habitat. Parts of Botswana's Okavango Delta are being sprayed with insecticides to combat the tsetse, an activity that may have ecological implications far beyond those envisioned by author-

---

*Estimates vary: TRAFFIC, the trade monitoring unit of the World Wildlife Fund, put the U.S. share of ivory consumption in 1988 at 12 percent of Africa's annual production, with Japan accounting for about 75 percent! Even the lower figure represents many thousands of dead elephants, however.

Hunted for its horn, the black rhino is on the brink of extinction. *Photo by Allen Bechky.*

ities. Other areas are destined to be dredged, like the Sudd in Sudan, or dammed, like the lower Zambezi Valley.

Finally, there stands the menace of political instability. As the Ugandan experience has shown, it takes only a few years of anarchy to wreak havoc on a country's wildlife paradises.

Although the threats are real, predictions regarding the "end of the game" have been rife since the early days of African independence. Yet there are still enough animals around to confound the old-time pessimists. Nor are gloomy current trends necessarily irreversible. Research suggests that elephant numbers were probably as low at the end of the last century as they are now, following an earlier period of ruthless ivory hunting. With protection, the elephants recovered from that holocaust, and may bounce back again if poaching can be controlled. That is a tall order, but it is possible that international awareness will reduce the demand for ivory. Moreover, African governments may recognize that it is in their self-interest to vigorously protect this valuable, and renewable, natural resource. There may even be hope for the black rhino; its cousin, the white rhino, was only saved from extinction by a hair's breadth, but is now common in the parks of South Africa. Emergency actions are being taken that will probably ensure the survival of the black rhino in at least a few locales. In all likelihood, the future of Africa's wildlife reserves will be a mixed bag: some parks will disappear altogether, some will be reduced to the status of wild animal theme parks, and a few will remain large and relatively wild.

Rather than abandon all hope, do what you can to aid the cause of African wildlife. A number of organizations fund and manage conservation projects in Africa (a partial list is included in the Appendix), and all of them need financial support. It also helps to stay informed and spread the word to friends that African wildlife needs help: the slide show that results from your safari could be used to raise a few dollars for your favorite wildlife group. More directly, you can refrain from buying wildlife products (especially ivory), and let your government representatives know how you feel about the importation of such products into the United States. Letters to foreign embassies can also be effective; ultimately, boycotts may have to be organized against the tours and products of countries that do not seriously support international efforts to control the wildlife trade.

4

Kenya: The Lion's Share

Boasting an astonishing assortment of wildlife amid an array of magnificent parks, Kenya more than fulfills all expectations for an African safari. Its awesome landscapes, startling in their diversity, have delighted generations of visitors. The land continues to enthrall everyone who has an eye for natural beauty. To the magnetism of the bush country is coupled the sun-drenched playground of the tropical Indian Ocean coast. These formidable attractions are backed by a modern infrastructure that delivers a high level of service and comfort. A network of good roads, an up-to-date fleet of safari vehicles, an abundance of delectable foods, and a whole constellation of game lodges allow a wide range of safari options. Indeed, Kenya has something to offer every visitor. From budget travelers to movie stars, whether holiday safarists or wilderness enthusiasts, international tourists have made Kenya their overwhelming choice. Of all African countries, Kenya receives the lion's share of tourism.

Geography is one important key to Kenya's appeal. Although positioned firmly on the equator, its temperatures are moderated by altitude, so the climate is pleasantly warm rather than torrid. The coast is frankly tropical and the deserts of the north searingly hot, but much of the game country is high enough for comfortable safari temperatures. The central highlands around Nairobi are blessed with an eternally springlike climate that suggests the finest days of an English summer. The scenery is as enticing as the climate. The Rift Valley cuts through the country north to south, forming a series of breathtaking escarpments that drop to a chain of scenic lakes. Mountains and hill ranges abound, the remnants of ancient East African volcanos. Best known are snow-capped Mount Kenya and towering Kilimanjaro, which although geographically in Tanzania, is most often viewed from Kenya's Amboseli plains. The alternation

129

of desert thornbush, sheer escarpment, and forested hills provides a scenic diversity that is rare in Africa. In the course of a day's drive, one can easily drop from cool mountain forest to bone-dry semidesert on the Rift floor, and climb again into grassy savanna gamelands. This startling variety of landforms and climates never ceases to amaze visitors, even those returning for the third time.

History adds to Kenya's charisma. The same seductive climate about which modern visitors rave also drew an earlier generation of European settlers. The colonists who came out to Kenya at the turn of the century sought land on which to build farms and estates on the model of those they knew in England. They gravitated to the fertile lands of the Kenya highlands, where both rich soils and bracing climate agreed with their sentiments. The romance of Africa—taming the bush, bringing civilization to savages, and hunting big game—appealed to a singular collection of eccentrics. Among them were some of unusual character and talent. These colorful people—footloose European gentry, gentleman ivory hunters, and a great many more humble folk—inhabit the writings of Isak Dinesen, Elspeth Huxley, and Beryl Markham. Their works have formed our portrait of the Kenya settler era, even as Hemingway and Robert Ruark have given us our stereotype of the big game hunting fraternity.

Hunting held a powerful attraction for many gentleman settlers and explorers. When Teddy Roosevelt led his 1909 hunting expedition, more than a hundred porters strong, from the Norfolk Hotel, Nairobi was forever established as the safari capital of the continent. Throughout the twentieth century, the rich and famous made Kenya their African playground. There, the safari mystique was born. Idealized in literature and film, the glamorous figure of the white hunter—fearless, independent, cultivated, yet cynical, hard-drinking, irresistible to women—became an icon of modern African mythology. The romance of safari, with its quasi-military paraphernalia and hint of danger, remains rooted in the hunt. Although trophy hunting is no longer allowed in the country, Kenya's status as safari capital lives on, nurtured by innumerable Hollywood feature films and wildlife documentaries. Now, with safarists stalking its bush with camera instead of gun, Kenya is still synonymous with "safari."

Although profiting from its reputation, Kenyans do not identify their country solely with game safaris, and their view cannot be ignored, as it was in the past. The white colonialists who came to Kenya aiming to settle new lands disregarded that it was already settled by black Africans. They took the land they wanted, designating the fertile high country as "white highlands," where Africans could work on European farms but not live permanently. The dreams of the white colonials dashed against the rocks of their blindness to the needs and desires of the black African people. When native land hunger and resentment spilled over into the violence of the Mau Mau Emergency in the early 1950s, the white settlers were rudely awakened from their colonial reverie. With black rule on the horizon, disaster was widely predicted for the future independent Kenya.

That disaster did not come to pass. From *uhuru* (freedom) in 1963, Kenya took a moderate, capitalist road to development under the leadership of Jomo Kenyatta. Foreign investment was encouraged and expatriates welcomed to help build the country. Kenya is one of Africa's few success stories, where economic growth has created an apparently prosperous nation. Paved highways crisscross the country, while schools, health clinics, and development projects are to be found in every district. In contrast with neighboring countries, where such essentials as food, fuel, clothing, and even soap are in short supply, Kenya's citizens seem to be living in great plenty. Aside from the unsuccessful coup attempt of 1982, Kenya's government has proved stable, and relatively democratic. Although it is a one-party state, lively elections are fought for parliamentary seats underneath the umbrella of the Kenya African National Union (KANU). Real power, however, resides with the office of the president. Kenyatta, known affectionately as the Mzee (the Old Man) governed from independence in 1963 until his death in 1978. His rule was prosperous and long. Some would say overlong, for the Old Man, the living symbol of independence, kept the reins of power long after he could properly grasp them. In his later years, the corrupt influence of his family somewhat dulled the luster of his good name.

The dire predictions for the fate of an independent Kenya have not proved true, but the doomsayers may yet have their day. The country's prosperity has not proved a boon to everyone. Tremendous inequities in pay and lifestyle exist among the simple people of the countryside, the unemployed underclass of Nairobi's slums, and the conspicuous "Wa-Benzi," the rich elites symbolized by ownership of a Mercedes. Education has fueled the expectations of the masses. People now want the jobs that lead to the good, modern life. Unfortunately, their expectations cannot be met, and wildly expanding population is exacerbating the problem. Tens of thousands of job seekers join the work force every year, but no jobs exist. New mouths increase land hunger among the farmers, but no more arable land can be effectively put under cultivation. The problem of the division of the economic pie is further complicated by Kenya's traditional bugaboo, tribalism, for the country is one of the most ethnically and linguistically diverse in Africa. The cornerstone of Kenyatta's policy was to "stamp out tribalism" in forging a national identity among all Kenyans. Although this campaign has been to some extent successful, tribal rivalries for political control are submerged rather than extinct. During Kenyatta's regime, the Kikuyu of the central highlands held most of the power. Government jobs, money, and privilege were showered on them. Since the death of the Mzee, a coalition of tribes backing President Daniel arap Moi has been pruning back Kikuyu power. Although serious tribal conflicts have so far been kept in check, they could well flare up when the rising tide of population and unemployment threaten the economic order. Pessimists still predict disaster, warning that the wonder of the national parks is a beauty already condemned.

Human settlement and development have already taken their toll on Kenya's wildlife habitat. Increasingly, the game is being pushed into the parks, which are becoming islands of wilderness separated by a sea of farms and ranches. Although the long-term pressures of development are serious, for the moment Kenya's parks are healthy and their animal populations thriving. Right now, it is Kenya's very success in attracting tourists that threatens to be its undoing as a safari paradise. The game parks are among the finest in Africa, but overcrowding is diminishing the quality of their wilderness experience. Complaints about a "circus atmosphere" and herds of minibuses are not infrequently heard. Still, the splendor of both wildlife and scenery will continue to gratify the majority of visitors. Wilderness aficionados need not be disappointed, either. Aside from a handful of annoyingly crowded parks, whole regions remain that are too remote, too wild, to be accessible to mass tourism.

Touring Kenya

Kenya has far too many attractions to be comprehensively visited without an extended stay. Nairobi is the transportation hub from which package safaris depart daily on regular tour circuits. These circuits can be meshed for visits to all the major reserves. The parks of central Kenya—Samburu, Meru, and the Aberdares—are often joined to various Rift Valley lakes and the Masai Mara to form one major game circuit. Amboseli and Tsavo make up the southeast safari circuit. The coast, where the main attraction is sun rather than safaris, is really a separate region, although it is easily combined with the southeastern parks. All other areas are too far off the beaten track for mass tourism. Although tours do operate to places such as Mount Kenya, Lake Turkana, and western Kenya, they are not on the popular minibus routes. To visit lesser-known reserves and wilderness areas, you really have no alternative to highly specialized tours or going it on your own.

SAFARI FACTS

Entry. Visas are required, and are easily obtained at any Kenya embassy worldwide. Although it is recommended to pick up your visa before departure, it is no problem to get a visa on arrival by air at Nairobi: you need a few minutes of paperwork and a $10 fee (payable in U.S. currency). No vaccinations are required for entry by air from Europe, but travelers arriving from other African countries may be required to show proof of vaccination for yellow fever and cholera.

Currency. Kenya shillings (1989 rate: KSh 19 = U.S. $1). Currency control regulations are in effect. You will be asked to declare your funds on arrival. Have all exchanges recorded on your currency declaration form, which you will give back on departure. Airport banks are always open. Make sure to change your money on arrival if you come at night or on a weekend. It is wise not to exchange at the bank inside the customs hall, as it is always crowded and slow; other exchange offices are located outside. Do not use the interior bank if you are a member of a tour group—you will delay other group members being met outside the customs area. There are many banks in town, all offering the same daily rate, which is fairly stable. Larger hotels change at a slightly lower rate. The black market runs about 10 percent higher than the official rate, but street exchange ripoffs and con games are extremely common.

Language. Swahili is official, among a great number of tribal tongues. English is ubiquitous, and will serve a traveler well.

Air Travel. Nairobi is a great hub for international flights. Jomo Kenyatta International Airport is one of the busiest airports in Africa, receiving numerous daily flights from Europe and serving most African countries with several flights weekly. Multiple Kenya Airways flights depart daily for Mombasa and Malindi, Kenya's popu-

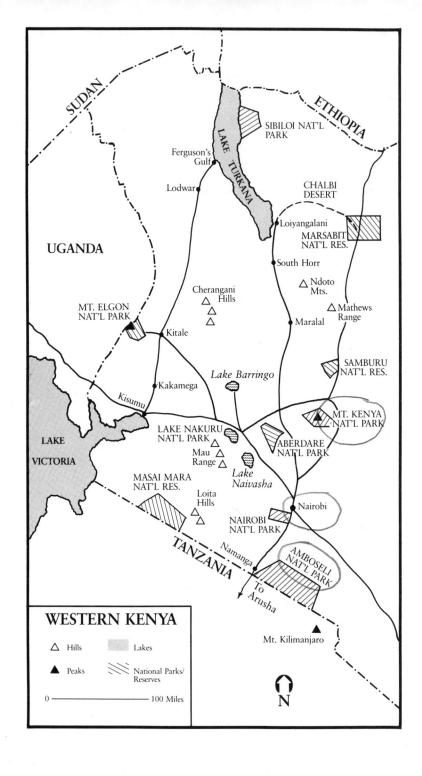

SUDAN

ETHIOPIA

UGANDA

SIBILOI NAT'L PARK

LAKE TURKANA

Ferguson's Gulf

Lodwar

CHALBI DESERT

Loiyangalani

MARSABIT NAT'L RES.

South Horr

Ndoto Mts.

Cherangani Hills

Mathews Range

MT. ELGON NAT'L PARK

Kitale

Maralal

Lake Barringo

SAMBURU NAT'L RES.

Kisumu

Kakamega

MT. KENYA NAT'L PARK

LAKE

LAKE NAKURU NAT'L PARK

ABERDARE NAT'L PARK

VICTORIA

Mau Range

Lake Naivasha

MASAI MARA NAT'L RES.

Loita Hills

Nairobi

NAIROBI NAT'L PARK

Namanga

AMBOSELI NAT'L PARK

TANZANIA

To Arusha

WESTERN KENYA

△ Hills   Lakes

▲ Peaks   National Parks/
              Reserves

0 ——————————— 100 Miles

Mt. Kilimanjaro

N

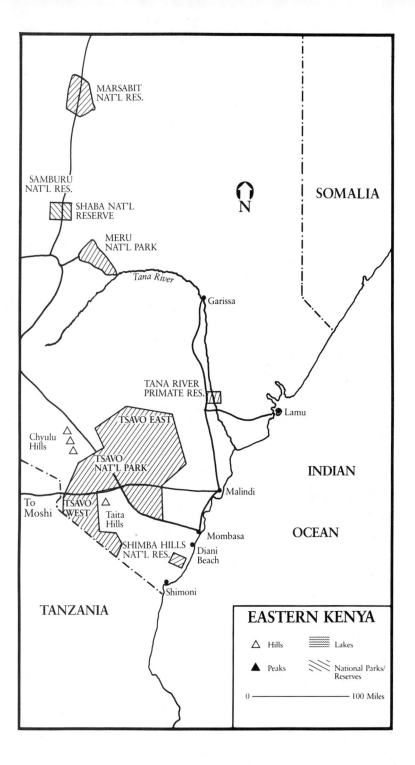

MARSABIT
NAT'L RES.

SAMBURU
NAT'L RES.

SHABA NAT'L
RESERVE

MERU
NAT'L PARK

Tana River

Garissa

SOMALIA

N

TANA RIVER
PRIMATE RES.

Lamu

TSAVO EAST

Chyulu
Hills

TSAVO
NAT'L PARK

INDIAN

To
Moshi

TSAVO
WEST

Taita
Hills

Malindi

OCEAN

SHIMBA HILLS
NAT'L RES.

Mombasa

Diani
Beach

Shimoni

TANZANIA

EASTERN KENYA

△ Hills

▲ Peaks

Lakes

National Parks/
Reserves

0 ———————— 100 Miles

lar beach destinations. Several small airlines (such as AirKenya, and Boskovic Air) provide regular service to the game parks and coastal resorts; their light aircraft are also available for charter. There is a KSh 50 tax on all domestic flights; the international airport departure tax of $20 is payable *only* in U.S. currency.

Transportation. Kenya has an excellent countrywide system of roads, many of which are paved. Public transport includes buses, long-distance Peugeot taxis, and an irregular collection of private vehicles. These *matatus,* which ply between towns and villages at rock-bottom prices, are well known for extreme overcrowding. Both the *matatus* and the Peugeots are legendary for wild rides and horrendous accidents. In Nairobi, deluxe Mercedes Kenatco taxis provide transport from the airport and major hotels at a fixed price. Other taxis have negotiable, hence cheaper, rates. A bus runs regularly between the airport and the downtown Kenya Airways office, stopping at the major hotels on request. Many rental car agencies have offices in both Nairobi and Mombasa. Advance bookings can be made with the major international companies such as Hertz and Avis; budget rates are available on older vehicles from local companies. Kenya Railways operates overnight service between Nairobi and Mombasa, with trains going each way daily. Sleeping berths (two people per compartment, first class; four people, second class) should be booked several days in advance. Porters fix up comfortable bedding at a slight extra charge. A dining car with bar service is attached to the train. The night train makes a pleasant one-way journey to or from the coast. Daytime trains now also operate daily, but they are *much* slower.

On Your Own. Kenya is the African country of greatest opportunity for independent travelers. Both in town and on safari, there are accommodations and styles to fit every pocketbook. Innumerable tour operators offer trips to all the big destinations. Most of these tours fit standard itineraries; for example, a one-week circuit of Samburu Game Reserve, the Rift Valley lakes, and the Masai Mara or a four-day journey eastward to Amboseli and Tsavo. The larger tour operators—United Touring Company, Abercrombie & Kent, Flamingo Tours, Rhino Safaris, and many others—offer a variety of tours that depart regularly each week. Budget camping tours are also operated weekly by Gametrackers, Scenic Safaris, and Safari Camp Services, among others. Bushbuck Safaris runs participatory camping trips with more interesting itineraries, at reasonable rates. Regular departures of walking safaris and Mount Kenya treks are operated by Tropical Ice. Other operators do not feature scheduled departures, but visitors can arrange personalized programs. Quality camping safari operators include Safaris Unlimited and Tropical Ice. The oldest safari operator, Ker & Downey, caters to the luxurious standards of the Hollywood set. All these operators, and more, have their offices in Nairobi; a list is included in the appendix.

For those not wishing to participate on a tour, car rental agencies may be the answer. Four-wheel-drive vehicles, minibuses, and a full range of sedans are available. Budget travelers should check the notice board at the Thorn Tree Cafe at the New Stanley Hotel for others looking to share the expenses of a rental.

Independent travelers are able to visit the populated areas of the country with relative ease. The coast, with its variety of activities and accommodations, is a magnet for those seeking rest and relaxation from the rigors of African travel.

Park Fees. Kenyan charges for nonresidents are less than half those in Tanzania. National Park fees are KSh 80 *per visit* for entry; KSh 50 for camping. The game reserves have different tariffs: entry to the Masai Mara is KSh 100 *per day*; each of the Samburu, Buffalo Springs, and Shaba reserves charge KSh 80 *daily;* KSh 50 for camping.

Nairobi

Nairobi is Kenya's metropolis, the nation's workplace and cultural center as well as the seat of government. It is a magnet for *wananchi*, the people, from across the nation. From a railroad supply depot founded in 1899, the city has grown to over 1.25 million inhabitants, with more coming in every day. Its population may number 2 to 3 million before the end of the century! In spite of this growth, Nairobi makes a favorable impression. Its center gleams in the African sun, a cluster of steel and glass towers housing government, international agencies, and modern hotels. The blossoms of frangipani, jacaranda, and bougainvillea lend a splash of color to roadsides and gardens. In the outskirts are lovely tree-lined suburbs where expansive homes are set among manicured grounds complete with swimming pools: the preserve of Kenyan elites and the expatriate community. Few visitors see the shantytown slums where the new immigrants live, although beggars are not an uncommon sight in downtown Nairobi. The faces on the street tell the story of a truly cosmopolitan community: white residents and tourists from every Western nation, government ministers and bureaucrats, businessmen and beggars, people stylish or ragged, bearded Sikhs, Arab mullahs, even the odd *shuka*-clad Masai.

Nairobi is a busy town. For the long-term visitor, it can be a fascinating place to live. It is headquarters and stomping grounds for a corps of journalists, conservationists, food relief workers, and others who follow the intrigues of Africa's political scene. For safari-bound travelers, a stay of a day or two is sufficient. Beyond that, the novelty of an African capital wears thin among the noise and crowds of a busy city center.

That center is a beehive of commerce dominated by offices and shops. The Parliament and Kenyatta Conference Center are the most important official edifices. It's worth walking over to the colorful City Market where a veritable cornucopia of luscious produce spills from the vendors' stalls. Neighboring Biashara Street has some of the atmosphere of an oriental bazaar, a feeling reinforced by the minarets of the nearby Jamia mosque. Many of the shopkeepers in this area are Asians (Indians); their wares include souvenirs and curios, colorful fabrics, and spice. In the River Road area, the shops and shoppers tend to be African.

Every visitor should visit the National Museum. It contains several superb collections exhibiting the natural and cultural wealth of the country. Guests are greeted at the door by a life-size model of Ahmed, the bull elephant whose colossal tusks earned him designation as a living national monument (a mandated armed escort served him well: unlike most giant tuskers, he died of old age). Inside, is a fascinating ethnological collection of tools, weapons, and typical artifacts from Kenya's numerous tribes. This display is complemented by a gallery of Joy Adamson paintings. Known primarily for her association with Elsa the lioness, Adamson recorded the native dress of the tribes of old Kenya in extraordinary detail. The stuffed animals in their habitat dioramas may seem stale to people bound for the parks, but naturalists will appreciate the closeup views of rare animals such as the bongo. Ornithologists will profit from study of a comprehensive collection of East African birds. Perhaps the most topical exhibits document human origin in East Africa, for the museum is a leading research institution in the field. Many significant discoveries have been made by the museum's director, Richard Leakey, as well as by his parents and other scientists working under the museum's aegis. It is particularly interesting to see original relics laid out in the context of their meaning and discovery. Just outside the museum is the Nairobi Snake Park, which houses an excellent collection of native Kenyan reptiles. As these are the only snakes that you are likely to see on your safari, it is well worth your while to take a look at these fascinating creatures.

Other places of interest around Nairobi are as follows:

Karen Blixen House. The house of the renowned writer (she used the pen name Isak Dinesen) was a school for many years, but because of all the attention given to her recently, has now been turned into a museum. The rather small house is found in a suburb named Karen, in her honor. It is now a green, residential neighborhood, a far cry from the wilderness farm described in her memoirs.

Bomas of Kenya. Also in the suburbs near Nairobi National Park, the Bomas of Kenya cultural theme park features representations of old-time villages (*bomas*) of various Kenyan tribes. Tribal cultural displays and dance performances in traditional native dress take place, and a variety of handicrafts are on sale. Perhaps a bit touristy, but none the less enjoyable and informative. A similar facility, Riuki Village, is a recreation of an old-time Kikuyu settlement. It is near Kiambu, just to the north of Nairobi.

Kenya Railroads Museum. A small museum with mementos of the construction of the Mombasa-Uganda railroad, one of the major engineering feats of its day.

Parks. The Arboretum features a collection of labeled botanical gardens, while the City Park contains a remnant of the beautiful native forests that once clothed the highlands to the north of Nairobi. Both are interesting for plants and birdlife, but can only be recommended guardedly because of their reputation for muggings. The same is true of the large Uhuru Park in the city center.

Bird Walks. If you happen to be in town on a Wednesday morning, be at the entrance to the National Museum by 9 A.M. to join local birders on a regular weekly outing. Conducted by a resident expert bird watcher, they are good excursions for beginners and experts alike. Participants meet at the museum, then car-pool to the site of the day's bird walk.

East African Wildlife Society. This worthy group has its offices and gift shop in the mezzanine of the Hilton Hotel. They have a selection of books, maps, and souvenirs. A great deal of useful information regarding the Kenyan parks, African natural history, and local tour operators can be gained by purchasing their wildlife magazine, *Swara*. You may want to join the society: your membership will help advance many local conservation projects.

Mountain Club of Kenya. Climbers and trekkers may be able to pick up useful information here, join an outing, or make contacts with local climbing partners. The clubhouse is at Wilson Airport; meetings take place every Tuesday night. Ring up to see what's on: telephone 501747.

Shopping. Perhaps Nairobi's most typical visitor activity is shopping. Souvenir stands and curio shops abound. At street stalls, and in the City Market, prices are negotiable. Shops tend to keep fixed prices, but even there deals can often be wrangled. Good buys can be had on woven sisal baskets (*kiondo*), which are currently used as very stylish women's bags in the United States. Carvings of African animals in wood and soapstone are ubiquitous. Monotonous in the mass, they make popular gifts back home, where they will seem unique. For higher-quality pieces, you have to go to galleries where you must pay much higher prices. Some of the better art shops are the African Cultural Gallery on Mama Ngina Street, Gallery Watatu on Standard Street, Kumbu Kumbu in the Hilton Hotel arcade, and the African Heritage House on Kenyatta Avenue. The best carvings and batiks are signed by the artists. Most of the ebony Makonde carvings on sale in Nairobi are imported from Tanzania and resold at much higher prices. The top galleries feature Makonde by artists resident in Kenya, and the quality of some of their work is evident. The best shops can be reliably depended on to pack and ship your purchases home. Many shops feature tribal curios such as gourds, beaded jewelry, shields, and spears. It is worthwhile to have a look at what is offered in Nairobi before going into the bush; Nairobi shops are generally cheaper for souvenirs, but the authenticity of their native crafts is often doubtful. African Heritage House sells a wide variety of authentic tribal curios from Kenya, as well as an extensive collection of art and ethnographic items from all over the continent. Many shops sell maps, and books describing Kenya's parks and tribal cultures. Nairobi's bookstores offer an excellent selection of natural history and safari literature. Field guides, maps, and large-format photo books that are hard to find in the United States are often on sale for a fraction of the U.S. price. Among the best bookstores are Prestige Booksellers and the Book Corner, both on Mama Ngina Street, and the Nation Bookshop on Kimathi Street.

Tourist Information. The government Tourist Information Office is located on Moi Avenue in front of the Hilton Hotel. Free magazines, *Tourist's Kenya* and *What's On,* full of ads for tours, restaurants, and information on local events, can be found at any of the large hotels. Tour agencies all have descriptive brochures.

Hotels. Nairobi has accommodation to suit every budget and style. The new Nairobi Safari Club is tops in luxury, while the Norfolk is dean of Nairobi hotels. Founded in 1904, it has played a part in a good deal of Kenyan history, including riotous drinking bouts at the bar (now named for the chief reveler, Lord Delamere), a bloody riot in 1922 that marked the birth of the independence movement, and a New Year's Eve terrorist bombing in 1980. The Tudor-style main building was badly damaged in the attack, but has been rebuilt in its original colonial design. The rooms are thoroughly modern. Two aviaries in the garden house an admirable collection of colorful African birds. Other top-grade hotels include the Hilton, Intercontinental, and Nairobi Serena. The New Stanley is a step down in quality, but is central, and its streetside Thorn Tree Cafe is a very popular meeting place. More moderately priced hotels include the Boulevard (near the Museum), the Ambassadeur, and the Jacaranda in suburban Westlands. The Fairview is good value, and a favorite with upcountry expatriates; so, too, is the Heron Court (which rents apartments with kitchenettes). The Oakwood (just across the street from the New Stanley), and the Azee Guesthouse (out near the City Park) are cheap and clean. Budget travelers will find plenty of cheap hotels in the River Road area; the Iqbal and New Kenya Lodge are favorites. Safer, but outside the city center, are Mrs. Roche's Guest House near the Aga Khan Hospital and the Youth Hostel on Ralph Bunche Road. Both are very popular meeting places for the budget set.

Restaurants. There is no lack of good eating from a wide variety of international fare. The top gourmet restaurants include Alan Bobbe's Bistro and the Chevalier (in Muthaiga) for French food, the Red Bull and the Horseman (in Karen) for German-accented European cuisine, and the Ibis Grill (at the Norfolk). The lively Carnivore features a feast of grilled meats, including exotic game. For seafood, try the Tamarind. It's no surprise that a town with such a large Asian population should have terrific Indian food: the best is found at the Minar and the Safeer, which serve Moghul specialties hot from the *tandoor* oven. Moderate and cheaply priced restaurants of every stripe abound. European- and American-style food such as pizza, hamburgers, and fries are well represented at touristy cafes such as the Thorn Tree and at numerous local fast food outlets. The Supreme Hotel on Tom Mboya Street and the Super Hotel on River Road serve wonderful vegetarian South Indian dishes— fiery hot—very cheaply. The African Heritage House presents good

African food. Its selection is heavy on Ethiopian dishes, which is certainly the most unique cuisine on the continent, and probably the tastiest. Local restaurants serve *ugali*, cornmeal, which is a staple starch at meals throughout black Africa. It is usually served with a saucy stew of meat or chicken. Cheap and upcountry restaurants offering typical Kenyan *chakula* (food) will serve *ugali* or rice dishes and a variety of fried snacks. The most common of these is the *sambusa*, a spiced tidbit of fried triangular crust with a minced meat filling. It's delicious when not too greasy. The yogurt is quite often good, too.

Entertainment. Nairobi can be lively after dark. Disco is found at the Florida 2000 Club. The Bubbles is favored by the young white set. A mixed and lively crowd savors live music at the Carnivore. The International Casino features cabaret and dining as well as games of chance. Several cinemas, a small national theatre, and lectures at the museum or various cultural centers round out the nighttime offerings. Facilities for golf, tennis, and other sports are abundant. A very lively horse-racing track is located on the Ngong Road.

Outfitting. All your safari food needs can be met at Nairobi's supermarkets, such as Uchumi on Kimathi Street (opposite the Thorn Tree). Dried and tinned foods can be supplemented with fresh produce or meat from the city market. In the suburbs, Westlands Shopping Center is convenient for one-stop food shopping. Colpro on Kimathi Street is noted for selling safari clothing. Tarpo Industries (Dar es Salaam Road) makes heavy-duty camping equipment for the professional safari outfits, but quality light camping gear is hard to come by. Virtually all kinds of accessory equipment—jerry cans, buckets, mosquito nets, etc.—can be found in shops along River Road, if not downtown. Camping Gaz butane containers are available in some supermarkets; white gas and kerosene are purchased at gas stations.

EXCURSIONS OUTSIDE NAIROBI

Langata Nature Education Center. Run by the African Fund for Endangered Wildlife (AFEW), the center is primarily designed to educate Kenyan schoolchildren to the need for wildlife conservation. Tourists come more to meet (and pet) the famous giraffe, Daisy Rothschild, and her kin. Luxury accommodation is also available on the estate at the exclusive Giraffe Manor.

Mayer's Farm. Choreographed excursions to this Masai *manyatta* were once popular tourist attractions: visitors toured the village and watched authentically attired Masai warriors perform their high-jumping dances. A daily event, it was a bit contrived, but many of the beautiful closeup photos of ochered warriors and girls in beaded necklaces that you see in glossy magazines were taken there. The price of admission allowed you to take all the pictures you wanted. The farm has recently been closed to the public, but will be worth visiting if it reopens.

Ngong Hills. The 8,000 foot-high hills of which Isak Dinesen wrote so lovingly are in Masai country, about 15 miles past Karen and the National Park's main gate. Legend has it that the hills are formed from the knuckles of a fallen giant who once plagued the Masai. The country surrounding the hills is mostly covered with acacia thorn and high grass. Except for relict patches, the highland forest that used to crown the hills has been replaced with small farms. With the forest, most of the buffalo have gone, but in the bushlands below the hills Masai tend goats and cattle, and wildlife is present. A rough track leads around the hills for a circular tour. You can walk up there, too, but be cautious about leaving your car unattended. A track continues down a sheer escarpment on the west side of the Ngongs, joining the road to Olorgasailie National Park, a site of prehistoric human habitation. A small museum and open air exhibits display the stone tools of the Acheulian Stone Age culture uncovered by Louis Leakey. Further on, the road descends to Lake Magadi, the lowest point in the Masailand section of the Rift Valley. Magadi consists mostly of caustic soda flats; its waters are too alkaline to support animal life except where freshwater springs seep at its edge. A modern factory processes the crystalline sodium carbonate for export as washing soda. Although the Rift scenery is fine, the country is blisteringly hot. Except the trucks transporting soda, few make the journey.

Nairobi National Park

On the drive from Nairobi's airport to town, don't be too surprised if you spot ostrich or giraffe in the grasslands to the left side of the road. You will be looking at free-living residents of Nairobi National Park.

From its inception, Nairobi Park has been justly celebrated as the place where Africa's wild animals can be observed only minutes from a major downtown center. Although the illusions of long-lens photography make the city's skyscrapers seem closer than they really are, it is nonetheless a wonder that gazelles and lions can go about their primordial business so near to civilization. Yet they do, drawing hundreds of eager wildlife watchers daily. This traffic has led to problems of overvisitation. Nairobi Park was one of the first reserves to suffer from the "Find the circle of minibuses, find the lions" syndrome. The explosion of tourism into the reserve caused it to be used as an early example of the evils of unrestricted tourism. Tight regulations have lessened those ills, though the volume of visitors has not diminished. But if the wild animals are disturbed by the influx of tourists, their numbers have not shown it.

The park is small, only 44 square miles in area, yet encompasses a good selection of wildlife habitats. The landscape is classic East African plains country: grasslands peppered with scatterings of acacia bush. Grassy plains and low ridges are cut by several seasonal streams, their beds marked by tree lines and stony *korongos* (ravines). The southern boundary of the park rests on the permanent Mbagathi River, which flows through rocky gorges and groups of graceful, yellow-barked fever trees (*Acacia xanthophloea*). Downstream, where the river is rechristened the Athi, are a hippo pool and picnic site. The park is fenced on three sides to prevent animals from wandering out into the suburbs of Langata or blundering onto the main Mombasa road. To the south, no fences block the animals from migrating seasonally to the Athi Plains and beyond.

African animal life is well represented. The fauna is dominated by "plains game," including Thomson's and Grant's gazelles, giraffe, and zebra. Kongoni, or Coke's hartebeest (*Alcelaphus buselapus cokii*), a sand-colored antelope with a long face and oddly curved yet symmetrical horns, are very common.* Eland, largest of the antelopes, are also customarily seen, and often relatively tame. In most places, eland tend to run from vehicles at long distance, so they are photographic subjects that should not be overlooked. Warthogs (*Phacochoerus aethiopicus*) are also normally quick to take flight, but those in Nairobi Park are exceptionally tolerant of approach. Don't miss the opportunity to observe and photograph

*Coke's hartebeest and the similar Jackson's hartebeest are usually referred to by their Swahili name, *kongoni*.

them up close! Ostrich are also quite common. Tourists, especially those on their first game drive, are anxious to spot lions. In this they are rarely disappointed at Nairobi Park. Predators, particularly lion and cheetah, are always in residence. They are seen on most visits because of the high density of search vehicles: once found, word goes out and everyone sees them. Cheetah have adapted to constant pursuit by tour buses, and are often observed at close quarters. Elephants long ago vanished from the surrounding Embakasi and Athi plains, and are absent from the park. A small herd of buffalo, composed mostly of reintroduced "orphans," are resident. Black rhino numbers have also been augmented by translocation from other parts of the country where they were deemed sure to fall victim to poachers. Although rhinos tend to lie up in the forest during the day, Nairobi Park remains one of the likelier places to see them. It is ironic that rhinos do better in small, highly popular parks, than in the huge wilderness reserves that were their former strongholds. The plain truth is that vast tracts of bush wilderness cannot be properly protected, while daily observation by large numbers of visitors creates the kind of high-risk situation that poachers find intolerable. Probably the smaller, well-protected reserves like Nairobi Park will soon have the only rhinos left in the wild.

Along the western park boundary, near the Main Entrance and the Langata Gate, is a tract of highland forest. This woodland, composed of African olive, croton, purple-flowering Cape chestnut and other evergreen trees, is now rare though it formerly carpeted many of the hills of East Africa. It provides ideal cover for rhino and leopard. This is an excellent area to patrol slowly at dawn or dusk, watching for those animals, as well as Sykes' monkey, baboons, and forest birds. It is one of the best places to get views or photos of bushbuck and bush duikers. Just beyond the forest's eastern edge, a good overview of the entire park can be had from Impala Point.

The game population of the park varies seasonally, as many of the grazing species migrate out of the park during the rains, dispersing southward through Masai country. Animal numbers are highest at the height of the dry seasons, when herds of zebra, wildebeest, and other antelope concentrate in the park. They are attracted to the water in the Mbagathi, and to several small manmade dams. At those times, it is worthwhile to park yourself at a dam to watch thirsty animals coming to drink. A good selection of animals is resident at any season, though, and the birdlife is best when the park is green with recent rain. More bird species have been recorded there than in all Britain.

Whereas Nairobi Park was at one time an essential part of every tour itinerary, it is now left off most. This is due more to cost cutting by tour operators than by any decline in the quality of game viewing. Today, the standard half-day tour is generally an optional extra to tour packages. Every local tour company operates them daily. It is easy to visit the park on your own, as roads are good and junctions are clearly marked with numbers keyed to a good park map. Tour groups do not arrive until the late afternoon, when the half-day tours (departing Nairobi at 2 P.M.) arrive. Plan your visit to be there at dawn, patrol the forest early, then go along the river, and loop back over the plains. You will likely have the park almost to yourself. Then take lunch in town, or at the Carnivore in Langata. Another possibility is an al fresco lunch at the riverside picnic site. If you have not had your fill of game viewing, or have missed the big cats, you can return in the afternoon when the veteran minibus drivers will have done your game scouting for you.

The Animal Orphanage is located at the Main Entrance to the park. Some of the resident animals were injured or orphaned in the wild and rescued by concerned people; others are former pets that grew too wild for their owners. You will see some adorable animal babies, as well as faunal oddities, such as bush pig, which are not likely to be seen in the wild.

Masai Mara National Reserve

The Mara ranks among the top game reserves in Africa. With its wealth of animal life and the magnetic presence of the Masai, the country has a physical brilliance that distills the essence of the African wilds. During and after the rains, the Mara flushes radiant green. In the dry months, the muted greens of bush and the dark ribbons of gallery forest are counterpoint to plains of golden grass. At any season, the Mara is a magic country of wide vistas, alive with wild animals.

The mile-high Mara region receives good rains: thunderstorms from Lake Victoria, 60 miles to the west, refresh its plains over an extended wet season. The rains nurture a 50-mile-wide expanse of rich savanna, framed between the Loita Hills and the steep Oloololo (or Siria) Escarpment, which abruptly marks the Mara's western

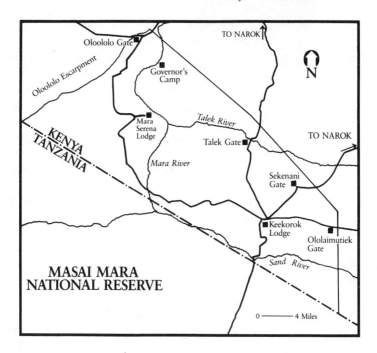

limit. Primarily open country, the Mara's tree-flecked grasslands are broken by occasional hillocks and patches of thicker bush. The Mara River, small springs, and marshes provide permanent water. It is ideal habitat for a wide range of animals, and thousands of gazelle, topi, impala, zebra, and Cape buffalo remain year-round residents. These are annually supplemented by the arrival of mass wildebeest herds from the Serengeti. For most of the year, the wildebeest are farther south, feeding on Tanzania's Serengeti plains (for a complete discussion of the migration, see the Serengeti section of Chapter 5, on Tanzania). With the onset of the long dry season, hundreds of thousands invade the Mara, seeking lusher grass and faithful sources of water. With this volume of prey animals, it is no surprise that Mara carnivores are abundant. Resident lion prides are among the largest in Africa, growing to an extravagant size: Mara prides sometimes number more than thirty individuals, with as many as five or six adult male members.

The Mara plains are legally Masai land. To reduce conflicts between herders and game, the Mara has been divided into an outer reserve, in which Masai graze their animals, and an inner National Reserve, which is the exclusive domain of wildlife. Although Masai cannot graze their cattle inside that territory, the wild animals do not respect boundaries: they wander freely into the outer Masai country. Game and herdsmen coexist pretty well, but both face a common menace: large, mechanized wheat farms are encroaching on the reserve's northern portions. These productive farms, which some believe absolutely necessary to the sustenance of the nation, represent a grave threat to the Masai way of life and to the health of the Mara ecosystem.

The Mara's qualities have not been kept secret from the traveling public. For many years the reserve could only be reached by fully equipped camping safaris. Now readily accessible by road and by air, it is one of the most heavily visited parks in Africa. More than a dozen permanent camps and hotels have been established in or around the reserve, providing accommodation for many hundreds of visitors. Demand is also high for official campsites. Crowding is becoming a serious problem. Packs of safari vehicles scour the countryside, while multicolored hot-air balloons drift through the morning sky. This unrestrained tourism is taking its toll on the Mara's pristine ambience. The park has long been a bastion of safari freedom, where you could go wherever your vehicle and your whim would take you. With the steady increase in vehicles, prohibitions on off-road travel are inevitable.

ACCESS AND ACCOMMODATION

From Nairobi, the drive to the Mara takes from four to five and a half hours depending on weather conditions and the route taken. Once out of the city, it's less than a half-hour's drive through Kikuyu farmlands and townships to the lip of a sheer escarpment. Views are stupendous as the Old Naivasha Road goes through a series of breathtaking hairpin turns, dropping 2,000 feet to the floor of the Rift Valley. Shortly thereafter, the Mara road turns off to the west, passing the dishes of Kenya's satellite communications station, as well as the extinct Longonot and Suswa volcanos, before rising almost imperceptably out of the Rift and arriving at the town of Narok. Narok is a major Masai administrative and trading center; safari vehicles universally stop for gas at the eastern edge of town, where a snack bar and lively souvenir market have sprung up. Ten miles beyond is the Ewaso Ngiro River, after which the road divides. The main left fork to Keekorok is paved almost all the way to the park boundary, while the rutted dirt track to the right skirts the northern edge of the reserve, heading toward the camps along the Mara and Talek rivers.

The northern road traverses a region of shrubby *oleshuba* bush until breaking into open country among the controversial wheat farms. The government is encouraging their development through the privatization of Masai land, a policy that may ultimately convert the Masai from self-sufficient pastoralists into hired herdboys and farmhands. Once past the encroaching farms, Masai and their stock become common, the children waving as they run after their skittish goats. Game starts to appear in numbers that would be acceptable in major parks, although still outside the borders of the National Reserve. Traffic is thinner on this section of the road, so you can take the time to stop at will.

A marked track turns southward toward the Talek Gate, on the Talek River. Many campsites are located along the river, which marks the boundary between the territory in which Masai graze their animals and the National Reserve, which is left entirely to wildlife. The Talek is a small stream, with steeply cut banks and a sprinkling of good-sized trees to shade the camps. In dry seasons it carries little more than a trickle of water. Numerous Masai *manyattas* are in the vicinity of the riverside campsites, and Masai can be expected to visit. Care must be taken with security: an unattended camp would be an invitation to theft. The thin woods along the Talek grow denser as you follow the river westward, passing Fig Tree Camp. Fig Tree is a permanent tented camp, less luxurious or costly than some of the other Mara facilities. Access from the Talek area to the rest of the park is good, as tracks lead from the Talek Gate to Keekorok, to the Mara Bridge at the Tanzanian border, and to the Musiara Gate.

Twenty miles beyond the Talek turnoff, the main road meets the Mara River, where it flows swifly at the base of the Oloololo Escarpment. Masai *manyattas*, lush gallery forests, and the backdrop of the escarpment wall make this the most scenic part of the Mara. Several permanent tented camps are located in the vicinity: Mara River and Mara Buffalo camps are reached before crossing the river, Mara Sara and Kichwa Tembo are on the far side. The river crossing can be difficult because floods gouge hollows around the edges of the concrete causeway. With the exception of Kichwa Tembo, all camps are located along the river, under the shade of riverine forest. Birding is excellent, and the Masai close, but for the best game viewing it is sometimes necessary to travel some distance to the inner reserve.

Kichwa Tembo, one of the largest tented camps, is nicely situated in a forest overlooking a grassy plain. This plain, which extends to the river a mile away, is something of a private hunting ground for Kichwa Tembo vehicles. Game drives are always good, for there is plenty of resident game, including lion and cheetah. Access to the rest of the reserve is slow, however, because the roads are so bad.

Also in the northwest corner of the reserve, are Governor's and Little Governor's camps, located near the game-rich Musiara marshes. The twin camps stand kitty-corner on opposite banks of the Mara River. Governor's is sumptuously set in cool gallery forest immediately above the river. Views of birds, hippos, and crocodiles are good, but overall game viewing in camp is better at Little Governor's. Vehicles can't get to Little Governor's; instead, guests are ferried across the river by boat. All tents face a small marsh, to which a parade of animals comes to drink or bathe over the course of a day. Both camps cater primarily to fly-in visitors. Game viewing is always excellent in the Musiara area, although it gets crowded with vehicles from all the nearby river camps. Access to the southern part of the reserve is very difficult, requiring fairly long drives via either the Talek Gate or crossing the Mara River to the Oloololo Gate.

Several extraordinarily beautiful campsites are located in the forest along the Mara River. These are usually reserved by professional safari operators.

Mara Serena Lodge is located in the western part of the reserve, on top of a hill above the meandering Mara River. A large hotel, the lodge's architecture is meant to simulate the rounded contours and dun coloring of a Masai *manyatta*. It has a stunning bird's-eye view. Heavily frequented by holiday safari groups, it is well situated for touring the west side of the Mara River, the escarpment tracks, and the Mara Bridge area along the Tanzanian border. Tour groups usually travel to the Serena via Keekorok—a longer road, but faster and smoother than the northern track.

The superluxury Intrepids Camp is situated in a rather secluded part of the reserve, along the Talek River. Being well away from other lodges and off the main roads, it offers the possibility of some remote wilderness touring and has good access to the Keekorok, Talek, and lower Mara River areas.

The eastern, or Keekorok, sector of the reserve is the closest to Nairobi and is reached by the best road. After crossing the Ewaso Ngiro River, the route crosses the wide Loita Plains, skirting the northern edge of the Loita Hills. About 5 miles short of the reserve boundary is the turnoff for Cottar's Camp, a large, tented facility. Although it takes some time to move into the reserve proper for the best big game viewing, Cottar's has some advantages. Masai visits can be arranged there, as can bush walks and night game drives. Another tented camp, the Mara Sarova, is located closer to Keekorok and is inside the park. The Mara Sopa Lodge is found outside the reserve boundary near the eastern Ololaimutiek Gate.

Keekorok is the oldest of the Mara's lodges. Its main building faces a small marsh, well visited by game. The hotel's capacity was extended by erecting luxury tents behind the lodge. This tented camp is comfortable but doesn't have much bush ambience: it is very close to the village for hotel and park maintenance workers, which bustles with administrative offices and workshops. Game viewing around Keekorok is good, especially when migration is centered along the Tanzanian border.

Many visitors prefer not to make the long drive to the Mara; instead they fly from Nairobi. Regularly scheduled air service departs at least three times daily, puddle-jumping from one Mara airfield to the next. Most of the permanent safari camps are geared up for fly-in visitors, with airfield transfers and game drives included in the price. Game drives are conducted by radio-equipped vehicles, and viewing is generally good to superb. There can be problems if you wish to explore distant areas or see the wildebeest migration when it happens to be concentrated in another part of the reserve. Camp managers are loath to send their vehicles far afield, preferring to keep them on short runs searching for resident animals in their own vicinity. You may be allowed to take a camp car (and a picnic) and go wherever you want, if you can find enough guests (usually seven) to fill a vehicle. This is not always easy, however.

TOURING THE PARK

The abundance of Mara wildlife is legendary. There is always plenty of resident game, much of it very accustomed to vehicles and their human occupants. It is often boasted that "the Big Five" can all be viewed in the Mara. Certainly there is no lack of lion and buffalo. Elephant numbers are not enormous, but enough are around for every visitor to get some close sightings. Rhino have been almost eliminated, despite the best efforts of special antipoaching patrols. These are responsible for checking up daily on each individual rhino, but have been unable to halt the decline of the species. Only a handful remain in the reserve. The Mara probably rates as the number one reserve in all Africa for sightings of unbaited leopards. Several of the stealthy cats have become exceptionally tame: one

A cheetah taking advantage of an old termite mound to search for potential prey, Masai Mara National Reserve, Kenya. *Photo by Allen Bechky.*

leopardess raised her cubs under the daily scrutiny of hordes of tourist-filled vehicles.

The Mara is superb cheetah country. The profusion of small-size antelope, especially gazelles, ensures a ready food supply. Resident cheetahs are known to drivers at all safari camps, so the odds are good that you will see them. In fact, you are likely to get good observations: once accustomed to cars, cheetahs tolerate close approaches and are easily followed when on the move (please allow enough distance not to interfere with their activities). Cheetah hunts and kills are regularly witnessed by tourists in the Mara.

Game tends to concentrate in pockets where grazing is best at any particular time. Herds of topi, Grant's and Thomson's gazelles, kongoni, zebra, and impala often mix together on favored open plains. These places also hold small herds of Mara's resident, non-migratory wildebeest. Defassa waterbuck are also common. Buffalo frequent places of higher, tougher grass. From afar, a large herd looks like a spreading black inkspot on a distant plain. Giraffe can be encountered anywhere.

One of the most typical of Mara antelopes is the topi *(Damaliscus korrigum)*. It is a handsome animal, gracefully proportioned, its red-brown coat trimmed with bluish-black markings on its flanks. Many visitors are surprised to learn that it is a very close relative of the ungainly wildebeest. Topi thrive in open country. They often congregate in large, loosely organized herds. It is common to see a sentinel topi gazing into the distance from the top of a termite mound, while its comrades feed oblivious and at ease, heads down in the grass.

The gallery forests of the northwestern Mara are a beautiful minihabitat. These thick woodlands are tropically luxuriant. Sustained by groundwater, they crowd the course of the Mara River and its seasonal tributaries. Game drives through gallery forest are less rewarding in terms of animal numbers than drives on the plains, but unusual species may be encountered. Leopard often shelter there, but you would be extraordinarily lucky to spot one in the forest shadows. More likely you will see bushbuck and waterbuck, small groups of elephant, and surly bull buffalo. You may also find the beautiful black-and-white colobus monkey *(angolensis* variety). Birders will definitely want to investigate the riverine forests carefully. Specialties include blue flycatcher, huge black-and-white casked hornbills, Schalow's and Ross's turacos, green coucal, and white-headed wood hoopoes.

The Mara River has many excellent hippo pools with high banks, for excellent viewing. The "river horses" usually remain coy, with only the nubs of eyes, ears, and nostrils above water. In cool weather, they often sun themselves on sandy banks, allowing thorough observations. Crocodiles are also generally shy, but occasionally present themselves without fear. Some Mara crocs are longer than 15 feet. It is awesome to see these veritable dinosaurs sunning themselves in full reptilian glory. It is especially sobering to see a monster croc guarding the carcass of an unfortunate drowned wildebeest, victim of a disastrous river crossing. Don't fall into the river!

River crossings by migrating wildebeest herds are one of the Mara's most dramatic events. Wildebeest can swim, but many are swept away by the swift current, especially when panic strikes a herd in midstream. Mass drownings are set off by the appearance of ambushing lions or by any number of false alarms. Close approaches by cars and people on foot can also trigger stampedes that result in the drowning of hundreds of animals. To prevent such unnecessary catastrophes, watch river crossings from a reasonable distance.

The westernmost reaches of the park, underneath the wall of the Oloololo Escarpment, are the least visited in the reserve. Game species otherwise hard to see in Kenya are found there. Most notable, for its powerful physique and curved horns, is the roan antelope. Small herds are sometimes encountered on the tracks to the west of the main Oloololo Gate-Keekorok Road. Oribi, too, are most likely to be spotted west of the Mara River, and the reddish-coated patas monkey is also occasionally seen.

Visitors staying on the Talek River or in the Keekorok area do most of their viewing on the Posee and Meta plains. Open grass predominates there, interspersed with bushy thickets that may harbor some of Mara's few remaining rhinos. This eastern country has plenty of buffalo, and lions frequently tackle this dangerous quarry in the area. The main track connecting the Talek River sector with the Musiara area leaves the Talek and passes over open plains. If you stay with the river track, it brings you to heavier bush country where thick forest fringes the stream. It is a good area for lion, elephant, and buffalo, a place where few tourists venture. You may spot less game overall, but the wilderness experience is stronger.

The timing of the wildebeest migration is very variable. In a dry year, the herds may arrive by the end of June. If rains are especially good, the wildebeest may not come till August, or never turn up at all in large numbers. Generally, by mid-July or the beginning of August huge herds are spilling over the border into the Mara. It is incredibly impressive to see the massed wildebeest on the move, walking in single files, one animal following another, like lengthy threads strung out over the plains. Sometimes they crowd into wide columns, moving in tight formations thousands strong. When they stop to feed, they spread over the landscape, their black bodies dotting the plain as far as the eye can see. If you hit it right, you can drive from the Mara Bridge at the Tanzania border clear to Keekorok, passing through wildebeest herds the whole way, a distance of 15 miles. When the wildebeest are in the Mara, their calves are about six months old, not yet independent of their mothers. The half-grown calves are a boon for the carnivores, who grow fat with easy kills. The wildebeest stay till they have mowed all the grass, then return southward. By mid-September, the masses are usually gone, leaving small groups of stragglers and bleached bones to mark their passage.

The Mara really has no "off season" for game viewing. It is at its best during migration time, which, to be safe, should be considered August. This month is therefore very busy; bookings must be made in advance. Some safari camps close during the April–May wet season, when mobility is impaired by mud and when high grass makes game spotting more difficult.

BALLOON SAFARIS

Balloon safaris are now the rage in the Mara. Balloons ascend daily at dawn from several locations, including Keekorok, Kichwa Tembo, and Governor's Camp. As a balloon junket, they rate highly, for the aerial views of the countryside are terrific. Claims for superior game viewing are more problematical. Balloons have no real control over direction, only altitude. They fly with the wind, surveying whatever happens to be below. Although some otherwise well-hidden animals may be more easily viewed from aloft, other creatures (such as elephants) are scared by airships, which are not silent, but hiss repeatedly, dragonlike, as their burners are fired to gain altitude. Flights last about an hour and a half (depending on wind speed and direction—they must come down before the Tanzanian border). A support vehicle follows the balloon to its landing site, where a champagne brunch is served.

The balloon safari is costly—the price of a short flight is as much as a full day's participation on a good-quality safari. A further cost to consider is not in money, but in time. Dawn is the best time for spotting nocturnal animals, and for witnessing predators on the hunt or on the remains of a nighttime kill. Since most people spend only two or three mornings in the Mara, it may not be worth giving up this prime game-viewing time. For the keen naturalist, it is ordinarily time lost to go up in the balloon. It is certainly worthwhile, and possibly the experience of a lifetime, to go up when migration is in the Mara, because the balloonist's-eye view is no doubt the best way to appreciate the scale of that extraordinary event. If you will be in the Mara in July or August, or possibly even in September, when migration has a good chance to be in full swing, by all means take the time for a balloon safari. It is advisable to book well in advance, as each camp launches only two or three balloons daily, with a maximum capacity of eight to ten passengers for each airship.

The Masai

Among westerners, the Masai are the most famous of all East African tribes. Since the first contacts, Europeans have held them in high esteem, admiring their self-sufficiency and indifference to the supposed benefits of modernization. Those qualities still make an impact today. Whereas most Africans have shed traditional religions, customs, and dress, the Masai have kept their cultural heritage intact and they remain visibly confident in their identity as a people. At ease in what seems a dangerous country, they are an integral component of their environment, as much a part of the landscape as umbrella-shaped thorn trees and herds of fleet-footed gazelles. The Masai exactly fit our romantic image of what an African tribal people should be. Attired in togalike robes, adorned with ocher and beaded jewelry, carrying swords and long spears, they *are* a part of a timeless African dream.

The Masai's natural conservatism, their clinging to an ancestral way of life, is not unique. Other pastoral tribes, such as the Rendille or the Turkana, remain equally steadfast in their customs, but have received much less recognition. That the Masai have become so much better known outside of Africa is partly an accident of geography: since they inhabited the richest rangelands of the Rift Valley, they became familiar to both English and German explorers, settlers, and hunters. The literary luminaries of the East African hunting era met and admired them, and brought the tribe to the attention of the rest of the world.

The Masai have always had a reputation as a fierce warrior tribe. In the old days, they were indeed a people to be reckoned with. When they moved into the Rift Valley three or four centuries ago, they carved out a huge territory stretching from the Laikipia Plateau on the north side of Mount Kenya to what is now called the Masai Steppe in Tanzania. Parties of raiding Masai *moran* warred continuously against neighboring tribes, driving most of their rivals from the valley into highland enclaves. Like other pastoral nomads, the Masai believed that their god had originally given them exclusive ownership of all the world's cattle. That was sufficient justification for endless cattle raids. The Masai social system reinforced an affinity for war. Young men remained bachelor-soldiers for 15 or 20 years. During that time they were encouraged to amass cattle with which to later buy wives and support families. Cattle raids offered the promise of the brightest future.

A young Masai girl, Tanzania. *Photo by Allen Bechky.*

Arab slaving caravans avoided the territory of the pugnacious warrior tribe, so the earliest European explorers likewise gave Masailand a wide berth. A young Scot, Joseph Thomson, was the first European to have extensive contact with the Masai. On his expeditions of 1883–1884, he found them armed and arrogant, but managed to reconnoiter throughout central Kenya without once having to resort to violence. He did so by showmanship, treating the Masai to fireworks displays and gramophone concerts. The Masai were impressed by his modern wizardry, much as they enjoy the gimmickry of today's consumer society. Shortly after Thomson's visit, an epidemic of rinderpest struck Masailand. Cattle died wholesale, with starvation quickly following for the people who were not struck down by a simultaneous plague of smallpox. When British and German administration reached the Masai, they were so reduced in numbers that the once-feared warriors put up no resistance. The colonial administration in Kenya soon decided to remove the Masai from the entire northern part of their territory, banishing them from the high Rift Valley between Naivasha and Laikipia. They were moved southward to the country along the border with Tanganyika, which at that time was considered worthless, lion-infested bush. Content to seize the lands they wanted to settle and to control cattle raiding against neighboring tribes, the British then left the Masai to themselves. On the Tanganyika side, the Germans did pretty much the same, though no mass territorial grabs took place.

The nomadic Masai life is very well suited to their environment, for large cattle herds must be shifted periodically according to seasonal grazing conditions. In former times, the Masai were more truly nomadic, moving their herds and their homes as they saw fit. Now they must remain within the confines of fixed tribal territories, so they are necessarily less mobile. Today, most Masai establish a home base from which their cattle are maneuvered as necessary between wet- and dry-season ranges. From time to time, home *manyattas* may be abandoned, the residents moving to establish a new headquarters in another area.

Although the traditional Masai diet consisted of milk, blood, and meat, modern Masai also eat cornmeal, which they buy rather than grow themselves. (This, too, is changing; increasing numbers of Masai are farming or hiring members of other tribes to work their land.) But livestock are still a prime source of sustenance. Milk is taken daily; curdled with a little cattle urine, it keeps well for several days. Every Masai woman has a good selection of gourds for use as milk containers. In wet seasons, when grass is green, cattle fatten quickly and milk is plentiful. With the arrival of the hot dry season, the udders of cows shrivel with the grass. Milk is then supplemented with blood from bulls or oxen. The blood is drawn by shooting a blunt arrow into the jugular vein and filling a gourd, then closing off the wound. The animal is released quite unharmed, although it takes quite a struggle to secure the bull. Blood-taking is not an everyday event. Blood is considered a recuperative source of strength: a gourdful is given to a woman just after she has given birth and to initiates after circumcision.

Masai are very fond of meat. Goats are often slaughtered, with cattle being reserved for special occasions. Various events marking the passages of Masai life—including marriages, births, and circumcisions—call for meat-eating festivities. The slaughter of a bull marks the occasion for feasting for everyone in the neighborhood. The greatest feasts take place at ceremonies marking the graduation of men from one grade of adult responsibility to the next. Then Masai from a wide area gather to form a temporary village called a *manyatta*. This word is now widely used to describe all Masai villages, although a Masai settlement is more correctly called an *engang*. A characteristic *engang* is very small, quartering only a few families. Their distinctive doughnut profiles—cattle pens at the center, ringed by flat-roofed mud huts and a prickly thornbush stockade—are a familiar sight throughout Masailand.

In addition to cattle, goats, and sheep, the Masai keep large numbers of donkeys. The donkeys are used almost daily for hauling water. Masai usually choose to build their homes in open areas (possibly a customary safeguard against surprise attack), so water and firewood must be transported over long distances. Men are responsible for digging wells if springs or streams go dry, but women collect water. They fill gourds and jerry cans, load the donkeys' panniers, and drive the animals home. Women are also responsible for gathering firewood.

Masai social structure revolves around a system of "age sets." The status of individuals depends on their passage into categories that are essentially based on age. Training for adult duties begins early in life. Children learn to look after goats almost as soon as they can walk. As they grow, their responsibilities increase; older boys look after cattle, while young girls help their mothers with wood and water collection. Adulthood is announced by circumcision, in joyous ceremonies that mark the rite of passage. Girls are circumcised* when they reach puberty, and married off shortly thereafter. Boys must wait until the elders decide that there are enough eligible candidates around to form a new age set of young warriors. That only occurs once every five to seven years, so the new age set will be composed of youths of varying ages, ranging from fourteen to twenty years old. Each boy is circumcised publicly at the gate to his father's *engang*. He is expected to endure the operation stoically. To flinch would be to invite disgrace, expressed by ridicule in nicknames and song. Boys who cry out have even been killed by their own mortified fathers. If this seems cruel, keep in mind that the Masai are physically and mentally prepared to endure pain. From a very young age, they are inured by mutilation of their bodies for decorative purposes. The cutting of ear lobes and scarification are part of the hardening process. In this way, the Masai are fortified for a rough life in the bush, a life without any modern medical care or comforts.

After a brief period of healing, the initiate warriors, called *sipolio*, wander the country dressed in ash-blackened goat skins. They shoot colorful songbirds, using the tiny feathered bodies to make elaborate headdresses that they wear in ceremonies signifying their acceptance as a new set of junior-grade *moran* (warriors). As *moran*, they embark on the most glamorous part of their lives. Traditionally, the *moran* formed the Masai army, responsible for the defense of the community's cattle from the raids of other tribes, as well as from rival Masai. Today's *moran* continue to fill that role. Although cattle raids are now officially frowned on, they do still take place. But now guns have been introduced into the game, and the Masai are the victims of cattle thefts as often as not. The *moran* must also protect Masai livestock from wild animals, such as lions. The spears (*empere*) and short swords (*olalem*) they carry are not just for show.

Moran have other, less martial social duties. They often drive cattle long distances to find proper grazing, living in the bush for weeks or months on end. Each warrior is expected to increase his personal herd. This herd starts at birth, when the newborn child is given livestock by relatives. As the boy grows, his animals grow too,

---

*Female circumcision consists of the removal of the clitoris and the outer lips of the vagina. The practice of clitoridectomy is controversial, but it is an accepted custom among many African tribes. Issues of morality, sexual politics, and cultural imperialism aside, the practice of female circumcision is dying out among modern, educated East Africans.

and hopefully reproduce. With proper husbandry and good luck, a *morani* will have enough cattle to start paying (on the installment plan) for his first wife.

Today's *moran* are as proud as ever. They spend a lot of time tending to their looks. Sisal thread is woven into their hair, and the whole is ochered into spectacular braided coiffures. By tradition, a man is not allowed to marry during the time he is a *morani*,* nor can he eat meat in the presence of a married woman. He can have as many girlfriends as he likes, however. Young girls shower the warriors with attention, giving their favorites the beaded jewelry they love to wear. Groups of warriors often bring young girls to their own *manyatta*s in the bush, where they feast on slaughtered cattle and enjoy very free sex lives. Pregnancy for unmarried girls is taboo, however; it is avoided by marrying girls off as soon as they begin to menstruate.

Girls relish the attentions of the *moran*, but they do not necessarily get to marry their boyfriends. If a beau is due to become an elder at the time of a girl's initiation, he may open negotiations with her family. If successful, he begins paying the bride price. Not all girls get a love match, though. Many become the second or third wives of older, prosperous men, often friends of their fathers. Such a marriage may be the source of pride for the girl, for she may fetch a very high bride price. The system ensures a girl's security while at the same time allowing some freedom of choice. A Masai woman may leave a marriage and return to their father's house, if the village elders agree that she has done so for good cause. Unlike men, women do not have formal age sets; their rites of passage are determined individually. The birth of children and the passage of their children through the ranks of society change a woman's status accordingly.

After the initiation of new groups of young warriors, the older generation of *moran* passes through the elaborate *eunoto* ceremony, after which they become junior elders. As such, they are allowed to marry and begin raising families. In later years they will achieve the status of senior elders. Although governments appoint local chiefs in order to identify responsibility for administration, the Masai traditionally do not have chiefs as such. Each age set has leaders who retain lifelong positions of influence, but no authority to govern. Disputes ranging from marital squabbles to grazing rights are settled by the consensus of elders at open meetings.

---

*This custom is relaxing: increasingly, men are marrying as *moran*, if they can afford to support a wife.

The Masai attitude toward wildlife has made their land synonymous with big game country. In contrast to many other African
tribes, the Masai do not eat wild game. Only in times of famine do
they make exceptions for eland and buffalo, which they consider
wild cattle. That is not to say that Masai do not kill wild animals:
young men sometimes hunt buffalo, rhino, and other dangerous
game just to prove their readiness for initiation, and occasional animals are killed for decorative purposes (such as ostrich, for their
plumes). Although the organized lion hunts that were once a feature
of *moran* society have long been banned, Masai still do hunt lions
with spears whenever they can. As cattleherders, they have no love
for the carnivores that are a threat to their livestock. Lion, leopard,
and cheetah are killed by Masai at every opportunity. Where Masai
are numerous, lions lay low, rarely being seen during daylight hours.
The value of certain game species to other people has not been lost
on the Masai: they have been known to kill rhinos and leopards for
profit. But by and large, most of the grazing animals that share their
range are ignored, so the entire wildlife community thrives.

The Masai god is named Lengai. In his benevolent manifestation,
he is the black god of the dark clouds that bring life-sustaining
rains. His harsher side is seen as the red god of the dry season's sun.
The *laibon* are spiritual leaders to whom the Masai look for wisdom
in times of communal or personal crisis. In the old days, the great
Laibon (chief spiritual leader, a direct descendent of the original
Masai ancestor) bore a heavy responsibility in warfare. The *moran*
consulted them for auspicious signs before embarking on raids, and
the *laibon* offered plans for their execution. Masai religion is earthy
and practical. The individual is concerned with this life, without
worries about a hereafter. Traditionally, the Masai do not bury their
dead, but leave the corpse in the bush to be disposed of by hyenas.
Only high personages such as *laibon* were buried. Today government encourages burial, but it is questionable how often the practice is observed.

The larger question remains as to how much longer the Masai
can resist the forces of modernization that would sweep their way
of life aside forever. Numerically weak compared to the other tribes
in Kenya and Tanzania, and politically unsophisticated, the Masai
have been in a poor position to defend themselves against postcolonial threats. They have been the victims of discrimination in the
name of progress. By and large, the Masai are looked down on by
their Western-dressed and -educated compatriots, and the demand
for better use of Masai lands for the national benefit is often heard

in both Kenya and Tanzania. In fact, the Masai have already made tremendous contributions to the economies of those countries. The best game parks, which are the major source of tourist dollars, are in Masailand. Far from being unproductive, they are pulling in more foreign exchange than any other acreage in either country. The Masai have lost considerable territory to national parks. They have been banished from some areas, like the Masai Mara, by negotiated arrangements that are supposed to produce economic benefits for their local communities but that bring far more revenue to the country as a whole. In either case, the practical effect is that the Masai are no longer free to use a large portion of their land for their own support.

Like their nation at large, the Kenyan Masai are visibly more prosperous than their Tanzanian relatives. Yet in Kenya their traditions are more threatened. Government schemes to privatize the Masai's lands are being strongly pushed. Formerly, the Masai never had any concept of individual ownership of land; all territory belonged to the community as a whole, with local councils deciding where individual families could settle. In the last few years, this system has been more formalized by the creation of jointly owned "group ranches." But plans now call for each Masai man to be given title to his own parcel of land. Without any idea of what this title means, many Masai men will be tempted to sell for short-term gain what are to them meaningless papers. This kind of story is familiar to historians of the American West. Within a few years of privatization, the most unsophisticated and traditional Masai will find themselves legally landless and turned out of their own pastures. Either they will work as hired hands for the rich developers who buy up all the individual plots, or they will migrate into the cities, joining the ranks of Africa's faceless unemployed. Never have the Kenyan Masai faced a graver crisis.

The Tanzanian Masai have less money or access to modern goods, and fewer services such as schools and clinics. They are less integrated into a modern economy and live more purely traditional lives. The government would like to push them into a monetary system, but no plans are afoot that would deprive them of their land. They have been subject to some official discrimination: at one time edicts required Masai men to wear trousers in towns. That campaign was unsuccessful; nevertheless, current regulations oblige males to wear trousers (instead of their customary robes) when attending school or visiting health clinics. Girls going to school also must wear Western dress. Both sexes also suffer petty unofficial discrimination: haughty drivers may refuse them entry onto country buses.

MEETING THE MASAI

It is now difficult to have quality experiences with Masai along the main Kenyan tourist routes. The people around the parks have seen many tourists before and are primarily interested in strangers from a commercial point of view.

The majority of visitors encounter Masai only at formally arranged "*manyatta*" visits near the gates of the Mara and Amboseli reserves. Too often, these visits are reduced to a formula: a song and dance in welcome, followed by frenzied negotiations for photos and souvenirs. Such episodes do not always put the hardy nomads in the best light. Yet even these canned encounters can be quite enlightening if you make the most of them.

Do not be put off by the *manyatta* environment. Since livestock and people live together in close quarters, animal dung and flies are omnipresent. The fly situation can truly be exasperating. Although the Masai are rarely bothered, the sight of flies crawling unheeded around the eyes of children is more than some tourists can stand. And house visits can be claustrophobic: the interior of a Masai hut is hot, smoky, and dark.

A Masai *engang* is surrounded by a thornbush stockade constructed as protection against marauding carnivores and cattle raiders. Inside are a number of low flat-roofed houses. Typically the Masai live in small groups: perhaps three or four adult men, and their families, sharing a single compound. Each man may have as many wives as he can support, but each wife must have her own hut. Additional houses quarter older children or aged relatives. Every adult man must have his own gate in the thornbush fence, through which his cattle and goats are driven in and out daily, to the pens at the center of the village. Dawn and dusk are ideal times to visit an *engang*, for the most intense activity takes place when the stock are being driven.

Each woman owns her own hut, which she builds and maintains herself. First she contructs a wooden frame; the walls and roof are then "plastered" with a mixture of cow dung and mud that hardens into a reasonably tough adobe-type material. Cracks must be repaired constantly during the rainy season, when women are often seen collecting cow patties, mixing them with mud, and applying them to their roofs.

It is fascinating to go into a Masai house. You enter through a tunnel-like passageway. There are no windows, just a few small slits for ventilation. It is dark, so pause to let your eyes adjust to the twilight before going in. (It's wise to bring a flashlight along, or you won't be able to see much inside.) Off the entrance passage are storage areas, where items such as donkey's panniers are kept. Don't be surprised to find a calf or baby goat penned inside, for newborn animals are carefully looked after at home rather than sent out with the herds. (This hand rearing has important consequences later. Masai stock animals are extremely tractable: large herds are easily controlled by one or two people on foot. Contrast the tight-knit formations of obedient Masai cattle with the wild range animals of North America!) A fire smolders in the center of the hut, where the woman of the house cooks. Shelves hold firewood and a few pots. Furniture consists solely of the husband's small three-legged stool. Two tiny chambers, each filled with a bed of hardened cow hide, adjoin the kitchen. One is the man's bedroom; the other belongs to the woman, who shares it with her young children. Milk gourds and water containers hang in the wife's room. Masai adults often keep a locked metal box in which they guard personal treasures: money, photos, and *dawa* (medicine such as aspirin or chloriquine tablets cadged from tourists). The keys you see worn on Masai necklaces unlock these personal strongboxes.

The best experiences with Masai are often spontaneous. If you have occasion to get off the main roads, or to stop in the bush, you are likely to attract groups of curious Masai. Offer food or water; take an interest in their cattle or activities. Admire their weapons and jewelry *without* emphasis on the purchase of souvenirs. Keep your camera at a low profile and display a friendly attitude, and you may enjoy some real exchanges. Masai can be overly vain. They often assume that you have stopped to sneak photos even if you are actually examining a bird or animal through your binoculars. Don't pay them if you are innocent, but don't try to poach photos either.

In Kenya, the Loita Hills are the best area for contact with Masai "unspoiled" by the effects of tourism. The 8,000-foot range rises to the east of the Mara reserve, separating the high plains from the heat of the Rift Valley. The hills are accessible by rough unmarked tracks directly from the Mara, but most visitors take the long way: a better route cuts off the main Mara road just beyond the Ewaso Ngiro River. The Loita track passes through the tiny village of Narosura, before continuing into scenic hill country. Landscapes are mostly grassy, with patches of mountain forest, including groves sacred to the Masai. The Loitas are the territory of the *Ilaiser* clan, from which many important *laibon* (spiritual leaders) come. Well off the beaten tourist track, the Masai of the Loitas are less affected by tourism, although they have seen enough visitors to know the value of photos and plunder from unguarded camps. A few days there, and a good attitude, could lead to remarkable cultural experiences. The Loitas also offer fine hiking through plain and forest, especially along the dramatic Nguruman Escarpment that towers above Lake Magadi in the Rift. Game has declined from what it once was, but antelope, giraffe, and zebra can still be seen. Masai-wise lions give humans a wide berth, but beware of buffalo when you take forest hikes.

The Rift Valley Lakes

The Rift Valley marks where the African continent is in the process of tearing apart. Its easternmost portion is separating from the bulk of the African landmass, just as the Arabian peninsula has done before it. The cause lies in the movement of great tectonic plates deep within the Earth's crust. As these disconnect, a narrow band of ground between them is slowly sinking, leaving the land on either side at its original height. The Rift, then, is not one continuous valley, but a loosely connected series of fissures, all at widely varying altitudes. The lowest point of the entire Rift system is actually below sea level, at the Dead Sea. In Kenya, which is neatly bisected from north to south by the Rift, the low points are Lake Turkana (1,230 ft.) and Lake Magadi (1,900 ft.). Where the Rift cleaves the Kenya highlands, the valley floor is more than 6,000 feet above sea level. Rift valleys are distinguished by the sheer walls of slip escarpments, which dramatically expose how far the valley floor has settled from its original elevation. These escarpments can be seen throughout the 5,000-mile course of the Rift's path through Africa.

The same geologic forces that created the Rift unlocked tremendous volcanic violence, especially in East Africa. Throughout Kenya and northern Tanzania, volcanic mountains, craters, cones, hot springs, and geysers are conspicuous features of the landscape. The highest mountain ranges are volcanic in origin. Mounts Kenya, Elgon, and the Aberdares are the eroded remnants of fiery giants, as is the extinct massif of Kilimanjaro. A few active volcanos remain, notably the Masai's sacred mountain, Ol Doinyo Lengai. In the course of their eruptions, the Rift volcanos threw up enormous amounts of ash, which was especially rich in sodium carbonate, commonly called *soda*. Over time, large quantities of dissolved soda concentrated in the basin lakes of valley floors.

The legacy of this vast geologic upheaval is the remarkable chain of East African Rift Valley lakes. In Kenya, these run from Turkana in the far north, through Baringo, Bogoria, Nakuru, and Naivasha, to Magadi on the Tanzanian border. Most of these lakes are distinctly sodary, but the degree of mineral content varies widely. Magadi, in the broiling sump of the Kenyan Rift, is so alkaline as to be almost sterile: the white expanses of exposed soda flats replace water over most of its surface. Naivasha—at 6,200 feet the highest of Kenya's Rift lakes—is thought to have an underground exit stream that prevents the buildup of soda concentrations. It is a freshwater lake, alive with fish and bird life. Fringed with green papyrus marshes, surrounded by tawny savanna grasslands and groves of yellow-barked fever trees, it has a garden atmosphere.

The lakes located in the central part of Kenya's Rift Valley are the most accessible and often visited by tourists. Each has its own character, molded by altitude and the mineral content of its waters.

LAKE NAIVASHA

Naivasha is one of the most beautiful Rift Valley lakes. Its broad valley is ringed by the bluish silhouettes of the Aberdares range and the hills of the Mau escarpment. Because of its altitude, it also enjoys a delectable highlands climate.

The lake is renowned as a birding paradise. Birds are everywhere. Pelicans and cormorants pursue fish in open waters, cruising among rafts of ducks and coots. Pied kingfishers hover and dive, while the tiny, gemlike malachite kingfisher awaits its chance to strike from a reed stem perch. Fish eagles are conspicuous in fever trees at the lakeshore, their piercing cries frequently announcing their presence. Goliath and purple herons, black crakes, and purple gallinules all stalk the edges of papyrus marshes. These water birds attract notice from even the most blasé visitors: many are large, gorgeously colored, and highly visible.

Naivasha has been victimized by ecological disasters. The accidental introduction of nutria, an aquatic fur-bearing South American rodent, resulted in the elimination of *Nymphaea* water lilies. These lovely flowers once bloomed in massed beds that were a characteristic feature of the lake. The lilies have been replaced by another South American import, the floating *Salvinia* fern. These weeds have exploded into choking mats that threaten Naivasha's ecological health. Papyrus swamps, ideal cover for many aquatic birds, have been largely cleared from the southeastern shore for hotel marinas. But even so, Naivasha still hosts enough bird life to impress dedicated birders and casual viewers alike.

Bird watching is not the only activity around Naivasha. Fishing is good, while boating, water skiing, and horseback riding can be arranged. The surrounding countryside has several good hiking possibilities. Close to the south shore are the extinct cone of Longonot Volcano (9,111 ft.) and the gorge known as Hell's Gate. Both have national park status, so entrance fees must be paid, but walking is permitted without ranger escort. (Take care to leave vehicles attended while you are hiking.) It's an easy walk to Longonot's rim for views of its crater. Scrubby foliage envelops the crater walls, while plumes of steam still issue from vents on the otherwise dormant volcano's floor.

Hell's Gate was once the bed of a stream that flowed southward from Naivasha, but was dammed by lava flows from Longonot. Near the entrance to the gorge, vertical cliffs converge around an odd granite pinnacle, Fischer's Tower. This volcanic plug is named for a German explorer, Dr. Gustav Fischer, whose expedition was repulsed at Naivasha by a Masai army. Today, the spire tempts experienced rock scramblers. Climbers are also attracted by challenging routes on the gorge's basalt walls. A rough track (open to four-wheel-drive vehicles) extends some 5 miles through the gorge to the volcanic Hell's Gate hot springs, and the whole area is well suited to experienced hikers. As well as the fascinating geological features—old lava flows, weird rock formations, and the thermal springs—Hell's Gate also has wildlife. Gazelle, giraffe, zebra, dik-dik, eland, and rock hyrax are all likely to be seen. Birdlife is particularly good. Verreaux's black eagle is commonly spotted in the gorge, where it feeds on the abundant hyrax. Huge flocks of Nyanza swifts swirl noisily among the cliffs, catching insects on the wing. The cliffs are the nesting site of a pair of resident lammergeyers, or bearded vultures. These handsome birds, known for their habit of dropping bones from high in the air in order to shatter them and get at their marrow, are quite rare in Kenya.

Naivasha is a convenient overnight stopping point between the parks of central Kenya and the Masai Mara. Although only a few hours are needed to visit the cliffs at Hell's Gate Gorge, relatively few people go. More often they take to the water on short cruises organized at their hotel's dock. This is a relaxed way to view Naivasha's birdlife and enjoy the snorts and dives of its resident hippos. The cruise makes a nice break from the routine of car travel and game drives. For an easy walking trip, there are tours to Crescent Island, a privately owned ranch and game sanctuary, where typical plains-dwelling species of game have been introduced. Here you can walk among gazelle, waterbuck, and ostrich without fear of encountering dangerous animals.

A variety of accommodation is available on the lake's south shore. The Lake Naivasha Hotel is a luxurious colonial-style facility, much favored by tour groups. Safariland Hotel has equally nice grounds, although food and accommodation are slightly less elegant. A very limited number of guests can be boarded at Joy Adamson's former home, Elsamere. Budget travelers will find a Youth Hostel and a campsite near the Safariland. Particularly recommended for budget travelers is the rustic Fisherman's Camp, on the southwest corner of the lake. It offers simple *banda* (hut) accommodation on a beautiful, undeveloped part of the lakeshore where considerable wildlife is still to be found.

LAKE NAKURU

Nakuru is renowned for the spectacle of massed flamingos feeding in its soda waters. The shallow lake is often literally ringed with a solid band of pink birds. When feeding conditions are right, flamingos may number more than 2 million.

Flamingos are not exclusive to Nakuru. They are found in good numbers at many soda lakes throughout the African Rift. Their presence, absence, or superabundance is dictated by the supply of blue-green algae. These thrive in nutrient-rich soda waters. As lake levels rise or fall according to local weather conditions, the chemical content of the water changes. Flamingos migrate from one Rift Valley lake to the next, seeking out those where vast blooms of algae provide a bountiful source of food. At most times, Nakuru's waters are chemically perfect for the growth of the microscopic plants; the flamingos filter out tons of algae daily. Although algae dieoffs sometimes force the birds to abandon the lake, the flamingo display at Nakuru is generally impressive, if not overwhelming. Two species of flamingo are present. The pinker lesser flamingo is by far the more numerous. Larger and whiter, greater flamingos feed on small crustaceans rather than on algae.

The display of other birdlife along Nakuru's shores is hardly less impressive. Human introduction of the fish *Tilapia grahami* has encouraged the ample attendance of every type of fish-eating bird. Larger animal life is also present, for the lake is protected within Nakuru National Park. Reedbuck and waterbuck are common on grassy swards along the lakeshore, while baboon troops frequent rocky outcrops. Rothschild's giraffe, a rare subspecies threatened with extinction in Kenya, has been introduced into the park. Nakuru has also been designated a special reserve for the protection of the black rhino. Considerable effort has been put into the construction of a secure perimeter fence to keep rhinos in the park, and poachers out. The hard-pressed rhinos are being translocated into Nakuru from other areas where it is impossible to protect them from extermination. Nakuru may ultimately be one of the few places in Africa where the black rhino will be seen in the wild.

Accommodation in the park is available at Lion Hill Lodge and Lake Nakuru Lodge, which features a floodlit saltlick and waterhole. There is also a public campsite. An overnight stay is highly recommended for birders and those wishing to get the best light for photography.

LAKES BARINGO AND BOGORIA

Located to the north of Nakuru, Lakes Baringo and Bogoria are just close enough to Nairobi and the game parks to be included on tour itineraries. Baringo is the more popular. A freshwater lake, it is prominent mostly for its birdlife. Aside from throngs of fish eaters, waders, and fowl, the woodlands surrounding the lake harbor interesting endemic species not found elsewhere in Kenya, such as Jackson's hornbill. Lodges at the lake all offer escorted bird walks or cruises. Although Baringo is primarily of interest to birders, it is a beautiful and relaxing spot, a nice place to take a break from the rigors of game viewing. Most visitors also want to call on a village of the local Njemps tribe. The Njemps are relatives of the Masai. Although they speak the same language, they have some very different social customs: they eat fish, something the Masai would never dream of doing. Settled along the lake's southern shores, the Njemps have learned to exploit its most valuable protein resource. It was at Baringo that the theory of continental drift was proven by John W. Gregory, a young Scottish geologist, when he examined a cross section of rocks on the escarpment walls surrounding the lake. The eastern Rift Valley is now called the Gregory Rift in his honor.

Fifteen miles south of Baringo lies the smaller Lake Bogoria. A scenic soda lake, it normally hosts a charming complement of flamingos. On its northern end, quite close to the shore, impressive hot springs erupt in boiling geysers. Greater kudu inhabit thick bush at the base of the Siracho Escarpment on the lake's eastern side. These magnificent spiral-horned antelope are only likely to be spotted at dawn or dusk. The track through kudu country is restricted to sturdy four-wheel-drive vehicles.

Virtually every visitor to the area stays at Baringo, where all the amenities can be found. Pleasant, well-shaded, privately owned campsites are available at the lakeshore. The Lake Baringo Club offers lodge accommodation. Island Camp is a very charming tented camp, well known for its scenery and wealth of bird life. Camping and entrance fees must be paid at Bogoria, which is a national reserve; a lodge is soon to be opened there.

Meru National Park

Meru is the least visited of major Kenyan parks. Located some 50 miles to the northeast of Mount Kenya, it is omitted from many tour itineraries simply because it is out of the way. This is a pity, for Meru is a delightful park, incorporating a splendid variety of landscapes and animals. Meru is situated on the north bank of the Tana River, which forms a geographical divide for Kenyan game species. Several handsome animals—the reticulated giraffe, Beisa oryx, and Grevy's zebra—are found only to the north of the Tana. Meru is best known as the home of Elsa the lioness. Raised from infancy by painter and author Joy Adamson, Elsa had to be painstakingly trained to hunt for herself before she was released into Meru's wilds. The success of the *Born Free* books and film led to international recognition for Meru. In Elsa's time, the park was in its infancy—a former hunting area just given protected status. Today, Meru is a favorite place for campers who want to get away from it all.

Meru is a bush country park in which woodlands and scrub prevail over grassy tracts. The most open areas occur in the northwest, where scattered trees and shrubs pepper plains of coarse grass. Massive baobabs, their bloated trunks and swollen limbs bare against the sky, distinguish the landscape, sturdy sentinels among the more slender acacias. Marshes, fed by underground waters flowing from the Nyambeni Hills, are important features. In the dry season, these marshes are conspicuous oases of greenery, surrounded by parched grass and leafless woods. Animals converge on them, seeking moist forage and relief from the heat in waterholes and mud wallows. Several small rivers flow eastward from the marshes. Each is fringed with lush riverine forest. In places, tall fig trees and feathery wild date palms line the banks. Elsewhere, streams are bordered with groves of graceful doum palms. One pocket of cool evergreen forest is found near the western park boundary, along the Rhino Alley track.

Thick bush dominates Meru's eastern reaches, a jumbled woodland of wait-a-bit thorn and combretum scrub. During and after the rains, this bush is a tangle of impenetrable foliage. In the dry season, many of the plants lose their leaves, creating a landscape of bare gray limbs and wicked thorns. Game viewing is difficult in the scrub, although it is good habitat for gerenuk and the lesser kudu. Skirmishes with tsetses and fierce heat do not make the combretum bush a favored tourist haunt. But the park's eastern tracks lead to the Tana River. The Tana is Kenya's largest, draining all of Mount Kenya and a good part of the highlands beyond. By the time it reaches Meru, the Tana is a wide river that forms the park's southeastern boundary. The 8-mile drive along the river offers views of hippo herds and basking crocodiles. You can picnic at Adamson's Falls, named for Joy's husband George, first warden of the park. The rocky falls are not so impressive for their height as for their wilderness setting.

Meru has recently been the scene of a conservation disaster. Up to the fall of 1988, the park was the refuge for Kenya's only white rhinos. These animals were introduced with the idea of creating a wild herd. Having been transported from South Africa, they were kept in a special enclosure near park headquarters. The experiment never quite worked, however: although the rhinos showed that they could survive in Meru, and even produce offspring, they suffered casualties from poachers even before they were fully left to fend for themselves. Consequently, they were never released into the wild, but were kept under twenty-four-hour guard by park rangers and penned each night for their own protection. They were so tame that they readily allowed themselves to be herded, photographed, and even petted! Unfortunately, a single bold—and particularly vicious—attack by poachers wiped out the entire rhino herd, and left one of their guards dead as well. The incident speaks volumes about the gravity of the poaching situation in Africa.

ACCESS AND ACCOMMODATION

The main approach to the park is through the town of Meru, to the east of Mount Kenya. From Meru a good road winds over the verdant Nyambeni Hills, which reach heights in excess of 8,000 feet, before descending to the park. Meru is low, hot country: altitude drops from a high of 2,600 feet along the western boundary to about 1,000 feet at the Tana River.

Virtually all accommodation and campsites are located in the northwestern section of the park. The comfortable Meru Mulika Lodge overlooks one of the permanent marshes most favored by game. Leopard Rock Lodge offers self-service accommodation in rustic cabins; guests must bring their own food. There are a number of attractive special campsites in Meru, exclusively booked by professional safari outfitters. The public campsite is well appointed with clean shower and toilet blocks.

TOURING THE PARK

Meru flushes brilliant green in the rains, but game viewing is at its best during the dry months. The plains of the northwest, with their marshes and permanent rivers, are the best game-viewing regions.

Meru is an ideal park for exploring on your own. A relative absence of visitors affords a sense of personal discovery and privacy. An excellent network of signposted roads combs the reserve. Visibility is somewhat obscured by high grass and patches of thick bush, making predators rather difficut to spot. But you should have no problem seeing elephant, buffalo, and a good variety of other game, especially around the marshes. Boldly marked reticulated giraffe and Beisa oryx are easily located. Grevy's zebra is more problematic, as its numbers are low. Gerenuk are plentiful. Meru is probably the best park in Kenya for views of the lesser kudu (*Tragelaphus imberbis*). This pretty antelope is about the size of an impala, with vertical white stripes marking its flanks. The males, brownish in color, possess extraordinary spiraling horns. Females are hornless. They have much brighter reddish-brown coats, dappled with delicate stripes. Lesser kudu browse in thick bush country, often favoring riverine thickets. They are generally skittish, but those around Meru's western parts sometimes allow a close approach.

You will not fail to notice baobabs (*Adansonia digitata*), Meru's most conspicuous trees. Baobabs grow where good seasonal rains allow them to store up water for periodic drought. For most of the year, they stand completely leafless, looking like the bloated corpses of prehistoric giants rather than living trees. The baobab's shape has earned it the nickname "upside-down tree": its bare, stocky branches resemble a twisted mass of roots, while the bulbous trunk tapers as it approaches the ground. The corpulent trunks of baobabs unanimously show the scars of elephant damage. Elephants eat the baobab's heartwood, a soft moisture-laden pulp. They attack the giant trees throughout the long rainless months. Look for the chance to watch elephants feeding on a baobab. Chipping away with their tusks, they excavate their way into the heart of the tree. The trunk is used to pull off strips of loosened bark and to delicately carry morsels of pulp to the mouth. Unlike most trees, the stripping of the outer bark does not kill the baobab, for the wounds heal themselves with a new layer of stringy bark. Repeated feedings eventually do weaken and topple the top-heavy trees—giant baobabs are sometimes completely devoured by gourmandizing pachyderms.

Elephants are also very fond of the crab-apple-sized nuts of the doum palm. It is amusing to watch the huge beasts forage for them. The elephant cannot see them, so the massive trunk carefully sniffs out fallen fruits and transports them individually to the mouth. Local legend has it that doum palms were spread by Arab caravans, and that groves mark their former campsites. It is more likely that the palm nuts were carried to remote waterside locations inside the insatiable bellies of wide-ranging elephants. The nuts often pass undamaged through the elephant's gut, to be deposited in a ball of excellent fertilizer. It is somewhat of a mystery that one never sees intermediate-sized doum palms: either there are scrubby thickets of seedling fronds, or groves of tall, branched trees. Indeed, the doum palm (*Hyphaene coriacea*) is unusual among palms in that it has many graceful, slender branches, rather than the customary single stem.

Samburu National Reserve

Vast, austere, and harshly beautiful, Kenya's northern desert is home to a great collection of wild animals and nomadic peoples. A journey to Samburu National Reserve is highly recommended for a taste of the north country. It is relatively accessible, and on the way you will encounter the peoples of several tribes. It is certainly the best place to view the wildlife of the desert.

Samburu is actually one of several refuges clustered along the Uaso Nyiro River. The Samburu National Reserve extends for more than fifteen miles along the north bank, while Buffalo Springs National Reserve fronts about 10 miles on the opposite shore. From the visitor's point of view, they can be viewed as one unit. The adjacent Shaba National Reserve protects an additional tract of wildlife country to the east. The river is of prime importance to all, for it lures water-dependent animals from a vast arc of bone-dry country.

The Samburu-Buffalo Springs reserves dramatically showcase the habitats of the desert realm. Away from the river, the landscape is most typical of the north country: stunted acacia thorn is scattered over miles of bare rocky ground. Richer areas support plains of bleached desert grass and stands of graceful flat-topped *Acacia tortilis*. Where underground springs seep to the surface, small marshes and pools are magnets for water-loving animals and birds. Here and there, rocky hills break the profile of thornbush flats. To the north, the eye is drawn particularly to a great granite block, the flat-topped Ololokwe. Imposing vistas of distant ranges lend color and grand scale to magnificent sunsets.

If the desert scenery is consistently dramatic, game viewing is equally extraordinary. It never ceases to amaze that such large numbers of wild animals can thrive in what appears to be an implacably hostile environment. But the animals have accommodated themselves to a regime of meager rain and thin grazing. Each species has made its own selective adaptations, and is capable of living quite happily with the prevailing arid conditions. The true desert dwellers are so specialized that they need never drink, receiving all their moisture requirements from the food they eat. They can be active, or at least visible, at virtually any time of the day. These water-independent animals include the Beisa oryx, gerenuk, and Grant's gazelle. Grevy's zebra and reticulated giraffe do need water, but manage to meet their needs. They, along with the Beisa oryx and Guenther's dikdik, are the specialty animals of northern Kenya, being restricted to the country north of the Tana River. All are regularly seen in the Samburu-Buffalo Springs reserves.

The unusual gerenuk (*Litocranius walleri*) has the qualities of a high-fashion model. It is very slender, with long delicate legs, and a remarkably extended neck. In fact, the name *gerenuk* is Afrikaans, meaning "long neck." This antelope lives in dry thornbush country, where it uses its height to browse a higher level of foliage than competing species can reach. It is often seen standing on its hind legs, balancing against the wiry branches of a young acacia to reach even higher morsels. This competitive boost is holding the gerenuk in good stead in country that is now heavily overgrazed by voracious goats. It is common and tame in Samburu, living in small groups.

Guenther's is a very large dikdik. This is not saying much, for dikdik are among the tiniest of antelope: adults are only slightly larger than hares. At a glance, Guenther's is virtually indistinguishable from the more widespread Kirk's dikdik. It does have a more elongated nose. Like its cousin, Guenther's dikdik (*Madoqua guentheri*) is a high-strung inhabitant of thickets. Its bulbous nose is ever twitching in response to unseen stimuli. Unlike the gerenuk, the little dikdik is no longer thriving outside the game reserves. It is suffering badly from competition with goats, which denude the thickets it depends on for food and safety.

Like other oryx, the Beisa is consummately adapted to dry conditions. It is found throughout northern Kenya wherever there is a thin cover of dry grass. It may be seen in herds of dozens, although it is not uncommon to encounter solitary bulls. Its long, symmetrical, scimitar-sharp horns and bold black-and-white coloration, make the Beisa oryx (*Oryx gazella beisa*) particularly photogenic.

Grevy's zebra (*Hippotigris grevyi*) is often found in association with Beisa oryx for it feeds on the same coarse annual desert grasses. Grevy's is a large animal, with a donkeylike head and a distinctive pin-striped pattern on its coat. It looks quite different from the common Burchell's zebra, which is also found in Samburu. Grevy's zebra is restricted to a range in northern Kenya and southern Ethiopia. Because of hunting for its pelt and habitat destruction, conservationists feared for a while that the species was approaching extinction. Although that alarm proved false, Grevy's *is* a rare animal. Studies are now in progress to document its life history and population status. It appears that Grevy's stallions establish territories through which groups of mares wander as food supplies permit. This lifestyle is in sharp contrast to the habits of the common zebra, which lives in close-knit family groups, a stallion and his bonded mares, which migrate together.

The reticulated giraffe must drink, but it has adapted well to the acacia-studded regions of the Kenya desert. The subspecies *reticulata* is by all accounts the most beautiful variety of giraffe. Its bold geometrical markings are clearly etched with white borders, as distinct from the haphazard blotches of the Masai giraffe. The reticulated giraffe inhabits suitable thornbush country throughout northeastern Kenya. It has been reduced in numbers over the years

Grevy's zebra at Samburu National Reserve, Kenya. *Photo by Allen Bechky.*

through overhunting and habitat destruction. Many of the nomadic tribes formerly used the long hairs of this animal's tail to make ornamental necklaces and household basketry. This practice has somewhat declined with government protection and a general dwindling in the number of giraffes available.

For many Samburu animals, the lifeblood of the reserve is the Uaso Nyiro. The name is apt: it means "muddy river" in the Samburu language. The water indeed flows brown, carrying the lost soils of the overgrazed Laikipia Plateau into the scalding low country of northeast Kenya. There the river dies, trapped in an inland delta, the remote Lorian Swamp. Brown though it is, the river carries life to the Samburu region, making it an oasis for humans and animals alike. Outside the reserves, the Samburu bring their thirsty cattle to its banks. Inside, elephants come to bathe and sate their ample thirst in its shallow waters. A ribbon of greenery follows the river's course. Except when in spate, the Uaso Nyiro runs low, its bed marked by exposed sandbars and flats of tender colonizing grass. In the upper, westernmost part of the reserve, the river is bordered by groves of tall *Acacia albida* trees. Lower down, and into the Shaba National Reserve, this shady riparian forest thins down to a narrow strip of branched doum palms.

The river oasis is a natural haven for water-dependent species that cannot adapt to the surrounding desert. Crocodiles bask on sandbars, where saddle-billed storks and other aquatic birds hunt frogs or fish. Waterbuck feed on the riverbed grasses, while impala are confined to the fringing forest. Vervet monkeys and baboons also forage riverine glades. They may venture into the margins of the desert, but retreat to the safety of the treetops for their nightly roosts. Elephants enjoy the shade of the forest's *Acacia albida* trees, but they also relish their taste. Large sections of riverine forest have been seriously damaged by their attentions. Elephants have to drink, and no finer experience can be had at Samburu than to witness the arrival of elephants at the river. As if by magic, herds of up to a hundred emerge from the desert scrub, enthusiastically bathing and drinking in a daily ritual.

Although all the major predators live in Samburu, seeing any is not guaranteed. Lion prides are small and reclusive, while cheetah are not particularly abundant. On the other hand, Samburu offers a good chance to view leopard. Because the spotted cats have been baited regularly for many years at Samburu Lodge, leopards in that area are much less shy than normal. If not seen at the lodge's nightly bait (there is about a 50 percent chance that one will turn up on any particular night), they might still be noticed by some sharp safari driver in the riverine forest. Word gets out fast once any of Samburu's predators are found, so expect a ring of vehicles to attend any viewing session. Samburu is a good area for seeing the striped hyena. A shaggy-maned, wolflike predator, the striped hyena is more solitary than its spotted cousin. Striped hyenas thrive in dry bush country, so Samburu is ideal for them. They are occasionally seen on late drives, and sometimes visit the leopard bait at Samburu Lodge, hoping to pick up scraps dropped from above. Its appearance does not generate nearly as much excitement as the leopard's, in spite of being one of the less often viewed carnivores.

ACCESS AND ACCOMMODATION

It takes about five hours to drive the 200 miles from Nairobi to Samburu, via the uplands town of Nanyuki.

The descent from the Kenya highlands into the northern desert is truly dramatic. From the flanks of Mount Kenya, the Timau road drops from almost 9,000 feet in altitude to 3,000 feet on the desert floor. Within 40 miles you pass from rolling wheat fields and verdant forests of mountain cedar to thirsty thornbush country, where red-robed nomads tend scrawny cattle and camels. Air temperatures noticeably rise as the road descends.

At the town of Isiolo, a new mosque is a conspicuous sign of the cultural influence of Islam. The market next door is interesting, for it bustles with people from half a dozen desert tribes. The selection of vegetables is paltry compared with highland markets, but many vendors sell neat little bundles of red-barked twigs. This is *miraa*, a mild stimulant drug. Grown by the Meru in the Nyambeni Hills, *miraa* is widely used by the peoples of the desert.

At Isiolo, all vehicles stop at a police barrier. Drivers must register with the police, who monitor traffic in both directions. Presumably plenty of hanky-panky is going on in terms of smuggled goods headed both north and south. While your vehicle is stopped, you will be besieged by scores of souvenir hawkers, all seemingly desperate to make a sale. Although negotiations take on a frantic, hurried atmosphere—for time is short until your driver returns—many interesting items are on sale. Excellent buys can be made. Specialty items include Somali swords with beautifully tooled camel-leather sheaths, Samburu milk containers woven from wild sisal, and bracelets of braided copper wire. Amber pieces are of dubious authenticity; they can well prove to be plastic counterfeits. Giraffe-hair bracelets and ostrich-egg jewelry are genuine, but are the products of poached animals, so do not buy them! Bargain hard for other items here, however. The lunatic prices first asked plummet as soon as your driver starts his van. The items are then thrown inside and can be purchased for a small fraction of the original price. You may feel like a thief for beating the vendor down too hard, especially when you return to Nairobi and see the inflated prices in the shops for the same items. But if you accept prices at face value, you will feel a fool. Warning: during the mass assault of vendors on your vehicle, hands and souvenirs enter the car from all sides. Take care that loose valuables, including cameras or backpacks, do not disappear in the confusion.

Beyond the barrier, you officially enter Kenya's wild north country, the old Northern Frontier District. The pavement is replaced by a heavily corrugated, washboard road that goes all the way to Marsabit and Ethiopia. After 20 miles, you will be happy to turn onto the more gentle reserve tracks, just before reaching the Uaso Nyiro. The Samburu and Buffalo Springs reserves are immediately west of the main road. Shaba National Reserve is to the east, just beyond its headquarters complex. The Shaba entrance track is very rough where it crosses an ancient lava field.

A variety of accommodation is available at Samburu. Samburu Lodge is one of the best in Kenya. It is not only comfortable but lively: the dining room's open verandah invites weaver birds, horn-bills, and starlings, almost as much as the feeders placed outside exclusively for the birds' use. Crocs and waterbirds are always within view on the riverside terrace. Nile monitors, the semiaquatic lizards that can reach a length of up to 7 feet, are frequent daytime scavengers below the terrace. They seek leftover scraps from the meat that is put out each evening to entice crocs for closeup viewing. These crocodile feedings are artificially showy, but interesting. Some of the leviathan reptiles are full size, and fully capable of devouring a human being. This capability is enhanced by the feedings: they have lost all fear of humans. It's wise for anyone camped near the lodge to stay well clear of the river's edge. The more publicized show is the leopard baiting. A goat is hung in a floodlit tree on the opposite side of the river. When a cat appears (of which there is roughly a 50 percent chance), it is not bothered by the huge cocktail party taking place at the lodge's riverfront bar. The rival Samburu Serena Lodge also baits for leopards. It is located on the south bank of the river, just west of the Buffalo Springs Reserve boundary. The tented Buffalo Springs Lodge is within the reserve; less luxurious than the other hotels, it is located in a very good game-viewing area, and elephants frequently browse through its grounds. The new Larsen's Camp got off to a rough start: no sooner was it opened than it was washed away by a Uaso Nyiro flood. This deluxe tented facility was subsequently moved to a higher riverbank location. Another big lodge, the Sarova Shaba, has just opened downriver, in the Shaba National Reserve.

Professional safari companies use scenic special campsites in the forest along the river, or the isolated site near Kubi Panya (the Hill of the Rat). The public campsites are found on Champagne Ridge, so-called because it was once the province of a more exclusive safari crowd. Precautions against thievery must be taken at all campsites; the local Samburu are not discouraged by a trek through the bush when raiding unattended camps.

TOURING THE PARK

Leisurely morning and evening game drives work well at Samburu, where the midday heat makes relaxation imperative. It's best to patrol the grassy plains between Buffalo Springs and Champagne Ridge in the very early hours. This is a choice area to spot cheetah, Grevy's zebra, oryx, and reticulated giraffe. Gerenuk can be encountered anywhere in areas of scrubby desert thornbush. It's good to work along the numerous river tracks in the later morning, when the elephant herds are most likely to arrive. This is also a good time to look for basking crocs. You can break up a hot game drive with a refreshing dip at Buffalo Springs. A low wall has been built around a natural rock swimming pool: its waters are refreshingly cool, and absolutely bilharzia free. Late afternoon drives are exceptionally pretty as the twilight colors engulf the superb desert landscape.

The nearby Shaba National Reserve equals or surpasses Samburu in scenery, but its wildlife is much sparser. As such, Shaba is almost completely overlooked by commercial tourism (though that could change with the opening of the new lodge). Visitors with their own transport and plenty of time will enjoy a wilderness outing down to scenic Penny's Falls (also called Chandler's Falls).

Game viewing in the desert reserves is dependably good. The numbers of elephant, oryx, zebra, and other animals may drop during the rains (which are rare and extremely erratic), but representatives of all species are invariably present.

SAMBURU VILLAGE VISITS

Just outside the Samburu Reserve's eastern Archer's Post Gate, several *manyattas* line the road, open for tourist business. Visits to these villages are apt to be little more than chaotic bargaining sessions for photos and souvenirs. All the livestock, including the camels that the Samburu have only recently adopted, are driven off for forage early in the morning. Photos of the Samburu are keenly sought, however, because of the extreme beauty of the people. Their lean frames and sharp features, bright red robes, and gaily colored beaded jewelry make them prized subjects for the camera. Neither the *manyatta* visits nor the dance performances put on by decked-out *murran** at Samburu Lodge are fully satisfactory as cultural experiences, but the photographic opportunities are there.

More meaningful encounters with the Samburu require that you get away from the immediate vicinity of the reserve gates, and devote some time to exploring their country. Several of the more adventurous tour outfitters are starting to take their clients bush walking outside the Shaba National Reserve, and to organize safaris to such Samburu strongholds as Maralal and the Mathews Range.

---

*The Masai share the same language, *Maa,* with the Samburu, but dialects and pronunciation vary. Thus "warriors" is *moran* for the Masai, *murran* for the Samburu.

Camel safaris through Samburu country are also catching on. These offer the opportunity to walk (or ride camels) for several days in the company of Samburu stockmen. The best-known (and fairly luxurious) camel trip is operated by Julian McKeand. It is booked through Flamingo Tours in Nairobi. Yare Safaris runs a budget-priced camel safari.

The Northern Frontier: Land of Nomads

For unspoiled country and peoples, few parts of Kenya can compare with the far north. The British called it the Northern Frontier District, a name that still conjures up considerable romance. Although that appellation is no longer officially used, the old NFD remains a raw country, the venue of wandering nomads, *shifta* bandits, man-eating lions, and intrigue.

The "deserts" of the NFD are by no means an empty wasteland of rock and dune. Although water and rain are rare, vegetation and animal life are not. Scattered thornbush is almost ubiquitous and tree lines follow the course of dry riverbeds. After rain the desert is briefly transformed: overnight, trees blossom and fresh grass sprouts on bare ground. Storms are very local, however, and the land may have to wait months or even years for its next refreshment. Desert animals and humans alike have had to adapt to the fiercest conditions of aridity. The hardiest of the wild animals are able to survive without drinking. People have learned where to find water, and how to maintain flocks of grazing animals in spite of near impossible conditions. For them the answer was and is migration. Northern Kenya is the land of nomads.

The nomads live in a bewildering variety of tribes: Samburu, Pokot, Turkana, Rendille, Gabbra, and Boran share the deserts surrounding the inland sea, Lake Turkana. Although ethnolinguistic overlaps exist (the Samburu, Pokot, and Turkana belong to the Nilotic group, while the others speak Cushitic languages), each tribe maintains a distinctive language and customs. Their most common denominator is the rigorousness of the environment. Most of these peoples depend completely on their animals to provide a diet of blood, milk, and meat. Their various strategies for survival are determined by the types of animals they keep. As they wander with their herds, tribal territories overlap. Although nomads mingle in the larger desert towns, relations among the tribes are not always good. The Kenya government enforces the peace, but cattle raids and retaliations still occur. Despite the best efforts of the government to bring the nomads into the national economy, most continue to lead independent lifestyles, aloof from the modern world.

SAMBURU

Best known of the desert tribes are the Samburu, an offshoot section of the Masai with whom they share language and many social customs. Like the Masai, they have an age set system that keeps men as bachelor-warriors for a large part of their lives. Living in a tougher range, with other nomadic groups competing for grazing and water resources, the Samburu have remained more martial than the Masai, and each of their lean *murran* usually carries a twin set of spears. Samburu prize cattle above other stock, though they also tend goats. Due to increasing population and environmental degradation in the north country, cattle are becoming ever more difficult to keep alive, so the Samburu are now starting to care for camels, as well—a custom picked up from their Rendille neighbors. Although most visitors come into contact with the Samburu around the game reserve that bears their most familiar name (they also call themselves *Loikop*), the tribe has an extensive triangular territory extending from the shores of Lake Turkana southward to the plateau around Maralal, and eastward to the Samburu National Reserve.

RENDILLE

The Rendille are few in number—only some 22,000—yet they hold a large territory stretching from the east shore of Turkana to Marsabit Mountain. Their land overlaps that of the Samburu considerably in the south; moreover, the two groups have been traditional allies, not enemies. Some of the southernmost Rendille have adopted cattle from the Samburu, but primarily Rendille depend on the camel. Camels yield much more milk than do cattle. They also feed on the foliage of trees and shrubs, which are more abundant than grass in the desert, and can go for much longer periods without water. The Rendille live in large semipermanent villages called *gob*, where married men remain with their families. Young boys and warriors may live apart for months, moving the valuable camel herds to the best forage. A Rendille man must pay a bride price of eight camels

A Samburu woman in her beaded jewelry. *Photo by Allen Bechky.*

to obtain a wife. Since raising camels is difficult, few Rendille can afford more than one bride. Excess girls are therefore often traded to the Samburu. Men tend and milk the camels, women are responsible for collecting water. They drive camels to distant wells, returning with each animal laden with up to 30 gallons. Women weave excellent baskets from the fibers of roots. These *jijo* are absolutely liquid-tight containers for water and milk. A married woman wears an elaborate cockscomb hairstyle once she has given birth to a male heir.

POKOT

The Pokot live along the western wall of the Rift Valley. Although those in the Cherangani Hills are settled agriculturists, the pastoral Pokot on the valley floor wander the country to the north of Lake Baringo. They share many customs with the Turkana, but they are frequently in conflict with these more powerful neighbors.

TURKANA

Some 200,000 strong, the Turkana are by far the most populous of the nomadic tribes. Although concentrated to the west of the lake, they are constantly pushing into the territories of their neighbors, a source of much friction. The Turkana are more adaptive than the other desert peoples: they keep all types of domestic stock, and have even settled as farmers and fishermen. Unlike the Samburu, Turkana have no aversion to eating wild meat, so game has disappeared throughout the country they occupy. Adult men adorn their hair with clay and ostrich feathers. To protect these unusual coiffures, they use wooden neckstools as pillows. Among the desert nomads, only the Turkana do not practice circumcision. Men are not shy about nudity, regarding only circumcised males as truly naked.

GABBRA

The Gabbra are a small, hardy tribe who have been squeezed by more powerful neighbors into the inhospitable country to the east of Lake Turkana. Their parched territory includes the Chalbi desert, a seemingly endless expanse of empty salt flats. The Gabbra must ceaselessly move their camels to find fresh browse, but always return to the same springs and deep wells for water. In contrast to the Samburu, who are very individualistic, the Gabbra social system places great value on cooperation. There is a remarkable level of social obligation and interdependence between members of very extended families. The Gabbra are related to the Boran and, like them, both men and women wear their hair in long ringlets, unusual among the desert peoples.

BORAN

The Boran came originally from Ethiopia, part of a wave of peoples who speak Cushitic languages, collectively known as the Galla. They wander large tracts of desert to the east of Marsabit, where they are most likely to be encountered by visitors. Like the Gabbra, Borana women are fond of jewelry fashioned from aluminum.

SOMALI

The Somali predominate in the low bushlands of northeastern Kenya. Fiercely Islamic, the half-million Kenyan Somalis have closer cultural links to their kin in the Republic of Somalia than to other Kenyan tribes. Somali nationalism has kept alive a simmering separatist movement. Outbreaks of *shifta*, bands of armed Somali raiders, occur periodically. The threat of *shifta* violence, whether politically motivated or simple banditry, makes travel in the northeast risky. The Somalis you are most apt to meet are more likely to be shopkeepers or traders than nomads.

JOURNEY TO LAKE TURKANA

Most expeditions to the north have Lake Turkana as their objective, for the region around the lake beams with scenic and ethnological interest. The most frequented access is via Maralal and the South Horr Valley. Intrepid explorers will want to take a circular route, returning through Marsabit and the Chalbi and Kaisut deserts.

Access and accommodation in the north are poor, so visitors are few. Several budget outfitters operate rough-and-ready camping safaris to the lake. The "Turkana Bus" departs regularly from Nairobi. This 8-day truck safari is the cheapest way to go. AirKenya operates daily flights from Nairobi to Loiyangalani; these save on the wear and tear of the overland trip, but also cut out much of the adventure. The region is best explored with time on your own. A good vehicle and good sense are indispensable for a trip to the lake. Public transport can take you to Maralal or Marsabit, from which you may be able to arrange outings with local tribespeople. Remember, this is not territory to be approached casually. But the scenery and, above all, the people are unforgettable.

Maralal is a main administrative and trading town in the heart of Samburu country. It is also the principal traveler's gateway to Lake Turkana. The town itself is merely a dusty collection of *dukas* (shops) patronized by Samburu and Turkana taking a break from the bush. Maralal, itself at an altitude above 5,000 feet, is surrounded by wooded hill country. In the dry seasons, the Samburu drive their herds into these and other high desert ranges to take advantage of better grazing and water resources. Some of the hills around Maralal are crowned with forests of African cedar, and game is still relatively abundant throughout Samburu country. Zebra, impala, and notably tame eland are frequent visitors to the Maralal Safari Lodge, located only a mile north of town. Leopard are sometimes viewed there too, because the lodge baits for them nightly.

North of Maralal, the road drops precipitously from the wooded Lorogi Plateau into desert thornbush country, where it passes over several *luggas*. These sand rivers are of prime importance to the Samburu, who must dig wells in them in order to find water. Beyond the dry El Barta Plains, the oasis-like South Horr Valley is squeezed between the Ol Doinyo Mara range and Mount Nyiru. High above the valley, the Kosikosi rock outcrop on Nyiru is thought to be sacred to the Samburu god, and religious rites sometimes take place on the mountain. Displays of tribal dancing are often arranged at the Kurungu campsite, near the village of South Horr. To the west of town is the brutally arid Suguta Valley and the soda Lake Logipi. Time permitting, a side trip there is justified to view the tortured desert landscapes.

For most visitors, the final approach to Lake Turkana is adventure enough. Miles of sandy track culminate in a mountain of fist-size pebbles that must be surmounted for the first spectacular views of the lake. Turkana has been nicknamed the Jade Sea because of the color of its waters. The color actually changes with the vagaries of the weather, giving multiple faces to an elemental vista of rock, sea, and sky.

When the explorers Count Samuel Teleki and his companion Ludwig von Hohnel first viewed the gleaming expanse of the lake, they were elated. But after a thirst-racked desert crossing, they were heartbroken to discover that the sodary water was undrinkable. It is comforting to know that cold beer now awaits you at the village of Loiyangalani. As you descend to the lakeshore over miles of pebbles and rocky rubble, the perfect volcanic cone of Nabuyatom is seen jutting conspicuously into the south end of the lake. This cone is often erroneously referred to as Teleki's Volcano, which the count reported in eruption during his visit. "His" volcano, now also quiescent, actually lies beyond Nabuyatom, in the Suguta wastelands. When Teleki saw the lake he named it Rudolf, after an Austrian prince, a name dispossessed by the winds of independence.

Although Turkana's bitter waters are distasteful to humans, fish thrive in the briny soup. The fish in turn feed Turkana's crocodiles, which number in the thousands. People also exploit the fish: the Turkana fish the west shore at Fergusons's Gulf and Eliye Springs. On the east side, the tiny El Molo tribe survives on the bounty of the lake.

The El Molo number no more than 400 people, living in a few tiny camps along the southeast shore. Their culture is still almost neolithic, entirely dependent (at least until the advent of tourism) on a hunting and fishing economy. They are adept at using the meager resources of the environment to fashion all the tools of survival. Palm fiber is used to make fishing nets and line, while the trunks are lashed into primitive rafts. Harpoon shafts are made from acacia root or oryx horn; only the iron tips are forged from materials brought in from the outside world. Fishing with both lines and nets, the El Molo are also amazingly skilled at spearing fish. They also use harpoons to hunt crocodiles and hippos along the lake's reedy shores.

Loiyangalani, a small village on the southeast shore, is the primary destination of Turkana-bound travelers. Its physical setting is impressive: it commands a magnificent vista of the lake and rugged South Island, while Mount Kulal overshadows the desert to the east. Comfortable accommodation is found at Oasis Lodge, which caters to fly-in guests.

The El Molo have a lakeshore village of reed huts at Loiyangalani, but this is obviously called on by lots of tourists. It is better to visit the village further north at El Molo Bay, or to arrange a crossing to El Molo Island. It is hard to have more than a look-see encounter with the El Molo, though you can watch them fishing near shore if you are up and about early.

Several adventurous excursions can be made from Loiyangalani. A track leads to Mount Kulal (7,522 ft.) which supports patches of mist forest high above the parched desert. Guides may be found for treks to Kulal or for the long day's walk to Nabuyatom Cone. Oasis Lodge charters boats for fishing trips. Nile perch, which reach weights of over 200 pounds, are the sportsman's principal quarry. Boats can also go out to South Island, but extreme care is necessary. Powerful winds can surge down the slopes of Kulal, whipping the lake into treacherous waves. These sudden gusts often prove catastrophic to the El Molo's palm log rafts, and are a danger to all small craft. Swimming in the lake must also be approached prudently. Although the lake is supposed to be bilharzia free, the crocodiles cannot escape notice. They are reputed never to attack El Molo, but the presence of numerous 14-foot specimens suggests extreme caution.

Students of our evolutionary history will want to make the trip to Koobi Fora, part of the Sibiloi National Park. This site, located about a hundred miles north of Loiyangalani, is where Richard Leakey's teams of anthropologists have uncovered some of the oldest human remains. The discovery of Skull 1470, a specimen of a *Homo habilis* dated to roughly 2 million years old, propelled Leakey to international fame. A small museum is instructive, and the actual discovery sites are marked by concrete posts. Guides and permits for visits are issued by the National Museum of Kenya. Research continues at Koobi Fora, as well as new sites on the west shore of the lake. Also at Siboloi is a vast forest of petrified cedar trees, testimony of a much wetter climate in former times. The wildlife at Siboloi includes oryx, gerenuk, zebra, and bluish-skinned Somali ostrich. Along the lakeshore a thin strip of green grass is grazed by zebra, topi, and hippo. Road access to Koobi Fora involves a rough track via North Horr. Because of the distance involved, most visitors prefer to organize a charter flight or boat trip from Loiyangalani. Simple *banda* accommodation is available at Koobi Fora; it should be booked in advance with the museum in Nairobi.

WEST TURKANA

The Turkana country on the west side of the lake cannot be reached by road from Loiyangalani. Would-be visitors must take the route via Lake Baringo, cross the Pokot country underneath the towering Cherangani Hills, and make the long drive to Lodwar, administrative center of the Turkana. From Lodwar, rough tracks lead to Turkana settlements on the lake, where naked fishermen set basket traps in reedy shallows and spear fish from palm log rafts. The desert behind the lake is flat country, without the dramatic relief of the eastern shore; the chief appeal is the Turkana themselves. Flights can be arranged to Ferguson's Gulf, where a small but modernized fishing industry has developed. A fishing lodge services sports anglers there. Boats may be hired for the trip to Central Island, the principal breeding grounds for Turkana's abundant crocodiles.

MARSABIT

Marsabit Mountain forms a gentle 5,000-foot-high island in the northern desert, about 90 miles east of Lake Turkana. Higher elevation accounts for richer grasslands on the mountain's flanks and a crown of highland mist forest that graces its uppermost heights. The volcanic origin of the mountain is much evidenced by numerous craters, locally called *gof,* that pock its slopes. Each crater has its own character, some being filled with grass and boulders, others dotted with ghostly forests of giant candelabra euphorbia. The best-known crater forms the bowl of Lake Paradise. Hidden in the topmost forest, this aptly named pool was made famous by Osa and Martin Johnson, the pioneer wildlife photographers and filmmakers of the 1920s.

The Marsabit National Reserve was once considered the home of Kenya's largest ivory-bearing elephants. Ahmed, the celebrated giant tusker who received presidential protection and constant armed escort until his death through natural causes, lived in Marsabit's forest, as have several successor "national monuments." Unfortunately, the mountain's once-abundant elephant population, and, wildlife in general, has decreased enormously in recent years. Poaching and settler encroachment, accelerated by the burgeoning growth of the town of Marsabit, have been responsible. Nonetheless, animals still inhabit the forest. Marsabit remains the best place in Kenya to see the magnificent greater kudu. They may be seen morning or evening coming to drink at Lake Paradise. Marsabit also offers excellent walking in open hill country, to visit the various scenic craters.

Marsabit's main attractions are now the surrounding deserts and the nomads who live there. With its better grazing and reliable wells, Marsabit is a magnet for the peoples of the eastern desert. Rendille patrol the country to the southwest, including the beautiful Kaisut Desert. While they may be encountered throughout that area, it is especially interesting to see them at Marsabit's Singing Wells. These are located on the track to Ulanula. The deep wells are hand dug: the singing takes place as a bucket brigade of Rendille men passes leather water bags up from the depths, an arduous cooperative task necessary to refresh their thirsty herds. The Boran, whose territory stretches to the north and east of Marsabit, can also be seen at singing wells around the base of the mountain. Gabbra territory extends as far as Marsabit, too. They can be seen watering their stock at wells near Maikona in the Chalbi Desert.

The Chalbi is the bed of an ancient lake, now dried into dazzling salt flats. Violent storms occasionally reclaim this wasteland, creating a shallow lake in the course of a few hours. But the ephemeral waters soon evaporate in the baking heat. The track from Lake Turkana to Marsabit crosses the Chalbi, passing through the small hamlet of North Horr. The glaring whiteness of the salt pans generates classic mirages in which shimmer the silhouettes of single-file Gabbra camel caravans. It is an otherworldly atmosphere. Because of the heat and the utter loneliness of the place, it is frightening to drive across the Chalbi in an unaccompanied vehicle.

Truly dauntless trekkers can elect to walk across, taking a route from North Horr to Loiyangalani. This trek, and possibly others, are informally arranged in the town of Marsabit. Ask around for a guide. Once word goes out on the grapevine of what you want to do, entrepreneurial nomads will present themselves as guides. Camels will carry the gear, but you must be prepared to walk, not ride. You must provide food for yourself and your guides, and your own equipment, especially water containers. Negotiate all details of cost and duration of the trip carefully with your guides before starting out. It is hard to get guides you can trust: they will not kill or abandon you on route, but they may play tricks such as pouring out your water in order to force you to walk faster. Once organized, you find a truck to North Horr and begin the trek. It takes three days to cover the 50 miles from North Horr to Loiyangalani. This is not a trip for the timid. Daytime temperatures are intense, even during the cool of the June–July "rainy" season. But for a true insight into the life of the desert nomads, such an adventure can't be beat.

To the south of Marsabit lies the Kaisut Desert, which is Rendille country. The scenery is dramatic, especially where there are views of the high desert mountains, but a section of the main road, from Marsabit to the crossroads at Laisamis, must be driven in dusty convoys escorted by Kenyan army vehicles—a measure to discourage *shifta* attacks. Some 70 miles south of Laisamis, you reach the Samburu National Reserve, back in more touristed country.

Additional adventures off the beaten track are to be found in the Ndoto and Mathews ranges, to the northwest of the Samburu National Reserve. These mountains beckon to people who seek isolation and encounters with both Rendille and Samburu nomads. Although they should really be explored in the company of skilled professional outfitters, hardy travelers occasionally organize their own camel treks directly with desert nomads. The hamlets of Baragoi (on the Maralal-South Horr road) and Barsaloi (on a major north country *lugga*) are the gateways to the Ndotos; Wamba is the jumping-off point for the Mathews Range (also called Ol Doinyo Lengeyo). The tented Kichich Camp has been established in a beautiful wooded Mathews Range valley that still harbors a few elephants and rhinos. These and other animals can be tracked on foot in the company of Game Department guards. Two campsites have also been designated along the small Nyeng River on the floor of the narrow Kichich Valley.

The Mountain Parks: Mount Kenya and the Aberdares

East Africa's high mountain forests and mist-shrouded moorlands are a world apart from the game country of the plains. Although Kenya has a number of ranges that reach above 10,000 feet in altitude—the Cherangani Hills (11,055 ft.), the Mau Escarpment (10,165 ft.), Mount Elgon (14,178 ft.)—the Aberdares and Mount Kenya are by far the most accessible. Located in the heart of central Kenya, only a short drive from Nairobi, these national parks are the best places to observe highlands wildlife.

Biologically, the mountain parks are islands of refuge, surrounded by a sea of grassland or cultivation. In past eras, when Africa's climate was generally cooler and wetter, the equatorial forest zone stretched right across the center of the continent. As climate changed, East African forest creatures retreated with their diminishing habitat. Rapid human increase in the last century spurred the process. As Kenya's highland forests were felled, animals common to lower elevations were banished to the mountain islands. Today, the mountain parks serve as reservoirs of specialized habitat, niches for some of the rarest animals.

The various highland habitats succeed each other as altitude rises. Lower slopes are covered with remnant forest of the sort that once clothed most of the noncultivated Kenyan highlands. This delightful forest consists of a variety of splendid trees, including African olive, camphor wood, crotons and pillar wood. Cape chestnuts are conspicuous when they produce masses of delicate pinkish blooms. Roadsides and forest clearings are crowded with shrubby thickets bright with the yellow flowers of *Crotalaria* and the orange tufts of *Leonotis*.

The lower forest, particularly where opened up into clearings, supports the most sizable numbers and variety of large animals. Waterbuck, bushbuck, black-fronted duiker, warthog, and Sykes' monkey are common, as are herds of buffalo and elephant. It is superb rhino habitat, and excellent for the stunning black-and-white colobus monkey (*Colobus guereza*) with its long particolored for coat. One very unusual forest dweller is the giant forest hog (*Hylochoeros meinertzhageni*). These hogs live mostly in groups, although boars, which weigh up to 500 pounds, may be solitary. Mainly a West African animal, this huge black pig is restricted in Kenya to high mountains. If glimpsed in flight, it can be distinguished from the warthog by the way it holds its tail: the warthog's tail always points upward on the run, the forest hog's hangs down.

Higher up in the mountains, tall stands of podocarpus and African cedar indicate the zone of montane forest. This in turn gives way to dense stands of giant bamboo. Above the bamboo, a misty transition zone of moss-draped hagenia trees (African rosewood) and yellow-flowered St. John's wort (*Hypericum*) merges into forests of tree heath. These 30-foot-high heathers (*Erica*) are only one of a number of plants that grow to giant proportions in Afro-alpine environments. The upper montane forest, bamboo, and transition zones are the habitat of one of Kenya's rarest, most reclusive, and spectacular antelopes. The bongo (*Tragelaphus euryceros*) has a bright reddish coat, boldly marked with tigerlike white stripes. Males have impressive horns, thick and mildly spiraled. A nocturnal browser, the bongo is restricted in Kenya to the Aberdares, Mount Kenya, and the Mau Escarpment. In western Africa, it is much more widespread, inhabiting rainforest and gallery forests throughout the equatorial forest zone. Because of its deep forest habitat and nocturnal habits, it is nowhere easy to see.

By roughly 11,000 feet, forest gives way to open moorlands. This zone has its own character, completely unexpected in an African environment. Alternately bathed in torrential rain, blanketed in cold mists, or broiled in the radiance of the equatorial sun, the moorlands change mood at the whim of the weather. Plants tolerate the stresses of nightly arctic cold and intense levels of ultraviolet radiation through adaptations that delight the botanist. Giantism is notable. Aside from the tree heaths, the 20-foot-tall spikes of groundsels (*Senecio*) and lobelias, which in other climes are no larger than houseplants, are bizarre testimony to the wonder of nature's imagination. Tussock grasses thrive on the boggy moorlands, and multitudes of "everlasting flowers," all varieties of the daisy-like composite genus *Helichrysum*, dress the moors with subtle color.

The animal life of the moorlands is not abundant, but interesting. Bush duiker (*Cephalophus grimmia*)—also called common or gray duiker—mountain reedbuck, and eland are among the larger residents. Small animals such as rock hyrax, porcupine and rodents remain mostly unseen but they are there. Buffalo and elephant migrate from the forest to the moors during the rains. Predators include wild dog, leopard, hyena, and occasional lions. Birdlife on the moorlands is not abounding, but is unusually tame. The scarlet-tufted malachite sunbird is as striking as its name. It feeds on the spikes of giant lobelias. The mountain chat is plainer, but as trusting as a house cat. The voice of Mackinder's eagle owl, a hunter with wild flame-orange eyes, is often heard on the moorlands. Augur buzzard and white-naped raven are far more often seen.

Above 14,500 feet, moorlands are supplanted by an alpine zone, a world of rock and ice. On Mount Kenya and Kilimanjaro, shrinking glaciers keep a tenuous hold against Africa's continuing warming trend. Although there has been much hoopla and speculation about the leopard found frozen on Kilimanjaro's rim (what was the big cat doing there, so far from its usual haunts?) the inhospitable alpine desert is not much frequented by animals. Glaciers and rock spires make it much more a paradise for the mountain climber or trekker than the naturalist.

THE FOREST LODGES

For a good look at the animal life of the mountain forest, the best bet is to visit one of the "tree hotels." Treetops and the Ark are located in the Salient section of the Aberdare National Park, while Mountain Lodge is on the southwest slopes of Mount Kenya. Game viewing takes place at the hotels, each of which overlooks a forest clearing where animals come to favored saltlicks and waterholes. Which animals show up on any particular night is purely a matter of luck. Generally the show is quite good, starting in the late afternoon and continuing under floodlights during the night. Elephant and buffalo are regular visitors. The big prizes are rhino, bongo, and very rarely, leopard.

Although some find the atmosphere too touristy, these hotels provide opportunities for great wildlife viewing. Aside from the possibility of seeing rare or nocturnal animals, the tree hotel concept encourages prolonged observation. You can't drive off in search of something new and more exciting if the only animal in view is an old buffalo. You are forced to watch the behavior of the various animals, and in so doing, you often observe interesting actions, or interactions, which you would ordinarily have missed. Elephants rule, chasing off buffalo and proceeding to the saltlick at their leisure. They kneel to mine the mineral-rich soil with their tusks. Rhino prefer to wait till all is quiet. They approach nervously, as befits animals hounded to the edge of extinction. Delicate bushbuck shyly probe the edges of the clearing, all senses finely tuned to the sounds and smells of the night. Hyena patrol the clearing, too. Hyena hunts, even kills, have taken place immediately in front of the lodges. At the Ark, an unfortunate rhino was killed by enraged elephants that thought the horned beast had threatened their calves. (It was an injustice: the real culprit was actually another rhino, who had prudently disappeared from the scene.) Although such dramatic events cannot be guaranteed, the wildlife viewing is generally excellent. Some species will probably be encountered nowhere else. These include the giant forest hog, and its cousin, the bushpig (*Potamochoerus porcus*). Bushpigs are common enough, even outside national parks. In fact, they are notorious agricultural pests, capable of destroying entire crop fields in a single night's feeding. Their bright reddish coloration, enhanced with bold black-and-white facial markings on the face of the boar, make them extremely attractive animals. Almost completely nocturnal, they are rarely seen on safari game drives. Other small animals appear under the floodlights: sightings of foraging white-tailed mongoose and genets are common. Genets become so tame that they often enter the lodges to be fed, much to the delight of guests. Birdlife is also excellent during the daylight hours. Unusual forest species—including turacos and boubou shrikes—are lured to well-placed feeders.

The three hotels are similar in operation and game-viewing opportunities. Rooms are tiny, with community bath facilities. Each hotel has a limited number of deluxe suites with private bath. (If you want a private bath and are booking on a tour from the United States, ask your tour operator to make a special request, at extra charge.) Guests at Treetops and the Ark must rendezvous at facilities outside the park. After lunch they are transferred on large buses to the game lodge. Hot drinks and snacks are available while guests wait on the various viewing platforms. Daylight game viewing is best in late afternoon when animals begin to arrive at the saltlicks.

Mornings are quieter, though bird activity is then at its peak. The night brings out the most unusual species, which are viewed under floodlights. Game spotters keep watch throughout the night: if any of the most notable species turn up, various systems alert guests who wish to be awakened. At the Ark, an electrical alarm sounds in guests' rooms: one ring for elephant, two for rhino, three for leopard or bongo. The alarm can be turned off at will.

Treetops is the original tree hotel, much celebrated for a visit by Princess Elizabeth. During her trip she learned of her father's death and her accession to the British crown. Because of its historic allure and colonial ambience, Treetops is still the most popular facility. As the oldest, its cabins are smallest and least comfortable. It also suffers somewhat in comparison through its location. When Treetops was built, it was placed just inside the national park boundary: the land outside the park was still virgin forest, alive with wild game. Sadly, by now the forest has been felled right to the park fence. Even though game viewing is still good, guests can see the nearby farms from the hotel, and hear the nighttime barking of *shamba* (farm) dogs. Occasionally, village cattle even visit the waterhole through holes in the park fence. Elephant, buffalo, and waterbuck are the most regular wild visitors. The rendezvous point is the colonial Outspan Hotel, former estate of Lord Baden-Powell, founder of the Boy Scouts.

The Ark is sited much deeper into the forest, at an altitude of 7,500 feet. This is appreciably higher into bongo habitat, so the striped antelopes are seen more frequently there. The bus ride up to the Ark is longer too, allowing a greater opportunity to spot such species as colobus and Sykes' monkeys, which are not seen at the waterhole. Leopard are more often seen on the approach ride than at the Ark itself. Unfortunately, the old schoolbuses used for transport are woefully inadequate for decent game viewing. Guests enter the Ark on an elevated boardwalk through the forest, guarded by a rifle-carrying "hunter." The hunter is a truly hokey touch, but the boardwalk is a boon to birders and dedicated game watchers. Stalk it quietly for sightings of bushpig and suni—a tiny forest antelope— and a wide variety of montane forest birds. Guests meet at the Aberdare Country Club for lunch before the ride up. There, you are encouraged to check all nonessential gear, taking only what you need for overnight. It saves time if you prepare a day pack or small bag in advance.

Mountain Lodge is the most modern and comfortable of the forest lodges. Hidden inside the forest of Mount Kenya, it has excellent game viewing and is the particular favorite of many birding groups. Guests may drive themselves to Mountain Lodge, unlike the other tree hotels, though tour groups rendezvous at the Thego Fishing Camp for lunch.

TOURING THE MOUNTAIN PARKS

Game drives are difficult in the mountain parks. Wet weather often renders park tracks impassable or treacherous, even for four-wheel-drive vehicles. Forest visibility is poor, a problem often compounded by thick cloud. Many of the interesting animals remain shy and nocturnal. Drives should be conducted very slowly, allowing plenty of time for scanning.

The Aberdares are well worth exploring by road. The lower Salient section of the park has plenty of resident game. Colobus and Sykes' monkeys are common, so it's good country to see the powerful crowned eagle that preys on them. Leopard are often sighted by careful observers. At twilight, brushy clearings may yield sightings of rhino and giant forest hog. Several tracks lead up narrow ridges into the upper montane forest, but it is necessary to make arrangements at park headquarters for a key to the locked barrier at the junction with the Eastern Ruhuruini Gate road, if you wish to continue onto the moorlands. The Salient is a favored area for luxury safari operators, who monopolize the handful of expensive special forest campsites. There are no public sites.

Moorland exploration in the Aberdares makes a terrific contrast to the rest of the Kenya experience. The approach from the east takes you up from high montane forest, through bamboo and the transition zone, into the moors. The Aberdares high country is an undulating plateau that rises to the rounded summits of Satima (13,123 ft.) and Kinangop (12,815 ft.). Nyandarua, the Kikuyu name for Kinangop, is now the official name of the entire mountain range and the park, but the colonial title, Aberdare, remains in much more common usage. The roads on the plateau are certainly a colonial legacy: they were built by the British army during their campaign against the Mau Mau who took refuge in the Aberdares. On the plateau, crystal streams plunge over scenic waterfalls. Most impressive is Karuru Falls, a 1,000-foot drop into an awesome basalt gorge. On sunny days, the snow-capped peaks of Mount Kenya can be seen to the east. Although the climate is distinctly temperate, the bizarre Afro-alpine vegetation and the animal life are uniquely African. Game is sparse but certainly present. Mountain reedbuck,

bushbuck, common bush duiker, and eland are the moorland antelopes. Buffalo, elephant, and lion are found up there, too. Moorland
lions are hungry specimens, unafraid of humans. Trout fishing and
trekking are touted activities, but take extreme care when you are
on foot. Several lion incidents have occurred, causing the moorlands
to be closed to camping. Cabin accommodation is still available at
the self-catering fishing lodge, which should be booked with the
Game Department in Nairobi (they also issue fishing licenses).

The moorlands are approached either from Naivasha, over the
fertile farmlands of the Kinangop Plateau, or via the town of Nyeri.
The road is often closed by heavy rain, so check conditions at the
Outspan Hotel in Nyeri or the Bell Inn in Naivasha before attempting the trip.

Mount Kenya is less suitable for vehicular exploration than the
Aberdares. Four tracks go up the mountain. None is really meant
for game drives, but they do provide access to the forest and the
high country beyond. They are mostly used by trekkers. The Naro
Moru and Chogoria tracks go only to the top of the forest. The
Sirimon and Timau tracks approach the north side of the mountain,
reaching high onto the moorlands.

Trekking Mount Kenya

The snow-covered peaks of Kirinyaga ("the mountain of the cock
ostrich") have traditionally been sacred to the Kikuyu and Meru
peoples of the Kenya highlands. Recently, an ill-clad Meru holy man
climbed to the summit pinnacle of icy Nelion to commune with his
god, Ngai. His was an extraordinary feat, as any mountaineer,
climbing for more profane reasons, will testify. Torrential rains, bitter nighttime cold, and rarified atmosphere are severe obstacles. The
challenge is worth the trouble, for Kirinyaga is a mountain of sur-
passing beauty. It captivates walkers, naturalists, and technical
climbers alike.

Although not as high as Kilimanjaro, Mount Kenya (17,058 ft.)
is in some respects a more interesting trekking area. Wildlife is more
abundant. The forest still supports elephant, rhino, herds of buffalo,
and the gamut of smaller woodland creatures. If you spend any time
in the forest, you are likely to see at least some of them. On the
moorlands, duiker and buffalo are regularly spotted, more rarely

elephant and leopard. The Mount Kenya rock hyrax, a sturdier, more furry model of the lowland variety, is a very common animal. Around huts and campsites, it has become very tame, even somewhat of a pest. The huts also harbor the African dormouse, a large-eyed nocturnal rodent. Stands of the strange giant groundsels are more prevalent on Mount Kenya's moorlands, where they thrive in marshy bogs. The high peaks are clustered in a small group, the granite-hard remnant of the ancient volcano's core. This peak zone is more easily circumnavigated than Kili's, allowing constant, splendid alpine views. The peaks are ringed with small glaciers. Retreating beneath a warming African sun, the glaciers have left numerous alpine tarns, small lakes dammed by glacial moraines. Glaciers, tarns, and steep-spired peaks are the stuff of alpine scenery.

As you trek through the forest, you must keep an eye out not merely for buffalo and elephant, but for the various spectral beings who are supposed to inhabit the mountain. Milihoi is a Kikuyu ogre with backwards-facing feet. He lures strangers into ambush, then nails them with his spiked palm and drinks their blood. Less threatening is Kivuluutu, the Laughing Devil—a pot-bellied little Kamba spirit who is quite naked save for his perpetually broad grin. Don't be alarmed if you see him—it's good luck!

ACCESS

The easiest access is from the towns of Nanyuki and Naro Moru, on the west side of the mountain. The Naro Moru River Lodge outfits hikers for a variety of trips. Permits and hut bookings can be obtained there; also porters and guides if you want them. You are free to roam Mount Kenya unescorted, but the altitude can make carrying a full pack an unpleasant chore. If you are considering any of the more exotic treks, think hard about your route-finding ability. Trails are cairned, but not always clear, and a guide might be nice to point the way. Transport to trailheads can also be a real problem because lodge vehicles and local taxis are relatively costly. The only other alternative to hitching may be walking, which will add another twelve and a half miles to your trek. If you want to avoid the same problem at trip's end, you should arrange with the lodge to be picked up there.

Naro Moru Lodge has both chalet and bunkhouse accommodation. A Youth Hostel is located near Naro Moru, about 4 miles toward the park gate. Closer to Nanyuki, accommodation can be found at Bantu Lodge, which recently began to organize treks on the Burguret and Sirimon routes.

Professionally guided treks on the Sirimon and Chogoria routes are operated by Tropical Ice of Nairobi.

LOGISTICS

If you are not participating on a catered trek, bring your own food from Nairobi. You'll need a gas stove, for wood is not available above the forest (where it is always wet) and burning groundsel is illegal. If you hire guides and porters, you should arrange for their transport to and from your trailhead. If you do a traverse, you can pay for their return on public vehicles.

There are a number of huts on the mountain, most of them clustered around the peaks area and along the Naro Moru route. The Meteorological Station cabins and Mackinder's Camp have bunk accommodations; Meru Mount Kenya Lodge offers comfortable two-person bandas (how water available). The Mountain Club huts are less comfortable: they provide narrow "bench" sleeping platforms. Refuse and rodents have become problems at the huts. All your garbage should be carried off the mountain. Trekkers on routes other than the Naro Moru should bring tents for use on the forest and moorlands approaches. Stony ground makes pitching tents difficult near the higher huts, but good campsites can be found lower down that are within striking distance of the peaks.

A ranger station is located at the head of the Teleki Valley on the Naro Moru route: rangers should be sought out in all emergencies.

Altitude sickness tends to occur more frequently on Mount Kenya than just about anywhere else. This is due to the fast access to the high country. It is possible to drive to 10,000 feet, commence hiking, and spend a first night at 13,700 feet, with a summit attempt the next day. That kind of ascent is guaranteed to make all but the fittest veteran mountaineers ill. Acute mountain sickness (AMS) syndrome—headache, nausea, insomnia—is very common among Mount Kenya trekkers. Cases of the more serious HAPE and HACE occur regularly. Plan a well-balanced approach for proper acclimatization, even if it takes an extra day or two. You will have a much better time.

Keep in mind that weather on the mountain is extremely unpredictable. Even in the dry seasons, storms can be expected: hail and snow are not infrequent on the moorlands. Generally, the south and western sides receive more rain than the north. Early mornings are often clear, with clouds building up to produce heavy rains in the afternoon.

Trekkers, and especially climbers, are well advised to obtain a copy of the Mountain Club of Kenya's *Guide to Mount Kenya and Kilimanjaro*, edited by Iain Allan (see the bibliography to this book). It contains a wealth of information in addition to detailed descriptions of all trekking and climbing routes. The best map of Mount Kenya is Andrew Wielochowski's (published by West Col in England—see bibliography). Also recommended is the Survey of Kenya 1:25,000 topo map of the moorlands and central peaks area.

TREKKING ROUTES

At 16,355 feet, Lenana is the highest of the summit peaks that can be reached by trekkers. There are many trek routes on the mountain. The following are the most important. The hours given for marches are estimates for fit walkers, without taking account of time for bird watching, botanizing, or photography. For descents, figure that you need at least half the time indicated for the ascent.

The Naro Moru Route. The Naro Moru route is the most popular, and the easiest logistically. It's 10 miles from the town of Naro Moru to the park gate; another 6 from the gate to the roadhead near the meteorological station at 10,000 feet. Most people drive, even though the walk through the lower forest is lovely, and good for proper acclimatization to altitude. If you walk, you must be alert for buffalo grazing along the track. Elephants can be there too, though you are more likely to encounter baboons, colobus monkeys, and hornbills. Animal watching is rewarding around the Meteorological Station, where bushbuck, black-fronted duiker, and Sykes' monkeys have become used to harmless tourists. The Meteorological Station cabins are pretty comfortable. Alternatively, you can camp.

From the Meteorological Station, the trail climbs through a magical moss-draped transition forest of hagenia and tree heath. Watch for the brilliant red blossoms of wild gladiola (*Gladiolus watsonioides*). The forest thins out as the trail disintegrates into a slalom path of mudholes through the infamous "Vertical Bog," where mounds of tussock grass emerge from waterlogged ground. Some trekkers leap from one tussock island to the next. If they miss, they are calf-deep in the muck. You may choose just to plow through. Either way, your feet will get wet, so it's best to wear running shoes, keep a change of socks handy, and save your mountain boots for the rocky summit walking ahead. After the bog, you mount a ridge

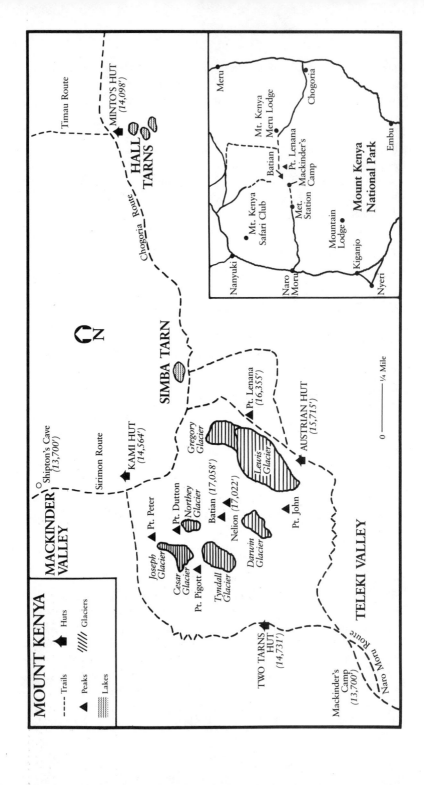

from which you get your first views of the Teleki Valley and, when clear, the mountain peaks. It is then easier going up the Teleki Valley, which is adorned with giant groundsels, lobelias, and everlasting flowers. In the upper valley is Mackinder's Camp at 13,700 feet: formerly double-layered canvas tents, it is now a large brick lodge. Operated by the Naro Moru Lodge, meals are catered only for guests. The Ranger Station is located a little further up the valley.

It's a three- to four-hour walk up to Austria Hut (15,715 ft.), on the eastern edge of the Lewis Glacier. Although it is less than a 1,000-foot elevation gain and a half a mile to the top, the ascent to Point Lenana (16,355 ft.) requires at least another hour. In the rarified air, it is hard walking. Nights are bitterly cold at Austria Hut, which is primarily a base for technical climbers.* Most trekkers set out from the Teleki Valley in the wee hours, hoping to attain the summit before cloud buildup obscures the views. They then descend to the huts in the Teleki Valley for the night.

It's best to plan a minimum of three days walking for the return trip from the Meteorological Station.

The Peaks Circuit. Using the Naro Moru access route, you can circumnavigate the peaks area, instead of hiking directly up Lenana. The circuit requires a lot more hard walking at high altitude and at least one additional night on the mountain. You will be rewarded with brilliant mountain scenery as you hike right around the alpine massif, circling the twin summits of Batian (17,058 ft.) and Nelion (17,022 ft.) before ascending Lenana on the return loop.

From the Teleki Valley, you climb the scree slopes behind the Ranger Station on a poorly marked path to Two Tarn Hut (14,731 ft.), a march of about two hours. If strong, you should be able to go on to Kami Hut (14,564 ft.) on the north side of the mountain, which takes another three or four hours. Keep in mind that two passes, Arthur's Seat and Hausburg Col, both in excess of 15,000 feet, must be crossed. From Kami Hut to Point Lenana it's a hard five-hour walk. You skirt to the east of the Gregory Glacier before climbing the scree (some easy rock scrambling is needed) to the summit. Do not try to cross the Gregory and Lewis glaciers unless you have the right mountaineering equipment and skills. If you don't wish to ascend Lenana directly, you can follow the porter route around via Simba Col to Austria Hut, which would also take

---

*Top Hut, just next door to Austria Hut, is reserved exclusively for members of the Mountain Club of Kenya. It is in very poor condition.

about five hours. From Lenana you rejoin the main Naro Moru trek route for the descent.

The Sirimon Route. The excellent Sirimon route approaches the mountain from its less frequented northwest side. It offers the scenic bonus of a traverse, for you can exit via the Naro Moru route. The Sirimon is logistically more difficult to arrange than the Naro Moru route. Although you can plan on staying at Mountain Club huts, you are better advised to bring a tent. Bantu Lodge is currently constructing bunkhouses at the top of the Sirimon track (Judmeier Camp) and at the head of the Mackinder Valley (Shipton's Camp); these will probably be reserved for the exclusive use of their own trekking parties.

The trailhead is approached where the Sirimon track turns off the main Nanyuki-Timau road on the north side of the mountain. It is about 6 miles from the junction to the park gate. The track continues on much further, snaking up through forest to about 13,000 feet on the moorlands. For acclimatization, it is advisable to make your first camp and start walking well below road's end. Camp can be made in the forest beyond the park gate, at about 8,000 feet.

The forest on the mountain's drier northern slopes is different from that of the western Naro Moru side: tall cedar and podocarpus trees thin out directly into moorland scrub, without a bamboo or hagenia zone. In places (notably along the Timau track), the forest is largely absent. Instead, acacia-grasslands reach high up onto the mountain, allowing access to plains animals. It is not uncommon to see zebra in the forest glades along the Sirimon track, and lions may be seen or heard in the forest camps.

Above the forest, a good campsite is located where a stream crosses the track at about 11,000 feet. From there, it is roughly a four-hour walk to the Liki North Hut (13,100 ft.). The distance can be cut if you drive further up the track, beyond the 12,000-foot marker, to start walking at the actual trailhead. The trail cuts southwestward, mounting a ridge separating the Sirimon Valley from the Liki North Valley. Aside from the planned Bantu Lodge bunkhouses, Liki North is the only hut on the northern moorlands, so you must plan to stop there if you do not bring a tent. It takes another three or four hours to reach the head of the Mackinder Valley, where there are good campsites. The landmark Shipton's Cave (13,700 ft.) lies near the valley's head, and from there it is a further one and a half to two hours to Kami Hut (14,564 ft.). If you camp in the upper Mackinder Valley above Shipton's Cave, it is a three-hour climb directly to Point Lenana. From either Kami Hut or the Mackinder Valley campsites, porters can take your gear around the mountain via Two Tarn Hut while you climb Lenana. Then, rendez-vous at one of the huts in the upper Teleki Valley.

You should count on four days of walking from a Sirimon forest camp to the meteorological station.

The Chogoria Route. Once the most popular route on the mountain, the eastern Chogoria approach is very seldom used today due to the extra difficulty of arranging transport and porters. Although parts of the magnificent camphor and bamboo forest on its lower slopes have been damaged by logging, the beautiful glades of the upper forest are intact and the moorland scenery on the east side is probably the mountain's best. The Hall Tarns area is particularly noteworthy. An east–west traverse from Chogoria to Naro Moru is a highly recommended trek.

Without transport, the trek begins with a 10-mile walk from the Chogoria Forest Station (where you can camp) through heavily logged forest to a campsite at Bairunyi Clearing (8,858 ft.). From there, it is about another 4 miles to the new Chogoria Lodge (9,898 ft.), which offers good banda accommodation for self-catering par-ties. (Also called Meru Mount Kenya Lodge, it is reserved through Let's Go Travel in Nairobi.) With a four-wheel-drive vehicle, you can motor all the way to the lodge. The glades of hagenia forest that stretch between the new lodge and the site of the old (and nearly ruined) Urumandi Hut (10,050 ft.) harbor quite a bit of wild-life: elephant, buffalo, bushbuck, and duiker can all be seen in the area.

Six hours of moorland walking brings you to Hall Tarns Hut, which is also called Minto's Hut (14,098 ft.). Hall Tarns, a cluster of small mountain lakes surrounded by tall stands of giant ground-sels, is one of the most scenic spots on the mountain. In clear weath-er it has magnificent westward views of the peaks. Nearby is a group of rocky outcrops called The Temple, which dramatically overlooks Lake Michaelson and the head of the deep Nithi Gorge. A walk of another three and a half to four hours is needed to go to either Austrian or Kami huts. Strong hikers can climb Lenana di-rectly from the east side and continue on to the Teleki Valley the same day.

A minimum of four days should be planned to cover the distance from Bairunyi campsite to the meteorological station. If you drive to Chogoria Lodge, it is probably a good idea to spend two nights there to acclimatize properly before going on to Hall Tarns. You could enjoy a very good day of moorland hiking, up to Lake Ellis and Mugi Hill (about 11,600 ft.), returning to the lodge for the night. Porters can be hired in Chogoria (for advance arrangements write to Mount Kenya Traversers at P.O. Box 83 Chogoria; telephone Meru 20781). Because of the problems and expense of getting porters and vehicles around the mountain, you might find it more practical to retrace your steps back to Chogoria rather than do a complete traverse. Strong hikers can reach Lenana and descend all the way to Chogoria Lodge in one long day. Others should plan on an additional night at Hall Tarns after the summit ascent.

TECHNICAL CLIMBING

There are many challenging climbing routes on Batian and Nelion. All require a high level of technical skill for both rock and ice climbing. The level of difficulty is compounded by high altitude and the extreme unpredictability of the weather. Plan for a two-day climb, with an overnight bivouac, on any technical summit route. Although clothing can be rented from Naro Moru Lodge, it's best to bring your own hardware, including ropes, ice axe, crampons, and other climbing items. Tropical Ice can be contacted to charter guided climbs; so can Mount Kenya and East Africa Guides in Nairobi. Details of all climbing routes are well described in the Mountain Club's guidebook.

MOUNTAIN RESORTS

Scenic beauty and balmy climate make the environs of Mount Kenya and the Aberdares an ideal locale for resort hotels. These country club retreats provide activities such as golf, tennis, and horseback riding in an atmosphere of genteel luxury. Although the typical leisure activities can be spiced with bird watching on estate grounds or game viewing on nearby private ranches, the resorts are designed more with a view to afford a relaxing break from safari routine. The grande dame of highland resorts is the Mount Kenya Safari Club, which has been a magnet for visitors since its founding by film star William Holden. Its colonial ambience, sumptuous cuisine, and superb setting against the forested slopes of the great mountain have kept this very expensive hotel a popular destination. It is located 5 miles from the town of Nanyuki. Nearby, a deluxe rival, the Secret Valley Safari Club, is supposed to be open soon, and plans are being made to open a variety of smaller lodges on private estates in the Nanyuki area. (The tented Sweetwaters Camp has already opened, with much fanfare.) The Aberdare Country Club, gateway to the Ark, is trying to broaden its appeal as an overnight destination by offering easy walking safaris in an adjacent private reserve stocked with unaggressive types of animals. Larger game (such as elephants) may be encountered on foot or horseback safaris at Lewa Downs, a cattle ranch located in the dry acacia country just to the north of Mount Kenya.

Amboseli National Park

Anyone who has seen the archetypal safari photo—an elephant backdropped by the white dome of Kilimanjaro—is already familiar with Amboseli National Park. Indeed, the reserve is renowned as much for splendid views of Africa's highest peak as for abundant wildlife. Neither disappoints the thousands who flock to Amboseli each year. Almost every visitor goes home with a rendition of the classic Kili shot that epitomizes the safari experience.

If Amboseli has a fault, it is only that so many come to admire it. The reserve is small, yet for its size hosts a greater volume of visitors annually than any other African park. As a consequence, fleets of minibuses throw up clouds of dust as they roam in search of wildlife, and game finding is often reduced to a jostle for position to photograph sleeping lions. The lodges are full, the tourists are happy. But what of the animals?

It is hard to calculate the effect of mass tourism on Amboseli's wildlife. Researchers have been studying and commenting on the question for years. Neither elephant, lion, giraffe, nor any other species seems to have declined in number as a result of overtourism, although some fear that vehicles threaten the long-range survival of the cheetah by obstructing its hunting. Yet cheetah seem to thrive, as often using vehicles for cover in stalking as having the approach ruined by thoughtless drivers. Rhino have decreased, but tourist volume can't be blamed: that was a result of Masai anger at promises broken by the Kenya government, and of the general mayhem of commercial poaching. Damage to grasslands through the continuous pounding of safari vehicles is another hot issue. Rules restricting vehicles to game tracks are often breached: telltale tire tracks are all over the park. But Amboseli's tough grasses revive with every rainy season. While the jury is still out on the seriousness of tourism's negative impact on habitat, there is no doubt that it adversely effects the esthetics of the safari experience. More than one visitor has left Amboseli disgusted by the traffic and dust.

"How can such enormous numbers of large game live in this extraordinary desert?" This question, originally posed by the explorer Joseph Thomson when he first described Amboseli, is often echoed by modern visitors. For at the height of the dry season, when the land is a desolate dustbowl, Amboseli teems with wild animals.

The answer lies with Kilimanjaro; the great mountain that dominates the park's skyline provides not only magical scenery but also life-giving water. Rain falling high on Kili's flanks seeps underground, eventually emerging in a series of springs. These feed Amboseli's permanent swamps, which attract animals from all over southeastern Masailand. Kilimanjaro is also responsible for the dustbowl atmosphere, because it laid down the light volcanic soils of the Amboseli basin. Pulverized by the passing of thousands of hoofed feet (and now by tires), clouds of chalky gray dust pursue both vehicles and herds across the plains.

Amboseli's core is a geologic basin, seasonally inundated by rainwater. The shallow bed of Lake Amboseli takes up a third of the park. Only during prolonged wet seasons does it actually hold water; ordinarily, the broad lakebed is a dusty sea sprinkled with spindly yellow grass—a spawning place of mirages. During the rains, many of Amboseli's animals migrate out of the park. Moving onto Masai group ranches to the north and east, they range as far as the Chyulu Hills. As the surrounding bush country dries out, the game returns to the plains and concentrates around the permanent swamps near Ol Tukai. The swamps are real oases on the dusty plain, their brilliant green makes an almost violent contrast to the gray ground, worn bare by the passing of animals and machines. Enkongo Narok Swamp is particularly striking. It is bordered by beautiful stands of yellow-barked fever trees. Where they have been killed by changes in the water table, and torn by elephants, the white skeletons of standing trees add a ghostly dimension to Amboseli's schizophrenic landscape. To the north of the swamps, the plains around Ol Tukai are covered with seasonal marshes. These are the principal feeding grounds for the thousands of zebra, wildebeest, and gazelle that crowd Amboseli in the dry season.

Amboseli was formerly much larger than it is today. It was part of a 1,259-square-mile reserve, shared by both wildlife and Masai. Although the cattle herders readily tolerated the animals, dry-season competition increased for the water and grazing of Ol Tukai's swamps. After much resistance, a compromise was worked out creating the present National Park of 150 square miles. The Masai were excluded from the swamps, the animals' critical dry-season range. In exchange, water was to be piped to areas outside the park boundary and the government undertook to provide more community services. Unfortunately, the construction of the pipeline was botched, and when the promised water was not delivered, a number of rhinos were speared in protest. As a result, the Masai were again allowed to water their herds in the park. Efforts have since been made to develop greater cooperation and communication between the authorities and local people, and projects to help the Masai benefit economically from Amboseli have been encouraged. With the completion of a new water project, it is hoped that the Masai will eventually remove their cattle from the park. Yet the solution of the water problem may not prove so straightforward, and the game must continue to migrate onto Masai land during the rains. The complex issue of land use for the benefit of both people and wild animals will be ongoing—a situation that must be monitored carefully and will require a pragmatic attitude to adapt to ever-changing environmental conditions. There is no doubt that Masai interests must be taken into account: as the rhino-spearing incidents proved, the survival of the animals is largely in their hands.

ACCESS AND ACCOMMODATION

From Nairobi, it takes about four hours to drive to Amboseli via Namanga. The road is paved to Namanga, at the Tanzanian border. Beyond, there is only a corrugated track through Masai country, and visitors must eat a lot of dust before stately Mount Kilimanjaro comes into view. The road then skirts the northern edge of the dry Amboseli lake. The acacia thorn woodlands on the approach to the National Park harbor interesting wildlife: gerenuk, fringe-eared oryx, Grant's gazelle, and giraffe are common residents.

Amboseli can also be reached by air: it is served daily by a scheduled morning flight from Nairobi, and charter aircraft are constantly coming in (often full of day trippers from the coast).

Amboseli Serena Lodge is sited at the edge of the lava springs on the south end of Enkongo Narok Swamp. Animals, including rhinos, often visit the pond in front of the verandah. Several lodges are set among impressive groves of fever trees around the Ol Tukai park headquarters and village. Amboseli Lodge and the more basic Kilimanjaro Safari Lodge both feature comfortable chalets and excellent mountain views. Ol Tukai Lodge has self-service *bandas*. Two other lodges are located outside the park, some distance from the main Ol Tukai area: the luxurious Kilimanjaro Buffalo Lodge on the road to Tsavo, and Kimana Safari Lodge on the northeastern Emali-Loitokitok road. Amboseli's campsites are all located beyond the park boundary on Masai group ranches: the government helped set them up so that local people could earn more income from visitors. The public campsites are not far from Serena Lodge, on the edge of Enkongo Narok Swamp. The Masai also lease special campsites to safari tour operators.

TOURING THE PARK

Kilimanjaro (19,340 ft.) looms above the Amboseli plains, which lie at an average elevation of only 3,700 feet. But, the mountain's twin peaks—the snow-crowned Kibo and rocky Mawenzi—tend to hide themselves behind a curtain of cloud. Early morning is the time for the clearest views and best photographs. Generally, by 10 A.M. the mountain is veiled; only its massive base can be seen. At sunset, the clouds usually drop, revealing the summit in twilight grandeur.

The main game-viewing tracks circle the permanent swamps. Amboseli's few remaining rhinos haunt the swamps, and groups of elephant go there daily to drink, bathe, and apply a new layer of gray Amboseli dust. On the Enkongo Narok Swamp circuit, you view a wonderful medley of Amboseli images. Ravaged woodlands, strewn with the skeletal litter of fever trees, rim the perimeter of reed-choked marshes. Buffalo wallow in the muck, while hippo grunts issue from hidden pools. A strand of emerald grass borders the long, narrow swamp as it drains toward Lake Amboseli. At midway, a causeway crosses the marsh, giving access to Observation Hill. Walk to the top for a good overview of the park. To the south, woodlands stretch off toward Kilimanjaro, excellent country for elephant and giraffe.

The Logenya Swamp, crowded with papyrus, is just to the east of Ol Tukai. It's a good place to watch a day-long parade of thirsty animals making their way to water. Zebra and wildebeest wade knee-deep into the swamp to drink, before wandering back to feed on the dusty flats. Flocks of white cattle egrets trail massive black buffaloes through the marshes, snapping up insects disturbed by the animals' progress.

It is worth seeking out fringe-eared oryx and gerenuk, especially if you will not be visiting the Samburu National Reserve. Gerenuk are common in the dry acacia country in the northern part of the park. Fringe-eared oryx are more evident in open grassy areas. These specimens are browner than the Beisa oryx of northern Kenya, and are distinguished by black tufts on the ends of their ears.

Amboseli's elephants are a noteworthy park specialty. They have been the subjects of years of study: much has been learned from them about elephant social structure and their ability to communicate over long distances by using super-low-frequency sounds. After so much observation by researchers and tourists, they are quite tame and allow extraordinarily close viewing. In contrast to so many other parks, Amboseli's elephant herds have been relatively free of poaching: it is one of the few places where you can still find really big tuskers.

The combination of swamp and dry-land habitats makes Amboseli an extremely rich birding area. Madagascar squacco heron are seen in the reeds, long-toed lapwings on the short-grass littoral of swamps. Around the lodges, busy colonies of brightly colored Taveta golden weavers cannot escape notice.

Ranger guides can be picked up at the Ol Tukai office. They are not really needed to find the way around this very compact park, but they know best where lion, cheetah, and rhino were most recently sighted.

The Tsavo National Parks

At 8,034 square miles in the area, the two Tsavo parks constitute Kenya's biggest protected game areas, and one of the largest reserves in Africa. History has made it one of the most famous.

Tsavo first gained notoriety because of the man-eating lions that plagued workers on the Uganda railroad in the 1890s. During World War I, it was the scene of savage fighting as German raiders from Tanganyika repeatedly attacked the Mombasa-Nairobi railway line. After the war, the Tsavo country was much favored by ivory hunters—among them Denys Finch-Hatton and Baron Bror von Blixen—so it found plenty of mention in safari literature. In 1947, it was declared a national park. The boundaries were drawn to include an enormous expanse of wild bush territory, almost all of which receives less than 20 inches of rain per year. Too dry for agriculture and infested with tsetse, Tsavo was made a permanent refuge for wild animals because it was deemed unsuitable for any other use—a familiar rationale for the creation of game reserves. The legendary warden David Sheldrick set about turning a wilderness into a park. Suppressing poachers was a major priority, for Tsavo was the hunting grounds of the Waliangulu and Kamba tribes, who employed poison arrows against elephants with deadly effect. It was a difficult undertaking: the area was vast, park rangers few, and roads nonexistent. Gradually, patrol tracks were built and native hunters excluded from the park.

As the struggle against poaching achieved results, Tsavo's elephant population began to rise. Large numbers moved into the park from the surrounding country where they were under pressure from big game hunters, poachers, and increased human settlement. The immigrants began to wreak havoc on Tsavo's woodlands. These woodlands—a mixed forest of commiphora, baobab, acacia, delonix, and other dry-country trees—were then the characteristic vegetation of the park. By the 1960s, when Tsavo was just beginning to receive a constant flow of international visitors, the woodlands, especially in Tsavo East, had suffered heavy damage from an estimated 36,000 elephants. Calls to reduce the herds in order to save the woodlands ignited the Great Elephant Controversy. Scientists, conservationists, and park wardens lined up against each other in an emotional fight over "culling" as a tool of game management. In the end, Warden Sheldrick won out: no culling took place. The elephants were spared a mass kill-off by official decree only to die by the thousands during the terrible drought of 1970–1971. Although 6,000 elephants starved to death, steady immigration from outside the park rapidly replaced the losses. At drought's end, the woodlands were badly damaged, but the number of elephants had not declined at all. Further famine would surely have followed if not for the tidal wave of poaching that began in the late 1970s. That unprecedented slaughter has reduced Tsavo's elephants to their current population of about 5,000 animals.

Even with such trimmed numbers, Tsavo is still a good place to see elephants, which remain the park's specialty.* Tsavo elephants are typically "red" in color, a result of dust bathing in the lateritic soils that predominate throughout the region. A good selection of other animals is also found, although not in the concentrations of the Masai Mara. The woodlands and bush tracts, in various stages of demolition or recovery, are the habitat for giraffe, dikdik, impala, and an extraordinary collection of brilliantly feathered birds. Buf-

---

*Poaching could soon change that, however: as Tsavo's elephants continue to suffer heavy losses. The jittery survivors are showing less inclination to stick around when approached by vehicles.

falo weavers, yellow-billed hornbills, golden-breasted starlings, and orange-bellied parrots are only a few of many startling woodland species. Open country supports zebra, hartebeest, fringe-eared oryx, and gazelle. All the carnivores are present, including striped hyena. One odd animal to keep look out for is the savanna monitor. This formidable lizard, darker and more heavy-set than the aquatic Nile monitor, prowls Tsavo's bushed grasslands in search of small animal prey.

Tsavo has a deserved reputation for rugged beauty. So immense a region necessarily has many faces. Where majestic mountains breach the plain, scenery is overtly grand. In other parts, Tsavo's charms are more subtle. Vast tracts in Tsavo East have been reduced to desolations of broken trees, where gray snags stand forlorn among resurgent bush and the vertical shafts of termite mounds. Such landscapes possess a quality of resurrection, in which the cycles of life and death are visibly entwined. Where mighty baobabs have survived the elephant onslaught, their swollen trunks are fanciful monuments to nature's imagination. No less whimsical are the red turrets of termite mounds, dotted castlelike over the bushland domain. The country's mood changes considerably with the seasons. During the rains, the green of rejuvenated bush complements Tsavo's red earth in a palette of vibrant color. Tones are more subtle in the dry season, but equally well composed. Then, the red ground blends autumnally with the peeling yellow bark of commiphora trees in the leafless *nyika* scrub. At any season, Tsavo's mountains and rock outcrops permit panoramic views of a seemingly limitless wilderness. This is partly illusion, for the park is no longer entirely wild. Roads, pipelines, and powerlines cut disfiguring swathes through the bush. Yet Tsavo's vastness swallows them all. Sheer size preserves its wilderness integrity.

The future of the Tsavo wilderness is uncertain. However, with the decline in elephant numbers, Tsavo's battered woodlands should recover, and it is only to be hoped that the merciless ivory war against the elephants will abate. Assuming that poaching can be controlled, it is projected that the elephant population would stabilize at about five thousand animals—a number well within the carrying capacity of the land. But Tsavo faces another serious threat. As Kenya's human population swells, there are sure to be demands to reduce the size of the park. Already large areas are being illegally used to graze cattle. It is likely that some parts will ultimately be excised: one day there may be a smaller Tsavo. It will be a tamer place.

ACCESS

Tsavo is divided into two separately administered parks, bisected by the Nairobi-Mombasa highway. Tsavo West is about a four-hour drive from Nairobi; two from nearby Amboseli. Tsavo East is only three hours from Mombasa. A rough dirt road links Tsavo East's Sala Gate directly with Malindi.

TOURING THE TSAVO PARKS

Tsavo is too large to be explored comprehensively without a very extended visit. A good sampling can be had by taking in the scenic Kilaguni area of Tsavo West, then scouting the valleys north of Ngulia Mountain, before following the Tsavo River to the gate on the Nairobi-Mombasa highway. The Galana River drive, with a southward loop through rejuvenating woodland scrub to the dams on the seasonal Voi River, produces the best game viewing in Tsavo East. It will also give you a taste of the immense, though rather flat and featureless, bush country predominating in the northeastern reaches of the park. This trip requires a minimum stay of at least one full day in each park.

On group tours, your Tsavo explorations may well be limited to the area in which you stay. Since all lodges and campsites have good game-viewing circuits nearby, there really is no need to charge all over the country. Game is varied and present in good numbers, though Tsavo's size allows the animals to spread out and game viewing is spotty. Long-distance drives may reveal little in the way of big game, until everything is suddenly encountered in one favored locality. During dry seasons, animals naturally tend to congregate around the permanent rivers and other water points.

Much of Tsavo is bush country, which is a further inhibitor to easy game viewing. Even Tsavo's "red" elephants are not always obvious. False alarms are common: at a distance a red termite mound is easily mistaken for an elephant, while real animals may be passed by unnoticed. The best strategy is to go slowly and expect to make some embarrassing misidentifications.

Because of their proximity to the beachside resorts of the coast, the Tsavo parks receive large numbers of tourists. Most come for only the briefest excursions. Somehow, aside from a few collection points around Mzima Springs and Voi Lodge, the parks do not seem crowded. One can always get off the beaten track and explore in solitude.

Tsavo's game tracks are well signposted with numbers that correspond to the official park maps. You'll appreciate that concession to civilization if you are on your own. You will never feel that you are in territory where you would like to be lost. This is true as much if you are driving through an interminable stretch of encapsulating scrub, or surveying the country from atop a high outcrop, with all Africa spread at your feet.

TSAVO WEST

Tsavo West has the most dramatic scenery, particularly in its northern section where impressive mountain ranges are prominent. In the Kilaguni area, the rounded cones of the Chyulu Hills and the rocky eminence of Ngulia Mountain are both close at hand, while Kilimanjaro, 50 miles distant, is visible in clear weather. Interesting geological features add spice to game viewing, so it is no surprise that this scenic country is the most heavily visited part of the park.

The Chyulu Hills are a 30-mile-long chain of relatively young volcanos. Reaching up to 7,000 feet in altitude, they form the northwest skyline of the Kilaguni region. Podocarpus forests on their misty summits are an important water catchment area, the source of Mzima Springs. A track climbs into the Chyulus, making a short loop that affords spectacular views of both Tsavo and Kilimanjaro. A longer four-wheel-drive track runs the length of the hills. Only their southernmost end is within Tsavo Park; the western slopes belong to Masai group ranches, and the eastern side has recently been gazetted as the new Chyulu National Park. The summit track is steep and can be dangerous in misty rain, but makes an interesting alternative route to Tsavo from Amboseli. It begins at Makutano, on Amboseli's northeast boundary.

Volcanic cones and lava flows dot the Kilaguni region, extensions of the eruptions that created the Chyulu Hills. The southernmost of the Chyulu chain is the black cone of Shaitani (the Devil) Volcano. You can climb Shaitani's crumbling lava slopes to view its crater. Nearby, an interesting nature trail leads through an underground lava tube. The walk is easy, but not for the timid: you pass the skeletons of animals that wandered into the cave to die, while roosting bats flit overhead, and weird insects scurry away from your torch's beam. The main Amboseli-Tsavo road crosses an extensive lava field laid down by Shaitani. Bare black rock, hardly colonized by plant life, indicates that the flow occurred within the last 200 years. Also near Kilaguni, the Chaimu Crater can be explored by foot on a marked trail.

Some of Tsavo West's best game tracks wind through the hills and valleys to the north of Ngulia Mountain (5,974 ft.) and its sister, Kichwa Tembo Peak. They stand sentinel above the tangled bush country along the middle Tsavo River. Their rocky outcrops are the best places to spot klipspringer (*Oreotragus oreotragus*), a dainty goatlike antelope. Look for them atop high boulders, silhouetted against the evening sky. Leopard are also common on the Ngulia massif. The gap between the two high peaks is ornithologically interesting: on migration, Palearctic birds are funneled through by the thousands. Many are netted, studied, and catalogued before being released to continue their journey.

Mzima Springs is one of the most famous sites in the park. Their waters come from the Chyulu Hills; heavy rains sink into their porous soils, to flow underground until they emerge at Mzima. The springs form a series of clear aqua-blue pools set within a luxuriant oasis of wild date and raffia palms. An underwater observatory allows visitors a chance to watch hippos and crocodiles in their true element. Although both creatures inhabit the pools, you will be lucky to catch a glimpse of them through the observatory's submerged glass windows; they rarely approach closely when visitors are around. You are sure to see lots of fish, however. These are mostly whiskered barbel, which feed on the manure abundantly deposited by hippos in the otherwise crystal water. The observatory offers a unique perspective, even if you don't get to see hippos walking on the bottom, as gracefully displayed in Alan Root's acclaimed underwater film, *Mzima, Portrait of a Spring*.

The Tsavo River is the main dry-season water source for animals in the northern part of the park. It rises along the western boundary, then picks up strength from Mzima's overflow, before passing through the thick bush country beneath the heights of Ngulia Mountain. Vegetation thins out to the east, where the stream is fringed by doum palms, tamarinds, and acacias as it flows through open semidesert country. Rock forts and gun emplacements dot prominent knolls along the river, reminders of First World War battles. Participants on foot safaris often uncover souvenirs of the fighting. Where the river meets the Mombasa road, it flows through Tsavo's man-eater country. It was here that a pair of hungry male lions acquired an appetite for railway construction laborers. Their depredations brought a halt to work on the "strategic" Uganda railroad, which was being built to protect British control of the sources of the Nile. After having caused a stir in Parliament, the lions were ultimately shot by Col. J. H. Patterson, who wrote a book about the epic hunt. The man-eaters—stuffed—are now on display at the Field Museum in Chicago, but their descendants are still frequently encountered on rock outcrops along the Tsavo.

To the south of the river, a large tract of flat country is called the Serengeti Plains. Wild animals are much less numerous here than in Tanzania's park of the same name, but game viewing can be quite good. This bush-flecked grassland is inhabited by herds of zebra, oryx, buffalo and eland, as well as Tsavo's ubiquitous elephants. Animals from the area tend to congregate around Lake Jipe in the dry season. Located on the Tanzanian border, Jipe has a beautiful setting: across the lake rise the 6,000-foot-high North Pare Mountains, while the summit of Kilimanjaro, some 40 miles to the northwest, is spectacular in the clear light of dawn. A belt of acacia woods behind the lakeshore harbors dry-season throngs of zebra, kongoni, and impala. They daily risk ambush by lions when they drink from swampy pools at the southern end of the lake. The lake itself is fringed with dense reedbeds. Birding is noteworthy at Jipe, where rafts of migrant waterfowl join resident storks, herons, geese, and ducks. The unusual black heron—also called the "umbrella bird" because of its unique habit of covering its head with its wings while hunting—is a Jipe specialty. The National Park keeps a boat on hand at Jipe for aquatic expeditions. The charge is reasonable, but the motor is not always working.

Accommodation. Two luxury lodges are located in the scenic country to the north of the Tsavo River. Kilaguni Lodge is particularly noted for its spectacular location. Its terrace overlooks a well-visited waterhole backdropped by the green Chyulu Hills and distant Kilimanjaro. Wildlife viewing is continual as a succession of animals come to slake their thirst: the arrival of hundreds-strong buffalo herds or family groups of elephants are not unusual, and groups of zebra, oryx, giraffe, impala, and baboons are in constant attendance. The waterhole is floodlit for nighttime viewing. Birdlife is no less interesting as hornbills, weavers, and swifts swarm to the food and nesting sites offered by the open-air verandah. Ngulia Lodge is located high on the northern slopes of Tembo Peak. Its vista does not include Kilimanjaro, but its waterhole is much closer to the lodge than Kilaguni's, allowing superior photographic opportunities and animal observations. Leopard are frequent nighttime visitors to Ngulia's floodlit waterhole. A third hotel, the Lake Jipe Safari Lodge, has just opened in the southern section of the park.

Public campsites are located near the various park gates. The Chyulu site is probably the most scenic and is closest to the Kilaguni-Ngulia game circuits. Its disadvantage: lava ground that does not facilitate tent setup. The site at Tsavo Gate is located on the banks of the Tsavo River. The Mtito Andei site is uncomfortably close to the main highway and the village, so both vehicle noise and theft are problems. Another campsite is found at Lake Jipe. Self-service *banda* accommodation is available at the Kitani Safari Camp near Mzima Springs and the Ngulia Safari Camp, on the mountain. Outside the park, modest hotel accommodation is found on the Mombasa road at the Tsavo Inn at Mtito Andei.

The Hilton chain operates two luxury hotels just outside the southern section of Tsavo West. Both Taita Hills Lodge and Salt Lick Lodge have access to Tsavo's Serengeti and Lake Jipe, but most visitors are content with observations within a 28,000-acre private reserve. Excellent wildlife viewing there is enhanced by the ability to do nighttime game drives, and (newly inaugurated) balloon safaris offer the bonus of Kilimanjaro views.

TSAVO EAST

Tsavo East, a vast wilderness region, is the larger of the two parks. Almost its entire expanse is unremittingly hot country, less than 2,000 feet above sea level. Aside from brief green periods during the rains, Tsavo East is agonizingly dry, a near-desert of red sand and *nyika* bush. *Nyika* is woody acacia-commiphora scrubland. Punctuated by baobabs and other deciduous trees, it lies leafless and thorny for much of the year. Game is sparsely distributed, but dry-season herds collect in the park's river valleys: the Galana, the Tiva, and the seasonal Voi.

Public access is pretty much limited to the territory south of the Galana, which still leaves ample Tsavo bushland to be explored. The best game tracks follow the Galana and Voi rivers. The Galana is Tsavo East's major river. It begins where the Athi, flowing along the base of the Yatta Plateau, joins with the Tsavo as it exits the western park. Bordered by doum palms and a tattered curtain of riverine forest, the Galana is a wide, shallow stream, laced with sandbanks except where it surges through a tiny rock crevice at Lugard's Falls. Monster crocodiles are always to be seen there on the rocks below the chutes. Views of hippos and crocs are surefire on the river drive, as are a good variety of herons and storks. The Galana country was once excellent for rhino spotting, but those times are gone. Still, it remains one of the premier areas for sightings of lion and lesser kudu. You will also see waterbuck and other riverine species, and a variety of game coming down to drink. The Voi River flows only during the rains, shriveling in dry seasons to a series of small pools, marshy swamps, and a lake impounded by Aruba Dam. These are popular watering places. Tsavo East's scrubby woodlands are excellent habitat for lesser kudu, gerenuk, dikdik, and bush squirrels, as well as elephants and giraffe. Buffalo and gazelle (in Tsavo East the local specialty is Peter's, a subspecies of Grant's gazelle) favor more open grassy areas. Mudanda Rock, a mile-long stratified outcrop, forms a good observation point. You can climb to its flat-topped summit, which overlooks a natural pool often visited by elephant herds.

For the most part, the land north of the Galana is closed to the general public. Vast and inhospitably dry, it is considered too risky to be explored by inexperienced tourists. By special permission of the warden, self-sufficient parties are allowed to camp along the Tiva River, the main dry-season watering point for game in the far north of the park. Although you might expect an utter wilderness experience, an esthetic intrusion mars the scenery: a power line accompanies the main track connecting the Tiva with the Galana. Nor is the wildlife completely undisturbed: Orma herders have been reported to graze their cattle in the Tiva Valley, deep inside the park. So, though you'll find no other tourists, game viewing is probably no better than in the more accessible areas to the south.

The Yatta Plateau is the most conspicuous topographic landmark of Tsavo East. Almost 200 miles in total length, it is considered to be the longest lava flow in the world. The Yatta forms a 3-mile-wide wall on the western edge of the park, dividing the flowing Athi River from the waterless tracts of the eastern scrublands.

Accommodation. Voi Safari Lodge is Tsavo East's principal hotel. Perched on a hilltop near park headquarters, it has a commanding view. An underground bunker provides close viewing of animals visiting the lodge waterhole. Aruba Lodge is a rustic self-service facility located on the impounded lake at Aruba Dam. It is a prime dry-season watering spot. Public camping is allowed near Aruba Lodge, and at sites near the main Voi Gate and the eastern Sala Gate. Two special campsites are located along the course of the Voi River; professionally organized safaris are sometimes allowed to camp along the Galana or Tiva rivers. Crocodile Camp is a tented camp located on the Galana River, just beyond the Sala Gate, on the road to Malindi. Another facility, Tsavo Safari Camp, is located on the Athi River, just at the foot of the Yatta Plateau. It is far from Tsavo East's main game circuits, but is a good place to break a road journey from Nairobi to the coast.

TSAVO FOOT SAFARIS

Tsavo West is the only national park in Kenya in which game-country foot safaris are permitted. Tropical Ice organizes five-day walks along the Tsavo River on which participants patrol in the company of armed park rangers. They also offer foot safaris on Masai land in the Chyulu Hills. So, too, does Richard Bonham Safaris, who operate from their private camp at the foot of the hills. The Tsavo Safari Camp does escorted day walks with camels in the Athi River area. Walking and camel safaris were formerly operated on the Galana Ranch, a huge private block of bushland just over the boundary from Tsavo East, but have been suspended by government order. On your own, you can make arrangements with the warden of Tsavo West to hire rangers for a hike to the summit of Ngulia Mountain. The walk takes only a few hours, starting from the Ngulia Safari Camp.

Western Kenya

Kenya's western districts are among the most valuable farmlands in the country. Kericho is a major center of tea production. It is surrounded by large plantations, carpeted with rows of neatly trimmed tea bushes. The hills around Kisii are thick with small *shambas* producing tea, coffee, and pyrethrum (discussed in Chapter 6)—all esteemed export crops. Sugar cane is grown on the plains around Lake Victoria. Although these areas are pretty enough, little wildlife habitat remains to attract time-conscious travelers away from the main safari circuits.

A few places stand out for natural interest. Lake Victoria is so massive that it almost qualifies as an inland sea. Its shores are home to the Luo people, the second most populous tribe in the country. As businessmen, intellectuals, and politicians, the Luo are energetic rivals of the highland Kikuyu. Around the lake, the Luo remain farmers and fishermen. Their livelihood has suffered from a man-made disaster. Nile perch were introduced to the lake through a suspicious "accident." The voracious perch gobbled up the native tilapia, virtually exterminating prized food species on which the Luo diet had formerly depended. Perch grow up to 200 pounds, but are not highly regarded for taste. Such huge fish are also much more difficult to smoke for marketing than pan-sized tilapia. Now Victoria's fishermen (in Uganda and Tanzania as much as Kenya) are complaining about torn nets and poor catches.

Victoria, at an elevation of 3,718 feet above sea level, has a rather hot, humid climate. The lake is infested with bilharzia, so swimming is not possible. Malaria and other exotic tropical diseases are also more common there than in other parts of Kenya. None of this has hastened the development of beach resorts. There are nice hotels in Kisumu, Kenya's third largest city, and at Homa Bay. An attempt is being made to capitalize on the Nile perch by flying tourists to Rusinga Island from the Mara for a day's fishing.

The Kakamega Forest is a relict patch of West African-type rainforest. This "jungle" is alive with unusual birds and animals, many of which cannot otherwise be found in Kenya. Spectacular species like great blue turaco, double-toothed barbet, and gray parrot are powerful incentives for birding groups to include Kakamega on their itineraries. Primates are also of interest. Beautifully marked redtailed monkeys share the forest canopy with troops of black-and-white colobus. De Brazza's monkey (*Cercopithecus neglectus*) is sometimes encountered on the ground. Adult males are striking: they sport long-flowing white beards. At night, potto (*Perodicticus potto*) can be picked out in the beam of a spotlight. Pottos are slow-moving nocturnal primates, closely related to the more agile bushbabies. Kakamega enjoys a reputation for snakes, but their numbers have been greatly reduced by cattle grazing and reptile collectors. A grid of forester's tracks facilitates explorations on foot; all larger and potentially dangerous animals have been exterminated. An unpretentious resthouse provides shelter for self-sufficient campers. Accommodation in the town of Kakamega is found at the Golf Hotel, but most visiting tour groups stay in Kisumu, about 30 miles away.

Another favorite with naturalists is Saiwa Swamp National Park. This tree-fringed marsh is Kenya's only refuge for the aquatic sitatunga antelope. Platform blinds have been erected in strategic places for improved viewing. Observations are best at dusk, when the animals emerge from the swamp to feed. De Brazza's monkey and Ross's turaco are also Saiwa specialties. Camping is permitted. Cheap hotels are found in Kitale; the nearest tourist-class accommodation is the lodge at Mount Elgon.

Geologists speculate that Mount Elgon was once the highest of the great African volcanos. After millions of years, all that remains of the giant is its broad base. That remnant forms a 50-mile-wide mountain on the border with Uganda. Elgon has no dramatic peaks or permanent snows, but reaches 14,178 feet, making it the fifth highest mountain in Africa. Although its lower slopes have been cut and cultivated, the upper forest and moorland zone on the Kenya side is protected in the Mount Elgon National Park.

Elgon's fauna, typical of mountain forests, is shy and difficult to observe. The park's most fascinating feature are caves that have been excavated by salt-hungry elephants over thousands of years. Working with their tusks in absolute darkness, elephant miners have pushed tunnels deep underground. Three caverns are open to the public. Mackingeny is the most spectacular; its wide mouth is a 50-foot-high arch graced with a tumbling waterfall. Kitum cave is visited almost nightly by elephants. It may be possible to spend a night inside, a very eerie experience, but special permission must be sought from the warden. More regular accommodation is found at Mount Elgon Lodge, a lovely colonial farmhouse just outside the park gate.

Walkers can trek to Elgon's summit for views of its 5-mile-wide caldera and baths in volcanic hot springs. The principal route begins at the park gate, from which a track snakes up through podo forest and bamboo to the top of the Endebess Bluff (about 8,000 ft.), then continues over the moorlands to the roadhead at 11,000 feet. From there it is a three- to four-hour hike following the valley of the Kimothon River to Koitobos (13,852 ft.), a flat-topped rock outcrop perched above the crater rim. With transport, the return trek can be accomplished in one long day. Because walking through the National Park is forbidden, those without a vehicle must find their way to the Endebess Forest Station (to the north of the park) or the Kimilili Station (to the south) before beginning the trek. From the forest stations, plan for two days going up and one to descend. Be advised that thefts by local children are a problem and that Ugandan poachers are active on the mountain.

The Tana River

Even if its wildlife had not suffered severely at the hands of Somali poachers, the hot lowlands of Kenya's northeast would attract only the hardiest travelers. Intermittent outbreaks of *shifta* violence ensure that what is overall an inhospitable country anyway is completely avoided by tourists. Its one significant drawing card is the Tana River, Kenya's largest stream.

The Tana makes a long loop through the dry eastern scrublands before flowing almost due southward to the sea. Extensive riparian forests once lined its floodplain. They have been seriously degraded by human activity, but one stretch of gallery forest is protected in the Tana River Primate National Reserve. Troops of red colobus monkey (*Colobus badius*) and crested mangabey (*Cercocebus galeritus*), both essentially West African species that are very rare in Kenya, are found there. The reserve is most accessible from Malindi, about a hundred miles distant. Accommodation was available at the riverfront Baomo Lodge, but it has now closed; camping is now the only option. Searches for the monkeys are conducted on foot. Rumor has it that Hunter's hartebeest (*Damaliscus hunteri*) have also been seen in the reserve. These lyre-horned antelope are one of Kenya's rarest animals, dwelling only between the Tana's east bank and the Somalia border. The Arawale National Reserve has been created just for their protection. Unfortunately, real access or game tracks are as yet nonexistent.

A few hardy adventurers have floated down the Tana in dugout canoes bought in Garissa. Such a trip should not be taken lightly. Although there are a few villages along the way where you could take out in an emergency, it is almost 150 miles to Garsen, the next town of any size. Hippos and crocodiles are abundant in the broad brown river, and likely to be testy when the river is low. During the river's spate, large tree limbs are carried along on the flood.

An interesting safari can be made on a motorized catamaran, cruising the waterways of the Tana Delta on a four-night camping expedition. The channels of the delta country are a paradise for birdlife and aquatic animals. Elephants and other game may also be encountered, as well as people of the Pokomo and Orma tribes. High sand dunes have piled up where the river meets the sea. The trip ends with a sail on the open ocean to the coastal village of Kipini, from which transport is provided to Malindi or Lamu. The safari is operated by Tana Delta Limited in Nairobi.

The Coast

For Europeans, the white sand beaches along the Indian Ocean are Kenya's main attraction. Thousands of refugees from Europe's winter fly directly to Mombasa and Malindi, filling charter aircraft and hotels built especially to receive them. Few venture to the interior game parks. They already have everything they need for a splendid holiday: tropical sun, palm-fringed beaches, clear blue waters, a wealth of coral reefs, excellent accommodations, superb seafood, and friendly natives. Americans tend to visit the coast as an addendum to their game country safaris. It is certainly the perfect environment to wind down from the rigors of the bush. But the coast can offer more than the standarized pleasures of a tropical beach vacation. Natural history adventures abound on both land and sea, while explorations of the distinctive coastal culture, rich in historic legacy, lend an added dimension to the African experience.

HISTORY

The Kenya coast is spiced with the flavors of the Indian Ocean. The seafaring peoples around its periphery have mingled their blood and traditions with those of indigenous Africans, creating a cultural melting pot.

Ancient Egyptian expeditions to the "land of Punt" (as the Egyptians called the east coast of Africa) probably did not reach as far south as the Kenya coast. But the record is clear that Greco-Roman merchants visited that part of the "Erythraean Sea" as early as the first century A.D. By the eighth century, Arab and Persian mariners were regularly sailing their dhows into East African waters. Traders founded a string of coastal towns between present-day Somalia and Mozambique. Tiny city-states flourished, sending ivory, gold, slaves, and myrhh from the African interior to the great commercial centers of Arabia. These Arab enclaves reached their heyday during the thirteenth and fourteenth centuries, by which time they had made a profound impression on the Kenya-Tanzania coast. Insulated from the hinterland by a barrier of hostile *nyika* desert, a narrow seaside strip had evolved into a separate cultural region, heavily influenced by Arab civilization. Islam was introduced to the coastal tribes and, gradually, through intermarriage and assimilation, Swahili emerged as a distinctive language and culture. The Swahili tongue, a hybrid of Bantu and Arab dialects, later spread as the vernacular of trade throughout huge sections of the African heartland. Ultimately, Swahili was adopted as the national language of both Kenya and Tanzania.

Hard times struck the Swahili coast with the arrival of the Portuguese in 1498. Two centuries of armed struggle ensued. It was a free-for-all, in which the Swahili towns were pitted as much against each other as against the Portuguese infidels. Marauding tribes from the interior also joined the fray. The entire region was left a shambles. Some mainland towns were completely abandoned, and the vitality of coastal trade languished until the rise of the Zanzibar Sultanate in the early nineteenth century.

Mombasa's star was eclipsed by Zanzibari domination. The old fortress town did not resume its paramount role until the English annexed the mainland and needed a deep-water port for their new Kenya Colony. The port prospered, growing into a metropolis of almost half a million inhabitants. Today it is the vital lifeline for the nation's trade (as well as that of Rwanda and Uganda).

The unique Swahili culture has survived to the present. "Upcountry" Swahili bears little resemblance to the intricate grammar and fluid speech of the coast, where the truest and most sophisticated dialects are still spoken. Other facets of Swahili culture also remain strong, particularly in Lamu and Old Town Mombasa. To this day, men can be seen wearing flowing *kanzu* robes and Islamic skullcaps, *kofia*, while women commonly dress in head-to-toe black garments called *buibui*. Architecture also retains an Islamic flourish, which is not surprising in a culture guided by the symbol of the star and crescent.

TOURING THE COAST

It would take weeks to visit all the places of interest on the Kenya coast, but most visitors budget no more than a few days. If time is a consideration, pick one or two of the major centers in which to concentrate your stay. Nowadays the beach hotels are always busy. Advance bookings are almost essential: don't wait till the last minute to plan a coast extension to your safari. If you desire only seaside relaxation, have your transfers arranged when you book your hotel. The larger beach hotels all have travel desks that can arrange any local excursions or tours. If you plan more wide-ranging adventures, it is best to rent a car. Finding beach accommodation on your own can be a real problem, especially at Christmas. Budget travelers can always manage something, but should be prepared to camp if necessary.

MOMBASA

For centuries, Mombasa was a door to the African interior. Today the gate swings more than ever both ways. From the bustling harbor at Kilindini ("Place of Deep Water"), ships carry Kenyan coffee overseas. A stream of autos, trucks, and oil flows inward. For visitors, Mombasa is the major gateway to the Kenya coast.

Mombasa is a fascinating city with a history dating back more than 500 years. The mix of African, Asian, Arab, and European influences creates a unique cosmopolitan ambience. It's well worth a visit, if only for a few hours. Because of the sultry tropical climate, plan your sojourn for the morning or late afternoon: Mombasa's residents all close up shop during the midday heat.

The Arabian influence is very evident in the dress, features, and lifestyle of the inhabitants of the Old Town. It's streets are liveliest in the early evening. Ramshackle houses, laundry billowing from sagging wooden balconies, frame narrow streets in which children spill from every doorway. Vendors dispense roasted corn and cassava root, or tiny cups of thick Arabian coffee. The architecture seems antique, but most of the buildings date from this century. The Mandhry mosque is genuinely ancient, going back to about 1570. Its whitewashed, phallus-shaped minaret is a striking ediface on Mbarak Hinawy Street, which runs from Fort Jesus to Government Square. There, the Customs House overlooks the Old Harbour, with its dock for wood-hulled dhows. On the square, shops specialize in curios from the Horn of Africa, such as ornate wooden chests, brass coffee pots, and carved Somali spoons. Each morning, a busy fish market displays the local fruits of the sea.

The great fleets of graceful lateen-rigged dhows are a thing of the past, but the northeast monsoon, the *kashkazi*, still blows in vessels from the Persian Gulf and Arabia from December to March. Their cargos include dates and dried fish, carpets and chests, and salt. When the wind turns, the *kusi* or southeast monsoon carries them homeward loaded with cow hides and *boriti* mangrove poles. No doubt a fair amount of rhino horn and ivory is also secreted in their holds. Although photography is officially forbidden inside the port area, you will have no problem getting permission to board any dhows at the jetty.

Fort Jesus is Mombasa's most striking historical monument. Constructed by the Portuguese between 1593 and 1596, the castlelike stone fort was their major stronghold on the East African coast. It

A *buibui*-clad woman—representative of the Arab influence on the Kenya coast. *Photo by Allen Bechky.*

was the site of frequent battles, for despite its imposing walls and ample armament, Islamic forces made repeated attacks on the Christian invaders. The Portuguese were finally ousted when their garrison was annihilated during the Great Seige of 1696–1698. The fort was thereafter occupied by a long succession of foreign and domestic armies—Omani Arabs, Portuguese (again), Mazruis (the local ruling family), Baluchis (mercenaries of Zanzibar's sultan), and British. Today an interesting museum documents the battle-scarred history of the fort and displays cultural artifacts of the old Swahili coast.

Curio shops, tour agencies, restaurants, and an official Visitor Information Bureau are concentrated along Moi Avenue, where Mombasa's emblematic monument, a dual pair of steel elephant tusks, arches across the road. People watching is a popular pastime from the terrace restaurant of the nearby Castle Hotel. There, tourists intersect with street vendors, hustlers, and hookers. The ambience is less tawdry around the city market on Digo Road. Biashara Street bursts with stalls selling colorful African cloth. *Kangas* are cotton prints emblazoned with enigmatic Swahili proverbs (often ribald) and bold designs. Used by local women as wraparound skirts, they have multiple uses on safari and at the beach: one light cloth functions as beach blanket, sarong, and cover on nights too warm for sleeping bags. The *kikoi,* made of thicker woven cloth, is a skirt worn by Swahili men. Sisal basket work is found in stalls outside the municipal market, which is also a good place to sample *madafu,* young coconuts delectable for their refreshing "milk" and sweet meat.

Accommodation. The luxury hotels of the north coast—notably the Nyali Beach, Mombasa Beach, Serena and Intercontinental—offer quick access to town. In the city, hotels catering to the business community are less fancy and more moderately priced: the Oceanic Hotel and Casino has a sea view location on the Kilindini cliffs; the Manor, Splendid, and especially the Castle are closer to the action. Budget hotels include the Savoy, Hydro, and New People's on Digo Road.

Restaurants. Tops in ambience, quality, and price is the Tamarind, located just north of town, across the Nyali Bridge. An outdoor dining room commands a view of Old Town's shore; the menu features exotic renderings of excellent sea fare. In town, the Singh Restaurant near the bus depot on Mwembe Tayari Road is unpretentious and cheap, but its Indian meals are authentic and delicious.

Swahili specialties—including kebabs, coconut curries, and Arab-bread—are featured at the Rekoda Hotel in Old Town: its outdoor street-life ambience is offset by its suspect cleanliness.

Dhow Sailing. Although international transit aboard dhows is officially frowned on, it is still possible to voyage on the venerable craft in the style of Sinbad. Small vessels ply the Kenya coast, and you may be able to catch one sailing to Lamu. This romantic sea adventure is only for the hardy: the deck is open to the sun, the head hovers precariously above the waves, privacy is nonexistent. Be sure to bring along a supply of fruit and other food as supplement to shipboard meals, a monotonous ration of *ugali* and salt fish. Neither the dhows nor the sailors' diet has changed much since the days of Sinbad. To make the voyage, you'll need permission from the registrar at the Old Harbour office. Tales circulate of dhow voyages to Zanzibar: the Old Harbour is the place to inquire.

Easier to arrange, and less rugged, are dhow cruises on specially fitted vessels chartered by various hotels and tour operators. Mombasa's Tamarind Restaurant caters daily lunch and dinner (the latter with dancing) sails on Tudor Creek, beneath Fort Jesus. Weekly cruises on modern sail boats are being offered in the Lamu archipelago; another makes a seven-day loop journey from Mombasa to Zanzibar via Shimoni and the isle of Pemba.

MOMBASA'S NORTH COAST

The beaches just north of Mombasa were the first to be developed for tourism, and large hotels dot the shore for some 15 miles out of town. Among the better-rated are the Nyali Beach, Mombasa Beach, Intercontinental, Serena Beach, Traveler's Beach, Reef, and Whites Sands hotels. Accommodation on the North Coast offers the advantage of easy access to Mombasa and Moi Airport. Aside from the tropical sea (which is a considerable enticement), the area has little to recommend to explorers. The newly created Mombasa National Park encompasses a 4-mile long section of coral reef between Bamburi Beach and Mtwapa Creek; the Mamba Village crocodile farm offers camel rides along the beach in addition to its reptiles. Baobab Farm is a wildlife sanctuary that hosts a variety of animals, both free-roaming and caged. Its site was once the barren quarry of the Bamburi Cement Company. Now verdantly reforested, it showcases the possiblities of ecologically sound land reclamation.

THE SOUTH COAST

Diani Beach is the chief resort area to the south of Mombasa. There, a 6-mile-long strand of white sand is protected by a parallel ribbon of coral reef, and backed by groves of coconut palms. The atmosphere at Diani is pleasantly relaxed, and there is plenty to do. The larger hotels all rent equipment for water sports, including windsurfing. Some offer scuba diving courses, too. Small *jahazi* dhows make access to the reef easy. Snorkling cruises often visit nearby Chale Island.

A wide selection of hotels, beach chalets (with kitchenettes), and camp sites is available at Diani and neighboring Tiwi Beach. Both beaches are some 20 miles away from Mombasa and separated by the mouth of Kilindini Harbor, which must be crossed on the Likoni Ferry. Neither area is convenient for quick forays into town. Boskovic Air serves Diani Beach daily with a flight from Nairobi to the village of Ukunda.

Diani is a naturalist's paradise. The junglelike Jadini Forest, haven to local wildlife, reaches right down to the beach. The forest rings with the calls of hornbills and orioles, and exceptionally tolerant black-and-white colobus monkeys allow themselves to be photographed at close range. Tiny suni antelope and bushbabies can be spotted with a good torch on night walks along the beach strip road.

Larger game is viewed 10 miles inland at the scenic Shimba Hills National Reserve. These gently rounded hills are clothed with tracts of *Brachystegia* woodland, interspersed with grassy balds and patches of coastal rainforest. From Giriama Point, a magnificent view of countryside covered with banana groves and palms sweeps all the way to the sea. Sable antelope, noted for their inordinately long, sweeping horns, are the park specialty. Restricted in Kenya to a few coastal areas, they are only protected in the Shimba Reserve. The sable are often spotted in grasslands and are not easily spooked. Roan antelope have been introduced, but are not numerous. Elephant, buffalo, leopard, and even lion are also found in the reserve, but they are not often seen. That situation may change with the opening of the Shimba Hills Lodge, which features nighttime salt-lick viewing. Otherwise, most visitors find game drives disappointingly sparse. Birders are attracted to Shimba Hills for the opportunity to see Fischer's turaco, trumpeter hornbill, African pitta, and other unusual species. The park is easily reached from Diani Beach via the town of Kwale. There is a campsite, and walking is permitted to an informal swimming hole at Shedrick Falls.

The best snorkeling on the entire Kenya coast is at Shimoni, 40 miles south of Diani Beach, where vast shoals of coral are protected in the Kisite Marine National Park and Mpunguti Marine Reserve. Pristine coral gardens nurture a fantastic variety of marine life, including abundant schools of colorful reef fish. Flamingo Tours operates a regular trip to the marine park that can be booked at any of the large beach hotels. It includes transport to Shimoni, a reef cruise on board a specially manicured dhow, and a sumptuous seafood buffet on Wasini Island. Less flashy but more indepth explorations of the reef can be arranged yourself, though not easily or cheaply. Boats can be chartered from the Pemba Channel Fishing Club and the Shimoni Reef Hotel. It is best to call ahead to arrange a charter, though phone connections to Shimoni are intermittent. An excursion to the reefs should be timed to coincide with low tide. Allow at least one hour for road travel from Diani, and an hour and a half for the boat ride out to coralline Kisite Island. If you fail to prearrange a charter, the National Parks office at Shimoni may be able to help you find a boat to take you out to some of the extensive inshore reefs. Plan on extra time to get everything organized. You can stay at Shimoni: moderate accommodation is available at the Reef Hotel.

The Pemba Channel Fishing Club is renowned for world-class marlin fishing. Boats and goodwill for snorkelers are in short supply, however, during fishing season, from November to March.

EXPLORING THE REEFS

Tropical reefs are among the most fascinating natural communities. A myriad of lifeforms compete and coexist in a habitat unrivaled in complexity and beauty. Except where broken by *mlangos,* "doors" formed at the mouths of coastal rivers, coral reefs fringe Kenya's coast for virtually its entire length. The reefs form a barrier between the open ocean and the beach. The leeward side is protected from high waves, strong currents, and sharks. Swimming is therefore very safe, although the sea bottom between shore and reef tends to be shallow, muddy, and choked with seaweed. This queasy bottom discourages visitors from walking or swimming to the reef, which is often only a few hundred yards from shore. On most resort beaches, small *jahazi* dhows are always on hand to carry walkers and snorkelers out to the reef at low tide. Strike a bargain with the captain before you set sail.

Whether beachcombing, reef walking, snorkeling, or diving, you should be aware of a few rules to prevent you from doing harm to yourself or the environment. The waters of the East African coast are fairly benign, though a few creatures can cause inadvertent harm to human beings. Sharks are absent on the landward side of the reef. One hears a lot about the dangers of stonefish and sea snakes, but serious human casualties in Kenya are almost unprecedented. Stonefish are well camouflaged and highly venomous if trod on, however. More numerous are urchins, whose porcupine-like spines are murder on bare feet. Tennis shoes and a cautious attitude are the best protection. Fire corals, stinging plankton, and jellyfish are all sources of potential discomfort, but the chief hazard is certainly overexposure to sun. Bring water-resistant sunscreens or wear protective clothing if you are at all photosensitive.

Cone snails are common. Although they are equipped with a lethally venomous sting, fear does not seem to discourage shell collectors. Shells and corals are eagerly sought as souvenirs, especially spider conch, cowries, and tritons. This has caused some devastating ecological effects by upsetting predator-prey population dynamics. A notable example: the wholesale removal of triton snails has resulted in an explosion of coral-eating crown-of-thorns starfish that threaten the health of entire reefs. Most of the reefs near popular beach hotels have been seriously degraded. Picked over by thousands of tourists and scoured by local vendors for salable shells, many creatures are virtually absent. Often the corals themselves are dead. It is now illegal to collect live shells, or to buy shells from unauthorized sellers. But collecting goes on, even in the marine reserves and national parks.

Snorkeling, locally called "goggling," is the most popular way to view the reef. There are any number of reefs to explore, both within and outside the marine national parks. Each area is different and what you see is a matter of luck, so multiple sessions are recommended. Aficionados may be frustrated in their efforts to experience a really good underwater session. Boats tend to visit the same coral heads, with consequent overcrowding and environmental destruction. Equipment can be rented at many hotels, and sometimes from dhow owners, but it is often badly worn. It is advisable to bring your own mask for a good fit: one can make do with fins, but a leaky mask spoils any dive.

Diving is the ultimate portal to the underwater world. Many hotels operate dive shops offering equipment rental, boats, and guided packages. They also have reasonably priced one-week courses for international certification by the Professional Association of Diving Instructors (PADI). Bring prescription goggles if you wear glasses.

Large shelves of reef are exposed at low tides. Although reef walking does unquestionable damage to live corals, many exposed flats are composed of fossilized coral rock. These can be walked on without damage, and offer great tidepooling and bird watching. Herons, egrets, and wooly-necked storks hunt on exposed reefs, while terns and other seabirds roost on coralline islands. Coral cliffs are worth exploring, too: scuttling crabs and slithering skinks share a world of sharply pitted rock with a variety of splash-zone sea creatures.

DEEP-SEA FISHING

Although big game hunting is banned in Kenya, sport fishing still thrives. Marlin (blue, black, and striped) and sailfish are the grand trophies. Yellowfin tuna, wahoo, kingfish, dorado (dolphin fish), and mako shark are also sought. There are numerous professional outfitters. The season coincides with the northeast monsoon, from November till March.

THE MALINDI AREA

In 1498 Vasco da Gama visited Malindi, where he hired a local pilot to guide his voyage to India. The stone cross he left behind is about all that remains of Old Malindi. The town has grown into the busiest of Kenya's coastal resorts, receiving thousands of European tourists annually. Sex and sun are the main attractions, and the atmosphere is decidedly hedonistic: bars and discos, as well as prostitutes and gigolos, abound. The beautiful sand beaches of Malindi Bay are also flawed by the outflow of the nearby Sabaki River, which reddens the sea with soils washed down from the distant highlands. Although those sediments have prevented reefs from growing to the north of town, Malindi has excellent snorkeling and diving in its offshore Marine Reserve. The lovely coral gardens of Malindi's Marine National Park are easily accessible from Casuarina Point. But aside from the marine parks, the town is mostly devoted to partying.

It's preferable to be based at Watamu, 12 miles south. With the exception of local party times (like New Year's), it's much quieter. The Turtle Bay Hotel is located on a lovely beach of the same name.

Nearby, the Ocean Sports Hotel is popular with white Kenyans, and the posh Hemingway's has just opened. Diving and deep-sea fishing expeditions are very much on at Watamu. The Turtle Bay is headquarters for one of the best diving operations on the coast, while Hemingway's caters to the sport-fishing set. The Watamu Marine National Park attracts snorkelers: local guides pass out bread so that you can feed shoals of tame fish. Nearby Mida Creek is also a marine reserve; this one devoted to a mangrove-rimmed tidal estuary rather than corals. Kingfishers and bee-eaters, among the most colorful of African birds, roost atop the mangrove trees, while mudskippers—bubble-eyed air-breathing fish—crawl out of the water onto protruding mangrove roots. The mud flats are the hunting ground of egrets and herons, as well as the crab plover, which is hard to see elsewhere. The mud flats occasionally teem with great masses of European waders on migration. Boats for touring Mida Creek can be hired from the hotels.

The Gedi ruins are also very close to Watamu. Gedi was a Swahili town that flourished in the fourteenth and fifteenth centuries. It was suddenly and mysteriously abandoned, to be reclaimed by jungle and ultimately turned into a national historical park. The evocative ruins of pillar mosques, Arab houses, and the town's fortified wall are set among the giant trees of a beautiful coastal forest. This undisturbed woodland is large enough to provide a good refuge for many rare coastal animals and birds. You'll need patience to catch a sight of the golden-rumped elephant shrew, a long-nosed, squirrel-sized insectivore that forages among the leaf litter of the forest floor. A good stalker might also spot suni and blue duiker. Watch for snakes off trail and among the ruins. It's imperative to visit early or late in the day to avoid heat and noisy tourists.

The nearby Sokoke-Arabuko Forest is another tract of relict (and fast disappearing) coastal forest. Although big game (elephant and buffalo) live there, it is more celebrated for its endemic birdlife and wealth of butterflies. A guide can be hired at the Gedi forestry station. A four-wheel-drive vehicle is necessary for confidence on the forest's sandy tracks.

LAMU

Lamu enjoys a reputation as an island that time has passed by. It is part of a small archipelago off the northern coast. Isolated from the mainland and the mainstream of modern Kenya, the island has no real roads and only one official vehicle. It remains a quiet place, where the old Swahili culture, with its strong Arabian influences, survives intact.

One of the most prominent of the old Swahili towns, tiny Lamu has preserved its architectural and cultural heritage to the present day. Colonial-style buildings line the shorefont esplanade, where dhow moorings and stacks of mangrove poles testify to the island's traditional commerce. A central plaza is dominated by a crenelated nineteenth-century fort. Long used as a prison, it is now being converted into a museum and cultural center. Emanating from a single main street, a maze of narrow lanes winds among attached houses of white coral rock. Dwellings conform to the two-story style of the traditional Swahili house: in the old days the upper level was the quarters of the master's family, while the ground floor sheltered his slaves. Some houses possess finely carved wooden doors inlaid with brass, which are the pride of Swahili craftsmanship. Lamu, boasting twenty-three mosques, is an important center of religious studies, noted for its Islamic college. Every year the Maulidi Festival celebrates the birth of the Prophet with music and song. Lamu's brand of Islam is not fiercely ascetic. Although women are clad in the black *buibui* and may be veiled, they are by no means cloistered. The people are known for their love of music and dance, and the atmosphere of the island is distinctly relaxed.

It is 2 miles from town to the village of Shela, where Lamu's seaward beaches begin. Shela is a quiet place, a tiny hamlet slowly being inundated by massive sand dunes. The mosque's conical minaret, gleaming white in the tropical sun, is an island landmark. Beyond Shela lies a 7-mile strip of deserted beach backed by high dunes. Finding shade is definitely a problem on this otherwise perfect beach, for there are no trees or refreshment stands and the sun is ferocious. Shela is a good place to stay because of its beach access. From town, it's about a forty-five-minute walk along the Manda Channel, though it is always easy to hire a small dhow to taxi the distance. Dhows can also be rented for visits to the interesting Takwa ruins, the site of an abandoned town on Manda Island.

Lamu has long been popular with budget and long-term travelers, giving the island a reputation as the Kathmandu of Africa. There are many low-cost hotels, and it is not difficult to find accommodation in residents' homes or to rent houses outside town. Petley's Inn, a nineteenth-century house, is the only tourist-class hotel in town.

Although Lamu is an easy place to pass time cheaply, it is not an ideal site for a typical beach holiday. The town is far from the beach, and seaside accommodation is limited. The renowned Peponi Hotel at Shela and the Ras Kitau Hotel across the channel on Manda Island are the only tourist-class facilities. *Peponi* means "paradise"—it is relaxing, unpretentious, and very heavily booked. Both hotels arrange boat charters for snorkeling and diving, providing the only real access for these activities.

Lamu is a six-hour bus journey from Malindi. Scheduled aircraft fly in daily from Malindi, Mombasa, and Nairobi.

Two exclusive camps have opened at Kiwayu, 35 miles north of Lamu and served daily by a scheduled AirKenya flight. The only lodges on the far north coast, they promise seclusion and opportunities for explorations in the pristine Kiunga Marine Reserve.

5

Tanzania: A Host of Edens

Tanzania is a country of safari superlatives, delivering every element of classic African adventure. Among its unspoiled wilderness landscapes, you can still find Masai nomads and impossibly huge throngs of wild creatures. Its celebrated parks are without peer: the bounty of Serengeti wildlife is as legendary as the astounding beauty of Ngorongoro Crater. The nation claims Kilimanjaro, Africa's highest mountain, and the Selous Game Reserve, largest on the continent. Such impeccable credentials support Tanzania's long-standing reputation as the ultimate safari destination.

The fly in the Tanzanian ointment has always been service: the country's hard-pressed economy simply does not deliver the amenities that mass tourism demands. Because the pendulum of economic chaos swings from better to worse and back again, a visit to Tanzania is always an adventure to be anticipated more for its natural charms than for its creature comforts.

Official policy toward tourism has blown both hot and cold. In the early years of independence, tourists were tolerated as a source of revenue, but were not welcomed with much enthusiasm. They were regarded as vectors of decadent ideas and temptations that did not jive with the ideology of African socialism. Nevertheless, a chain of modern game lodges was built, and by the early 1970s overseas visitors were streaming to Tanzania's wonderful parks. Most flew into Nairobi to join tour packages operated by Kenyan companies. The "milk run" was the most spectacular game-viewing itinerary imaginable: beginning with a stop in Amboseli for Kilimanjaro views, safaris then entered Tanzania on a whirlwind loop through Manyara, Ngorongoro, and Serengeti before recrossing the border into the Masai Mara on the return to Nairobi. Although its lodges were full, and the national parks were collecting fees from thousands of visitors, this tourist influx did little to help Tanzania's forlorn economy. The lodges had been very expensive to finance (though built with the aid of international development funds), and the costs of safari infrastructure—gasoline, food, road and car maintenance—were hardly sustainable when the bulk of tourist dollars remained in Kenya. With the collapse of the jointly owned East African Airlines, the Tanzanian government closed the border. It was hoped that the newly constructed airport at Kilimanjaro would draw tourists directly, enabling the country to reap all the rewards of an independent safari industry. Instead, the border closure was the deathknell of Tanzanian tourism. Without the Kenyan traffic, Tanzania's facilities went into rapid decay. The lodges were empty, the parks went broke, and worn vehicles could not be replaced, but were cannibalized or endlessly rebuilt.

Although its economy had hit rock bottom, Tanzania's appeal for safari aficionados remained undiminished. A trickle of visitors continued to report on the fantastic quality of the parks, where a few hardy outfitters provided rough-and-ready safaris. Vehicles were tattered and breakdowns common, but participants found they had the magnificent parks all to themselves. As word got out, the number of visitors gradually picked up and, when the border with Kenya was reopened in 1983, tourist volume surged. Today, Tanzania is once again a booming tour destination.

With success have come significant advances in services—and fresh problems. International tour companies have been flooding the country with new vehicles, addressing one of the major failings of the previous era. But improvements in transport have not been matched with gains in accommodation. Although a few lodges have been scheduled for refurbishing, so far even the best can muster only a modest and irregular degree of comfort. In some of the leading game lodges, hot water remains as rare as leopard sightings, and cold water may not be as forthcoming as guests might expect. A more serious problem is overbooking. Whereas hotels used to stand empty, tour groups are increasingly finding themselves turned away and having to make unexpected itinerary adjustments. In attempting to cope with full houses, hotels are overstretching their ability to provide adequate service to those guests who do get the rooms reserved for them. Over time, the situation may get better, for plans are being made to construct more hotels and improve the management of government lodges. Nonetheless, visitors should always expect some surprises or inconveniences.

Camping safaris have long been the mainstay of the Tanzanian tour scene. Indeed, visitors often discover that service and comfort are more dependable in their own camps than in lodges. In the past, campers had to be willing to accept some hardships as a trade off for an authentic safari experience. That is no longer necessarily the case: with the awakening of the economy, tour operators can now offer luxury safaris to match the best Kenyan standards. But a dramatic increase in the volume of tented safaris has meant that campers are frequently encountering overcrowding: most Tanzanian parks have only a limited number of designated campsites, and those are now being booked beyond capacity—a disappointment in a country renowned for the purity of its wilderness environment.

Governmental caprice is another source of potential exasperation: regulations change often, and usually without prior notice. Park fees may be raised overnight, or certain types of vehicles suddenly be restricted from use in the parks. Although such actions in themselves may not be unreasonable, the heavy-handed manner in which they are imposed can cause great inconvenience, especially when itineraries have to be adjusted at the last minute.

Whatever minor frustrations visitors may encounter are nothing compared to the everyday hardships that Tanzania's citizens have to endure. Yet they are an exceptionally friendly and resourceful people. Perhaps that is because hardship is not a new element in their history: current economic woes seem trivial in comparison to the scourges of slavery and war that belong to the country's past.

Slavery was inextricably linked to the rise and fall of the tiny sultanate of Zanzibar. For centuries, the sultans of Oman had enjoyed nominal authority over the Arab towns along the East African coast, but real control languished until the reign of Seyyid Said. Indulging a preference for Zanzibar's balmy tropical climate to the desert harshness of Oman, Said moved his capital there in 1832. At his direction, clove trees were brought to the island, and their cultivation became the lasting pillar of the island's prosperity. But trade in ivory and slaves was also expanded as caravan routes were pushed to Lake Tanganyika and beyond. And it was the slave trade that brought Zanzibar to the attention of the outside world. All the great African explorers—Livingstone, Burton, Speke, and Stanley— used the island as their starting point, following the sultan's established caravan routes. Their reports settled the geographical mysteries of the continent and set off an uproar about the horrors of slavery in the African interior. Said's successors found themselves in an increasingly uncomfortable position as the abolitionist British consul at Zanzibar, Sir John Kirk, relentlessly pressured them, against their will and their own commercial interests, into suppressing the slave trade. Even that concession could not prevent Zanzibar from being swallowed up in the European rush to empire.

The Germans were late in joining the colonial game and established their East Africa dominion in an almost offhand manner. Carl Peters, a secret agent for the German Colonization Society, sneaked onto the mainland from British-controlled Zanzibar. Proceeding to the Kilimanjaro district, he got a number of local chieftains to sign treaties (meaningless to them, of course) ceding their land to his society. Prior to that time, Germany's Iron Chancellor, Bismarck, had been opposed to the establishment of overseas colonies. But seeing a chance to gain diplomatic leverage against his great power rivals, Bismarck seized on Peters' treaties to declare a German protectorate in East Africa. That resulted in the infamous Berlin conference of 1884–1885, in which the European nations finally and completely partitioned the entire continent among themselves. The sultan lost all his mainland possessions, which were divided between the English and Germans, and ultimately, Zanzibar itself officially became a British dependency.

The Germans promptly set about the exploitation of their new domain. The private German East Africa Company, under the direction of Carl Peters, was given carte blanche to run that colony. Land was distributed to white settlers, who were encouraged to grow sisal for export as a cash crop. Sisal cultivation is extremely labor intensive, so the colonists were allowed to forcibly conscript unwilling natives for unpaid plantation labor. This stiffened African resistance, which had already been strong from the start. The coastal towns, loyal to Zanzibar, had immediately revolted against German rule. No sooner were they crushed than the Hehe of the southern highlands rose up bloodily. Between 1905–1907, the entire southern part of the country was engulfed in the Maji-Maji rebellion, which was only quelled after the death of an estimated 120,000 Africans. Reforms were instituted in the wake of the great revolt. The German government took over administration from the company, forced labor was restricted solely to public works (and had to be compensated), and a school system for Africans was established. Railroad lines were built connecting the coast to both the Kilimanjaro district and Kigoma on Lake Tanganyika. By 1914, some 5,000 German settlers were living in a pacified and well-organized colony.

The outbreak of war in Europe brought armed conflict to the colonies as well, and German East Africa became the locale of one of the war's most bizarre campaigns. Cut off from all supplies and communications with the home country, German forces conducted a guerrilla war that succeeded in tying up huge numbers of British, Indian, and South African troops. Under the brilliant leadership of General Paul von Lettow-Vorbeck, the Germans managed to hold out until word arrived of the 1918 armistice in Europe. At war's end, a wrecked colony was turned over to the British, who renamed their new protectorate Tanganyika. English settlement and development schemes followed, although never on the scale lavished on neighboring Kenya.

Independence was granted to Tanganyika in 1961. A year later, Zanzibar received its freedom, whereupon a bloody revolution promptly ended the reign of the sultans. In 1964 the radical government of Zanzibar formed a union with the mainland, creating Tanzania. Julius Nyerere led the new nation on a unique path of African socialism. His philosophy of *Ujamaa* ("family") saw the nation as an extended family, sharing common African values and working together toward communal self-reliance. Known as *Mwalimu*, the teacher, Nyerere's integrity and ascetic lifestyle earned him considerable moral authority both at home and abroad. But despite his good intentions and an impressive record in advancing education (the nation's literacy stands at an amazing 85 percent), his determined efforts to keep the country on a socialist road did not lead to economic prosperity. Even with massive infusions of foreign aid, the overly controlled economy remained stagnant. The people suffered serious hardships as scarcity became a way of life. Everything was rationed, and such basic commodities as cooking oil, sugar, kerosene, and soap became available only on the black market. Gasoline shortages repeatedly brought the country to a complete standstill. By the early 1980s, the economy was a shambles and corruption had become almost institutional. Mighty Kilimanjaro seemed a perverse symbol of the nation's plight: like the mountain, the country's head was in the clouds, its shoulders bent against constant storms, its feet stuck in the mud.

In 1985 Nyerere left the presidency to Ali Hassan Mwinyi, a former president of Zanzibar and an economic pragmatist. Nyerere has retained his post as head of the Chama Cha Mapinduzi (CCM), the official (and only) political party. It is questionable where the real power now lies, but since the transition there have been real steps toward economic reform. The availability of food and consumer goods in the shops has improved dramatically, and the climate for business has revitalized Tanzania's tourist industry.

From the earliest days of independence, when President Nyerere

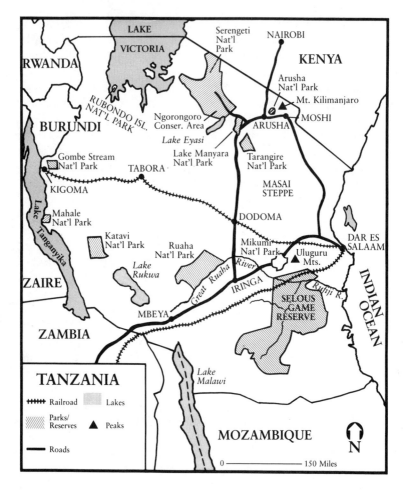

issued his Arusha Declaration, the government has been pledged to the preservation of the country's wildlife heritage. Towards that end, it has devoted more than 10 percent of the nation's land to national parks and game reserves. Overall, wildlife has done very well: even in the depths of the economic crisis, while Tanzania was a hard place for people to live, it was a very good country for wildebeest. With the nation beyond the point of insolvency, the game parks had to make do on a regime of almost benign neglect. Little or no money could be given to parks, especially when declining revenues from entry fees produced less than the sums needed to operate them. International conservation groups stepped in to help keep park administrations running, but it was natural fecundity rather than technical efficiency that kept the animals abundant. Shortages of vehicles and gasoline brought most antipoaching patrols to an end. Elephant, and especially rhino, declined as a result, but most of the other species continued to thrive. In the case of the Serengeti, a decade of good rainy seasons saw game populations increase astronomically—the wildebeest herd alone reaching a peak population of about two million. With economic revival, and a hefty increase in park entrance fees, the Tanzanian parks are again getting financially on their feet.

Safari Facts

Entry. Visas are required and obtainable at any Tanzanian embassy. Regulations regarding the issue of visas on arrival change often: currently they cannot be procured at the Namanga border to Kenya. Although it may be possible to get one at Kilimanjaro International Airport, it's safer to get one before you go. No vaccinations are required if you fly direct from Europe; yellow fever and cholera vaccinations *may be* needed if arriving from other African nations.

. *Currency.* Tanzania shillings (1989: TSh 139 = U.S. $1). All visitors, including those on prepaid safari tours, must officially exchange a minimum of $50 on arrival. All exchanges should be recorded on a currency control form, to be surrendered on exit from the country. National park fees *must* be paid in foreign currency. Locally purchased safari and hotel services are also supposed to be paid in U.S. dollars (or traveler's checks) and recorded on your currency form, but this rule is not strictly monitored. The black market is pervasive. In the past, its rate was five or six times the official rate, but has now dropped down to about double. Visitors are barraged by requests to change money: take care, for black market exchanges are illegal and tourists who break the law have been arrested, temporarily imprisoned, and heavily fined. That said, you should note that it is useful to bring in some undeclared U.S. cash, even if you do not plan to deal with the black market: foreign currency is always useful in an emergency, and tips to safari drivers and staff are much more appreciated when made in dollars. Tanzanian money is worthless outside the country. In practical terms, you will not be able to exchange unused shillings back into dollars when you leave, so do not get more than you will need. You can obtain shillings officially at hotels. The rate is lower than the bank's, but the process at a bank is interminable.

Language. Swahili is official; English is widely spoken.

Air Travel. Most safari visitors arrive at Kilimanjaro International Airport (mountain views on takeoff and landing are often spectacular, when planes fly right over the Kibo summit). Kilimanjaro is served weekly by KLM (Royal Dutch Airlines) and Air France; three times a week by Ethiopian Airlines. Visitors to the southern region can fly directly to Dar es Salaam on a number of carriers. Air Tanzania flies a network of routes around the country, and has scheduled service from Kilimanjaro to both Nairobi and London. It is, however, a notoriously erratic airline: it is difficult to get confirmed reservations in advance; flights are regularly overbooked and are often canceled. Tight vacation schedules and Air Tanzania do not mix well. Light aircraft can be chartered between Nairobi and Kilimanjaro. There is a U.S. $20 departure tax on all international flights; TSh 300 on domestic.

Land Transportation from Kenya. Since Kenyan and Tanzanian registered tour vehicles are not allowed to operate across their respective borders, travelers must switch vehicles at the border post at Namanga. This procedure is routine for tour groups, but quite expensive to prearrange for individuals. Local tour operators charge as much as $200 per vehicle, one way, on *each* side of the border. It is much cheaper, and not difficult, to arrange your own transport on the spot. Shared taxis (*matatus*) run frequently from Nairobi (at River Road and Haile Selassie Avenue) to Namanga, where Tanzanian *matatus* are waiting to go on to Arusha (and vice versa). Normally, these vehicles are thoroughly packed and make frequent stops along the way, but you can hire them for private use at a fraction of the cost of having your U.S. tour operator prebook a transfer.

Some Kenyan car rental companies (such as Hertz in Nairobi) will allow you to take their vehicles into Tanzania. In addition to the regular rental costs, you must pay extra for special insurance (1988 cost: U.S. $390), Tanzanian road tax (U.S. $100), Tanzanian parks fees (if any, at U.S. $30 per day for the vehicle), and a Kenyan rental surcharge. These hefty charges may be worth it if you want to take the risks of doing it on your own, for self-drive rentals are not available in Tanzania (see below).

Transportation. Roads in Tanzania are generally poor, with public conveyances to match. The main northern road linking Namanga, Arusha, Moshi, and Marangu (for Kilimanjaro treks) is an exception: it is paved and well served by ramshackle buses and *ma-*

tatus. Public buses go from Arusha to Lake Manyara and Ngorongoro, where vehicles can be hired to the tour parks. Self-drive car hire is impossible: rental vehicles all come with drivers, and charges are very high at the official rate of exchange. The risks of breakdown or gas shortages would make self-drive impractical for all but the most self-assured, anyway. Railroads connect Dar es Salaam with Moshi, Zambia, and Kigoma on Lake Tanganyika, but trains depart only half as often as scheduled. Trains are slow and very heavily booked.

Books and Information. The National Parks have published an excellent series of guides to the major parks. These are sold at all park entrance gates and offices. Supplies are spotty, so it's advisable to pick them all up wherever you find them available.

Tours. Tanzania does not have the variety of travel services available that exist in Kenya. Only a handful of safaris operate on a regular basis from Arusha to the game parks; these lodge trips can be booked through the larger tour companies in Nairobi. In Arusha, you usually have to go around to the various tour companies looking for a vehicle to hire. People who want to join up with others to share a vehicle should check out the snack bar at the New Arusha Hotel, where Star Tours solicits clients for pickup safaris at budget rates. Tracks Tours operates a budget truck-camping safari that can be booked locally. It is difficult to find vehicles for hire during peak periods such as February, when everyone wants to go to Serengeti, and July–August (the busiest season for U.S. travelers). Forget about it during the Christmas holiday—the one week in the year when everything in the country is fully booked. Tanzanian tour operators are supposed to require payment in dollars: most are scrupulous in this regard, but there are always exceptions.

Shopping. The best buys are Makonde carvings and Masai artifacts. These are generally cheaper in Tanzania than Kenya, especially if paid for in dollars or barter goods. Clothing is always much in demand, and useful for negotiating deals with market vendors. Shops tend toward fixed prices and legitimate cash transactions.

Tanzanite, the country's endemic gemstone, is not easy to find. It is sold exclusively at a few selected shops, and is then available only as cut stones (which is unfortunate, because of the dubious quality of the cutting). Still, if you know stones well, you may find good-quality gems at a fair official price. It is a serious offense to purchase gems from unofficial sources.

The Makonde tribe, who live in Tanzania's southeast corner on the Mozambique border, are celebrated for their ebony carving. The heartwood of the African ebony tree, *mpingo,* is heavy and dark. Sculptures are often slicked up with boot polish to make them black, which is unfortunate because their natural color is a lovely deep russet-brown. On some pieces the lighter outer wood and bark is left on, with the darker central carving seeming to literally emerge from a part of the tree. There are several styles. The "family" or *Ujamaa* style depicts intertwining figures woven around male and female parents. *Shaitani* ("devil") figures are frightening spirits, traditionally associated with water, trees, and animals. On these grotesque figures, the parts of body and face are often interchangeable: eyes may double as nipples, a leering mouth for a foot. A modern *mawingu* ("clouds") school has developed that molds traditional forms into graceful abstract shapes. Of course, plenty of junk is mass produced for the tourist market, but pieces of remarkable skill and imagination may be found. Check for good craftmanship, which is indicated by plenty of open space (arms carved free, etc.), details on faces, and quality of finishing. Sadly, Makonde carving is not highly regarded by professionals in the African art world. That could change, but for now you should buy solely on the basis of taste, not as an investment. Ebony is very brittle, so take extra care in packing for safe transport.

Although the availability of imported foods, liquors, and consumer goods has improved dramatically, you should bring all needed safari gear with you rather than rely on local purchase.

Photography and Video. The animals rarely object to photos, but people often do. Ask permission, and expect to contribute something. Don't shoot any buildings, airports, army bases, bridges, railroads, or anything remotely official—it can result in a lot of hassling and the confiscation of your film. Normal video cameras are no problem, but advanced models may be lumped in the category of professional cinema cameras, for which the fee to shoot in the national parks is $800 for the *first week.* You can get away with shooting video on safari, but keep a low profile around around customs, park gates, and official guides.

PARK FEES AND SAFARI PRICES

It is a paradox that Tanzania, one of the poorest countries in Africa, is notoriously expensive for safaris. Government control of prices and currency rates ensures that costs remain artificially high: whenever the government devalues the shilling, it raises prices for hotels and gasoline, so tour costs are immediately passed on to visitors. The government strategy to milk the market for every dollar it will bear is abetted by a carpetbagger mentality among private tour operators. Heavy investments in safari vehicles have to be recovered as quickly as possible, for no one knows when the tourist boom will again collapse. The ironic result is that visitors must pay higher prices for a lower level of service than in neighboring Kenya. But the country has undoubted attractions and, so long as a minimal level of service is provided, visitors will continue to arrive.

National park fees are undoubtedly the highest in Africa. Nonresident entry fees are U.S. $10 per day; camping is $6 in official campsites, $12 in remote "nonestablished" sites, $30 on the floor of Ngorongoro Crater. (In all likelihood, park fees will be substantially increased.) To prevent the loss of income to the black market, fees are payable in U.S. currency at park gates. Most prepaid tours include fees in their cost. Although these fees seem high, and are considered exorbitant by budget travelers, keep in mind that the money goes to support badly underfunded parks. Compare the value of a day in Serengeti to what $15 will buy at home. The question should be not whether Tanzania's fees are excessive, but whether other African nations are undervaluing their parks. In any event, and despite the outcries of tour operators, park fees are not the major cost of a Tanzania safari: they still don't equal the sums that are siphoned off on foreign exchange scams before the tourist ever reaches the country.

THE MASAI

Tanzania's Masai are more attached to a traditional life than are their kinspeople in Kenya (for a complete discussion of the Masai way of life, see the Masai section of Chapter 4, on Kenya), but it is difficult to make contact with them on the main safari route. Photographing them is officially frowned on, if not outright forbidden. Safari drivers consequently do not like to stop for anything more than quick shots, for fear of being harassed by government officials. Naturally, those Masai living on the safari circuit are totally familiar with tourists: they charge exorbitant rates for photos and village visits, and are not automatically friendly. Nonetheless, good experiences await if you extend yourself properly. The key is really to get off the main Arusha-Serengeti road.

TOURING THE COUNTRY

Of the two major tourist areas in the country, the northern one is the overwhelming favorite. It includes several of Africa's most renowned attractions: Ngorongoro Crater, Serengeti and Lake Manyara parks, and Kilimanjaro. Scenery is consistently stunning and the area can't be beat for vast numbers of wild animals. Arusha is the safari capital of the region: it is easily accessible by land from Kenya and by air through Kilimanjaro International Airport.

Dar es Salaam is the jumping-off point for safaris in the south. The parks there are among the finest in southern Africa, but difficulty of access, unreliablity of transport, and heavy expense have kept them from being developed into an active tour circuit. The best-known attraction is the Selous Game Reserve. The coast, including the island of Zanzibar, has not been well developed for its tourist potential.

The Northern Safari Circuit

For breathtaking scenery and volume of wild animals, few places compare with the parks of northern Tanzania. Paradoxically, due to the expense and travails of safari in the country, tours and individual travelers generally try to keep visits there as brief as possible. In the old days, when Kenyan vehicles could cross the border in the Masai Mara, the safari circuit was a one-way journey: entering Tanzania at Namanga and exiting into the Mara, visitors could see Lake Manyara, Ngorongoro, and the Serengeti on a short four-night trip. Now it is necessary to double back along the main road that connects Serengeti with Arusha, and a well-paced itinerary calls for a minimum visit of about six nights in the bush. Certainly, a much longer stay would be rewarding. Serengeti alone is so large that many days could be devoted to exploring it fully, and there are plenty of other interesting places beyond the three best-known parks. These include Tarangire and Arusha National Parks, and the Lake Natron region in the Rift Valley. To visit all these places requires a safari of about two weeks.

Two major parks in the northern region are greatly affected by seasonal game migrations that should be taken into account when planning or selecting a safari itinerary. Serengeti is at its "best" during the December–March tourist season, a period of intermittent rains. At that time huge herds of wildebeest and zebra are centered

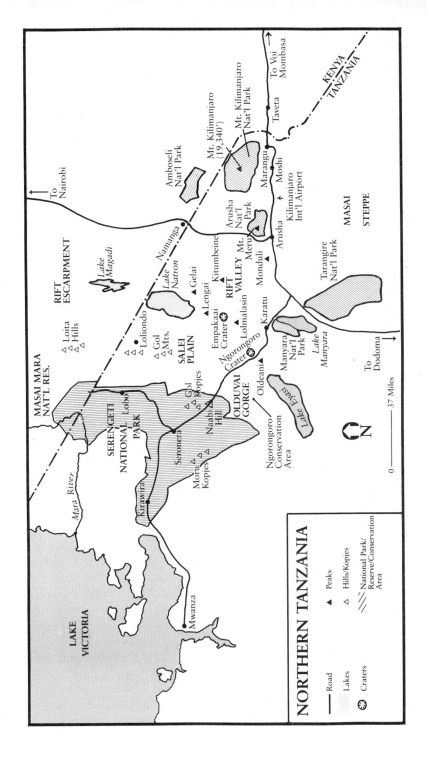

NORTHERN TANZANIA

Legend:
- — Road
- Lakes
- ✳ Craters
- ▲ Peaks
- △ Hills/Kopies
- /// National Park/Reserve/Conservation Area

0 — 37 Miles

N

Labels on map:

KENYA
TANZANIA

To Voi
Mombasa

Taveta

Mt. Kilimanjaro
Mt. Kilimanjaro Nat'l Park
Mt. Kilimanjaro (19,340')

Marangu
Moshi

Amboseli Nat'l Park

Kilimanjaro Int'l Airport

To Nairobi

Arusha Nat'l Park

MASAI STEPPE

Arusha

RIFT ESCARPMENT

Lake Magadi

Namanga

Lake Natron

▲ Gelai

▲ Lengai

Kitumbeine
Mt. Meru
Monduli

RIFT VALLEY

△ Loita Hills

△ Loliondo

△ Gol Mts.

SALEI PLAIN

✳ Empakaai Crater

▲ Lolmalasin

Karatu

Tarangire Nat'l Park

MASAI MARA NAT'L RES.

✳ Ngorongoro Crater

Oldeani ▲

Manyara Nat'l Park

Lake Manyara

To Dodoma

SERENGETI NATIONAL PARK

Lobo

△ Gol Kopies

OLDUVAI GORGE

Naabi Hill

Lake Eyasi

Ngorongoro Conservation Area

Seronera

△ Moru Kopies

Mara River

Kirawira

LAKE VICTORIA

Mwanza

on the open plains in the southern part of the region. Spectacular masses of animals, along with attendant predators, can then be found with more certainty, and the open nature of the country makes visibility better, allowing the spectacle to be viewed to its most impressive effect. After the end of the heavy April–May rains, the herds move northward to their dry-season range. In the "woodlands," the animals find higher grass and permanent water sources. There, the big herds are relatively inaccessible: they are often found far from the lodges, in areas where there are few game tracks. During July and August, the Serengeti's southern plains are dry. Although the dusty plains are not lifeless, visitors making the long crossing are sometimes disappointed, especially if they see the migrating herds in the Masai Mara on the same trip. On the other hand, Tarangire Park is fantastic during the June–October dry season, when game concentrates around its namesake river. Dry-season itineraries should therefore include Tarangire and shorten Serengeti stays. Ngorongoro and Lake Manyara have largely resident animal populations that make game viewing dependable year round.

Arusha

Arusha is the safari headquarters of the northern region. The town is located in a green and fertile district dominated by the extinct Mount Meru volcano, and inhabited by members of the Wa-Arusha and Meru tribes. The Wa-Arusha are an offshoot of the Masai, with whom they share language, dress, and customs; they differ in that they have a primarily agricultural way of life.

Arusha is easily accessible by road from Kenya (it is only an hour and a half from the Namanga border post) and by air through Kilimanjaro International Airport (28 miles to the east). Tour operators and safari outfitters all have their offices clustered in the area around the Clocktower traffic circle, or in the Arusha International Conference Center office building. The Tanzania National Parks also have their headquarters in the Conference Center: it's a good place to purchase park booklets, maps, and logo pins. There, too, is a government "dollar shop" (where only foreign exchange is accepted) selling imported liquors and foods, but these items are now easily available at cheaper private stores.

Aside from booking a safari, there is not much to keep visitors in Arusha. A few souvenir shops near the Clocktower feature Makonde carvings and Masai artifacts. The same area swarms with street vendors and clinging black-market hustlers. The town is interesting to those who have never visited another African city, and is certainly good for a leg-stretching walk after a long international flight. A river runs through the middle of town, and views of nearby Mount Meru are very pretty from along its banks. Between the Mount Meru and New Arusha hotels lies a neighborhood of nice homes with wooded gardens where early morning birding is good. Going downhill from the Clocktower is the city's commercial district, which is filled with many Asian (Indian) shops, a city vegetable market, and a great variety of people. Tanzanite is on sale in the lobby of the Mount Meru Hotel, and meerschaum pipes are a local specialty. They can be purchased at hotel shops, or you can visit the factory where they are carved, kitty-corner to the most important building in town: the brewery.

The New Arusha Hotel, located on the Clocktower circle, has an outdoor garden restaurant that is a favorite meeting place for travelers, but rooms are generally poor and noisy. The "best" accommodation is found at the Mount Meru Hotel, a highrise on the eastern edge of town. It is the flagship of the Tanzanian Tourist Corporation's (TTC) chain of luxury game lodges. Although it is attractive and modern, service is indifferent: don't be surprised if your room has no shower fixture, or lacks a hot-water tap. Inspect your room thoroughly before you unpack, in case you want to change rooms. Even then, you may not find a better one. The Motel Seventy-Seven is just across the road from the Mount Meru. It was hurriedly built to provide lodging for delegates to the opening of the East African International Conference Center in 1977. An Israeli company got the construction contract, a cause for major embarrassment when discovered by Arab delegates. You can still see Hebrew lettering stenciled onto walls and fixtures. It is nothing fancy, just rows of concrete blocks, but is just as comfortable as the Mount Meru. The mosquitos are worse, but Mount Meru has "mossies" too, and is generally noisier. All three hotels have large menus, but most items are perennially "not available." There are many cheap and very basic local hotels and restaurants in town: the Golden Rose Hotel is clean and serves good food.

Several lodges are clustered in the vicinity of Usa River, 13 miles east of Arusha, midway between town and Kilimanjaro International Airport. Ngare Sero Lodge is the most charming: a restored German colonial farm (one of the cottages is a conical brick "fort" to which the settlers could retreat when the natives got restless), it is run by a family and has good food and service. On the grounds, a lake and tract of highland forest host an active heronry, a troop of colobus monkeys, and an excellent collection of hard-to-see forest birds. Small and exclusive, it is difficult to secure a booking, and has a reputation for bumping reserved guests in favor of their own safari clients. The Mount Meru Game Sanctuary is another small colonial hostelry. A private zoo gives it spice: the lions roar periodically all through the night. It, too, is very small and difficult to reserve. Next door, the Tanzanite Hotel is more used by tour groups. It is favored because of the dependability of bookings, not by superior service or cuisine, both of which are decidedly mediocre. But it is no less comfortable than any of the hotels in town, and the country atmosphere makes it a more pleasant place to recuperate from an international flight. Mountain Village is the area's newest hotel and should prove a welcome addition. Scenically set among the coffee farms that fringe Lake Duluti, a small water-filled crater, it features boating and horseback riding, as well as mountain views. It is located a mile off the Arusha road, about 5 miles toward town from the Usa River. The more remote Momela Lodge has a stunning position at the foot of Mount Meru, with a splendid view of Kilimanjaro to the east. Accessible only via a rutted dirt road from Usa River (10 miles), it is almost surrounded by Arusha National Park, so giraffe, buffalo, and other wildlife are close at hand. This lodge would score top ratings for location and charm if it were not so sadly run down.

Unless you are planning to visit Arusha Park, there is little need to stay more than one night in Arusha or the Usa River area. They are often necessary rest stops—buffers between flights and the bush—at the beginning and end of a safari.

Lake Manyara National Park

Sandwiched between a dramatic 1,000-foot Rift Valley escarpment and a soda lake tinted pink with masses of flamingos, Manyara is one of the most beautiful parks in Africa. A remarkable diversity of microhabitats support an extraordinary abundance of animals in an area of only 125 square miles (of which more than two-thirds is taken up by the lake). Beneath the wooded escarpment, a narrow strip combining dense forest, palm-filled glades, and acacia woodlands opens up to grassy flats along the shore of the lake. A series of small rivers are oases in an otherwise seasonally dry country.

They provide permanent water to game and sustain the lush vegetation of Manyara's groundwater forest. With its giant trees, buttressed roots, and snaking lianas, this vibrantly tropical woodland lends the park an extra touch of the exotic, for it is as close to "jungle" as anything you'll encounter in East Africa. Although Manyara was once a celebrated hunting area, its animals are now extremely docile and permit excellent closeup observations.

The park's most famous attraction is undoubtedly its tree-climbing lions. Lions are heavy animals—adult females weigh about 250 pounds—hardly suited to an arboreal life. Yet the Manyara lions typically scale trees for postmeal cat naps. No one is sure why. The most commonly advanced theory asserts that they climb to avoid biting flies, but it is equally possible that they simply like the view or are trying to catch cooling breezes. The big animals certainly look silly draped precariously among the acacias, with legs and oversized paws dangling in the air. When their bellies are bloated with feasting, they look decidedly uncomfortable. Tree climbing is not unique to Manyara, but it is the most accessible place where lions regularly take to the air.

The mixed Manyara country supports good numbers of buffalo, impala, and giraffe, which all thrive at the intersection of grassland with woodland. The park would seem to be baboon heaven: troops fifty or sixty strong are everywhere. The Manyara variety is the olive baboon (*Papio anubis*), which is the most common type in East Africa. Their numbers are particularly large at Manyara because they are so good at exploiting the resources of the park's many habitats. You can observe baboons eating grass in the glades, feeding on acacia flowers or pods in the woodlands, or foraging for fruit in the forest. That same versatility is responsible for the success of elephants at Manyara. The park is supposed to have one of the highest population densities of elephants in all Africa,* and likely compares favorably with other locales for the number of baboons it can sustain, too.

Manyara is the finest place for elephant watching in Tanzania because you can get fantastic closeup observations of cow-calf groups. Its elephants are so well habituated to cars that it is not

---

*A 1973 census put Manyara's elephant population at 453—an astounding 14 per square mile of dry land! That figure may have been the result of severe overcrowding. By 1987, poaching had reduced the elephant count to 180 animals, or about 5 per square mile.

unusual to be able to park in the center of a herd with little ones all around you. Whether they are stripping trees, frolicking in mud, or determinedly devouring grass, the natural rhythms of elephant life make this one of the most fascinating safari experiences.

In the days when Ernest Hemingway hunted at Manyara, rhinos were the favored trophy. Its well-watered bush is still perfect habitat for black rhino, but poaching has almost driven them into oblivion. Only a handful are left, and they are extremely wary. They are occasionally spotted at sunset among the palm thickets on the periphery of the lakeside grasslands. Since this is just the time when the park closes, and the authorities are strict about locking the gate at 6:30 P.M., you are not likely to be on hand to catch a glimpse of what were once one of Manyara's most characteristic residents.

Birdlife at Manyara is simply too spectacular to be ignored. Tens of thousands of aquatic birds crowd the lakeshore and periodically build vast nesting colonies atop nearby fever trees. The collection of woodland species matches any other area on the continent, and to those must be added the specialties of the groundwater forest. Manyara is one of the hottest birding spots in East Africa.

ACCESS AND ACCOMMODATION

Manyara is only 72 miles from Arusha, but you may need up to 3 hours to cover the distance. The time depends on the state of the road, which is usually bad: the pavement is so potholed that drivers often prefer to negotiate the dirt shoulder rather than the roadway. A new paved road linking Arusha with Dodoma is under construction, and should eventually reduce the driving time to Manyara by about half (the routes diverge after 50 miles). This part of the Rift Valley has no eastern escarpment: the land gradually falls away from the highlands around Arusha and becomes beautiful savanna countryside, well populated by Masai and their cattle. As you approach Manyara, its grand escarpment looms dramatically on the horizon.

Just at the foot of the escarpment is the village of Mto wa Mbu, "Mosquito River." The town has been undergoing explosive growth in the last few years, with unfortunate effects on the park. Farms are blocking animal migration routes, poaching has increased, and the inhabitants are denuding the escarpment woodlands in search of firewood. The largest souvenir bazaar on the northern tour circuit has developed next to the village's lively vegetable market. Vendors are very friendly and ever ready to negotiate, but you'll have to bargain hard to get good deals for Makonde carvings or Masai artifacts. Another souvenir market has grown up atop the escarpment, at the turnoff to the hotel.

The road snakes up the escarpment, passing huge sentinel baobabs. At the summit is an awesome viewpoint from which the park is spread out at your feet. From on high, the gray shapes of miniature elephants can usually be seen among the forest glades, and the colonies of nesting birds look like so many white blossoms in the treetops.

The views are also fantastic from the Lake Manyara Hotel. It is one of the better-run TTC hotels: rooms are comfortable, food is okay, but hot water is not always available, though not crucial in Manyara's hot climate. It takes about twenty minutes to drive from the hotel down to the park gate. The only alternative high-quality lodging is in Karatu (a further one-hour drive toward Ngorongoro) at Gibb's Farm. Budget accommodation is found at the Rift Valley Hotel in Mto wa Mbu, where you can ask around about hiring vehicles for touring the park.

The park gate is just off the main road, about a mile beyond Mto wa Mbu. Several simple *bandas* are available for rent there. Bedding is supplied but you must bring your own food or be prepared to go to the lodge or town for restaurant meals.

Manyara's public campsites are also located at the gate, tucked just within the groundwater forest. Shady and alive with the calls of hornbills and blue monkeys, the sites are very pleasant indeed. At night, elephants may come near camp, and you are likely to hear the cries of bushbabies and the alarm calls of baboons disturbed by marauding leopards. Baboons are major pests: they are adept camp thieves, almost lacking any fear of white tourists. You must keep your tent zipped shut and constantly guard your food. Camps should never be left unattended anyway, because human thieves from Mto wa Mbu also regularly check out the sites. With the current boom in camping safaris to Tanzania, the two regular sites tend to be overcrowded with tour groups. A special campsite has been established deeper into the forest, on the edge of the Mahali pa Nyati glades. Other special luxury sites are located near the Msasa, Bagayo and Endabash rivers.

TOURING THE PARK

Game viewing at Manyara is dependably good. In a short drive, you can easily tour the northern two-thirds of the park, where you can pretty much count on getting close views of elephant, buffalo, giraffe, impala, baboon, and a great many other birds and animals. Lions in trees are not always guaranteed: they are sighted somewhat less than half the time.

The level of the lake greatly influences the number and variety of animals that may be seen. After exceptionally rainy years, the lake floods most of the grassy flats along its shores. When the grasslands vanish, zebra and wildebeest migrate further into the Rift Valley and the Simba River hippo pool is absorbed into the lake, making close viewing impossible. Flamingos abandon the lake at high water, but fish-eating birds—pelicans, cormorants, and yellow-billed storks— then converge in vast numbers. Nesting colonies of many thousands carpet the high fever trees behind the shore in a wonderful, if smelly, display of avian color. During dry cycles, a shrinking lake leaves green lawns of succulent grass that provide excellent fodder for herds of wildebeest, zebra, and gazelle, as well as resident hippo, elephant, and buffalo. In very dry seasons, numbers of elephant may wind their way up narrow paths to the top of the escarpment where they forage in the Marang Forest Reserve. Big herds are then scarce and difficult to find in the park.

Because Manyara is small, even a half-day tour can be sufficient for a satisfactory overview. A full day is better, but morning and evening drives are recommended to avoid the hot midday hours. Early morning runs are best for bird watching and for catching views of hippos out of water. Elephants usually come to the various rivers during the late morning or early afternoon, so you may need to expose yourself to some heat if you want to see them drinking and bathing. The lions also tend not to climb into trees until the day heats up. They are somewhat more likely to be seen on after-noon drives, by which time they may have been discovered by some sharp safari driver. Once found, word of their location gets around fast. Photography at Manyara is superb in the late afternoon, when the sun comes from behind the escarpment and the lake reflects the intense colors of the evening sky. That is by far the best time for shots at the hippo pool. The park's small size has its drawbacks for game watching: tracks are few and Kenya-style traffic jams can oc-cur, especially around tree-napping lions.

The park's only entrance is located on its northern end, and it can take some time to get through the gate if there are other safari parties present. While fees are being paid, you can inspect the mu-seum's aging collection of stuffed specimens or search for live birds and monkeys in nearby trees. Beyond the gate, a single track leads through the groundwater forest. The forest casts its best spell just at dawn, when it rings with bird song and leopard are sometimes fleetingly seen. The road is often clogged with baboons and the lush vegetation harbors many esoteric birds. But species such as Narina's trogon, green pigeon, and crested guinea fowl are not easy to see, and lengthy observation is often impossible because of vehicle jams. Blue monkeys (*Circopithecus mitis*) are common in the forest. Their coats are an attractive grayish-blue; the males are twice as large as the females. They are easily passed by when they are sitting quietly in the shady forest foliage. If you watch a troop, you will notice that they communicate with a distinctly birdlike twitter.

The forest is cool and dark, yet tropically luxuriant: it is quite unlike any other woodland you will encounter on the northern park circuit. Many of the trees have been numbered to correspond with a list of Latin names in the national park booklet. The most conspicuous are the huge sycamore figs. These giants grow near streams and have smooth yellow bark. Looking high, you will see their round fruits growing in clusters attached to the trunk. These figs are highly attractive food items to monkeys and birds. Waterbuck and bushbuck are likely to be seen in forest clearings.

The forest melts into a series of open glades, liberally dotted with *Hyphaene* palms and wild mango trees. This area is known as the Mahali pa Nyati, the "place of the buffalo." Buffalo are indeed present in the lightly wooded grassland, which is also favored by impala, zebra, warthog, and giraffe.

Beyond the glades, pure grass flats extend toward the lake. The track continues down to the narrow channel of the Simba River. Its banks are lined with cormorants, ducks, pelicans, and Egyptian geese. Herons, storks, and ibises hunt in the marshes of *Typha* reeds downstream, while blacksmith and crowned plovers stalk the stubbly grasslands on the near shore. Two neighboring pools crammed with hippos provide the best viewing of these animals in northern Tanzania. In cool weather, early visitors may see them piled like pink logs on the far shore, where they like to warm up in the morning sun. More often, you will see them in the water, resting in tight huddles that dissolve with grunts and splashes each time a hippo shifts position. Access to the lakeshore is cut off by impassable swampy ground. Flamingos, which are often present in multitudes, can only be viewed at a great distance.

The treeless floodplain behind the hippo pool often has a large herd of buffalo grazing on it, as well as zebra and wildebeest. Where the grass flats meet the woodlands, wild date palms, graceful with long feathery fronds, grow among yellow-barked fever trees. These stately acacias are often festooned with the nesting colonies of pelicans and other waterbirds. Groups of ground hornbills—rather grotesque, turkey-sized birds—quarter the ground at the edge of the woods, gobbling up any small animals they meet. Their deep, drum-like calls, which African legend holds are the voices of the dead, are familar sounds in the Manyara dawn.

The acacia country at the foot of the escarpment is much favored by tree-climbing lions. The woodlands have been badly torn by elephants, so an effort has been made to protect the lions' favorite trees: the trunks of selected *Acacia tortilis* have been wrapped with screens of chicken wire. Aside from lions, the acacia woods are the place where you find the greatest variety of game. Animals as diverse as vervet monkey, dikdik, giraffe, and mongoose are common among the thickets and trees. Barbets, woodpeckers, starlings, and doves keep the woods alive with sound. You may contribute an outcry to the local chorus, too—for this area is well populated with biting tsetses. Their distribution is patchy; some places are bad, others not. The flies are definitely an annoyance, but if you want Manyara's sugar, you may have to take its lumps!

As you go southward, you cross each of the rivers that run down from the escarpment. Forest and glades follow their courses far onto the lakeshore grasslands. These riverine glades are always crowded with baboons. Lions can occasionally be seen there—sometimes they climb into the thick foliage of *Rauvolfia caffra* trees. The stream beds are excellent places to see monitor lizards, which sun themselves on grassy banks or overhanging trees. Good luck may also reveal a python. More conspicuous are kingfishers—both the pied, a black-and-white specimen that hovers helicopter-like over water before it dives, and the malachite, a tiny red-and-blue gem that perches on twigs.

Elephants can be found in every park habitat, as they wander widely between the escarpment woodlands and the lakeshore. The Ndala River is a particularly good place to look for them in the late morning. A ranger post overlooks a pool to which the river plunges from the escarpment in the rainy season. Iain Douglas-Hamilton lived there during his landmark study of the African elephant, and other researchers may be resident now, in which case visitors are not welcome. This is a pity, for it is not only a pretty spot, but also a choice place to watch elephants bathe. Lower down, the Ndala is a broad sand river in which the animals must dig for water. When rain showers fall, the area is well endowed with mud puddles in which elephants love to wallow. The beautiful Bagayo River, about

1 mile south of the Ndala, is another excellent place to observe elephants drinking. Beyond the Bagayo, you reach Little Maji Moto Hot Springs. If you have already seen plenty of game, this is a good place to turn back. The road continues on to the larger Maji Moto hot springs, but the country southward to the Endabash River is thick with tsetse and is best avoided unless the elephant herds are known to be found nowhere else. Special permission is needed to exit at the ranger post on the south end of the park, from which it is possible to do a backroads trip around the lake to Tarangire.

Ngorongoro Crater

Ngorongoro is universally acclaimed one of the natural wonders of the world. On the verdant crater floor, thousands of wild creatures live a fishbowl existence in a setting of almost sublime beauty. Spread over treeless pastures, the animals are displayed in glorious, unobstructed view. The crater has it all—mighty bull elephants, dour-faced buffalo, beleaguered rhinoceros, lions galore, even a sparkling, flamingo-thronged soda lake. Everything is enclosed within the velvety green walls of a perfect volcanic bowl. In this mile-high caldera, where the mountain air is as fresh as at the Creation, billowing cumulous skies dip close enough to touch the crater rim, sealing Ngorongoro in a misty world of its own. The crater casts a spell of overwhelming tranquility that invites inevitable comparison with the Garden of Eden. It is certainly as close to that earthly paradise as we can ever hope to get. If you have only one day in your life to visit an African game park, that day should be spent at Ngorongoro.

The crater is not a national park. It is part of the Ngorongoro Conservation Area, a 3,200-square-mile tract of Masai land that includes the whole of the Crater Highlands as well as a good portion of the Serengeti plains. The aim of management is to balance the needs of both its human inhabitants and wildlife. Although there are inevitable conflicts between game animals and cattlemen, a multiuse land concept has so far proved workable, if not always easy. Masai formerly lived on the floor of the crater, but were forced by Conservation Area authorities to abandon residence there. When resentful *moran* speared rhino in protest, it become obvious that there would have to be an accommodation: today the crater is officially reserved for the exclusive use of wildlife, but the Masai are periodically allowed to drive their cattle down to drink from the soda lake.

Ngorongoro is the relict of a gargantuan volcano that once dwarfed the 10,000-foot peaks that now compose the Crater Highlands range. About a million years ago, the giant collapsed in on itself, leaving only the base of its walls to ring a caldera 10 miles wide. After the volcano's fires had smoldered to extinction, the land was softened with tropical vegetation and colonized by animals. Today, it remains the largest intact caldera in the world not filled by a lake. The floor of the crater is reckoned to be 102 miles square and about 5,600 feet above sea level, with the height of the rim averaging 2,000 feet higher. The animals are not trapped inside. Time-worn game tracks enable elephants, buffalo, and rhino to regularly pass between the crater floor and the forests of the eastern rim, while zebra and antelope occasionally move in and out from the Serengeti plains.

The crater floor resembles a miniature Serengeti. On its treeless grasslands, the species of the open plains—zebra, wildebeest, and gazelles—are the most abundant animals. A resident ungulate population of about 25,000 head migrates within the confines of the crater. In wet months, antelope and zebra prefer the nutritious short grasses that thrive on the alkaline soils surrounding the soda lake. Marshes become important to them in the dry season, when the herds spend a lot of time grazing on their margins. Fed by permanent rivers or springs, the marshes are reliable sources of water and remain moist and green throughout the year.

The marshes also provide important habitat for other types of animals. Elephants are almost invariably present. All are bulls, for the females keep their precious young hidden in the concealing forests of the rim. It is hard to say why cows learned to avoid the crater floor: was it too open, too much used by Masai, or holding too many lions? In any event, cow-calf groups never venture down. The bulls spend a lot of time feeding in the marshes, eating *Aeschynomene schimperi*, a favored swamp grass. Rhino, too, use the swamps, and hippos take refuge in ponds tucked within the sheltering reeds. Cape buffalo (*Syncerus caffer*) prefer neighboring tracts of damp ground where "rank" grasses grow too high to attract other grazers. The crater specimens—bulky, black animals, with chronically sour expressions—are no more appealing than those elsewhere, but are extremely photogenic as they plod through the wet grassland attended by flocks of white cattle egrets.

Like so many ephemeral bodies of water in their territory, the main Ngorongoro lake takes its name from the Masai word for soda, *magadi*. Lake Magadi is subject to wide fluctuations in water level. It never attains a depth of more than a few feet, but occasionally dries out entirely. Most of the time, it is perfectly ringed with stupendous masses of flamingos. They are joined on the lakeshore by other interesting birds: spoonbills sift the mud, while stilts and avocets probe, and terns wheel overhead. In the grasslands, bustards and ostrich are conspicuous for their size, and whirling swallows fill the air. Undoubtedly the most spectacular crater bird is the crowned crane, which is named for the golden head-tuft worn by both sexes. During the dry season, hundreds of these splendidly coiffed birds congregate on the crater grasslands. In the wet season, they pair off and perform elaborate mating displays.

The Lerai Forest, just below the lodges on the southern rim, is the only really significant woodlot on the crater floor. It's canopy is formed by huge fever acacias, which are particularly striking when their yellow bark glows with evening light. Within the forest, waterbuck graze in grassy clearings and there is an extensive swamp that is popular with bull elephants. Vervet monkeys and baboons live there, too. These primates are closely confined to Lerai's vicinity, where they are marooned in a sea of lion-infested grassland. A second, much smaller, patch of fever tree forest is located at the freshwater Koitoktok Springs.

Game viewing in the crater is always extraordinarily good because the unobstructed nature of the country facilitates the search for specialty species. The animals are also completely at home with vehicles, so you can get exceptionally close without disturbing their activities.

Rhinos are one of the crater's major animal attractions, and you can still pretty much count on seeing them. This is not to say that crater rhinos are safe from poaching. Far from it! They have been hit very hard over the years, in spite of official efforts to maintain a 24-hour guard inside the crater. It is just too easy for poachers to walk down under cover of darkness, fire a quick shot, and escape with a couple of kilos of horn. The official estimate of rhino numbers is sometimes quoted as high as thirty, but that is overly optimistic. It includes rhinos supposedly living in the forest above—animals that may no longer be there. Rhinos are definitely safer on the crater floor than in the forest. In fact, their guardians have tried to physically block them from climbing upward. It is a sad commentary that rhinoceros cannot be guaranteed protection at Ngo-rongoro, where conditions for maintaining a vigilant antipoaching effort are optimum. If rhinos can't be preserved in the wild at the crater, where can they be? Even with the overall situation as desperate as it is, the crater is still one of the best places to view rhinos. At least a dozen rhinos live on the crater floor, and they are continuing to produce offspring. On a good day, you might actually see them all.

There can hardly be a better place for observing lions than the crater floor. Although their actual numbers vary—at one time, disease had reduced them to a mere handful—the usual estimate of lion population is about a hundred animals, roughly one per square mile. With so many big cats around, good sightings are almost guaranteed and it is not impossible to see as many as sixty in a day. Crater prides are large—counting juveniles and cubs, they can total thirty or more individuals. Territory is all-important: each pride must keep to its own area. When good numbers of grazing animals are in their territory, the lions enjoy the fat life. But when grass gets sparse and the herds move to the other side of the crater, such large prides have a hard time feeding all members. As everywhere, starvation is the lot of many cubs.

Hyenas also have the crater floor divided into rigid clan territories that they defend against outsiders of their own kind in noisy pitched battles. Crater hyenas are active hunters: working in concert, they are adept at pulling down anything from warthog babies to adult zebras. Their efforts are closely monitored by lions, who often appropriate the kill for themselves. When there are many hyenas and only one or two cats, however, the shoe may be on the other foot, and the lions may have to yield their kill.

Although cheetah lose a high proportion of kills to lions and hyenas, a few are regularly seen in the crater and have even succeeded in raising cubs. They are tame and can often be very closely observed. Many of the smaller carnivores can also be seen to advantage. Serval cats frequent rocky areas around the crater walls and the high grass on the edge of swamps. The common (locally called *golden*) and black-backed jackals are not shy. Less often encountered is the side-striped jackal, which is largely nocturnal and lives in areas of long grass.

The crater floor is not good leopard country, although they are occasionally seen in the Lerai Forest. They are much more common on the rim, where they are often glimpsed along the main road in the early morning or evening. Lions too are sometimes seen on the rim, but the animals most often encountered in the forest glades are buffalo, bushbuck, waterbuck, and elephant. The forest is natually a good place for unusual birds. Notably pretty species include the golden-winged sunbird, olive thrush, and several varieties of robin chat.

ACCESS AND ACCOMMODATION

The road from Manyara to Ngorongoro passes through fertile farm country belonging to the Mbulu tribe. The Mbulu, or Iraqw as they call themselves, are thin-boned, Cushitic-language-speaking people who originally came from the Horn of Africa. They inhabit a high plateau beneath the Crater Highlands, on which they grow rich crops of coffee and wheat. Beyond Mbululand, forests cover the eastern faces of the highlands massif. A vital water catchment, the forest is protected within the Ngorongoro Conservation Area.

Immediately on entering the forest, you encounter the entrance gate. All vehicles and occupants must pay park fees, even if merely passing through. This is extremely irksome to budget travelers, but nothing can be done: the gatekeepers have heard every story before. Entry fees are the same as for national parks (U.S. $10 per day) and, as usual, are payable in foreign currency.

The road climbs up the southern flank of the Ngorongoro volcano, passing through thick montane forest. Tall, silvery-trunked pillar wood (*Cassipourea malosana*), flat-topped *Albezia gummifera,* and *Croton macrostachyus*—distinguished by large, heart-shaped leaves that are always well chewed by insects—are the most conspicuous forest trees. The roadside blazes with the yellow flowers of *Crotalaria* bushes. The ride is intoxicatingly beautiful, with impressive views of Oldeani Volcano (10,000 feet high and covered with bamboo) and distant Lake Manyara. On reaching the rim, you get your first breathtaking vista of the crater floor. The road then circles around the rim through forest and glades offering tantalizing glimpses of the caldera below. Elephant and buffalo are often seen in the forest, and excitement runs high at the prospect that a leopard may dart across the road.

Beyond Crater Lodge and village, the forest thins out into pastures of tussock grass. Sprinkled among the meadows are gnarled *Nuxia congesta* trees, wrapped under heavy robes of gray-green moss. With the grasslands come the Masai and their herds. Unlike their kinfolk in the Rift, these highland Masai have the advantage of year-round water sources but must contend with bitter cold: they endure the chill of wind-driven mountain mists with nothing more than blankets for protection. At the Seneto Crest, where the descent road begins, there is another awesome overlook from which to examine the crater floor and its pink-fringed soda lake. You also have an impressive view looking toward the Serengeti. In the grass-filled Malanja Depression, between the crater rim and Ol Makarut Volcano, Masai cattle graze among zebra, eland, and flocks of black Abdim's stork. To the northwest, the Serengeti Plain shimmers in the haze.

It is only 35 miles from Manyara to the lodge area on the crater rim. Tour vehicles cover the distance in about two hours; the public bus takes much longer. Only four-wheel-drive vehicles are allowed to descend into the crater. Most visitors will therefore be giving their minibus driver the day off while they transfer to Land Rovers, which are usually at the hotels by about 8 A.M. Because so many different groups are scheduled at the same time, there is often considerable confusion: picking up lunch boxes and getting tour members found and boarded delays snappy starts. Be ready *and* be patient. Land Rovers are locally available for hire by independent travelers. Charges are high, so most attempt to join others in sharing the cost. Check the lodges for like-minded souls, and try to book the previous evening at the State Travel Service office in Ngorongoro Village. Their vehicles are not in great condition, but there is not a lot of choice. You can also try the Ngorongoro Conservation Area office, which is just next door: it has several cars for hire and its drivers are definitely a cut above. Don't take a half-day tour if you can help it; take a full day. During peak periods, such as Christmas, you may have no choice—if you can find a car at all.

All lodge accommodation is found on the crater rim. Crater Lodge is one of the great old safari hotels. Built of hand-hewn logs, with trophy heads looking down from the walls and an ever-blazing fire in the bar, the lodge has a rich old-time safari atmosphere. Its cabins have fine crater views and are equipped with gas heaters (needed for defense against the evening chill, as well as for providing hot water). The menu features exotic game meats—either zebra or wildebeest, depending on the luck of game department hunters. Early morning wake-up tea or coffee is no longer brought to the room, but the flower-decked grounds are still conducive to wandering in search of birds. The brave may even elect to walk downhill to the Fig Tree Bar. There is no longer any service in the treehouse, just the peace of the forest, and you must stay alert for buffalo as you walk down. The "buff" that graze in the lodge compound itself are familiar with people, but you should show proper respect for their capabilities. They will not bother anyone who does not go out of his or her way to pester them, but at least one tourist has paid the ultimate penalty for harassing a bull. Forest hog and serval cats can also be seen on the grounds at night.

Ngorongoro Wildlife Lodge is the modern TTC hotel. Its bar and dining hall offer stunning views from picture windows that protrude over the crater rim. The lodge has central heating and a reputation for better service than other state-owned facilities. Aside from the parking lot, it has no grounds in which to wander.

Rhino Lodge is a much more basic and cheaper facility, located a few miles down the main road toward Manyara. Budget travelers can also find rooms and food in the village of Ngorongoro, at local hotels that serve safari drivers. The Simba campsite is located on the crater rim. Fees are only U.S. $12, compared to $30 per night for sites on the crater floor.

Ngorongoro Safari Lodge, better known as Gibb's Farm, is located at Karatu, in fertile farm country midway between Manyara and the crater. An old coffee estate, it is an oasis of colonial gentility—a great favorite with tourists, expatriates, and members of the diplomatic corps. The main house and bungalows are built around a garden bursting with tropical blooms and birds, which overlooks rows of fragrant coffee trees. Close behind is the Ngorongoro Forest Reserve, from which leopards sometimes stray onto the hotel grounds. Guests can walk to a lovely forest waterfall (the daily park entrance fee must be paid). It is about a one-hour drive to either the crater rim or Manyara, so Gibb's is not perfectly situated for game drives. It is more a haven of quiet luxury, a place for a break from safari life. It features tasty foods and hot water in a country where both are hard to find. Gibb's coffee—just picked, freshly roasted, perfectly brewed—rivals the best in the world. Worth a detour, even if you are just passing by!

The Kifaru Safari Club is planned for construction near Karatu, and promises to be a nice hotel with a resort ambience: it will offer swimming, tennis, riding, and hiking on its coffee farm.

The crater floor is a delightful place to camp. Access to game drives is immediate; in fact, animals may be viewed from camp both by day and night. The number of campsites has recently been expanded to meet increased demand. Even so, there are more camping parties than sites, advance bookings are not always honored, and private campsites cannot be guaranteed. Each overnight party must be accompanied by a Ngorongoro Conservation Area guide. Unarmed, he is along more to protect the crater from tourists than to guard people from animals. In any event, the well-fed crater lions have little cause to prey on tourists.

The Fig Tree campsite is beautifully sited among specimens of giant strangler figs that have completely overgrown the thorn trees they originally parasitized. Both Fig Tree and the nearby Acacia site are situated just outside the Lerai Forest, with splendid views across the crater. The frightening nocturnal screams heard in these camps are made by tree hyrax, which live in the figs. More genuinely disconcerting are lions, which regularly come to drink from leaky water taps. Two newer sites are tucked within the Lerai Forest, where elephants and vervet monkeys are the most common visitors. The plaintive sound of the red-chested cuckoo—known as the rainbird because its three-note call is supposed to warn that "It will rain"—is familiar in all these camps. Another camp site is located among the fever trees at Koitoktok. This is a lovely place, where hippos are neighbors and Jackson's widow birds perform jack-in-the-box courtship dances. It would be paradise, if it were not for the occasional annoyance of biting flies.

TOURING THE CRATER

Most visitors staying on the crater rim descend for a full-day tour. It takes about an hour to drive from the lodges to the crater floor. The descent is remarkable. Because of the dramatic dropoffs, the access road looks scary, especially when it is wet. Actually, the track is buffered by an embankment and a careful driver will have no trouble making a safe descent. The track winds down the crater wall through a forest of giant candelabra euphorbia trees. At the bottom is the lovely Seneto Pool, backed by a small grove of fever trees. By this point, you may already have spotted your first lions!

Normally, tours take a clockwise route around the crater. First you drive through plains of short grass between the western wall and the lake. This is a favorite area for territorial wildebeest bulls and gazelles, and has a resident pride of lions. The lions are often found in the vicinity of small seasonal pools, which are also attended by flocks of red-billed ducks, Egyptian geese, sacred ibis, and wintering ruffs. You then proceed to the lake to view the flamingos.

At a freshwater spring near the western shore, the exquisite pink birds venture especially close to wash soda from their feathers. Just beyond, they parade in tight-knit formations, performing a mass courtship dance. Jackals and hyenas have learned to hunt flamingos by playing dead near the springs. When a predator approaches, the birds move further out into the lake. If the hunter lies down on the shore, even though in full view, the birds soon return and fail to recognize the brown lump as an enemy. With great patience and good luck, a wily predator is sometimes rewarded with a flamingo dinner. However, the pink feathers that line the flats are more the result of preening than predation. Caustic soda quickly damages feathers, but you may be lucky enough to find a few in pristine condition. Do not get out of your vehicle on the side facing the lake, or the birds will retreat to deeper water—the whole mass imperceptibly fading into the distance.

Depending on game locations, you will then cut to one side or another of the extensive Munge Swamp. Lionesses with newborn litters keep their young hidden in such places. If you are lucky, you may get to see tiny cubs. Saddle-billed storks are often seen hunting at small pools on the edge of the swamp, while black-headed herons stalk the high grass. An excellent hippo pool is accessible in dry weather. Bull elephants are almost always to be seen in the marsh, sunk chest-high among the reeds.

From atop the eroded ash cone called Round Table Hill, you will have a good overview of the Munge Swamp. The area between the hill and the crater wall is good for eland, but even in the crater these large antelope are too timid to allow a close approach. From the hill you finish circling round the swamp and proceed along the Munge River, where a eucalyptus grove marks the site of a colonial-era German farm. Another lion pride lays claim to the country on either side of the small tree-bordered stream. The main circuit road then continues past a small hill to the idyllic Koitoktok Springs, where you are allowed to stretch and picnic. This is a welcome break, because guides are overly zealous in forbidding visitors to get out of cars anywhere else, even in completely open, animal-free zones. Toilets offer overdue relief. Koitoktok's reed-fringed pool is a delight. Floating islets of papyrus are pushed across it by the wind, and unseen hippos splash in the screening vegetation along the shore. While lunching, you must beware of the black kites, which have lost all fear of humans and will readily snatch food from your hand. They learn this trick from people who purposely tempt them with scraps.

Game tracks crisscross the rolling grasslands between Koitoktok, the Munge Swamp, and Lake Magadi, an area that is often thick with game. After checking out those herds, you follow the main road from Koitoktok toward the Lerai Forest, skirting waving fields of 3-foot-high Rhodes grass (*Chloris gayana*). This is the crater's best place for rhino.

The Lerai Forest is a favorite nighttime haunt for rhino. In the morning, they come into the open and head for the high grass, where they spend the day. If standing, their gray shapes are easily picked out at a distance with binoculars. They are much harder to find when they are sleeping, which they like to do stretched out in the sun on a patch of bare ground. Once located, they would be easy to approach were it not for the warning cries of the tick birds that escort them everywhere. Certain individuals may trot away nervously—tail sticking straight in the air—at the first hint of a car's arrival. But more often, a rhino will turn blindly toward the oncoming sound, trying to sense what the disturbance is all about. Most will tolerate a slow and quiet approach. Crater rhino only make serious charges when deliberately provoked. Even then, the charge will remain a bluff so long as the vehicle stays in place. Once a rhino has begun its assault, however, cars are likely to be chased some way if they attempt to move off.

A picnic site in the Lerai Forest is the last stop on the crater floor. Vervet monkeys and bright yellow Speke's weavers patrol the clearing, which is shaded by stately groves of yellow-barked acacia. Directly behind the forest, the exit road begins its zigzag up the crater wall. It passes through a lovely wooded canyon where giant spike-leaved *Dracaena* plants and the dangling aerial roots of strangler figs lend a jungle atmosphere. Stop a while when you reach a little stream as it tumbles through a deep forest glade. A flash of color among the foliage may betray the presence of Schalow's turacos, cinnamon-chested bee-eaters, or blue monkeys.

The opportunity for undisturbed game observation in the crater is greatly enhanced by the animals' tameness. It's worthwhile to spend time parked among the herds, quietly watching and listening as the animals go on unconcernedly with their lives. Zebras luxuriate in rolling dust baths, wildebeest bulls cavort in mock combats, baby hyenas let you approach right to the mouths of their dens. Action can explode when you least expect it, too: lions can surge from the high grass to execute an ambush to the surprise of both you and the intended prey.

Half-day tours barely have time for such prolonged observations and should be assiduously avoided. This is not always possible, especially at Christmas, when shortages of four-wheel-drive cars can force unlucky hotel residents to descend on abbreviated schedules. Vehicles then zoom from one pride of lions to the next, staying only long enough for a quick photo, before buzzing on like a swarm of angry bees. This is not the way to enjoy the crater.

Campers can pursue a more relaxed strategy of game viewing. The crater's size makes it an ideal location for shorter drives, with returns to rest in camp. You should wake in the darkness, and be out on your way at first light. This is the time to catch rhinos emerging from the Lerai Forest, to find lions on the night's kill, or still in the process of stalking. You can have a very full drive and be returning to your camp for breakfast just when the people from the lodges are reaching the crater floor. Later you can make a full tour of the crater, or slowly canvass a particular area. On your first circuit, you will be able to determine the location of various lion prides and the state of their appetites. If you find bloated lions with bellies in the air, you can be sure that you will see very little activity from them during your stay. If they look lean and hungry, it will be worth returning periodically to check up on them, for they may very well hunt. Plan to spend two nights on the crater floor. This allows plenty of time for leisurely game viewing on three consecutive days. A longer stay could begin to get repetitive because the crater is really not terribly large, but would greatly increase your chances of viewing a lion kill. Campers can visit the flamingos in the late afternoon, when the play of evening light on lake, birds, and sky creates a magical display of color. The gabbled voices of thousands of birds are then absorbed into the quiet of the almost deserted crater, deepening a sense of profound serenity. This is the perfect way to close out a crater day.

CRATER HIGHLANDS EXCURSIONS

Although the Ngorongoro caldera is the scenic masterpiece, six other major volcanos in the Crater Highlands reach elevations in excess of 10,000 feet. The range is well worth exploring, particularly on a trip to Empakaai Crater.

Empakaai is most easily reached by driving through the Ngorongoro Crater to the track that leaves its northeastern side. Beyond the red thorn (*Acacia lahai*) woodland that spills over the rim, the country opens up into tussocky mountain grassland, composed of tall makutian (also called manyatta grass) and wire grasses. Game is sparse—the odd bushbuck or mountain reedbuck will appear—but there are plenty of Masai. The road goes through the Masai hamlet of Nainokanoka, where the Munge River waterfall can be seen plunging from the flanks of nearby Olmoti Volcano

(10,167 ft.). To the east stands Lolmalasin (11,969 ft.), tallest of the crater peaks. Soon Empakaai's cone comes into view, and the track narrows as it runs around the circumference of the crater's knife-edged rim.* The rimroad is often shrouded in mists but, when clear, the views are astounding. On one side, you look straight down into the Rift Valley. The cones of Lengai and Karamasi volcanos are immediately below, with Lake Natron close behind. Further to the east is Mount Meru, with Kilimanjaro visible a hundred miles away. Just on the other side of the track, Empakaai's thickly forested walls plunge to a crater floor shared by a 259-foot-deep lake and virgin grasslands. You must bring along an armed guide if you want to hike into the crater, which is heavily grazed by buffalo. The trip to Empakaai is long and rough: when clouds close in, as they often do, the moorlands take on a somber mood. A round trip from Ngorongoro can be done in a day, but an overnight camp is recommended if you want to do the crater hike and catch the best Rift Valley views, which are most reliable at dawn and dusk.

Another rough highlands track leads to Endulen and fantastic views of the remarkable escarpments above Lake Eyasi. Eyasi is the territory of the Hadza, Tanzania's last tribe of hunter-gatherers. Special permits must be obtained in Arusha to visit them at Mangola, which is reached from Oldeani.

Olduvai

From Ngorongoro, the road winds down through grassy hills toward the Serengeti plains. The upper slopes are dotted with spindly forests of seedling whistling thorn (*Acacia drepanolobium*), readily distinguishable by their conspicuous roundish galls. The galls, which are hollow and make a subtle high-pitched sound when the wind blows, are inhabited by biting ants that help protect the plant from browsing animals. Lower down, whistling thorn gives way to mature stands of *Acacia tortilis*. Eland, zebra, kongoni, and steinbok are all likely to be seen on the way, but above all, this is splendid country for giraffe. These animals are absent on the treeless crater floor, but here they are both plentiful and tame. Within a few

---

*The track may no longer be open beyond the Embakaai Ranger Post and picnic site, but the most scenic vistas are to be had from there.

miles of where the hills level off to dusty plain, you come on Olduvai Gorge. Lying in the rainshadow of the Crater Highlands, it is a hot, desertlike place for most of the year.

Olduvai is a world-renowned site for research into our human origin. Its crumbling walls have revealed a continuous record of human occupation that goes back almost two million years. The gorge attained international fame when Mary and Louis Leakey discovered the remains of *Zinjanthropus,* "East African man," in 1959. That event was the culmination of a search begun in 1931, when Louis found stone tools on his first visit to Olduvai. Thereafter he returned annually to look for fossil remains of the hominids who had chipped those ancient artifacts. The discovery of "Zinj" *(Australopithecus boisei),* dated to 1.6 million years, was an international sensation. Zinj was proclaimed the long-sought "missing link." Overnight the Leakeys became celebrities, and the search for human origins developed into a media obsession. The Leakeys later unearthed two new species in the gorge, *Homo habilis* and *Homo erectus.* After Louis's death, Mary continued to work at Olduvai, far from the media limelight and the controversies that had wracked the field of anthropology since the 1970s. The gorge was being overshadowed by other fossil sites in Kenya and Ethiopia, until she unearthed footprints, identical to modern humans', in a 3.5-million-year-old bed at Laetoli. That put the Olduvai region back on center stage. Today, research digs are continuing under the direction of Donald Johanson, discoverer of "Lucy," the *Australopithecus afarensis* who is the current candidate for the oldest in the direct line of our human ancestors.

Whatever the ultimate resolution of the puzzle of human evolution, Olduvai adds a special significance to any Serengeti safari. A million and a half years ago, Olduvai's protohuman residents lived in a natural community much like the one found there today. They inhabited the shores of a soda lake, alongside prototype elephants, hippos, rhinos, antelopes, lions, baboons, and warthogs. Some animals, such as the black-backed jackal, have not changed one whit in form since ancient times. A visit to the gorge strongly reinforces the notion that a Serengeti safari is a trip back to our primordial roots.

While the lives of thousands of generations of our ancestors were being played out, the great volcanos were spilling the layers of ash that buried Olduvai's secrets. Recent faulting reversed the region's drainage. The soda lake was replaced by Olduvai Gorge, which was cut by a stream that flows from the Serengeti plains to the Olbalbal Depression at the base of the Crater Highlands. In a mere 30,000 years, the seasonal river had cut through soft layers of ash and clay to reveal the five beds of strata that have contributed so much to our understanding of prehistory.

Black lava signals the 1.8-million-year-old basement of the gorge, on top of which rest the grayish Beds I and II. The oldest *Zinjanthropus* and *Homo habilis* fossils come from Bed I, dating back at least 1.65 million years. *Homo erectus* appeared later, in Bed II. The distinctive red soils of Bed III contain few relics, but the more recent Bed IV and the Ndutu Beds each yield widespread human evidence, especially beautifully crafted stone tools. Today, Masai and tourists are depositing artifacts that may one day become part of the fossil record. Perhaps future archeologists will be as fascinated by our refuse dumps—filled with plastic film cannisters and broken soda bottles—as today's scientists are with the ancient habitation sites of Bed I.

The five beds are clearly visible from the overlook at the Olduvai Museum. At that point, the gorge is about 250 feet deep, and well covered with dry-country vegetation—aloes, commiphora, and spiky wild sisal. It is the wild sisal (*Sansevieria robusta*), called *oldupai* by the Masai, from which the gorge takes its name. A shady *banda* (shelter) at the lip of the gorge is the usual place to receive an informative lecture from local Antiquities Department guides. The little museum houses replicas of hominid remains, original stone tools, and a fascinating collection of skulls from the ancient fauna. The *banda* is a popular picnic spot. Beautiful red and yellow barbets perform elaborate musical duets in the sisal, where they are enticed by tourists' breadcrumbs. Masai live all around Olduvai and water their cattle in the gorge. A few are perpetually in attendance at the museum, hawking trinkets and posing for pictures. Unfortunately, the regulars often put on phony makeup in order to attract more business.

You can drive into the gorge to see the nearby Zinjanthropus discovery site. Several other sites—including the Bed I Stone Circle, the earliest known human-built shelter—are in the vicinity, but require more time and are primarily of interest to specialists. At least a full day's expedition is needed to visit the new site at Laetoli, where the ancient footprints are to be opened to public view. It is in a remote area near Endulen, far from the closest accommodation at Ngorongoro or Ndutu.

Serengeti

Serengeti is arguably Africa's premier game park. The sheer volume of its wildlife is staggering. More than a million and a half wildebeest live there, as do a quarter million zebra, almost half a million gazelles, and thousands of attendant predators. Yet the impact of Serengeti herds goes beyond the quantitative: spread over its seemingly boundless plains, wild animals extend as far as the eye can see. Where else can that be found? Such sights are gone from the plains of Asia and North America, vanished now even from the rest of the African continent. Serengeti is our last vestige of the Pleistocene, the Age of Mammals, a remnant of an abundant nature unfettered by omnipresent humankind. To cross the plain, surrounded by enormous hosts of free-living animals, is the quintessential African experience.

Serengeti is one of the largest parks in Africa, with a total area of 5,500 square miles. It is divided into two distinct geographic zones. In the south is the celebrated Serengeti Plain. Roughly 40 by 50 miles wide, the plain—which the Masai call *Siringet,* "the empty place"—is a vast sea of grass, punctuated only by outcrops of sensuously rounded stone (called *kopjes*). At Seronera, in the center of the park, grassland changes abruptly into "woodlands" that stretch northward through Lobo and the Kenya border. Woodlands also bound the western edge of the plain, extending through the long Western Corridor that takes the park boundary almost to the shores of Lake Victoria. These woodlands are not primarily dense bush, but open, tree-peppered savannas, among which are scattered small grass-covered plains.

Although the Serengeti grasslands support the most massive concentrations of animals, a greater diversity of vegetation enables the woodlands to sustain a wider variety of species. Trees and bush provide shelter to baboons and monkeys, forage for browsers as diverse as giraffe and dikdik, and shade for elephant and buffalo. Some species are present in tremendous numbers: an estimated 70,000 impala inhabit the Serengeti woodlands, and 20,000 buffalo are thought to live solely in the northern half of the park. Permanent sources of water permit these woodland animals to remain resident year-round, unlike the water-dependent species of the Serengeti Plain, which are forced to migrate to the woodlands in the dry season.

The profusion of plant-eating animals ensures an abundance of carnivores. Indeed, Serengeti has been called "a Kingdom of Predators." An estimated 1,500 lions live in the park. Large prides have established permanent residence in all suitable territories, while hundreds of migrant cats follow the herds as they move between woodlands and plain. Serengeti is superb cheetah habitat. The park boasts the largest population in Africa, and it is one of the few places where that sleek hunter can be considered a common animal. It also seems to be the ideal habitat for spotted hyenas, which are superabundant on the open plains.

Serengeti lions were quarry for trophy hunters until the British declared the region a national park in 1951. In recognition of Masai rights, the boundaries were readjusted in 1959, when the Ngorongoro Conservation Area was established. The entire eastern half of the Serengeti Plain, crucial wet-season habitat for the migratory herds, was then excised from the park and the northern Lobo section was added. Concerned about the fate of the herds, Bernard Grzimek and his son Michael conducted the first aerial surveys of the migration. Michael was killed when his plane collided with a vulture, but the father went on to complete the film and book versions of *Serengeti Shall Not Die*, which first brought the park international renown (see bibliography). Since then, a constant stream of wildlife research projects and documentary films have made Serengeti a household name all over the world.

THE MIGRATION

The herds of the great migration are primarily composed of three species: zebra, Thomson's gazelle, and wildebeest.

The hero of the Serengeti story is the wildebeest (*Connochaetes taurinus*). Although zebra and Thomson's gazelle form concentrations that can number in the thousands, the outlandish-sized herds of wildebeest dominate the flood of migration. The ungainly wildebeest, or gnu, with its big bearded head, humped shoulder, and too-short hindquarters, looks like a beast "designed by a committee." But although the individual is comic, the mass aggregations of tens and even hundreds of thousands that carpet the plains are simply beautiful. There are few things in nature more spectacular than this display of Serengeti wildebeest.

Despite its size, Serengeti National Park does not fully encompass the range of its migratory herds. Their ecosystem stretches from the foot of the Crater Highlands through Kenya's Masai Mara Game Reserve—a south-to-north distance of almost 150 miles. In the course of a year, the herds make two great treks between the poles of their wet and dry season ranges. But the migration should not be thought of as a strictly seasonal event. It is really a constant flux of animals in search of grazing and water. Generally, the gnus are on the short grass of the southern Serengeti Plains between the November wet season and the heavy rains of April–May. The intervening months are a time of intermittent showers that keep the grass fresh and replenish shallow depressions that are the sole sources of water on the whole of the Serengeti Plain. During those rainy months, the plains around Naabi Hill and Lake Ndutu are often black with wildebeest. When showers fall, the herds advance to the southeast, reaching beyond the Gol Kopjes and even down to Olduvai. In drier periods, the wildebeest gather themselves into long lines to march westward, skirting or passing through the Ndutu woodlands to the marshes and watercourses of the Maswa Game Reserve. Heavy rain will always bring them back to the short-grass plain.

When the long April–May rains come to an end, the Serengeti desiccates rapidly. The herds then abandon the yellowing plain and begin the great trek to their dry-season range. The wildebeest break into great arms of migration. Huge columns file past the Moru Kopjes into the woodlands on the west side of the plain, following the Mbalageti River. Another arm flows northward through Seronera. The herds pause in the Western Corridor, massing on the grasslands along the Grumeti River and on the low Ndabaka Plain near Lake Victoria. As the Western Corridor's rivers dry up, the migration turns to the northeast. Great numbers of animals move out of the park, passing Fort Ikoma—an area of human settlement—where they suffer heavy losses to poachers. They then push resolutely northward toward the Mara River and Kenya. Extended rains or good grazing can keep the animals anywhere on route, but normally large numbers are crossing into the Mara Reserve by mid-July. From that time through September, it is generally easier to view the big herds in Kenya. By September and October, the animals have devoured much of the Mara's grasses and are just as likely to be found in the vicinity of Lobo. With the onset of the November rains, the herds again march southward, returning quickly to the short grass of the Serengeti Plain.

The wildebeest rut takes place during the long rains, and continues on the northward trek in June. Mating activity is then frantic. After every march, males establish temporary territories on which they vainly attempt to incarcerate any females that enter. In defending these territories, the bulls perform elaborate ritual displays rather than engage in real fighting. Facing each other on their knees,

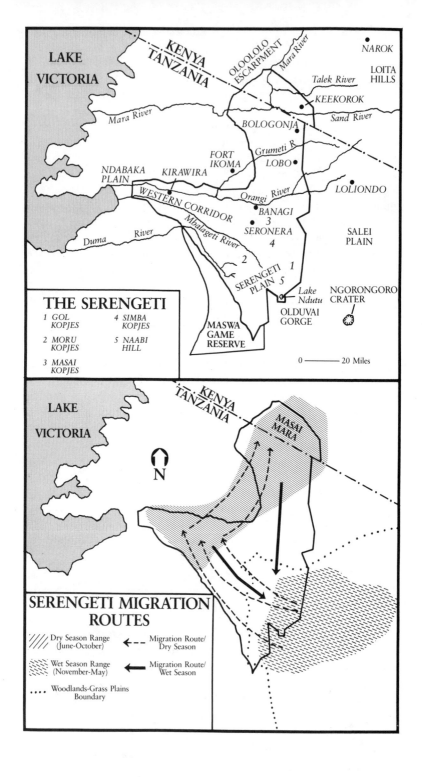

THE SERENGETI

1 GOL
  KOPJES

2 MORU
  KOPJES

3 MASAI
  KOPJES

4 SIMBA
  KOPJES

5 NAABI
  HILL

0 ——— 20 Miles

LAKE
VICTORIA

KENYA
TANZANIA

OLOOLOLO
ESCARPMENT

Mara River

NAROK

LOITA
HILLS

Talek River

KEEKOROK

Sand River

Mara River

BOLOGONJA

Grumeti R.

FORT
IKOMA

LOBO

NDABAKA
PLAIN

KIRAWIRA

WESTERN CORRIDOR

Orangi River

LOLIONDO

BANAGI
3
SERONERA
4

SALEI
PLAIN

Mbalageti River

Duma   River

2

SERENGETI
PLAIN 5

1

Lake
Ndutu

NGORONGORO
CRATER

MASWA
GAME
RESERVE

OLDUVAI
GORGE

SERENGETI MIGRATION
  ROUTES

///// Dry Season Range
      (June-October)

Wet Season Range
(November-May)

.... Woodlands-Grass Plains
     Boundary

←-- Migration Route/
    Dry Season

← Migration Route/
  Wet Season

LAKE
VICTORIA

KENYA
TANZANIA

MASAI
MARA

N

Wildebeest in the Serengeti's Western Corridor. *Photo by Allen Bechky.*

they thrash the ground with their horns. The frenzied expense of energy in constant herding, territorial displays, and mating is very comic.

Calves are born on the Serengeti's short-grass plain. The birthing season usually runs from late January through February, but starts late if conditions are dry. A baby wildebeest gets to its feet within minutes of birth. Even so, new calves are sitting ducks for Serengeti's numerous predators. To increase the individual's chances, all calves are born within a period of a few weeks. Those delivered early or late usually do not survive, but with every female wildebeest giving birth, the predators are simply overwhelmed by the number of newborns: they can't eat them all. Mothers cluster together in large nursery herds in which each has a little reddish-brown calf at her side. In the year that follows, there is steady attrition in the crop of young ones, but as long as grazing conditions are good, more than enough survive to adulthood.

For all their success in maintaining their numbers, the great wildebeest herds show a marked profligacy with the lives of individuals. Stampedes and chaotic river crossings take a heavy toll in accidental deaths and lost calves. These regular mishaps leave the impression that death is of no importance to the wildebeest, that they are too stupid to care. This is an exaggeration. To some extent, the Serengeti wildebeest are victims of their own success: where there are so many, they are necessarily subject to the madness of numbers. In this they are not so different from humans. Witness the chaos in the panic of a theater fire, in which people are crushed in the rush to escape. Is it really any wonder that there are apt to be useless deaths when disaster strikes a massive wildebeest herd? Certainly, in places where gnus live in more manageable herds of twenty to a hundred head, they are not prone to lose many calves through separation from their mothers, which is a major cause of mortality in the Serengeti.

Among the big Serengeti herds, the attack of a predator can create numerous orphans. In such an attack, the herd scatters in a confused cloud of dust. Each calf must manage to stay at its mother's side. If separated for an instant, it will be very difficult for mother and calf to find each other among the thousands of wildebeest in the immediate vicinity. Calves run around frantically checking each adult by turn, while their mothers move about the herd sniffing any young that approach. If a calf's scent is recognized as her own, there is a happy reunion. More often, a calf's enthusiastic advances are met with impatient rebuffs by strange cows, or even bulls, which it has mistaken for its mother. Lost calves are often attracted to vehicles, and it is one of the saddest safari experiences to be followed by such a doomed animal. The trusting little creatures have even been known to walk right up to lions in the hope that they will prove to be the missing parent. That is probably merciful, for those that are not taken quickly by predators are inevitably left to the dubious mercies of starvation.

Zebra *(Hippotigris quagga)* and Thomson's gazelle *(Gazella thomsoni)* are the other principal migratory species of the Serengeti. Each moves in somewhat different patterns from the wildebeest. Zebra disperse more widely and some remain in the woodlands throughout the dry season. Their herds do not approach the size of those of wildebeest. Bands of zebra are always found mingled among the gnus, but thousands may concentrate separately on different parts of the plain, where feeding conditions suit them better. Zebras prefer to graze at a higher level of growth than gnus, so they are the first to enter areas of taller grass. "Tommies," on the other hand, prefer very short, tender grass. They therefore tend to mass farther out on the eastern Serengeti, where the grass is shortest. Because the little gazelles can go for much longer periods without drinking, they can stay on the plain during those intermittent dry spells that force the other two species to retreat to the woodlands. With the arrival of the true dry season, Tommies are the last to abandon the plain, but eventually they too go north. Unlike many of the wildebeest and zebra, they do not push all the way to the Mara, but spread out in the woodlands above Seronera.

Tommies can be found in mind-bogglingly large congregations, but these are temporary and very loosely structured herds. Zebras live in small family groups that have a great deal of permanence and cohesion. Each is composed of a dominant stallion and his mares, which are strongly bonded to him in lifelong attachment. When you see herds of zebra, consisting even of thousands of animals, it is impossible to recognize the structure of individual families, but it is there. Like wildebeest, zebras often travel single file. They are extraordinarily cautious and, when traveling into the wind, can detect predators a long way off. It is hard to say if it is superior intelligence or sense of smell that seems to hold zebra back for second thoughts, while other animals forge ahead toward danger. Zebra vocalizations are surprisingly doglike. Their high-pitched barks and the persistent grunts of wildebeest are the soundtrack of migration.

Eland are common on the open plains. Shy as ever, the big antelopes will begin fleeing from a car as far away as half a mile. Ostrich are often encountered in flocks of a dozen or more. They too are shy, and rarely permit a close approach. Grant's gazelles are far outnumbered by Tommies during the wet season, but their herds are much more tightly structured, and it is not unusual to see groups of several hundred together. When the Tommies leave in the dry season, the plain is left to the Grant's gazelles, which are completely water independent.

Everyone hopes to see Cape hunting dogs, which have become associated with the Serengeti Plain by the films of Hugo van Lawick and Jane Goodall. In fact, they are not common Serengeti animals and they range very widely. Unless they have a den for sheltering pups, they can only be found through dumb luck. They tend to lay up near water during the day and to hunt in the late evening. Periodically, a pack dens up on the plain in the vicinity of Naabi or Ndutu. Once the lair is discovered, the better safari drivers all get to know its location. A patient wait in the late afternoon is usually rewarded with views of pups and the elaborate bonding ceremonies that precede the evening hunt. Hunts are high-speed chases, with a very good percentage of successful kills. The end is bloody, as the victim is disemboweled and torn apart by the pack. Wild dogs are remarkably tolerant of vehicles, and you can get very close, undisturbed views of these highly social predators.

Hyenas are much more common than wild dogs, though visitors make less of a fuss over them. Admittedly, they are not very graceful, and their fondness for lying in muddy pools leaves them looking very sloppy. But they are interesting social animals. They live in close-knit clans, usually headquartered at a den near a water-filled depression. Although they are much despised in hunting lore because of their scavenging habits, they are also terribly efficient hunters in their own right. Tiny cubs are black, older offspring spotted. If you find a den of youngsters, even the most hardened hyena hater will have to admit they are truly cute. You can count on seeing hyenas in a wide variety of situations: competing with vultures at kills, hunting, resting at their dens. Most Serengeti hyenas are shy of vehicles. They will run out of their dens to escape when approached too closely.

Serengeti skies are filled with birds of prey. Tawny eagles, harriers, and kestrels are all very common, but it is vultures who rule the air above the plain: the silhouettes of these cruising scavengers are rarely out of sight. Among the tremendous game populations of the Serengeti, animals die of natural causes every day. Vultures are often the first to find carcasses, and devour them before hyenas or lions arrive. On any morning drive, you will see vultures on a "kill," engaged in a milling free-for-all. They are inevitably joined by tawny eagles and marabou storks, which look rather fittingly like undertakers.

The common, or steppe, jackal (*Canis aureus*) is very abundant on the plains. Scruffy, coyote-like in appearance, they are usually seen resting outside their dens. Often observed scavenging at kills, they are also hunters. A pair is needed to hunt baby gazelles efficiently: while one distracts the mother, the other has a chance to rush in for the kill. They also catch small animals, such as rodents, especially in the dry season, when there is little left to scavenge.

Many other animals form the wildlife community of the plains in the green wet season. The Kori bustard is a stately (3½ feet tall) bird that hunts on the ground. In display, males evert the feathers of neck and tail, appearing at a distance like an oddly painted post. The African hare seems too vulnerable to survive on the open plain. In *extremis,* it employs speed to escape, but first uses discipline to avoid detection by enemies. When danger approaches, the hare freezes. Without moving a muscle, it will allow a vehicle to drive right to it. This tactic is also employed by baby gazelles. While the mother retreats to watch from a discreet distance, the scentless calf lies absolutely still. The mother's behavior may be designed to draw away a would-be predator before it discovers the calf's location, so its best not to stay near too long, in case a hyena takes interest in what you are looking at. Honey badgers roam the open grasslands. They are extremely shy, and can only be well observed with binoculars. If approached, they will run. If pursued, they may, true to their pugnacious reputation, attack the wheels of your car.

Birdlife on the plains is surprisingly abundant. Aside from such giants as ostrich, Kori bustards, and secretary birds, there are many varieties of nondescript larks and wheat-ears to puzzle enthusiasts. Sandgrouse, inconspicuous until disturbed, are present by the thousands. In March, the eastern plain is carpeted with huge flocks of Caspian and Senegal plovers, gathering for their migratory flights back to northern breeding grounds. They go unnoticed until disturbed by a vehicle's approach, when they all rise to wheel and resettle in amazing unison.

Even when you cross the plains at the height of the dry season, when the herds of black gnus are gone, there is plenty left to see. Ostrich and Grant's gazelle remain. The ostrich lay their eggs at that time, several hens placing their eggs in a communal nest. The gazelle are prey for the resident cheetah that guard their territories throughout the lean months. A search of a group of *kopjes* may reveal tattered lions, lean with hunger, hanging on till the rains bring the return of the wildebeest. Giraffe, elephant, buffalo, and other animals can still be found in the Ndutu woodlands. Less noticed but superabundant at that time, are *Avicanthis niloticus*, grass rats. It has been estimated that their dry-season biomass, or total weight per acre, equals that of wildebeest during the wet months! These little rodents are then preyed on by African wild cats, serval, and caracal. Tawny eagle depend on them as food for their young. Jackal and hyena also remain common on the dry plains, and no doubt supplement their diet with grass rat, too.

ACCESS AND ACCOMMODATION

Beyond Olduvai, the road continues across the short-grass plain of the eastern Serengeti. After 6 miles, you reach the track that turns westward to Lake Ndutu (also called Lake Lagaja). That track goes over open plain for another 10 miles before entering the Ndutu woodlands. Then there are another 4 or 5 miles of torturous winding through the woods in order to get around the lake. Never graded, the track is nothing more than a series of dusty ruts in the dry season or a slog through mud puddles in the wet. Getting to Ndutu can be a real piece of safari adventure!

Serengeti's main roads are easier because the national park keeps them well graded. From the Ndutu junction, the main road goes on straight to Naabi Hill, a prominent outcrop where the park entrance gate is located. From Naabi, it's a 30-mile drive across the center of the plain to Seronera. Lobo is a further 50 miles into the northern woodlands.

There are currently only four hotels in the Serengeti region. Ndutu Lodge is located near the lake on the boundary between the park and the Ngorongoro Conservation Area. It is a simple rustic lodge (it was formerly a tented camp, but the badly deteriorated tents have been mostly replaced by cabins). Accommodation is uneven—the older cabins are more charming than those in the new wing—but supplies of hot (though sodary) water and decent food are fairly dependable. Ndutu looks scruffier than the chic Seronera Lodge, but overall it is more comfortable. It is *the* place to stay when migration is on the southern plain, because it is very central to the herds' preferred wet-season feeding grounds around Naabi Hill and to the southwestern plains to which they retreat in dry spells. Elephant are seen in the woodlands around Ndutu, and lion and cheetah are common in the fingers of marsh that drain into the lake. The Ndutu region holds little resident game during the July–October dry season, when the big herds are in the north.

Built into a *kopje*, Seronera Lodge is a breathtaking piece of architecture. Boulders protrude into the dining room and bar, from which there are splendid views of the surrounding savanna countryside. Wildlife viewing at the lodge is great, particularly of the small animals that live on *kopjes*. Hyrax sun themselves atop boulders, while dwarf mongoose forage in crevices, and baboons peek into the dining room. Seronera is at the center of the park, so it can be used as a base to explore in any direction. It's the only lodge from which to explore the Western Corridor during the dry season. Unfortunately, Seronera Lodge is notorious for discomfort and poor service. A number of the rooms are too derelict to be used by tourists, their fixtures having been cannibalized for parts during Tanzania's lean years. The lodge has chronic water problems: it seems to have a regime of availability every other day. On offdays, guests are restricted to one full sink basin. Forget hot water at *any* time. Food supplies are sometimes short: meals, particularly breakfasts and picnic lunches, can be very meager.

In the north, Lobo Lodge is architecturally much like Seronera. It too has a spectacular location: it is so well built into its *kopje* that the lodge is almost invisible until you drive up to the entrance. It is more comfortable than Seronera: sinks and showers always flow, albeit not with hot water. Both Seronera and Lobo are TTC hotels, so when the water or food situation at Seronera has totally broken down, reserved guests are diverted to Lobo. This is a major inconvenience if game is concentrated on the southern plains or the Western Corridor, for Lobo is 50 miles north of Seronera, a long way from the main action. Lobo is really only a proper base for exploring the north of the park. A fair amount of resident game lives in the area, with peak concentrations of migration occurring erratically throughout the dry season.

The Grumeti River Camp, a tented lodge, has just opened near Kirawira in the Western Corridor. Another new lodge may soon be put up at Banagi, just north of the Seronera area.

Camping safaris with flexible itineraries are the ideal strategy for exploring the Serengeti. You can then stay closest to game wherever it is concentrated at the time of your visit. "Established" campsites within the park are found only at Seronera, Naabi Hill, Lobo, and Kirawira in the Western Corridor. These sites are "established" in little more than name: at best, they provide drop toilets; water must be drawn at nearby ranger stations. Permission can be obtained to set up special campsites virtually anywhere in the park, at twice the normal fee. From December to May, camps at Lake Ndutu or Naabi Hill are best for access to the migration. Naabi is a particularly good site, because lions and cheetahs often shelter on the little hill and you have very fast access to finding them on the hunt in open country, first thing in the morning. Camping in the Ndutu woodlands is a little complicated because fees are considerably higher in the Ngorongoro Conservation Area than in the national park, and the boundary is not always clearly marked. The north shore of the lake is safely within the park. It is very exciting to camp among the herds, listening to a nighttime cacophony of wildebeest grunts and zebra barks. Seronera camps are especially exciting, for the night always reverberates with the roars of lions, which often wander through the campsites. The sites at Lobo are high on the *kopje*, and exposed to the wind; nights are very cold in June and July. A special site at Klein's Camp, 10 miles north on the Grumeti River, is then worthwhile: it is warmer and the little river draws game.

TOURING THE PARK

The Serengeti is too vast to be fully explored on a single visit, so efforts must be concentrated in those areas that are seasonally best. In the December–March rainy season, you will want to maximize your time on the Serengeti Plain, and investigate the woodlands around Seronera. June and early July is the time to be sure to visit the Western Corridor; from late July through October, it is best to count on going up to Lobo in search of migration. Safaris during that long dry season can be disappointing: distances are vast and game concentrations sporadic. With the grass burnt to a dusty stubble, the Masai characterization of the plains as the "empty place" seems apt. Visitors have then been known to wonder, "Why have we come all this way? There is nothing here." That, of course, is not true: more species of mammals will be seen on a drive across the "empty" plain in the worst of seasons than could be observed in a prolonged stay in the best North American park. But if you must see constant masses of animals, better come back in December.

Off-road travel is permissible in Serengeti, except within a 10-mile radius of Seronera. That zone is prime habitat for cheetah, lion, and leopard, and subject to heavy tourist traffic. The restrictions are meant to minimize unsightly environmental damage to one of the prettiest parts of the park, and are strictly enforced. Any type of vehicle can negotiate the short-grass Serengeti Plain, when it is dry. If conditions are at all wet, four-wheel drive is essential for long-range exploration, particularly on the western side of the plain, where there are patches of sticky black cotton soil. To explore off-road on your own, you need to take note of the *kopjes* and hills that will be your landmarks. The plain undulates, so that hills are not always in sight, but most often some feature is visible and you can get a bearing if you know what you are looking at. In that regard, traveling over the Serengeti is much like cruising at sea.

You are allowed to get out of your car anywhere you like, except within the restricted Seronera zone. This facilitates picnics and rest stops in the bush, which are logical in such a vast reserve. *Kopjes* make magnificent picnic sites. It is best to choose a small one, and check it out thoroughly for hidden predators before exploring on foot.

Regulations concerning the necessity for accompaniment by park rangers are whimsical. Although not required for most touring, park officials *may* insist on the presence of ranger-guides for camping in special sites or for driving off the road, even beyond the restricted

Seronera zone. For maximum freedom of exploration, you are safest if you bring a ranger-guide.

With the exception of resident fauna in the vicinity of the lodges, Serengeti animals are generally more car shy than those in other parks. Observations must often be conducted at a distance, if the subjects are not to be scared away. For the most part, those close-up portrait shots will have to be taken in the crater, where the animals are completely tame.

Because Serengeti is so large, its diverse sectors must be described in some detail.

THE SERENGETI PLAIN

The Serengeti Plain is itself so vast that it would take many days to explore the whole. Few visitors get to see the remoter parts, but the main road passes through its center, so everyone sees a good cross section.

The plain is divided into two major types of grassland. On the "short-grass" plain, the prevalent *Sporobulus* and *Digitaria* grasses never attain a height of more than a few inches. The "long-grass" plain is dominated by red oat-grass, *Themada triandra,* which reaches up to about 3 feet. Short grass covers the southern and eastern Serengeti, from Olduvai and the Ndutu woodlands to the stony Gol Mountains on the easternmost edge of the plain. Naabi Hill marks a transition zone between the short- and long-grass regions. Beyond Naabi, the grass grows higher, and from the Simba Kopjes, 10 miles north, the long-grass plain sweeps unbroken to its junction with the Seronera woodlands.

From the summit of Naabi Hill, you get a wonderful overview of the geography of the plain. Behind Olduvai, the high blue silhouettes of the crater volcanos dominate the southeastern horizon. Looking east, the lonely islets of the Gol Kopjes are scattered on the short grass, while northward, the outcrops of the Simba Kopjes are clearly visible straddling the main road to Seronera. The Moru Kopjes are much less conspicuous against the background of hills on the western edge of the plain, and the Ndutu woodlands are lost in haze, so the flat prairie seems to stretch on to infinity toward the southwest.

In the wet months, Naabi Hill is a fine vantage point from which to observe the direction and magnitude of migration. Black dots often carpet the plain below like a horde of ants on a kitchen counter. A circular track leads around the hill, along the edge of the acacia-commiphora woods that crown its rocky summit. Lion and cheetah often rest in these woods, taking advantage of shade during the day and descending to hunt among the great herds that flow around the base of the hill.

Kopjes are a very distinctive feature of the Serengeti. Geologically, the plain is the creation of the Crater Highlands volcanos. Their massive eruptions laid down successive layers of ash that covered ancient African basement rocks. The *kopjes*, lonely isles of wind-carved stone, are the emergent summits of long-buried hills. *Kopje*, an Afrikaans word meaning "little head," is very descriptive of the piles of rounded boulders that dot the plains. *Kopjes* are found in groups that form small archipelagos in the grass sea.

Kopjes not only look like islands, but they also are genuine refuges to marooned communities of specialized plants and animals. Fig trees and succulent aloes cling to the rocks, and acacia or commiphora trees sometimes grow at their bases. Subterranean rocks trap sufficient water to enable these trees to survive on *kopje* mounds: just a few yards away, on the porous soil of the plain, a tree would never be able to push its roots down to the water table. Small animals that cannot survive in the surrounding grasslands spend their whole lives on these rocky islets, or within one close-knit island group. Hyrax sun themselves on top of the boulders, while dikdik inhabit the brush found at the base of larger *kopjes*, and small carnivores, such as serval and African wild cat, like to shelter in the rocks. Whole flocks of migratory kestrels perch atop isolated trees growing on *kopjes*, and owls roost in small crevices. Always check out *kopjes* carefully; you will inevitably find something interesting.

It is no accident that lion enclosures at zoos try to simulate the rounded, rocky contours of Serengeti *kopjes*, for they are excellent places to find the big cats. Predators find shade and seclusion on *kopjes*, making them ideal fastnesses on which to lie up during the heat of the day. Not every outcrop will harbor a lion, but the chances are good that you will find one or another of the big cats within a cluster of *kopjes*, if there is prey to be found in the vicinity. Lions or cheetahs sometimes perch prominently atop the rocks, bathing in the afternoon sun or drying after a rain shower. But they are not always so conspicuous. It takes a sharp eye to spot them when they are lying in brush at the base of the rocks.

Each range of *kopjes* has a distinctive character. The spartan Gol Kopjes have the esthetic quality of bonsai gardens in which gracefully balanced stones and an occasional wispy tree seem to have been placed just so by some skillful hand. Pruned by a relentless wind, the *kopjes* exactly suit the spareness of the surrounding treeless plain. The Gol are one of the more accessible off-road *kopje* groups, because only 5 miles of short grass separate them from Naabi Hill. They are a favorite haunt of cheetah, especially in the wet months, when the eastern plain teems with Thomson's gazelle. Cheetahs there are usually very shy and should be watched only at a distance, especially if they have small cubs.

The grass is longer around the Simba Kopjes, where nearby marshes keep grazing animals present further into dry periods. These *kopjes* are therefore much favored by lions. The main road passes through them, and tracks divert to make a circuit of the closer outcrops. The largest is the massive Mlima ya Fisi (Hill of the Hyena). Lion often rest at its foot, and a troop of baboons, unusual on the plain, use it as a base. Bohor reedbuck (*Redunca redunca*) are frequently seen among the *kopjes*, on which they shelter after feeding in the marshes. Cheetah are also found, but usually on the smaller rockpiles, far from the road. Large numbers of topi are seen around the Simba Kopjes in the wet season.

Kongoni, and especially topi, prefer the long-grass plain, which is dotted with the humps of worn termite mounds. Topi lookouts are always conspicuous on top of these hummocks. Cheetahs, too, regularly use them for spying out prey. When traveling on the main road between the Simba Kopjes and Seronera in the late afternoon, it is especially useful to stop to scan the mound-pocked plain with binoculars. Distant cheetahs, which would have been missed from a passing car, are often in full view.

NDUTU

The Ndutu woodlands are a pocket of distinctive habitat on the southern Serengeti Plain. Thorny acacia-commiphora woods ring the marshes and soda lakes that are the headwaters for the seasonal Olduvai stream. The woods, in turn, are surrounded by the open plain. During the wet season, this wooded enclave is often the fulcrum of migration. Huge concentrations are almost always to be found within striking distance of Ndutu, and columns of wildebeest frequently file through the woods on their endless peregrinations.

Game tracks wind through the woods and fingers of marsh that feed Lake Ndutu. These marshes have many different faces. Some are reed-filled swamps, stalked by crowned cranes. Others are gray soda pans covered by a thin mat of grass on which knots of kongoni graze. All are good places for predators to lie up. Lion and cheetah take up residence in these wet-season marshes, holding territories while the migration streams back and forth to the surrounding plains. They depend primarily on the gangs of wildebeest and zebra that file through, but impala, steinbok, giraffe, and buffalo are also potential prey. The marshes drain into Lake Ndutu and neighboring Lake Masek. Flamingos feed in their soda waters, and Ndutu's southwest shore is piled high with the bleached bones of wildebeest—the souvenirs of disastrous lake crossings.

Several routes can be taken through the Ndutu woodlands, depending on the direction of migration. All involve considerable winding to get around the various arms of the lake or its feeder marshes. Once out of the woods, you can often travel cross-country. Several tracks lead to the eastern plains that spread toward Naabi Hill and the Gol Kopjes. The "Makao" track leads southward, past Ndutu's tiny airstrip. Another, goes west past the landmark Three Trees.

During dry spells, the herds march to plains to the south and west of Ndutu. In many places there, grass gives way to clumps of foot-high bush. Eland browse these herbaceous plants, and large nursery herds, even hundreds strong, are sometimes encountered on the western plains. Rain puddles in the area are often guarded by lions, hyenas, or wild dogs. The edge of the grass plain is signaled by small, bushy *kopjes* along the course of a small stream. Lions are frequently found near these *kopjes*, which mark the usual turn-around point for tour vehicles venturing from Ndutu Lodge.

There is no regular track, but if you follow the stream and tree line northward, you enter wild country that is very seldom explored. Animals are shy in this region, but game can be very abundant. When the eastern plain is dry, large herds of wildebeest and zebra water in the Simiyu River. The thin stream meanders amoung sausage and fever trees, a pretty landscape much like the noted leopard country around Seronera. Indeed, trees along the Simiyu should be carefully searched. Lion and cheetah are both common, and big herds of buffalo are present. You may see impressive cow-calf groups of elephants, numbering over a hundred. These elephants are harassed by both sport hunters and poachers in the neighboring Maswa Reserve, so they are apt to be very nervous and unapproachable. By keeping close to the edge of the grass plain, you come to a lovely group of nameless *kopjes*. Set atop high, rounded hills, they offer magnificent vistas over the western plain and the tree lines that follow the branches of the Simiyu. If the big herds are in the area, it is a terrific place to picnic or camp, quite remote from the normal paths of safari traffic. You can return to Naabi or Ndutu by crossing directly over the plain, passing through Secret Valley.

THE WESTERN PLAIN

Secret Valley is hidden on the plain between Naabi Hill and the western woodlands. Its arms are almost unseen until you reach their edge, when a broad shallow depression comes into view. It holds water only during the wet season, when lions take up temporary residence. The valley drains the western plain, and is itself the head-waters of the Mbalageti River, which flows past the Moru Kopjes into the Western Corridor.

The Moru are the highest and most remote of the well known *kopje* groups. Located at the edge of the long-grass plain, with rugged hills and wooded bush country immediately behind them, they have a tough wilderness character and are not often visited. They are usually approached on a lonely track from Seronera, which passes an ephemeral soda pool, Lake Magadi. They can also be reached by a rough crossing of the plains from the Simba Kopjes or Ndutu. The grass around them is high, so the wildebeest avoid the area during the wet months. But when the great northward trek begins, huge herds file through, following the course of the Mbalageti into the Western Corridor.

SERONERA

At Seronera, the junction of grass plain and woodlands fashions some of the most beautiful landscapes in the park. In the proximity of the Seronera River, fingers of trees trace the course of small streams among waving fields of tall grass and gleaming granite *kopjes*. The diversity of habitat in the broken Seronera countryside ensures a good variety of animal life at any season. The big wildebeest herds only pass through occasionally, but resident game includes the whole gamut of woodland species. Park authorities periodically burn the high grass on the local plains to improve both grazing and visibility. This encourages a carpet of tender new grass, to which Thomson's gazelles readily flock. The area is perhaps at its most appealing when zebra gather by the thousands to water in the Seronera River.

Seronera is prime habitat for the big cats. Resident lion and chee-tah are both common and tame, but leopard are the real area specialty. With an extensive menu of small prey, long grass in which to conceal the stalk, and trees for sanctuary from competing predators, Seronera is indeed superb leopard country. At one time, its leopards were extremely tame and excellent sightings could almost be guaranteed to every visitor. Poaching spoiled the show for a number of years, but lately the leopards are becoming more tolerant and are again being seen with some regularity.

Leopards are most likely to be found when they are resting in the trees along the Seronera River. Even there, they are not easy to spot when they climb high into the canopy of fever acacias or hide in the thicker foliage of sausage trees. Leopards are particularly attracted to the river when there is an abundance of gazelle in the vicinity. At other times, they may hunt reedbuck in the riverbed, but are just as likely to be prowling elsewhere. Similar tree lines follow all the seasonal streamlets in the Seronera country, but game tracks do not. Since it is forbidden to drive off road there, checking all suitable trees is impossible. Good leopard photos are hard to get, even if you do find one up a tree. The cats do not stand for a great deal of talking or fuss, and are likely to slip into the high grass at the slightest disturbance. It is usually a tough photographic situation, anyway; shooting into a bright sky while the subject lies in the concealing shade of the tree's crown. Be content if you get a good view of the secretive cat through your binoculars.

There are three distinct sections to explore along the Seronera River. To the east of the main road, the upper river has two forks: the main Seronera stream, which meanders from the open plain, and the Wandamu, to its north. Both drain open grasslands, so the thin fringes of trees that line their courses are convenient sanctuaries for many animals and give shade to a resident pride of lions. Between the forks rise the polished granite blocks of the Masai Kopjes, which are much favored by the latter. Herds of topi, kongoni, and gazelle are likely to be seen in the surrounding grasslands. The upper river is one of the finest places for good views of reedbuck, which shelter and feed in the lush grass of the streambed. Vervet monkeys and baboons roost in the riverside trees and forage on the plain. They have to be careful: lions take them by opportunity, leopards by design. Bateleur eagles, so often seen on the wing, can be examined at close range when they roost in such isolated trees. Their ferocious red faces are terribly impressive at close range.

To the east of the Masai Kopjes is a wide country of undulating savannas, dotted with small stone outcrops. Game prospects there are not much different from the Seronera River area. If you see good-sized herds at a distance, there will be predators, but if game looks sparse it is more productive to turn back to the river tracks.

The Seronera and Wandamu forks meet at a small dam where the main road crosses the river. The pool is enclosed by dense reedbeds in which hippos grunt but most often remain hidden. Going westward, the main track parallels the middle section of the Seronera River, while others branch off to follow thinner tree lines along subsidiary streambeds. By this point, the river is fringed by tall fever trees and lush groves of wild date palms, and umbrella acacias appear in the fringing grassland. Waterbuck, buffalo, and giraffe become more common, and dikdik pop up from the occasional thicket. The nests of white-backed vultures are very noticeable in the high riverbank trees, which are also good places to view some of Africa's most impressive birds of prey. Crocodiles live in the river, but they are shy and hard to see. Just where the track rejoins the main road, there is a pool where you can get good views of a resident hippo herd.

A track continues down the lower Seronera River, where the ground is rockier and the bush thicker. Game is abundant, though lion and leopard are harder to see because of concealing foliage. Large tight-knit formations of impala—as usual, divided into separate male and female groups—become a characteristic of the woodland country. Birdlife is particularly interesting: magpie shrikes, little bee-eaters, and rollers seem to perch atop every bush, while flocks of guinea fowl crowd the track. Seasonally, this bushier stretch of the river harbors tsetse flies.

Seronera is the park headquarters. A small museum, housing dusty natural history exhibits, shares the grounds with the park office and gas pumps, and a picnic site is located on an adjacent *kopje*. Bird watching is terrific among its rocks and trees. A fair-sized village has sprung up at Seronera to support lodge workers and park employees. It is visible on the way to the campsites. Also near the campgrounds is the Serengeti Research Institute. Many ground-breaking animal studies have been conducted under the auspices of SRI, including George Schaller's work on Serengeti lions, and scientific monitoring of the park's ecology continues. No facilities at the institute are open to the public, so don't drop by uninvited.

Even those who are camping will want to stop in at Seronera Lodge. Aside from its imaginative design and the prospect (often disappointed) of a cold drink, there is no finer place to observe and photograph the smaller *kopje* inhabitants—particularly hyrax and agama lizards. The brightly colored male agamas are especially striking: the most common Serengeti variety has an orange head and shoulders; its body and legs are blue. Males perform aggressive pushup displays meant to frighten others of their kind out of their territories, but they direct these haughty shows at humans, too. There are also wonderful views from atop the lodge's *kopje,* and excellent birding to boot.

Elephants occasionally wander into the Seronera area. Park officials do not welcome them there because they are destructive of the riverbank trees and their replacement seedlings. In the past, they were sometimes shot in order to discourage such visits. Although no longer officially fired on, they remain more wary than elephants in many other places. Only some 400 are estimated to inhabit the Serengeti, and they are most frequently seen between Banagi and Lobo. Because of poaching, they are often concentrated in large herds and are very shy. Cow-calf groups are particularly nervous and must usually be viewed at a distance, trunks in the air, tasting for the offensive human scent.

RETIMA HIPPO POOL

From Seronera, the main road pushes deeper into Serengeti's northern woodlands. At any season, you will want to continue at least as far as the Retima Hippo Pool on the Orangi River. The trip provides a good sampler of Serengeti's woodland habitats. When flushed green, the whole route is lined with an astonishing parade of wildlife: here a small plain grazed by mixed herds of topi, kongoni, and zebra; there a wooded tract streaming with golden impala and watchful giraffe. The variety of woodland birdlife is always amazing. Most startling are the flocks of brilliant green lovebirds that constantly flash across the road.

The most direct route to the hippo pool follows the Lobo road to Banagi, the original park headquarters. Its ruins are on the Orangi River, about 11 miles north of Seronera. From there, a track leads 4 miles westward through thorny bush country in which spiky stands of wild sisal mix with acacias and *mswaki (Salvidora persica),* the bush that Africans use to make an excellent natural toothbrush. The track parallels the river, but does not closely follow its banks. It is permissible to drive off the road to peek into the many bends in the river, which are good places to spot basking crocs and wallowing buffalo. Off the road, take extra care not to hit stones and stumps hidden in high grass. A large resident lion pride is usually encountered on the way to the Retima Hippo Pool, which is located at the junction of the Orangi with the Seronera River. Retima is also accessible by a turnoff from the Western Corridor road.

This hippo pool is the Serengeti's finest, and a popular picnic site. The bank above the pool is quite high, so you'll have good closeup views of the resting hippos, which are well accustomed to people. Since you can get out of your car, it's a good place to examine the trails that hippos habitually use to come and go from the water. Note that bushes and tree trunks along these trails are amply covered with hippo dung: on leaving the river, the animals distribute feces with rapid flicks of the tail, to mark their exit path. This territorial behavior has given rise to a good African story: when God created the animals, the hippo asked if it could live in water. God at first refused, out of concern that the great beast would soon devour all the fish. The hippo won its case by promising never to eat fish, and forever after has spread its dung on land to show that it contains no bones—proving that it has kept its bargain. (In fact, however, hippos defecate in water as well as on land.)

In spate, the Orangi's brown waters run high, enabling hippos to disperse more widely all along the river. As the dry season progresses and the river falls, hippos crowd the few pools that maintain suitable depth for daytime resting places. At the height of the dry season, more than sixty animals occupy the small Retima Hippo Pool. Fights between territorial bulls then occur, and the big males inflict terrible wounds on each other with long, sharp tusks. The loser is driven from the pool. Weakened from its wounds, and stressed by food shortage because the herd has finished all grass within miles of the river, he may die, especially if he cannot find another pool in which to escape the burning African sun. Serengeti hippos are rarely taken by lions, but the relative lack of dry-season refuges definitely limits their numbers.

Careful observers can sometimes spot crocodiles on the rocks below the hippo pool. Also to be seen are water dikkop, nocturnal plovers with extraordinarily large eyes, and several types of kingfishers and bee-eaters.

THE WESTERN CORRIDOR

West of the Retima Hippo Pool, the Orangi flows into the Grumeti River, one of the principal streams in the Western Corridor. Riverine habitat, hill country, and a spotty blend of grass plains with thick bush give the Western Corridor a unique character. Most of it is trackless wilderness, cut off from easy access by the rocky ridges of the Central Ranges. Their brush-covered slopes confine the corridor's only road to a narrow strip of broken country along the Grumeti's south bank. The corridor road starts at Seronera and proceeds to the Orangi, then follows the rivers to the Ndabaka floodplains bordering Lake Victoria.

Some animals are found in the Western Corridor that are rarely encountered elsewhere in the park. The terrestrial patas monkey (*Erythrocebus patas*) inhabits savanna grasslands. It has a striking rusty-red and white coat, and long racer's legs, which suit its role as fastest member of the primate order. Two small antelopes, oribi and bush duiker, also live in areas of long grass and light bush. Roan antelope primarily keep to the corridor's remote Ndoha plain, so they are very seldom seen. Several birds are particular to the corridor, especially those of the riverine forests. Along the road, groups of gray-backed fiscal shrikes, with bold black-and-white markings and long tails, are common and very noticeable as they perch atop small trees.

The lower Orangi and Grumeti rivers are fringed with high gallery forest. Where the road goes close, it is worth leaving the track to explore the forest edge. Giant sycamore fig and mahogany trees provide shade for superb picnic spots and are excellent places to see black-and-white colobus monkeys.

Kirawira is famous for its incredible crocodile pool. Full-sized monsters, up to 18 feet in length, inhabit a riverine pool that shrinks to a slimy mud puddle in the dry season. The Western Corridor road is the main highway connecting Lake Victoria with Arusha. Although there is not a great deal of traffic, the crocodile pool is a favorite rest point for local travelers. To avoid harassment, the shy crocs scuttle to water at the sound of the human voice. A campsite is located near the ranger station at Kirawira. It is a fine place to stay when migration is in the corridor. A bridge allows access to the Ruana Plain on the north side of the river, while the main road continues through the Ndabaka floodplains at the westernmost end of the park. Both can hold large numbers of wildebeest when conditions are right. The Ndabaka Plain has game year-round, including a small resident wildebeest population. But its black cotton soils turn into soupy mud during the rains, when travel there is barely possible.

Kirawira is a long 50 miles from Seronera. The trip requires a full day of hard travel through hot country, but there is always plenty to see and lots of shady places to rest along the way. If migration is in the Western Corridor, the journey is a must. At other times, you may not feel like traveling so far. If you stop where the road first reaches the dense gallery forests on the Orangi River, 10 miles west of the Retima Hippo Pool, you will have seen a very full range of corridor habitats. West of the pool, there are really no game tracks, so all explorations will be off road.

The Western Corridor is at its best for wildlife in June and July, when the big herds file through on their northward trek. They mow the high grass, and stay as long as there is water in the Grumeti River. At other times, there is always plenty of resident woodland game. Bushier parts of the corridor are heavily infested with tsetse fly, especially in the wetter months, when long grass and thick bush create ideal resting and breeding places. Always travel there prepared with repellent or long sleeves and pants.

LOBO

From Seronera, it is 50 miles to Lobo in the north of the park. Beyond Banagi and the Orangi River valley, the country is heavily wooded and broken by rocky hills. These brush-covered *kopjes* are excellent places for klipspringer, the antelope that takes the niche of mountain goats in Africa. Hard to see unless silhouetted against the sky, they typically rest atop large boulders where they have a good all-around view. This wooded country also harbors most of Serengeti's shy elephants. They may stay hidden, but you will see evidence of their presence in the number of trees that have been overturned. In recent years, heavy browsing by elephant and giraffe has been reducing parts of the northern park to "relict woodlands" in which only a few large trees remain scattered among open grass. The situation is not irreversible: places such as the Togoro Plain are covered with regenerating acacia seedlings, each tree defended by oversized thorns.

The Lobo country is exceptionally pretty, much like the eastern Masai Mara, which it adjoins. Lobo is a boulder-piled *kopje*, perched atop a high savanna-covered hill. It is an outlyer of the broken range on the park's northeastern boundary. Springs seep from the base of the hills, providing permanent water to game. Resident species are similar to those at Seronera and the Mara. It is good country for buffalo, impala, waterbuck, giraffe, cheetah, and lion. Mountain reedbuck (*Redunca fulvorufula*) live in the hills and are sometimes encountered at Lobo. Klipspringer can be seen right around the lodge, as can baboons, and even leopard on occasion. The country below the hills is open savanna, in which numerous slender acacia seedlings do not hinder visibility. Grass is high during and after the rains, but is quickly mowed by the herds when they arrive, or burned by park authorities. A good system of game tracks has been developed in the area around the lodge.

Although game viewing can be superb around Lobo, it is a problematic area for finding the big migratory herds. During the dry months of July through October, they wander back and forth over the whole northern Serengeti and Masai Mara. Whether they are accessible from Lobo is largely a matter of luck. About 12 miles north of Lobo is Klein's Camp, where the Grumeti River flows into the park from its headwaters in the eastern hills. Another 8 miles farther on, gushing springs give rise to the Bologonja River, which flows westward into the Mara River. Both the Grumeti and Bologonja attract game while they flow, but largely disappear in the dry season. It is difficult to follow the Bologonga stream westward, but a rough track leads from Klein's camp to the Mara River, a distance of about 35 miles. The open country is gorgeous, consisting of gently rolling hills speckled with small trees and, possibly, by herds of animals. Along the river, there are good hippo pools, crocodiles, and riverine forest. It takes four-wheel drive to reach the Mara, and an armed ranger is a necessary escort because poaching gangs often operate in that area. Keep in mind that it is a long way to the Mara River and back again, a frustrating journey if the big herds are not found.

From the ranger post at Bologonja, it is only a few miles to the Sand River, where the Kenya Police have their border post. Ordinarily, vehicles are not supposed to be able to pass, yet they do. Overland expeditions are successful at crossing at this post because their vehicles are neither registered in Kenya nor Tanzania. Kenyan vehicles can cross, if they have paid their Tanzanian road tax and are carrying only Kenya residents. Arrangements have been made, however, where the presence of tourists has been ignored. The Tanzanians do not have immigration officers at the border, only at Lobo and Seronera. So although the Sand River border has been officially closed to tourists for many years, where there has been a will there has been a way.

Tarangire National Park

Overshadowed by the fame of Serengeti, the Ngorongoro Crater, and Manyara, Tarangire has never received the attention it deserves. Nevertheless, it stands on its own as one of the finest parks in Tanzania—which is saying a lot.

Tarangire is located in the Rift Valley, not far from the eastern shore of Lake Manyara. A large park, with an area of more than a thousand square miles, Tarangire is a scenic gem. It is a country of expansive views, in which wide panoramas of wooded savanna stretch in every direction. The baobab-studded grasslands of its northern plains are particularly beautiful. Tarangire's outstanding feature, its raison d'être, is its river. The river itself is a very small stream, but permanent. Although in places it loses itself in the sand of its bed, to flow underground, it is the only reliable dry-season source of water available to wildlife in a vast stretch of Tanzania's Rift Valley. As such, it attracts tremendous seasonal concentrations of animals. Between June and October, game floods into the park from as far north as Lake Natron and from all over the wide tracts of the Masai Steppe. Thousands of zebra, wildebeest, buffalo, elephant, eland, and oryx migrate into the park, and can be seen in herds of impressive size.

In the wetter months, much of Tarangire's game disperses into the surrounding countryside, leaving only scattered groups of resident animals, such as giraffe, impala, warthog, baboon, and kongoni. With the rains, the park is at its scenic best, however. It bursts with greenery, and Tarangire's extraordinary birdlife decks itself in breeding colors.

Tarangire harbors several animals that are not seen in the other reserves of northern Tanzania. It is the only park where a visitor can expect to see fringe-eared oryx, or have the chance to view lesser kudu. Tarangire is primarily wooded bush country that was, at one time, famous for abundant black rhino. Unfortunately, rhino have been all but eliminated during the last decade and are very rarely encountered. You may have better luck searching for giant python, which is a park specialty.

Elephants are abundant at Tarangire. Although they disperse in the rains, good numbers can still be found inside the park throughout the wet season. The behavior of Tarangire elephants contrasts sharply to that of Manyara's tractable pachyderms. They tend to cluster together in huge groups: it is not unusual to see herds of more than two hundred. This behavior is an indication of heavy human pressure outside the park, and poaching within. Consequently, the Tarangire elephants tend to be skittish. This is especially true of the cow-calf groups. Although you may get very close to bulls, wary matriarchs are apt to head for thick cover as soon as they sense a vehicle approaching. They often put on intimidating displays, with trunks raised to catch the wind and ears flapping in annoyance. Failure to heed the warnings can provoke a charge—and Tarangire charges are by no means all bluff. Take no chances with these elephants! As usual, bulls are much less nervous, especially in areas where they feel at home. Bulls frequently visit the lodge in order to feed on the acacias and baobabs that shade the tents.

Despite its great attributes, Tarangire is often left off tour itineraries. This is partly due to the seasonality of game viewing, but there are other factors as well. Tours are often designed with a view to keeping the number of costly days in Tanzania to a minimum, so deserving places like Tarangire get the axe for budgetary reasons. The park is also the habitat of one resident animal that is not a great favorite with tourists: Tarangire's bushy thickets are rife with tsetse flies. Although they are important conservators of African wildlife—and certainly enliven any game drive—they can be terribly vexing, especially during the wetter months when they are abundant and larger game is not.

ACCESS AND INFORMATION

Tarangire is about a three-hour drive (71 miles) from Arusha (it will take half that time when the new Dodoma road is opened), or an hour and a half from Manyara (43 miles). Its relative proximity to town makes it a good alternative to Arusha as an overnight stop at the beginning or end of a safari.

The road from the entrance gate to the lodge passes through some of the most beautiful country in the park. Ancient baobabs are scattered in the high grass of the Lemiyon plains. The giant trees have been much scarred by elephants; one displays a hole eaten right through its massive trunk. In the thirsty dry months, herds of zebra and gnu are very much a part of the landscape. Animals are then constantly filing across the road as they move between the plains and river valley. When thunderstorms clear the air, Kilimanjaro can be seen from the Lemiyon road—a hundred miles in the distance.

Tarangire Lodge is in the northern part of the park, about 6 miles from the entrance gate. It is a wonderfully situated tented camp. Perched atop a bluff, it has a commanding view of a lovely stretch of the river valley. In the dry season, troops of zebra and wildebeest thread their way to the water in a daylong procession, and it is sometimes possible to see hundreds of elephant immediately below the lodge. At night, bull elephants often come into camp to collect acacia pods or nibble on baobab. Dikdik then emerge from the hillside thicket to leave territorial middens along the visitor's path, and the "dustbin" outside the kitchen is regularly raided by honey badgers. The tents are set up in a line along the edge of the bluff, allowing a constant intimacy with the sights and sounds of the river valley.

The established campsites are located near the lodge, on a bluff overlooking the Matete section of the river valley. Water must be obtained at the lodge or park headquarters. Camps may be set up in other areas by special arrangement with the warden.

TOURING THE PARK

Most visitors restrict their tours to morning and evening game runs. A single drive easily combines the Lemiyon plains and the adjoining Matete section of the river valley. These game-rich areas are very scenic and close to the lodge. Lake Burungi and the lower river gorge are also nearby and can be included on short drives. If you visit all these areas, you will see a wide sampling of Tarangire habitats. With more time, it is worth taking a picnic and heading to Larmakau in the remote southern part of the park.

During the dry season, large herds of zebra and wildebeest, mixed with smaller groups of oryx, kongoni, and Grant's gazelle, feed on the open Lemiyon plains. Lions spend the day in the bush of the nearby river gorge, making nocturnal hunting forays onto the grasslands. Cheetah are rare in Tarangire, but are occasionally seen on a track that goes past the airstrip to the fringing woodlands on the park's eastern boundary.

Between the lodge and park headquarters, parallel to the main road from the gate, a winding track follows the gorge along the edge of the Lemiyon plains. It affords good views into a narrow and heavily wooded river valley, where you may see quite impressive herds of elephant. You may also spot bushbuck on the brushy hillsides, or encounter steinbok in the high grass on the lip of the gorge. Where the track dips down to the valley bottom, the country is heavily bush covered. This is an excellent area for a great variety of birds and animals—mongoose, dikdik, impala, and lesser kudu, as well as elephant and giraffe. But it is tsetse infested, so be well prepared to do battle before you descend. When the river is dry, four-wheel-drive vehicles can cross a sandy ford to join the track to Lake Burungi. Otherwise, you have to return on the main road, which can bring you very quickly back to the lodge.

The river valley to the south of the lodge and campsites is the most popular area for game drives. Leaving the Lemiyon plains, a track descends a baobab- and acacia-covered bluff, then crosses the river on the small concrete Engelhard Bridge. This is a good place to stop to look for monitor lizards, which sun themselves in the rocky riverbed. Just beyond the bridge, the track forks at a small *kopje* where klipspringer and rock hyrax are regularly seen. The right-hand track goes to Lake Burungi; the main road continues along the river valley, which at this point becomes much broader. Its edges are bordered with parklike groves of *Acacia tortilis,* well trimmed by giraffe. Impala, baboons, and vervet monkeys also feed among the trees. In the valley below, the high *matete* grass that grows along the river bank gives the area its name. Tall *Hyphaene* palms dot the grassy floodplain. Troops of baboons forage among the palms, while the green beds of *matete* are the place to spot reedbuck or lion.

Tracks leave the main road to loop through the valley, crossing areas of high grass to stands of riverine forest in which tamarind, sausage, and *Acacia sieberiana* trees line the banks of the river. (The sausage tree [*Kigella africana*] gets its name from the cylindrical shape of its woody hanging pods; tamarind [*Tamarindus indica*] is used as a tangy, sour flavoring for food and drink.) At one pool, vultures regularly come to bathe. Dozens may be seen standing in the riverbed with wings outspread to dry. Elephants prefer to quench their thirst where cleaner water flows beneath the ground. They kick holes in the sand, then wait for the water to seep upward before drinking. This behavior is interesting to observe, so it's better to remain at a nonthreatening distance than to try to get too close. If you see elephants in the riverbed, approach carefully so as not to scare them away. If elephants are not present, you will notice copious amounts of dung where they visit daily to dig and drink.

Riverine thickets and bush-filled gullies are the habitat of lesser kudu. These striped antelopes are as shy as they are beautiful. It is worth making a special effort to see them, but you must do so with deliberation: keep silent and drive very slowly, because they often run from fast-moving vehicles. Their haunts are also good places for leopard. Naturally, these cats are not often seen, but they are common in Tarangire. It is perfect country for them, with bush and long grass giving plenty of cover and a large menu of small animals and game birds as prey. Tarangire's woodlands are filled with suitable leopard trees, so keep your eyes peeled for a twitching tail dangling from a branch.

Lions are often seen on the river drive, either lying up in the long grass or resting under trees on the edge of the valley. Tarangire lions tend to be shyer than those of other parks, so you may not be able to get too close. The dry season is their time of bounty. In the greener months, they are forced to go for resident animals—such as impala, reedbuck, and warthog—which are difficult to catch and don't go very far toward feeding a hungry pride. In the hot months, there is an abundance of large game and the cats are more successful in surprising thirsty animals attracted to the river.

The early morning is the best time to see lions in the river valley; later on, when the day heats up, big herds of buffalo and elephant make their way to water. Tarangire buffalo herds can be really impressive, running hundreds or even a thousand strong. Such large aggregations are easily panicked, filling the woodlands with dust clouds and the rumbling sound of heavy hooves.

The main park road continues southward for 25 miles to the Kuro ranger station, formerly known as Lamprey's Camp. The road hugs the edge of the river valley the whole way, with consistently excellent views. Several side tracks cut off from the road to explore the meandering loops of the riverbed.

At the Kuro ranger post, a bridge allows you to cross the river and go on to the edge of the Larmakau *mbuga*. This is a wide plain of black cotton soil, which becomes a flooded morass in the rainy season. Tasty grasses fill the *mbuga* as it dries out, and it is sometimes possible to see hundreds of elephants spread out on the marsh. Animals come to pools at the western edge of the *mbuga,* so watchful lions like to rest under the acacias that line the rim of the swamp. Keep a sharp eye on the branches of these trees: large pythons often seek refuge there from the trampling feet of ungulate herds. Although an adult python can attain a length of up to 20 feet, it is unlikely to present any danger to a human. It prefers to lie in wait for more manageable-sized prey such as small antelope, young warthogs, guinea fowl, or baboons. Even if no lions or pythons are present, the shady acacias make an ideal picnic spot. To the south is a region of waterholes and bush country in which there is a slim chance to see greater kudu and gerenuk, both of which are rare in the park. Since this southernmost region is quite undeveloped, few parties explore further south than Larmakau.

The grassy acacia woodlands near Lake Burungi are the best place to see fringe-eared oryx, especially during the wetter months. The full Lake Burungi Circuit is a long one—about 50 miles. You drive up the river valley almost all the way to Kuro, then turn westward near the pyramidal Tarangire Hill, heading toward the park's western boundary. On route you pass through a belt of orchardlike combretum-dalbergia woodlands, which are characterized by small, evenly spaced, shrubby trees. The multistemmed, smaller-leafed tree is African ebony (*Dalbergia melanoxylon*), from which the Makonde statues are carved. Groups of eland can be seen along the way, but game is generally scarce until you reach the fringes of Burungi. Burungi is a small soda lake that usually has its complement of flamingos. Beyond Burungi, you can see Lake Manyara in the distance, backed by the towering wall of its escarpment. You continue north on the park boundary road until it meets the river gorge, then loop eastward through another stretch of combretum-dalbergia woods to the Engelhard Bridge and the main road. You can cut down the time and distance considerably by going directly to Burungi from the Engelhard bridge, and returning the same way.

Journey to Lake Natron

Tanzania's northernmost Rift Valley is among the wildest and most beautiful parts of Africa. Although dauntingly hot, the country is a constant feast to the eyes. Dust devils swirl on the parched valley floor, while thunderheads drop slanting windrows of rain on distant mountains, and the eroded cones of ancient volcanos are never out of sight. Accessible only on a rough four-wheel-drive track, the Lake Natron region is almost virgin territory. It retains the feel of old Masailand, as it was before the advent of roads, hotels, and national parks. The quality of Masai contacts in the area cannot be beat. Whenever you stop for a travel break, people will appear from nowhere, curious to meet strangers. With no traffic on the road, you can stop at will, be it to talk to laughing Masai women or admire the finery of passing *moran*. You may even wind up accompanied by Masai hitchhikers. Being off the main tourist route and outside the parks, with no hotel schedules to keep, you have total freedom to dawdle and wander. This is really the way safaris were meant to be!

The Natron route is not for everyone, however. The climate is often brutally hot; the road is long and poorly maintained. Devoid of hotels, it is the exclusive preserve of camping safaris. Even by their standards, conditions are rough: luxury camping operators rarely take clients there because it is impossible to guarantee comfort. Furthermore, although there are plenty of interesting birds and animals, game is sparsely distributed and quite untame, so wildlife photography is difficult. The Natron trip must be appreciated more for the magnificence of its scenery and the unspoiled character of the Masai. The route strengthens a safari itinerary because it permits a loop trip through the game parks, eliminating the necessity of retracing your steps. Ideally, you should visit Lake Natron first, and save the parks for the return. That way the excitement of game viewing continues to build throughout the journey.

The Natron track turns off the Arusha-Manyara road and passes through the village of Monduli. Skirting the hilly flanks of Monduli Mountain (8,727 ft.), you arrive at the lip of an escarpment from which a tremendous Rift panorama is spread dramatically at your feet. In the hazy distance is Lengai Volcano, which will be your beacon to Lake Natron.

Descending into the valley, the bush is thick with wait-a-bit thorn and acacia scrub. This is the only good country on the entire northern Tanzania circuit for gerenuk. If you see them, go off road for a closer look. They will be shy, so approach cautiously. Knots of giraffe, zebra, ostrich, and gazelle will also be seen, but there will be better opportunities for their portraits in the parks, so save your film and concentrate on scenic shots. Birdlife is surprisingly abundant in the dry bush, and enthusiasts will find it difficult to make rapid progress because hornbills, bee-eaters, go-away-birds, and rollers are constantly flying over the road. Everyone's favorite is the lilac-breasted roller. A tame and regally bright bird, it always perches in the open where it shows off its colors to maximum photographic effect.

The Masai have a tough life on the drought-stricken valley floor, where rains are sporadic and very local. Their scrawny cattle—often reduced to little more than bones—have badly overgrazed the land. In the vicinity of water tanks, deep furrows have been worn into the dusty ground by the constant pounding of hooves. When grazing is poor, the young men drive the cattle to pasture on the greener heights of the volcanic hills, leaving only the odd bullock or cow and flocks of voracious goats at the family *manyattas*.

As you pass beneath Kitumbeini Volcano (9,377 ft.), you have to cross numerous *korongo*, gullies, where rain-swollen streams repeatedly wash out the road. At times, some digging and pushing

may even be necessary to get through. Forests of tortured commiphora trees—trunks stunted and peeling, branches leafless—give
way to vistas of open grass as you round Kitumbeini and head north
up the Engaruka Plain. When green with rain, its treeless grass flats
are rich with wildebeest and gazelle—a precursor of the Serengeti.
It is an excellent area for fringe-eared oryx, which is an uncommon
antelope in the parks. Be sure to scan for them with binoculars.

As you drive up the Engaruka Plain, you pass through Tanzania's
awesome avenue of the volcanos. To the east, the eroded peaks of
Kitumbeini and Gelai (9,652 ft.) spring from the valley floor. In the
west, the giants of the Crater Highlands form a green wall, with the
heads of Lolmalasin and Empakaai volcanos usually lost in cloud.
At the north end of the range, the perfect cones of Kerimassi
(7,546 ft.) and Lengai (9,442 ft.) stick up boldly against the sky.
Beneath Kerimassi, a short detour leads to the crest of a spectacular,
but hidden, sinkhole crater.

The active Ol Doinyo Lengai, the Masai "Mountain of God," is
the most impressive of the volcanos. Its last major eruption was in
1966, though it put out a small plume of ash in 1982. When it
blows, it can blanket the neighboring country with alkaline ash,
forcing the nomads to move their herds to greener pastures. The
Masai are properly respectful of its power. Pilgrims go there to offer
prayer for rain, cattle, and children. Lengai's steep slopes are fluted
with cracks where torrential rains have gouged deep crevices in the
soft ash. It is tough going as the road rounds the mountain: you
must cross numerous "ash rivers" that wash down from the volcano
toward Lake Natron. As the lake comes into view, so too does a
startling Rift escarpment that sweeps from behind Lengai to the
western shores of Natron. In the colors of twilight, it is a landscape
that could make you weep for beauty.

Seven miles beyond Lengai, the tree-lined Ngare Sero River
("dirty water"), is the logical camping place near Lake Natron. The
river is distinctly sodary, but a nearby spring is the source of fresh
drinking water. There are many *manyattas* in the neighborhood, and
the area remains a great place to meet traditional Masai. The local
people, though exposed to the lure of trade and giveaways, are remarkably friendly. (For a detailed discussion of Masai life, see
Chapter 4, on Kenya.) They bring their herds daily to the river,
where a camp soon attracts a crowd of curious onlookers. In the
last few years, there has been a gradual increase in tourism and
development. A road maintenance camp has been established, a
small mining operation takes soda from the shores of the lake. Stone

bungalows are the monuments of one desultory attempt to create a permanent lodge. Another rustic camp has been successfully set up by Sengo Safaris for the exclusive use of its own clients. Everyone else sets up camp under trees along the river. Shade is an absolute necessity in this broiling region. Heat and sun can be positively dangerous, so activities are usually confined to the morning and late afternoon. The hot midday hours are rarely boring, however, because Natron camps are routinely filled with Masai.

Given the excessive heat, the river is a lifesaver. It is swift and shallow, with a gravelly bottom, but you can find places to comfortably stretch out for refreshing dips. Its fast-flowing alkaline water is bilharzia free.

The river flows from the flanks of Embakaai Volcano via a spectacular gorge that it has cut into the Rift escarpment. The gorge is the focus for an interesting hike. On the walk to its mouth, you may see giraffe feeding among the scattered acacias of the Lengai plains. Inside, towering cliffs hem in the little river. The path is narrow and rocky, so the easiest way to proceed is to continually cross and recross the river. The stream is nowhere more than waist high, but has an uneven, pebbly bottom. Wear shoes that can get wet and be very careful with photo gear: soda water is terminally corrosive to cameras. The walls of the gorge are covered with succulent euphorbias and dry-country scrub, including thickets of twiggy *mswaki* bush, the African toothbrush bush. More dramatic is an oasis that clings to the canyon wall. From a jungle of overhanging wild date palms and fig trees, a waterfall plunges to the chasm floor. For a delightful bath, you wade beneath a natural bridge to a swirling jacuzzi-like pool. It is a paradisiacal spot, well worth the effort to get to. This hike should be done in the morning. Start as early as possible, for you will want to be back in camp before the sun reaches its ferocious zenith.

Several other hikes in the area are best reserved for the cooler months of June and July. It is then easy to climb to the top of the Rift escarpment, following twisting cattle trails that begin at the mouth of the gorge. It is also possible to trek from Lake Natron to Ngorongoro, a four-day walk through the heart of Masailand. It must be emphasized, however, that the first stage of the journey is *very* long, and can be a veritable ordeal of heat and thirst. The route starts with a 15-mile hike through the devilish Lengai country on the floor of the valley, before scaling the escarpment. The going gets much more pleasant as you ascend the forested slopes of Embakaai, and proceed through the Crater Highlands to the rim of Ngorongoro. Dorobo Safaris of Arusha outfit this trek, using Masai donkeys to carry equipment. They also arrange guided climbs of Lengai Volcano. This too is no light undertaking, due to the difficulties of route finding on the fissured mountain and the dangers presented by slippery ash slopes and fierce daytime heat. A Lake Natron camp makes a good base for an attempt on Lengai's summit. An unmarked route approaches the mountain from the Eledoi Valley on its south side, about a 15-mile drive from the Ngare Sero River. You should drive that ground at night and be prepared to start the climb in predawn darkness or possibly by the light of the full moon. Take a good walking stick or ice axe and a minimum of 2 liters of water per climber.

Late afternoon is the best time to drive to the shore of Lake Natron. The lake is the principal breeding area for the Rift Valley's flamingos. The birds can always be seen in shallow bays at its southern end, but their nests are located on inaccessible soda flats in the middle of the briny sea. You can't hope to reach the nests, but it is extremely interesting to walk on the flats of crystallized soda. Sunset colors on the lake, when the Lengai and Gelai volcanos are reflected on its glassy surface, are unforgettable. On the way back to camp, stop near a *manyatta* to watch the cattle being driven in. Without light to distract you with thoughts of photography, you can absorb an essential vignette of Masai life.

The road from Natron to Serengeti continues up the west shore of the lake before passing into desolate badlands on the way toward the Rift escarpment. After rains, the hair-pin turns of the escarpment track are briefly decorated with the yellow blossoms of *Delonix* trees, and you may notice odd cactuslike plants topped with round black balls. These weird flowers have a rotten-meat odor, meant to attract pollinating flies. They are aptly named *Caralluma foetida*. Klipspringer can sometimes be seen on the escarpment road. From the top of the escarpment, there are great views of Natron, its vast soda flats and algae-rich waters flushing pink in the haze of blistering heat. The Serengeti road goes westward to the walled village of Sonjo, which its occupants have fortified against Masai cattle raiders. Mounting a low range of hills, the track continues into the mile-high savanna country around Loliondo. A missionary-run clinic at Wasso provides medical care for the local Masai. It is the closest place to Natron for emergency evacuation by the Flying Doctors. Beyond Wasso, the country grows wilder as the road passes through the woodlands of the Loliondo Hunting Area before entering the Serengeti National Park at Klein's camp, near Lobo Lodge.

Another route to the Serengeti, via Ol Kerien Gorge, makes an excellent alternative during the December–May wet season. A track cuts southward from the main Loliondo road just before the village of Sonjo. It leads through thorny woods to the tiny Masai hamlet of Malambo. Beyond, the woodlands open onto the grasslands of the Salei Plain. Situated between the Gol ("stony") Mountains and the Crater Highlands, its scenery is magnificent. There are dramatic views of Lengai's cone and summit crater. Periodically, large herds of migrating wildebeest and zebra visit the Salei Plain, which they share with throngs of Masai cattle. There are always good numbers of gazelle, so cheetah are present as well. Where seasonal watercourses emerge from the Gol Mountains, tree lines meander onto the plains. One such riverbed comes from the mouth of Ol Kerien Gorge. It makes a wonderful campsite: Masai and wildlife are both in the vicinity and, with an eastern prospect of Lengai, its sunsets and sunrises are among the finest in Africa. There is no water except that which can be dug from the bed of the sand river, so campers cannot expect a good wash.

The main attraction of the gorge itself is the colony of Ruppell's griffon vultures. Griffons are one of the commonest Serengeti vultures, but their nesting sites are limited to a few suitable cliffs. Hundreds of birds roost and nest at Ol Kerien. In the mornings, they can be seen slowly circling above the gorge, waiting to catch the thermal air currents that will carry them effortlessly to the great Serengeti herds. The gorge is also used by the Masai, who drive their cattle in to drink at wells that are laboriously dug in the streambed. It is quite remarkable to be hiking in the narrow defile during such a cattle drive, when the lowing of stock mingles eerily with the whistling of the herders. The Masai around Ol Kerien see very few visitors, so contacts with them are completely authentic rather than canned tourist experiences.

From Ol Kerien, the track continues down the valley to Olduvai, but it is more interesting to cut cross country through Angata Kiti ("the little plain"), a pass in the Gol Mountains. Grassy prairies and hills of gleaming quartz-rich rock make the scenery reminiscent of Montana's butte country. Lines of migrating animals use the pass to move between the Salei Plain and the Serengeti. With luck you may follow good numbers of wildebeest, zebra, giraffe, gazelle, and eland all the way. At the western mouth of the pass, you emerge onto the Serengeti Plain. A line of *kopjes* is a good place to rest and savor the moment. From there, you drive cross country toward the Gol Kopjes, Naabi Hill, or Ndutu. When migration is on the eastern plain, there is no better way to enter the Serengeti than through this back door: driving off road over the wide plain, with thousands of gazelles spread out in every direction and not another vehicle in sight, you feel as though you were the first explorer to discover Africa.

Arusha National Park

No visitor arriving in Arusha could fail to notice Mount Meru. Its imposing summit (14,979 ft.) completely dominates the skyline of the entire region. Yet few bother to investigate the beautiful national park nestled on its eastern flank.

From town the volcano presents a typically cone-shaped profile. But that view is deceptive: an eastern prospect reveals that half the mountain is missing. A quarter of a million years ago, Meru exploded. Its entire eastern wall was blown away in a holocaust similar to the recent eruption of Mount Saint Helens. Over time, forests grew up in Meru's crater and the Momela lakes formed among depressions in the rubble thrown out by the blast. A landscape of utter desolation metamorphosed into one of the prettiest spots in Africa.

Today, the Arusha National Park is a showplace of that geological and biological resurrection. It is more like a North American park than the typical African reserve in that the principal focus of interest is scenery rather than wildlife. That is not to say that there are no animals: the park hosts many species particular to both forest and aquatic habitats, as well as such African favorites as zebra and elephant. It is a great place to photograph either giraffe or dikdik, both of which are exceedingly common. The dikdik here are Kirk's (*Madoqua kirki*), the most widespread variety in East Africa. But a relative paucity of big game—there are no lions—signals why holiday safaris generally avoid the park. This is a pity, for the beauty of its scenery and the access to forest habitat make it an extremely worthwhile addition to any in-depth Tanzania itinerary.

ACCESS AND ACCOMMODATION

The park is ideally situated for day trips from any of the hotels in the Arusha region. The main gate is about 20 miles from the town of Arusha; seven from the lodges at Usa River. Momela Lodge has a fantastic location on a small salient of private land that juts between the Mount Meru and Momella sections of the park. The lodge was used as a set in the film *Hatari,* and from it you have an unobstructed westward view right into the Meru Crater. The vista at dawn, when the mountain lights up with pinkish alpenglow and Kilimanjaro is visible in the east, is sublime. Unfortunately, Momela suffered mightily in the years of Tanzania's economic distress. The white-washed, thatched "rondavals" (from their shape) would be the definition of charm if they were not so badly neglected. As it is, Momela is in a perpetual state of disrepair, and the lodge can only be recommended to those who truly value scenery over comfort. Rumors continually circulate that it will one day be brought back to its former glory. Meanwhile, a tiny neighboring hotel, the exclusive Ol Doinyo Norok Lodge, is scheduled to open soon.

The park's campsites are nicely located at the base of Mount Meru, an area well visited by buffalo and other wildlife. They front a fast-flowing soda river, but have no drinking water. Some budget camping groups prefer to pitch up on the lawn of Momela Lodge in order to take advantage of washing facilities.

TOURING THE PARK

The three attractions of prime interest are the Momela Lakes and Ngurdoto Crater in the eastern section of the park, and Mount Meru in the west. The park is quite small, but roads are very rough, so you should not underestimate the time needed to get around. The eastern sector can be toured in half a day. The Meru Crater also requires a half-day visit, though a full day's outing is needed if you expect to do any serious hiking up there.

Most visitors enter Arusha National Park by the gate located at the base of the diminutive Ngurdoto Volcano. Its slopes are heavily covered with highland forest, a good place to spot black-and-white colobus monkeys and the huge crowned eagle that preys on them. From the crater rim, you look into a small and very pretty volcanic bowl. You may be able to see buffalo and warthogs on its marshy floor. Tour literature often touts Ngurdoto as a mini-Ngorongoro, a teeming wildlife sanctuary in which human intrusion is banned. That people are forbidden access to the crater floor is true, but Ngurdoto's animal population has sadly declined since the time it was declared a national park.

From Ngurdoto, the track to Momela passes through deep forest before skirting a series of pretty papyrus-filled pools where bushbuck, warthog, and spurwing geese are often seen. The going is slow as the road continues over mounds of bush-covered volcanic rubble. It is rare to pass through this area without encountering many giraffe, which are superabundant in the park. A turnoff to the right leads through a seemingly manicured grove of African olive trees before emerging at the beginning of the Momela Lakes circuit. That one-way track winds through a wonderland of lakes and swamps, each separated from another by hillocks of volcanic debris. Dikdik pairs and flocks of guinea fowl are very common in the scrubby bush, while waterbuck, bushbuck, and buffalo feed on the grassy lakeshores. Each of the several lakes has its own charm. Hippos have a favorite refuge in Little Momela Lake; Big Momela is more sodary and usually has a flock of greater flamingos. Both attract impressive numbers of waterfowl, especially during Europe's winter months. Rafts of migrant shovelers, pintails, and garganeys then mingle with African red-billed, pochard, and Maccoa ducks. At all times, cormorants and pelicans can be seen fishing the open waters, while a collection of waders and herons hunt marshes and shores. The trilling cry of the dabchick, or little grebe, rings continually over the lakes region.

If the lakes circuit is a birder's paradise, the rest of the park is scarcely less interesting. Because of its patchy mix of forest and bush, avian life is extremely rich. The augur buzzard, a bird of prey with a red tail that makes identification unmistakable, is very common throughout the park and the brilliantly colored white-fronted bee-eater is especially noticeable around Momela. Forest birding is harder, but views of Hautlaub's turaco, olive pigeon, and red-fronted parrot await the patient observer.

The highpoint of any visit to Arusha National Park should be Mount Meru Crater. Unfortunately, few visitors get to see it because it is necessary to use four-wheel drive to ascend the steep mountain track, and even then many tour operators are hesitant to send their Land Rovers up. The Meru track begins at the Momela Gate. You splash across the Ngare Nanyuki River, then drive through an area of rich open glades in which buffalo, giraffes, crowned cranes, and saddle-billed storks are usually seen. The road climbs into mountain forest with an open parklike understory, which is a good place for black-fronted duiker and bushbuck. Both are shy antelopes, but the Mount Meru track is as good a place to see them as any, particularly if you are descending from the crater late in the day. The track passes right through a "tunnel tree"—a giant strangler fig that arches over the road. Strangler figs get their start from seeds deposited in bird droppings among the leafy detritus that collects in the crotches of large trees. The fig grows in both directions: it sends roots toward the ground, wrapping woody bonds around the trunk of the host tree, while its foliage grows up toward the light. Eventually, the fig can get large enough to block the life-giving sun from its host. In the case of the Fig Tree Arch, two trees died to support the giant parasite. The curtain of aerial roots through which you drive is kept open by the browsing of elephants. Beyond the arch, the track rises through forests of African cedar and podocarpus, until it emerges at Kitoto, a forest bald from which there is a grand view toward the Momela lakes. From there, it winds upward through lichen-covered stands of giant heath, until it reaches the floor of the crater at an altitude of about 8,500 feet.

It would not be an exaggeration to say that Meru Crater presents one of the most startling landscapes in Africa. It is an amphitheatre, enclosed on three sides by the unbroken wall of the volcano's western rim, which towers 6,000 feet above the crater floor. In front of those sheer cliffs stands the dormant Ash Cone (12,030 ft.), a volcano that sprouted after Meru's massive explosion. Scudding afternoon clouds often hang on to the summit of the Ash Cone, hiding the cliffs until wisps of wind dissolve the mists and reveal the full panorama of the crater wall. Although it hasn't erupted in more than a century, it is probable that the Ash Cone is still alive and may have been responsible for creating the Ghost Forest on the crater floor. There, tall cedars and podos, draped in forest moss, look like living trees, but they are all dead—probably killed by a plume of ash spit from the dormant cone. In other portions of the crater, where the trees are alive, there are sacred groves to which the local Meru people formerly came to perform rain-making ceremonies. The ghostly trees, the swirling mists, the ominous-looking volcano, and the high cliffs, create a mystical atmosphere suitable to the performance of such magic rites. From the road's end, you can walk up to a scenic overlook, from which you have a grand view of the entire crater.

Elephant and leopard are sometimes seen in the crater, but buffalo are much more common. For that reason, you should really have an armed guard to accompany you on the walk to the overlook. It is actually extremely worthwhile to hike up the mountain from the Fig Tree Arch, and have your vehicle pick you up in the crater or at the Kitoto viewpoint. Walking in the forest is pleasant and there is no better way to appreciate its subtle beauty. Carpets of purple balsam flowers (*Impatiens papilionacea*) grow on the shady forest floor, along with delicate violets and orange black-eyed

Susans (*Thunbergia alata*). The bright red blooms of fireball lilies (*Scadoxus multiflorus*) are most conspicuous after the rains. Walking also makes it easier to spot colobus monkeys and observe forest birds such as Narina's trogan and red-fronted parrot. Inquire about hiring a ranger at the Momela Gate or the nearby park headquarters; it's best to do so a day in advance.

CLIMBING MOUNT MERU

Terrific views await anyone who climbs Mount Meru. The park has built two simple mountain huts (with bunk beds) to facilitate two- or three-day treks. The route takes you up the road to Meru Crater, on the northeastern edge of which is the first hut. The next day's effort brings you to a hut on the saddle below Little Meru Peak (12,538 ft.). From there you proceed to Meru's rim, which you circumnavigate to the summit point. Some exposed scrambling is needed to reach the top, so this last part is only suitable for intrepid hikers. An alternative route goes up the mountain from Olkokola on its west side. This route is steeper and shorter—which could save a day's park fees—but is not as scenic.

Kilimanjaro

Kilimanjaro, Kilimanjaro, Kilimanjaro,
Kilimanjaro, mlima refu sana.

Kilimanjaro, Kilimanjaro, Kilimanjaro,
Kilimanjaro, very tall mountain.

—The Mountain Song

The origin of the name Kilimanjaro is unknown. It has been variously interpreted to mean "shining mountain," "white mountain," and "mountain of springs," but even the language to which the word belongs cannot be decided with certainty. Whatever the derivation of the name, the image of Kilimanjaro's glacial dome soaring above the plains is instantly recognizable worldwide as Africa's highest mountain.

For the African people who lived around Kilimanjaro, its unattainable white peak was a forbidding region of mystery and magic. To the outside world, nothing was known of the great mountain until 1848, when the German missionary Johannes Rebmann became the first European to lay eyes on Kilimanjaro. When Rebmann and his compatriot Ludwig Krapf reported the discovery to their sponsors, the Church Missionary Society in London, the news was met with ridicule by leading members of the Royal Geographical Society. Objections were raised concerning the impossibility of snow on the equator. This must have been a puzzling argument even then, for the existence of the equatorial Andean peaks had been confirmed 300 years before! The real problem was that Rebmann and Krapf were neither English nor gentlemen, two important requisites for credibility in some explorer circles.

Of course, the missionaries were ultimately proved right. But continued English disdain for Germany later gave rise to a great tale about Kilimanjaro. The well-known story goes that Kaiser Wilhelm wrote to Queen Victoria asking that Kili be assigned to German East Africa. He pleaded that the British Crown already had one snow-capped peak in its Kenyan domain, while Germany had none. The queen, in a typical English spirit of fair play, magnanimously assented, giving the mountain as a birthday gift to her grandson, the future Wilhelm II. It's a great yarn, one that has endured the test of time. But there is no truth to it; the Germans stole Kilimanjaro fair and square. Carl Peters had sneaked into Tanganyika and persuaded various Chagga chieftains to sign treaties agreeing to cede their territories to his Society for German Colonization. When Bismarck pressed these claims for inclusion within the German East African protectorate, the British accepted them in exchange for recognition of their own equally dubious land grabs in Kenya. The deal was merely part of the diplomatic horsetrading involved in the colonial division of Africa.

Kilimanjaro's German legacy remains strong. Ever since Hans Meyer made the first ascent in 1889, Germans have led the way in establishing most of the major climbing routes, and German place names on the mountain still abound. Perhaps because of its place in climbing history and literature, Kilimanjaro is a favorite with German trekking groups today.

Kili is a great volcanic massif. On its 50-mile-wide base are the remains of three once-mighty volcanos. The most ancient was Shira, now reduced to a series of rocky ridges emerging from the plateau on the mountain's western flank. Next eldest is Mawenzi, whose cone has eroded into a broken cluster of craggy pinnacles. Although often dusted with snow, it holds no permanent glaciers. At 16,893 feet, it would be one of Africa's most significant peaks if it were not overshadowed by neighboring Kibo. Separated from Mawenzi by a 3-mile-wide plateau called the Saddle, Kibo (19,340 ft.) is the highest and youngest of the volcanos, famous for its magnificent glacier-crowned dome. Deep within its summit crater, fumaroles still smolder in remembrance of its fiery past.

Although Kili supports the life zones typical of Africa's high mountains, it is dryer than Mount Kenya and the other East African giants. That makes for some ecological differences. There is no bamboo zone or distinct band of transitional *hagenia* forest. Instead, Kilimanjaro's forest thins out rapidly into groves of giant heath that mark the beginning of the moorlands. On Kili, rainfall increases steadily with altitude up to the top of the forest zone, which receives up to 118 inches per year. Beyond that, rainfall decreases markedly as elevations rise. The moorlands are rather dry compared to those of Mount Kenya, and there are far fewer stands of giant groundsels. By 14,700 feet, annual rainfall amounts to a mere 12 inches. Only a handful of wiry grasses and hardy flowering plants survive on the Saddle's alpine desert. Most of the animals found on Mount Kenya are present, with some notable exceptions. Bongo and giant forest hog are absent. So are rock hyrax, which are extremely common on Mount Kenya. (See the Mount Kenya section for a general discussion of the natural history of East African mountains.)

The forest belt is not very prominent on Kilimanjaro's more arid north side. Forests thrive between 6,000 and 10,000 feet on its southern slopes, but because of human interference, few large animals remain. On the main trek route, only blue monkey and colobus are likely to be seen in the forest, while duiker or eland are occasionally sighted on the moorlands. Elephant and buffalo are now pretty much restricted to the northwest slopes above the Amboseli plains—an area quite unfrequented by trekkers.

Below the forest, Kili's southern slopes are the territory of the Chagga tribe, who farm the mountain intensively. The soil is fertile and the rains are good, so Chagga *shambas* burst with bananas, beans, maize, vegetables, and coffee, which is their big cash crop. Since the land is crowded, Chagga families typically keep only a cow or two, which are penned at home. Grass is cut on the plains below, and the straw brought up to the animals. Since the days of exploration, the Chagga have had a reputation as sharp businessmen. Their chiefs overwhelmed a succession of early visitors with hospitality: guests were not allowed to leave until they had been relieved of the bulk of their trade goods. That entrepreneurial Chagga spirit remains unchanged. Work as porters and guides on the

Kibo—the summit dome of Kilimanjaro. *Photo by Allen Bechky.*

mountain is eagerly sought, and every legal device is used to part trekkers from their possessions.

The Chagga have their own version of Kilimanjaro's origin. In the old days there were two neighboring giants, named Kibo and Mawenzi. Kibo was a serious, responsible sort; Mawenzi, a more frivolous character. He liked to drink *pombe* and carouse, and did not always carefully tend his hearth. One day, Mawenzi came home to find his fire had gone out. He visited Kibo, who gave him bananas as well as burning embers to rekindle his home fire. Mawenzi ate the bananas, but again let his fire burn out. Once more, Kibo gave him both bananas and fire, but this time with resentment. When Mawenzi again returned with the same request, Kibo lost his temper. With a great club, he gave Mawenzi a series of mighty whacks on the head. The result is Mawenzi Peak's broken summit, in contrast to proud Kibo's perfect shape.

As the highest mountain on the continent, Kili is the number one trekking destination in Africa. Thousands come annually to attempt to reach Kibo's summit. Almost everyone takes the Marangu route, which has become a regular trekker's highway. Although it is a walkup, the ascent remains a real challenge, for altitude and cold are both formidable obstacles. One of the rewards is great scenery. The alpine panorama on the Saddle between Kibo and Mawenzi is world class, and the views from Kibo's rim are breathtaking. The satisfaction of standing on Uhuru Peak, the roofbeam of Africa, is immense.

ACCESS AND OUTFITTING

Kilimanjaro is literally adjacent to the international airport that bears its name. The closest city is Moshi (21 miles from the airport), but the real base for trekking activities is the town of Marangu, near the national park headquarters and main gate. The Marangu route is overwhelmingly the most popular, and the easiest to organize.

Several local organizations outfit catered treks on the Marangu route. They provide porters and guides, who not only carry your baggage but also bring and prepare food. Accommodation is found in the various national park huts. None of the locally organized treks includes park fees in their cost. The Marangu and Kibo hotels in Marangu are the principal trek outfitters. They provide transport to and from the park gate (about 3 miles), at extra cost. The YMCA in Moshi also organizes treks, and can arrange transport up to the park (about 40 miles). You can outfit your own trek if you wish. Guides and porters can be hired at the National Park gate, but you will have to provide your own food. You must hire a guide; porters are optional.

The outfitters arrange treks for any number of people.* You can have a private climb with your own guide and porters, but the cost is cheaper with a larger party. Most trekkers are cost conscious: they join pickup groups on the shortest possible (5-day) trip. Although this arrangement offers the advantages of price and companionship, you should weigh the potential problems of dealing with strangers' personalities and paces. If you want a layover day on the way up, you will find it much more difficult to find others to join you. Food on catered trips is adequate but unexciting. The same meals turn up with maddening regularity: tasteless dinner combinations of meat, potatos, carrots, and cabbage; eggs for breakfast; thin sandwiches for lunch. Even if you are on a fully catered climbing safari, plan to bring along some supplements or treats to spice up your diet. The guides are well briefed on keeping trekkers adequately hydrated—you will be served plenty of good Tanzanian tea.

---

*Recent national park regulations are supposed to limit each party to a maximum of ten people, but it is doubtful if this limitation is zealously enforced.

Only the Marangu route has regular hut accommodation. The Mandara and Horombo sites are both small communities, where numerous wooden cabins nestle around central mess buildings. The little huts are attractive Norwegian-designed A-frames, divided into two compartments, with four platform beds in each. Foam mattresses are provided. Generally, separate accommodation is booked for each party: if you are two people, you will have a compartment to yourselves; larger groups bunk four per room. At busy seasons, when all the huts are booked, the overflow (the last to arrive) sleep in dorms above the dining halls. When space is available, a tip to the ranger-caretaker may get you a private cabin. Kibo Hut is a stone building. Accommodation there is in dormitory rooms with double-tiered bunk beds.

PARK FEES

Fees are payable at the gate in U.S. dollars or other hard currency *only*. Fees have to be paid for daily park entrance (U.S. $10 per day), huts or camping ($15 per day), rescue ($15 per trip), porters ($20 each per trip), guides ($25 each per trip; maximum one guide for five climbers), and park concession fee ($5 per trip). These fees, I'm told, are about to rise $5 or so. Be sure to bring your currency declaration form when making payment. If your trek has been organized by a U.S. tour operator, the fees may have been included in the prepaid tour cost. Even so, it is a good idea to have cash on hand, just in case there is a problem with the paperwork. If necessary, you can pay, keep all receipts, and get a refund later on.

GUIDES AND PORTERS

Regulations require that you be accompanied by an official guide. Depending on the size of your group, you are likely to have one guide and several assistant guides. Guides are trained and licensed by the national parks. They are quite competent, both at managing your expedition and looking after your welfare. Their English is generally adequate, but they are not naturalists, nor experts on the climbing history of the mountain. They are courteous and friendly, and familiar with the routine of trek organization. A guide or assistant will always remain with the slowest member of your party. Respect your guides' judgment when it comes to safety. In other matters, they may want to organize things more for their convenience than for your enjoyment. If you wish to detour onto one of the slower, more scenic trails, they will go if you insist. Guides are magnificent morale boosters on the summit hike. They set just the right pace to get you to the top. *"Pole pole"* ("slowly, slowly") is their constant refrain. They are generous with encouragement, and will gladly carry your day pack if necessary.

Porters carry loads of up to 40 pounds, which is the baggage limit for two climbers. With the commissary, plus their own food and equipment, the ratio of porters to climbers usually works out at 1:1 or higher.

You will probably be very pleased with the work of your porters and guides. It is customary to give them a tip in addition to their official wages. It is best if your party pools funds and comes up with a gratuity that ensures that porters all get the same amount. Guides and assistant guides naturally should receive more. Tips should run from $20 to $50 per party member, depending on the size of your group. Gifts of clothing are much appreciated in addition to cash gratuities. This is harder to organize equitably. If you make group contributions of clothing, the chief guide will oversee its distribution. That is because the social organization of the crew is very hierarchical. The head guide largely picks his own assistants and porters, so his position as chief should be recognized.

The Chagga are just as industrious today in cajoling gifts out of visitors as they were in the days of Rebmann and Krapf. Toward that end, they will go to great lengths. Porters often wear their worst clothing and shoes on trek, hoping that you will give them yours at journey's end. This can be annoying. On the other hand, a promise to surrender some coveted item can yield remarkably attentive service. All guides play the "missing porter" game, so you can expect to be an unwilling participant. When it is time to hand out tips at the end of the trek, you will be informed that one porter is not present. He has invariably already gone home, requesting that his tip be given to the head guide for later payment. It is best to get a head count of your staff from your outfitter before starting out, and to take a second census personally while on the mountain. Otherwise, just count on paying an extra tip to the missing porter.

Also at trip's end you can expect your crew to sing you a chorus of the pretty "Kilimanjaro Song" (verses at beginning of this section). It's worth hearing more than once, so ask them to sing it during the trek. They *might* oblige.

EQUIPMENT

If you are inadequately prepared for rain and cold, your trek will be miserable and, most likely, unsuccessful. Nighttime temperatures on the moorlands drop below freezing—a chill heightened by relentless dampness. It's much colder (but drier) at the Kibo Hut. The nighttime summit ascent is bitterly cold: temperatures can dip well below 15° F, and the chill factor is severe because of high winds. You need real winter camping equipment: a wind- and rainproof parka-pants set as an outer shell, plus several layers of warm clothes (polypropylene clothing is ideal), and a good sleeping bag. A wool hat or balaclava (better) and gloves are essential. Polypropylene or warm wool socks are highly recommended, because the feet really feel the cold on the summit hike. Gaiters are also useful to prevent pebbles from getting in your boots on the final ascent. The local outfitters rent clothing and equipment, but it is hard to count on its availability or quality. Equipment rented at the park gate is generally in bad shape. There really is no substitute for bringing your own gear if you plan to climb the mountain. You are limited to the 15–20 pounds of baggage that your porter will carry. Bring two complete changes of clothing so that you will always have something as backup if you get caught in a soaking storm. Plastic bags for double-packing your clothes and sleeping bag are also advised. Carry a day pack for your lunch, water, and emergency clothing. Weather conditions change rapidly on the mountain, so keep a sweater and rain gear with you at all times. The normal weather pattern is for the day to start fine, with clouds building up to afternoon rain in the lower and mid-elevations. Carry at least one water bottle with you (two are better). Your guides will fill your bottle with tea if you like. Your outfitter will give you a bamboo walking stick free of charge. Take it along, even if it seems inconvenient. The sticks are very useful for negotiating the scree on the summit ascent.

At the entrance gate, it is sometimes possible to pick up trek maps (1:100,000). A booklet, *Kilimanjaro, Tanzania Notes and Records,* filled with information on the mountain's history, geology, biology, and Chagga lore, may also be available for sale.

THE MARANGU ROUTE

Overwhelmingly, the route of choice is the Marangu route. Most trekkers attempt it on a five-day hike, with four nights on the mountain. An extra night spent at Horombo Hut on the ascent is strongly recommended for acclimatization; it will significantly increase your chances of making it to the top.*

The hike begins at park headquarters at 6,000 feet. It is a walk of about 5.5 miles (three or four hours) to Mandara Hut. Most trekkers, and all porters, follow the main trail, which is an old vehicle track. It is more interesting to take an alternative found just to the west of the main trail (to the left as you climb). Tell your guide you want to take it. He will probably demur, but will follow you on it if you insist. (If it is raining, take his advice to avoid it because the trail will be a slippery mess.) If the weather is nice and the guide is reluctant to show you the way, you can find it by keeping alert to small trails that go down to the stream paralleling the left side of the main track. At one point, there will be a small bridge. Your guide *will* join you if you take this path. It follows the stream up for several miles before rejoining the main trail. It is a more pleasant path, shady and beautiful, with constant views of the rushing stream and several waterfalls. It is also uncrowded, being hardly ever used by tourists, and never by porters.

Mandara Hut is located at 8,858 feet, near the upper edge of the forest. After getting settled into your cabin (and weather permitting), you may want to explore. The best plan is to follow the marked path to Maundi Crater, one of the many parasitic cones on the eastern flank of the mountain. It is reached after a short 15-to-30-minute walk through a lovely podocarpus forest (excellent for birds and monkeys). The crater is rimmed with mossy giant heather forest, and wildflower displays—of beautiful ground-dwelling orchids, red-hot poker lilies, and anemones—are often quite good. There are also vistas of rounded volcanic hills in a countryside mingling grasslands with patches of heath forest.

The next day, you walk to Horombo Hut. Start via Maundi Crater. The trail is slightly longer, but much less crowded and more gradual than the main route, which is steep and extremely slippery when wet. If you haven't seen the crater already, you can do so on the way. Then, continue on the trail to Horombo, which is clearly marked (you should have a guide with you, anyway). You soon rejoin the main trail, where you will have your first view of Kibo's snowy summit, if the weather is clear. You then leave the last of the moss-strewn heath trees behind as you push into the moorlands,

---

*Because of the increasing volume of trekkers and the limited number of beds in the huts, park authorities may refuse to book an extra night's accommodation at Horombo.

where there are many interesting plants and shrubs, including lobelias, proteas, and various daisylike flowers. The trail is long, requiring 5–6 hours to cover a walk of about 10 miles. It passes beneath the rocky southern face of Mawenzi. On the way, keep a sharp eye out for eland, which the guides erroneously call "buffalo." As you approach Horombo, the trail goes up and down several small ridges, and you will begin to feel the altitude.

Horombo Hut is at an elevation of 12,200 feet. It rains there almost every afternoon, making it a rather cold and damp place. Even so, it is worth spending an extra night there to acclimatize for the summit walk. On your layover day, you can hike up to the Saddle and return to Horombo, or just spend the morning exploring nearby. A rushing stream passes just behind the hut complex. In its boggy valley is a very good stand of giant groundsels—the largest grouping to be seen on the Marangu route. Don't break off the old woody branches to burn in the hut's potbelly stove. It damages the plants, which take a very long time to grow, and will produce more smoke than warming fire. Birdlife is good at Horombo. Scarlet-tufted malachite sunbirds buzz around the groundsels, white-naped ravens scavenge at the kitchens, and the mountain chat is common and very tame. The rare bearded vulture, or lammergeyer, often hovers just above camp, looking for bones. Whatever you do, make sure you are inside when the rains hit: bring reading material, stay warm, and take it easy. Horombo typically has magnificent sunsets and nighttime views, when a skyfull of stars outshines the lights of distant Moshi.

On leaving Horombo, take the Upper Route—a continuous and direct climb to the Saddle. You pass a spring, marked "last water," where you should be sure to refill your bottles. When you reach the top, you will be quite winded, but rewarded with a startling panorama. The soaring peaks of Kibo and Mawenzi are close at hand, facing each other across a 3-mile-wide flat. Hemmed in by vast banks of cloud that hug its outer rim, the Saddle seems a world of its own, beyond which one would fall off the ends of the earth. It is a magical place. As you cross the alpine desert, you'll notice beautifully colored lichens and the odd plant pushing up from the bare ground. Eland sometimes visit the Saddle, and Cape hunting dogs have been seen on Kibo Peak, but ordinarily you can't expect to see any animal life. You'll meet a constant stream of refugees descending from their summit attempt. You'll probably find the last few hundred yards very slow going, as you start to ascend Kibo's base to reach the topmost hut.

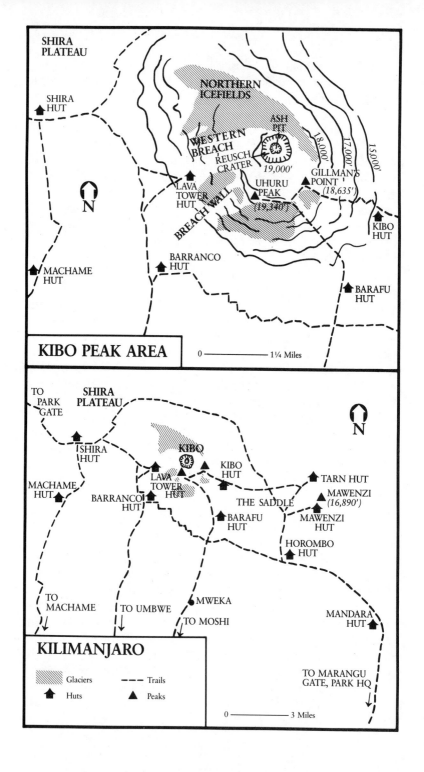

KIBO PEAK AREA

SHIRA PLATEAU

SHIRA HUT

NORTHERN ICEFIELDS

WESTERN BREACH

ASH PIT

REUSCH CRATER

19,000'

LAVA TOWER HUT

BREACH WALL

UHURU PEAK
(19,340')

GILLMAN'S POINT
(18,635')

18,000

17,000

15,000

KIBO HUT

MACHAME HUT

BARRANCO HUT

BARAFU HUT

0 —————— 1¼ Miles

KILIMANJARO

TO PARK GATE

SHIRA PLATEAU

KIBO

SHIRA HUT

MACHAME HUT

BARRANCO HUT

LAVA TOWER HUT

KIBO HUT

TARN HUT

MAWENZI
(16,890')

THE SADDLE

BARAFU HUT

MAWENZI HUT

HOROMBO HUT

TO MACHAME

TO UMBWE

MWEKA

TO MOSHI

MANDARA HUT

TO MARANGU GATE, PARK HQ

Glaciers   — — — Trails

Huts   ▲ Peaks

0 —————— 3 Miles

Kibo Hut is a stone building at 15,430 feet. It is bitterly cold there at night. Snow melt is collected from the roof, but there is no reliable source of water. Because all water and fuel must be carried up, it is logistically very taxing to remain there more than one night. This partly explains why trekkers climb at night, although the reason most often given is to get to the summit for sunrise. With a morning start, it would be impossible to reach the top and walk down to Horombo in one day. The night at Kibo Hut is often not very pleasant. The tradition is to have a light dinner—usually porridge—and turn in early for whatever sleep you can get. Do not supplement your meal with sausage or other greasy foods—they do not digest well at such altitude.

You will be awakened at 1 or 2 A.M., given tea and biscuits, and hustled outside to begin the climb. Your guides will carry kerosene lanterns. You should have your own flashlight or (preferably) headlamp, with extra batteries. You will be freezing as you start, but you will soon warm up on the merciless uphill hike. Layer your clothes in such a way that you do not get overheated walking, but have something extra warm that you can throw on easily as soon as you stop for a rest. (I wear my windbreaking parka while walking, and whip my down jacket on *over* it, rather than take anything off). Hands and feet get especially cold. The guides are full of encouragement and set just the right pace: "*pole pole*" is the only way to go. It is better to proceed with a steady "one step-one breath" rhythm than to walk quickly and rest often. The trail switchbacks up a steep scree slope. Fortunately, the path is well used, so most loose pebbles get knocked off it early in the climbing season. Otherwise, loose scree would present a frustrating "two steps forward, one step back" scenario. The Hans Meyer Cave marks an approximate half-way point. Anyone who is vomiting, or feeling extremely ill, should probably descend. One of the assistant guides will help you get back down to the hut. Dehydration from vomiting can lead to serious problems. If you are throwing up, be sure to take frequent *sips* from your water bottle. That way you might keep some fluid down. The climb in the darkness is tedious, but it can yield some positive experiences. A full moon brightens the walk, illuminating the two great peaks, and making a flashlight practically unnecessary. On moonless nights, the stars seem close enough to pluck, and you can easily follow the course of the Southern Cross through the sky. The lines of climbing groups, marked by the glow of lanterns, make a memorable impression as they snake up the slope.

The rationale for the nighttime climb is to arrive for the sunrise, before clouds obscure the views. But don't worry too much about making the crater rim before daylight. You will welcome the sun wherever you are (it will rapidly warm you up), and the views from the top will be rewarding in any case. If it is clear, you overlook a vast chunk of African plain, broken by the Pare Mountains to the southeast and Mount Meru to the west. If you are late, you will look down on a sea of clouds, with the peaks of Mawenzi and Meru grandly emergent. Strong climbers may reach the crater rim at Gillman's Point (18,635 ft.) in four to five hours, but it can take a lot longer.

From Gillman's it is another 2 kilometers to the true summit at Uhuru Peak (19,340 ft.). The gradient is much more gradual than the climb to the rim, but many hikers have had enough by the time they reach Gillman's. You'll have to judge your strength. It will take a minimum of two hours to make the round-trip journey. If you are going to do it, start off as soon as possible. Really strong climbers may want to walk down to to the Reusch Crater for a look at the Ash Pit within. Just remember that whoever goes down into the crater must come up again, and that will be a lot harder.

The glaciers on Kibo's summit are probably unlike anything you will have seen before. At that elevation, ice does not melt, but sublimates, turning directly into water vapor. The resultant glaciers, which have been steadily shrinking in historic times, look very much like huge ice cubes set directly on the rocks.

Whatever extent you explore on the summit, you still have a fairly long day in front of you. It should take only an hour to an hour and a half to descend from Gillman's Point to Kibo Hut. Some trekkers literally run back down the scree slope. Be careful: although going down is much easier on the lungs, it can be very hard on the knees. Depending on the time and your physical condition, you may want to crawl back into your sleeping bag for a short nap before continuing on your way to Horombo. Take the Lower Route; it is downhill all the way.

The last day is a long walk back to the Marangu Gate. You'll be spurred along by the thought of a hot bath and a cold beer.

THE MACHAME ROUTE

The Machame is a far superior trekker's route. A wilderness traverse beneath Kibo's south face, it offers consistently spectacular alpine scenery. It is a longer trek than the Marangu route, taking a full six days' walking. It is also much more difficult to arrange. Your porters, gear, and party must be transported to the roadhead from either Marangu or Moshi. (You must pay your fees at the Marangu Gate, which is about 45 miles from Machame.) This alone will add very considerable expense. Porters also demand higher wages to work the route. Several rudimentary tin huts, with dirt floors, provide the only shelter from the weather. Most trekkers bring their own tents, and leave the huts to porters and guides. Larger parties should note that level ground at several campsites is at a premium, so only tiny tents are practical. Another thing to consider before choosing this trek is the absence of any easy exit. Should you have a problem, all possible retreat routes are steep and will leave you far from transport at the bottom.

The trek begins about 4 miles beyond the village of Machame. (You might have to start at the village if you do not hire a 4-wheel-drive vehicle for your transport.) Rangers check your permits at the Machame Gate, where you sign into the park. It's possible to drive another half a mile up the track to the jumping-off point at 6,400 feet. From there, the path climbs steeply through thick forest, until it eventually breaks into giant heath near the Machame Hut campsite (about 10,000 ft.). It is a walk of about five hours. Transporting an expedition by road almost invariably leads to a late start. The porters will have to stop to purchase their rations in the village of Machame. Try not to let them get tanked up on *pombe* (banana beer) there, or it could be very slow going. Under normal circumstances, you will probably get to camp late in the day. Water is available at a nearby stream.

The next day's trek is relatively easy. You ascend through heath and moorland to the Shira Hut (12,598 ft.), a walk of about four hours. You overnight there, with fine views of Kibo's western flank and the wide Shira Plateau. In the morning, you proceed toward Kibo Peak, then turn southward just before reaching the lava outcrop beyond which the Lava Tower Hut is located. After a strenuous walk of five to six hours, crossing several ridges and valleys, you arrive at the lip of the Great Barranco. Views from the camp at Barranco Hut (12,795 ft.) are spectacular. Looking to the head of the steeply cut canyon, you see Kibo's sheer Breach Wall and the ice sheets of Uhuru Peak. (Note that the best sites on which to pitch tents are in the valley, rather than next to the hut.) The following day, you descend into the gorge, then climb its vertical eastern wall, which requires some easy rock scrambling. You then have a wonderfully scenic walk beneath Kibo's southern icefields, the largest glaciers on the mountain. It's easy going until the path descends into the shallow Karanga Valley (last water), after which it is a steady slog up a lava ridge to the Barafu Hut. *Barafu* means "ice," and at 15,092 feet, the windswept campsite lives up to its name.

You begin the summit climb in the frigid postmidnight hours. The path from Barafu is even more strenuous than the Gillman Point approach—a stiff climb of at least six hours. After winding up a boulder-strewn ridge, you pass through a gap between the Rebmann and Ratzel glaciers to arrive at the rim near Stella Point, about midway between Gillman's and Uhuru. You then proceed to Uhuru Peak and descend via Gillman's and Kibo Hut to Horombo for the night. The last march brings you to the Marangu Gate.

OTHER TREK ROUTES

The Shira route begins on the distant northwest side of the mountain, and leads directly to the Shira Plateau. There are two additional routes on the southern side of the mountain, with road access from Moshi. The Umbwe route climbs steeply to Barranco Hut, while the Mweka route leads directly to Barafu. Any of these routes, or the Machame approach, can be used to tackle Kibo Peak via the Lava Tower Hut (15,092 ft.). From there, a route penetrates Kibo's Western Breach on a lava staircase. Although, this route does not involve any really difficult climbing, there is a lot of strenuous rock scrambling at high altitude. An ice axe could come in handy in case snowfall obscures the way. It is also possible to trek all the way around Kibo on the North Circuit. At least an extra three days of hard walking are needed for a circular route from Horombo. The route from Loitokitok in Kenya is closed.

TECHNICAL CLIMBS

Many challenging technical routes on both Kibo and Mawenzi are detailed in the Mountain Club of Kenya's *Guide to Mount Kenya and Kilimanjaro* (see bibliography). Climbers must be in top shape and completely self-sufficient. Professionally guided climbs are very difficult to organize. Mountain Madness (based in Moshi) sometimes has guides available to lead technical Kili ascents. Mountaineering guides may also be hired in Nairobi, though at considerable expense: try Tropical Ice or Mount Kenya and East Africa Guides.

The Tanzanian Coast

Despite the allure of tropical beaches, the historic isle of Zanzibar, and excellent nearby game parks, Tanzania's coast is not a favored tour destination. That it has failed to live up to its potential is mostly due to the country's mismanaged economy. Official exchange rates make Tanzania relatively expensive, and its hotels do not provide a level of comfort to compare with that of Kenya or other seaside destinations. Nor is the infrastructure for holiday activities well developed. Facilities for snorkeling, diving, water sports, and fine dining are not universally available: frustration is too often the rule of the day. The gateway to the coast is Dar es Salaam, which is itself a barrier to tourism, for it can be an unpleasant place to visit. For now, the coast is best left off your Tanzania itinerary unless you are planning to visit the southern parks or "must see" Zanzibar.

DAR ES SALAAM

Dar es Salaam was established by the Zanzibari Sultan Seyyid Majid as a "Haven of Peace." Today the name seems like a cruel joke to anyone who has to spend time there. It is a city rife with discomfort and problems for the traveler, where nothing seems to work as it should. The climate is sticky hot, and any mechanical or human service that can break down, will. As Tanzania's capital,* it is a major transportation hub, unavoidable to travelers going to the southern part of the country. Make your sojourn there as brief as possible.

Accommodation. None of Dar's several tourist-class hotels can be totally relied on for satisfactory service or comfort. Designed for air conditioning, they have no window screens, fans, or mosquito nets. Unfortunately, the air conditioning often does not work, so you are left with the choice of sleeping in a sauna or opening windows, which invites hordes of mosquitos. Central city hotels are crowded with government bureaucrats, making it difficult to book a room and impossible to be sure that a reservation will be honored. Beach hotels are more relaxed, but a long 45-minute drive from town or the airport. They are especially inconvenient if you have an early morning flight, for which you must check in two hours before departure. In the city, the best hotels are the Kilimanjaro and the

---

*The capital is eventually supposed to move to Dodoma, in the center of the country.

Embassy, but they are often fully occupied by officials and resident businessmen. The New Africa is lively (its sidewalk coffee shop is a major local hangout); its standard of comfort is notably poor. The Agip Motel lacks personality but is a much better bet for comfort. The Oyster Bay Hotel, in a well-to-do suburb just across the Selander Bridge, offers comfortable seaside accommodation close to town. All these facilities have pretty good restaurants. There are many smaller hotels and guesthouses, all of which seem perennially full. The YWCA is a particular favorite with budget travelers.

Activities. Don't despair should you find yourself in Dar with time on your hands, for there are some places of interest. The town has a few charming old buildings left from the Arab and colonial eras, and the streets' shade-covered sidewalks are conducive to central city walks. The scenic waterfront is crowded with steamships waiting to load in the modern port, while sailboats tie up at the old Dhow Wharf. In the cool of dawn, it's worth strolling northward along the beaches of the Kivukoni Front, where fishermen sell their night's catch to an eager crowd at a lively market. You'll see plenty of unusual fish brought off the boats, including large rays and sharks. A big Makonde carving center and crafts market has been set up near the university, just off Bagamoyo Road, which leads to the beach hotels. This is one of the best places to buy Makonde sculptures; upcountry shopkeepers go there to purchase their stock. Look for genuine masterpieces among the mass of touristy items. Also off Bagamoyo Road is the Village Museum, where various tribal dwellings have been authentically reconstructed and dance performances are held on Sunday afternoons. In the city center, the National Museum houses both archeological and ethnological collections. The colorful Kariakoo Market is the center of Dar's bazaar district, where vendors sell everything from fruits and vegetables to utensils and textiles.

Safaris. None of the tour operators in Dar is terribly good, but they can provide a vehicle and driver (at devastating cost) to visit the southern game parks. The TTC has its headquarters in Dar; you can make reservations there for any of its lodges or tours. All the camps in the Selous Game Reserve have offices in Dar that arrange all-inclusive safaris.

Dar Beach Hotels. Dar's beach strip is located 12 miles north of town along Bagamoyo Road. The beaches are beautiful, but the hotels provide indifferent services. The TTC-operated Kunduchi Beach Hotel, with its pure white Moorish-style architecture, is the most attractive. The Bahari Beach Hotel is the only other tourist-class facility: both have air-conditioning (hopefully working) and offer reasonable protection against mosquitos. The Silversands is less costly and permits camping on its grounds. So does the cheaper Rungwe Oceanic, making it a favorite with overland safari groups. The Africana Vacation Village is really a local residence hotel. Seafood is prominent on all hotel menus, though too often only marginally prepared. Take care walking on the beach beyond hotel grounds—muggings are commonly reported.

The Kunduchi Beach Hotel rents equipment for windsurfing and other water sports, and hires out boats for trips to nearby coralline islands. Snorkeling is good among a fine collection of colorful fish, but the reefs have suffered heavily from the use of dynamite by local fishermen. The site of a ruined mosque and Arab cemetery is also located near Kunduchi.

Bagamoyo is 30 miles further along the potholed coast road. The old town was Zanzibar's mainland terminal for slave and ivory caravans, and the place from which the explorers Livingstone, Burton, Speke, Grant, and Stanley began their various expeditions. It has a quiet charm: many houses possess ornately carved Swahili doors and a few buildings remain from the colonial era. One is the church tower to which Livingstone's body was carried from the interior. There are nice beaches and Arab ruins in the vicinity, and it is a good place to get on a dhow bound for Zanzibar. Unfortunately, Bagamoyo apparently suffers from a plague of muggings and thievery.

ZANZIBAR

Zanzibar has firm credentials as an exotic destination. As the last bastion of the African slave trade and the center for the cultivation of cloves, it acquired a reputation as an entrepôt of evil tinged with the scent of paradise. The island's ruling sultans used their fabulous wealth to erect bathhouses and pleasure palaces. Sultans and slaves are gone now, but mementos of their era abound, and the island is still thick with the fragrance of spice. It is a lovely place, green with plantations of clove and cinnamon trees. The ruins of palaces, baths, and ancient mosques dot the countryside, and the coastline is ringed with coral gardens set in turquoise tropical waters.

Although postindependence construction of highrise apartment blocks has cost the city much of its former charm, some of the flavor of old Zanzibar is still found in Stone Town, on the city's western-most tip. Its narrow streets are lined by Swahili houses, with their typical overhanging balconies. Some still have beautifully carved wooden doors, ornately inlaid with brass. The three-story Beit-El-Ajaib, or House of Wonders, is an interesting palace built by the Sultan Barghash. Also worth visiting are an Arab fort dated to 1700, the slave market, the old British Consulate (1841–1874), and the Livingstone House, in which the missionary lived before setting off on his last quest.

Travel to Zanzibar has always been awkward for one reason or another. The government now encourages tourism, but strict currency regulations continue to make things somewhat difficult. So does transport from the mainland: Air Tanzania is the main link, but it is always fully booked. Failing to get a flight, you might be able to hire a plane reasonably (in local currency) from Tanair Charters at the airport in Dar. Daily ferries run from Dar, and it is still possible to catch a dhow from the capital or Bagamoyo. Top-class tourist accommodation does not exist. The closest approximation is the modern Bwawani Hotel, a concrete block on the shore near the Livingstone House. In Stone Town, are the older Africa House (a former British Club), the Zanzibar Hotel (once a sultan's guesthouse), and the Spice Inn. No hotels are found outside town, but the Tourist Bureau has several self-catering beach bunaglows available for rent in more remote parts of the island.

Touring the Island. Exploring the island is fairly difficult because of the awful state of the roads. Public transport is painfully slow and overcrowded. The Tanzania Friendship Tourist Bureau (with an office in town and a representative at the airport) can assist in booking tours, or you can hire a taxi to take you around. The main sites of interest, in addition to the delightful countryside and deserted beaches, are the domed Persian Baths, the Mangapwani Slave Caves in which human chattel were penned underground, and the Shirazi Mosque Dimbani, which dates back to A.D. 1107. Everywhere, you will see villages in which cloves are being dried and plantations where *Eugenia aromatica* trees (of which cloves are the flower buds) reach a height of 50 feet. Naturalists may want to visit the Jozani and Kichwele forests, the habitat of rare endemic animals such as red colobus monkey and Zanzibar duiker. At the port, you can hire a boat to take you to Changu Island (also called Prison Island after its abandoned old jail) for snorkeling. Several captive giant land tortoises are kept there.

OTHER COASTAL DESTINATIONS

Pemba Island is another center of clove production. Located just beneath the Kenya border, it is as yet completely devoid of tourists. One day, it will be discovered by resort developers. The TTC has a lodge on Mafia Island that caters to big game fishing. On the mainland, the whole southern coast is completely undeveloped. Kilwa, once an important Swahili town, is the site of Tanzania's most extensive Arab-Portuguese archeological ruins.

The Southern Safari Circiut

Tanzania's southern parks remain largely undiscovered by commercial tourism. Although they cannot be compared with Serengeti and Ngorongoro for masses of game or ease of viewing, they are nonetheless impressive reservoirs of African wildlife. Ecologically, they have more affinities to the reserves of south-central Africa than to the typical East African parks. In them, open savannas and acacia country are replaced by deciduous woodlands and the floodplains of large rivers. They are superb elephant country and the habitat of Africa's most magnificent horned animals—the greater kudu, roan, and sable antelopes.

Large portions of Tanzania's inland plateau are covered with *miombo* forest. These woodlands are named for the deciduous *Brachystegia* trees that are their dominant vegetation. Just before the rains, *miombo* trees put on new leaves that create a color display worthy of a New England fall. At other times, when the trees are bare or the woodland grasses stand 8 feet high, extensive travel through *miombo* can be rather monotonous. *Miombo* country is heavily infested with tsetse flies, making it inhospitable to humans and cattle. Huge tracts have therefore been left over entirely to wildlife. Although few large animals live in the *miombo* forest proper, the shallow valleys that drain the woods are filled with nutritious grasslands that support good concentrations of game. Hosting a large but widely dispersed population of elephant, buffalo, big cats, and trophy antelopes, such regions are really more suitable as hunting reserves than national parks. Tanzania has several huge hunting reservations, the most famous of which is the Selous Game Reserve, the largest wildlife area in all Africa. Its northeastern portion can be combined with the excellent Mikumi and Ruaha national parks to form one of the continent's most interesting game circuits.

For all its potential, the southern circuit has not been well developed for tourism. Distances between the parks are considerable—it takes a full day to travel by road from one to the next—and tour companies based in Dar es Salaam have never been notable for creating interesting safari itineraries or providing reliable transport. Those obstacles, plus the high expense of Tanzanian safaris and the discomforts associated with Dar, have discouraged international tour operators from offering the southern parks on their itineraries. Despite the logistical difficulties, it must be emphasized that the parks themselves are first rate. Their variety of habitats and species nicely complements those of the northern parks and they compare very favorably with the best reserves of southern Africa. Veteran safarists and keen naturalists will find an expedition on the southern circuit extremely worthwhile, so long as it is well planned and participants know what to expect.

The Selous Game Reserve

The Selous is another Tanzanian superlative: almost 22,000 square miles in extent, it is the largest and wildest game reserve in Africa. Vast tracts are covered with roadless tsetse-infested *miombo*, inaccessible even to ranger patrols, much less tourists' safaris. This immense no man's land has wildlife to match its size. A decade ago the Selous's elephant population was estimated as high as 120,000 and the reserve was proclaimed a last stronghold of the black rhino. Although poaching has since all but eliminated rhino and elephant numbers have been substantially trimmed,* the Selous remains ecologically intact and supports a healthy wildlife community.

The Selous's impressive statistics can be deceptive to would-be visitors, however. It is indeed immense and has plenty of animals, but game is widely distributed and not to be seen with the same ease as in national parks. Furthermore, all safari camps and game-viewing tracks are confined to the northeast corner of the reserve, a small fraction of its total area. The rest of the vast wilderness, including all the territory south of the Rufiji River, is the domain of sport hunters.

---

*The 1987 United Nations Environment Program (UNEP) report puts their number (inclusive of the neighboring Mikumi population) at 55,000, which represents almost half the elephants remaining in all of East Africa.

Only a reserve devoted to the chase could honor Frederick Courtenay Selous, who was one of the most famous big game hunters. Although he lived in an era when the pursuit of wild "game" was more widely accepted, his memoirs reveal a remorseless taste for slaughter that the most ruthless of today's ivory poachers could hardly equal: more than a thousand elephants and countless other animals fell to his gun. Although he actually carried out his shooting exploits further south, in old Rhodesia, he was killed in the reserve during a bizarre campaign against the German army during the First World War. Afterward, the British established the Selous Game Reserve, and it was expanded to its present gargantuan size almost single-handedly by the legendary warden, the eccentric C. J. P. Ionides. Today, the Selous is still highly regarded by professional hunters. Its bull elephants carry a heavy weight of fine ivory, and the other most sought-after trophies—greater kudu, sable, buffalo, lion, and leopard—can all be obtained there. Although there is not much shooting north of the Rufiji, even there the animals are considerably shyer than those in fully protected national parks.

The Selous is ecologically quite different from the parks of northern Tanzania. It is hot, humid country: almost the entire reserve is below 2,000 feet in elevation and receives generous seasonal rainfall. Vast stretches, especially in the remote southern and western regions, are covered with *miombo* woodlands. Game is scarce in the *miombo*, but abundant on the floodplains along a network of wide, shallow rivers—the Luwego, Mbarangandu, and Kilombero—that drain the southwestern wilderness. These flow into the Rufiji, which at its confluence with the Great Ruaha becomes the largest river in Tanzania. The mighty Rufiji then gushes through narrow Stiegler's Gorge before spreading out on a wide floodplain in the reserve's extreme northeast. Although not really the most "typical" Selous habitat, the Rufiji floodplain is wonderfully scenic country and well endowed with game. It is the only truly accessible part of the reserve.

The Selous is such a large chunk of real estate that various schemes have inevitably been proposed for its development. A dam project at Stiegler's Gorge has at least temporarily foundered for lack of funds; extensive oil and gas explorations have likewise yielded no results. So far, wildlife has proved the sole viable economic resource of the region through the revenues generated from big game hunting. Although many find it unpalatable, the Selous exemplifies the potentially positive role of hunting safaris in the conservation of African wildlife.

ACCESS AND ACCOMMODATION

The Selous's northeast corner is about 100 miles by road from Dar. Except during the height of the June–October dry season, a four-wheel-drive vehicle is needed to get around inside the reserve, if not just to get there. Visitors also arrive on the TAZARA (TAnzania-ZAnzibar RAilroad) railroad (to be picked up at Fuga Station by prior arrangement with any of the safari camps) or by chartered aircraft.

The Rufiji River Camp is located just inside the eastern reserve boundary. This rustic tented camp is a favorite with the expatriate community. Mbuyu Camp is 10 miles upriver. It too is perched on the banks of the Rufiji, its tents hidden among palm thickets and shaded by riverine trees. Mbuyu's dining area is underneath the enormous baobab for which the camp is named. Activities at either camp include game drives, motor launch cruises on the river, and foot safaris. Mbuyu is slightly more expensive, but better located for touring the reserve. At Stiegler's Gorge Camp, accommodation is not in tents but in handsome wooden chalets that were originally built to house Norwegian engineers doing a pilot study on the Rufiji dam. The rocky, wooded country around Stiegler's is attractive, though not as beautiful as the floodplain on which the other camps are located, nor as productive for game drives. For that reason, Steigler's is attempting to establish two small satellite camps—Kidai and Mloka—further downriver for the use of clients on walking and boating safaris. Behobeho Camp consists of small cabins, which are now too run down to attract foreign tourists.

Campers will find a wonderful campsite at Lake Tagalala, either on the lakeshore or at the nearby hot springs. There are no formal facilities, but you can soak with pleasure in warm mineral pools, shaded by the feathery fronds of *Phoenix* palms.

Few people visit the virgin wilderness region south of the Rufiji, where it is possible to conduct whole safaris without encountering another party. Such expeditions are logistic nightmares and terribly expensive to arrange professionally. They require special permission from the reserve warden and the accompaniment of an armed game scout. If you have your own vehicle, you can inquire at the headquarters at Matambwe, at the reserve's northern entrance near the Fuga railroad station, or with the Tanzanian Game Department in Dar. Because you must be completely self-sufficient, however, it is probably more realistic to count on keeping your explorations to the north side of the river.

TOURING THE PARK

As a game reserve, the Selous operates under different rules from those governing the national parks. There are no restrictions on off-road travel, and licensed expeditions, camps, or rangers are allowed to shoot for the cooking pot. The Selous is also the only game area in Tanzania where foot safaris are regularly featured activities. Although reserve fees were formerly much lower and could be paid in local currency, prices and conditions of payment are now being changed to conform with those of the parks.

Game viewing in the northeast Selous takes place in a variety of scenic habitats. None is more striking than the Rufiji and its floodplain. On the flats, the big river winds through a maze of swamps, lakes, and sand-choked cutoff channels. Its banks are fringed with stately borassus palms (*Borassus aethiopum*), which display a characteristic swelling midway up their tall, straight boles. Many have been illegally tapped by local tribesmen, who use the sap to make a potent palm wine. Tapping quickly kills the trees, leaving the tall headless trunks to line the river like an avenue of ancient Greek columns. Even in the dry season, the wide brown Rufiji usually runs as high as the shoulder of a bull elephant. Big tuskers can sometimes be seen fording the river, and good herds can be encountered anywhere in the floodplain country. Hippo, crocodile, and birdlife are much in evidence all along the river.

Terminalia woodland is the dominant vegetation in the eastern Selous, where it thrives on higher ground with "hardpan" soils. Massive baobabs are conspicuous among the smaller terminalia trees, as are giant termite mounds, which often have tamarind or ebony trees growing on them. In the lightly wooded terminalia country, the grass is kept cropped by small herds of blue wildebeest, impala, and zebra. Giraffe are common, although for reasons unknown they do not occur on the south bank of the Rufiji. Lichtenstein's hartebeest (*Alcelaphus lichtensteinii*) is a "*miombo* antelope" that also inhabits terminalia woodlands and is probably best seen in the Selous. This animal's horns are oddly curved with an angular inward kink. When spooked, hartebeest depart with a stiff-legged, bounding gait that carries them to safety with surprising speed.

Mbugas are also typical of the eastern Selous. There are large depressions of black cotton soil that flood during the rains, when they are turned into quagmires of sucking clay. As they dry out, a succession of succulent grasses spring up in the wake of the shrinking pools. Waterbuck and impala then flock to them for fresh forage. Buffalo, elephant, and warthog are also attracted. They not only feed, but also come daily to wallow and bathe in the cooling mud. The heavy tracks of countless elephant and buffalo churn deeply into the muck. As the dry season advances, their footprints become frozen in the clay, which turns cement-hard and gets furrowed with treacherous cracks. These obstacles render a dry *mbuga* impossible to drive across, and uncomfortable to negotiate even on foot.

The spiral-horned greater kudu (*Tragelaphus strepsiceros*) are one of the Selous's prized photographic trophies. The big antelope keep to the margins of thickets and forest, where they are well camouflaged by the broken coloration of their striped flanks. In the Selous, they remain extremely wary and it is not easy to get more than a brief glimpse of them before they disappear into deeper cover. Sable are also present in the reserve, but are very rare on the north side of the Rufiji. Although occasionally seen in hilly areas between Matambwe and Stiegler's Gorge, they are much more common in the southwestern *miombo* country.

Boat rides on the Rufiji provide a unique perspective on Selous game viewing. They are particularly good for close encounters with hippos and crocodiles. Herds of hippos wallow at every shallow pool, the weighty beasts snorting and splashing to deeper water at the approach of your boat. Bulls sometimes cause real excitement by throwing their mouths wide in toothy threat display. Enormous crocodiles, jaws open to dispel the heat, bask on sandbars while Goliath herons stalk the reeds at water's edge. Waterbuck, elephant, and buffalo are all commonly seen along the river.

Walking safaris are a Selous specialty. Naturally, they must be accompanied by an armed guard. Each of the permanent camps has game rangers on duty to take guests around on foot. Because animals can be widely distributed, the best strategy is to drive to an area where game is concentrated before starting your walk, rather than just hiking out from camp. Stiegler's Gorge Camp is offering longer treks, using "fly camps" on a meandering four-day journey from the main lodge to Kidai.

Game drives are most rewarding in the floodplain country, because it is fairly open and has the largest concentrations of animals. Tracks skirt the edge of a string of large lakes created by the Rufiji's meanderings. Near the water, beds of tall elephant grass (*Hyparrhenia spp.*) and palmetto thickets make ideal lying-up places for lions, though it is hard to spot them there. Bird-filled swamps fringe beautiful Lake Tagalala. Closeby are the hot springs that make a favorite picnic or camp site. West of Tagalala, the terrain gets hillier and more thickly wooded. Rhinos are still occasionally reported on the Behobeho ridge, though they are now extremely shy. Selous's grave rests among the doum palms below Behobeho, where he was slain by a German sniper while having his breakfast—unexpectedly shot down like so many of the elephants he claimed as trophies. It now seems crazy that armies once clashed in such a remote and beautiful place. But in 1917 Behobeho blocked the British advance to the Rufiji, where the Germans were holding out with the aid of supplies salvaged from the warship *Königsberg.* Scuttled lower down in the Rufiji Delta, the cruiser's ghostly wreck was visible until just a few years ago. A steam engine used to help power the German war effort (by grinding grain for the troops) still lies rusting in the bush near the Selous gravesite.

If you make arrangements for an inclusive safari at one of the permanent camps, don't expect to tour the entire reserve. The Rufiji River and Mbuyu camps concentrate game drives on the floodplain area, ranging as far as Lake Tagalala and Behobeho. Arriving by rail, you will travel through a lot of terminalia woodland on the way from the station to either camp.

Behobeho and the lakes circuit are a long way from Stiegler's Gorge if the direct track via Kidai Ranger Post is closed by rains. But Stiegler's Camp has its own system of woodland tracks, which are good for buffalo, elephant, lion, and kudu. An electric cable car spans the gorge at Stiegler's. It is exciting to be suspended above the chasm, but you must give full trust to Tanzanian machine maintenance. The cable or the nearby ferry at Kidai Post is the only means for transporting vehicles to the south bank of the Rufiji.

The Selous is virtually inaccessible during the November and April–May rainy seasons. It is at its prettiest between January and March, when it is green and crowded with animal life. The many seasonal pools then attract a marvelous collection of waterbirds. The open-billed storks are surely the most unusual. These wholly · black birds are named for the gap in their mandibles through which you can plainly see the sky—an adaptation that is somehow useful for catching snails. A flock makes a bizarre sight when perched on a bare snag. Even more spectacular is a tree festooned with dozens of carmine bee-eaters. In their most brilliant breeding plumage, they light up their perch like a Christmas tree. Also during the wetter months, cassia trees are very prominent because of their bright clusters of yellow flowers and long, beanlike seed pods. Tour groups tend to schedule visits during the sere July–October dry season, when transport is more certain. The entire reserve is then singed by raging bush fires. Although it may be distressing to see the nighttime sky lit with flames from one horizon to the next, the fires do little permanent damage. Game viewing is made somewhat easier, because the high grass has been burnt off and the woodlands have lost most of their leaves.

RIVER SAFARIS

Sobek Expeditions operates float safaris on the Rufiji. All the whitewater action takes place on the brief run through Stiegler's Gorge. Below the rapids, there is plenty of paddling among hippos and crocs, with ample time to make foot safaris ashore. Stiegler's Camp is attempting to make rafting the gorge a regular lodge activity, and is offering more extended motorized raft trips between its Kidai and Mloka camps, but similar plans have foundered before under previous managements.

Mikumi National Park

This small park richly showcases a variety of animals and habitats not seen in northern Tanzania. Ecologically, it has much in common with the northeastern Selous, and has the advantage of being easily accessible from Dar es Salaam.

The heart of the park is the game-rich floodplain of the Mkata River valley. The Mkata is not large, but at Mikumi it receives the flow of many smaller streams that run down from surrounding hills. When these hit the valley floor, they sluggishly weave their way through bottomlands of black cotton clay. In the wake of seasonal flooding, tall *Hyparrhenia* grasses flourish on the Mkata flats, while marshes fill permanently moist areas. Slightly raised hardpan ridges provide places for trees to take root above the waterlogged clay. These areas are lightly wooded with baobab, acacia, and tamarind, as well as the *mikumi* palm (*Borassus flabellifer*) from which the park takes its name. Denser stands of forest and thicket occur along the edge of watercourses. The Mkata Valley is enclosed by scenic *miombo*-covered hills. To the southeast, a fine backdrop is provided by the Uluguru Mountains. Their lower slopes have been worn into the shape of open-spread fans, while the jagged spires of their high peaks are visible in the far distance.

Rank grass and mud wallows attract herds of buffalo to the Mkata Plain. Joining them on the lightly wooded grasslands are good numbers of zebra and wildebeest. Like those of the Selous, Mikumi's wildebeest are more handsome than the white-bearded northern race. The Nyasa or blue gnu is paler, with noticeably dark stripes on the neck and shoulder, a black beard, and tan leggings. Some individuals have a white "chevron" blazed across their muzzle. Blue wildebeest occur in reasonable-sized herds of twenty to a hundred animals, rather than the massive groupings of their Serengeti cousins. The southern parks' yellow baboons (*Papio cynocephalus*) are also dissimilar to their northern relatives: they are leaner and, as their name implies, lighter in color. Mikumi hosts plenty of elephant, impala, and eland. It is a good place to see greater kudu and is probably the most likely park in Tanzania in which to encounter sable antelope. Because of an abundance of resident prey, it has a good complement of lions.

ACCESS AND ACCOMMODATION

The main road from Dar es Salaam to Zambia runs right through Mikumi. It is well paved, so the park is an easy 180-mile drive from the capital. That ease of access makes Mikumi a favorite weekend getaway spot, but during the week you will have the park completely to yourself. Mikumi Lodge is beautifully situated among the wooded Uluguru foothills, which overlook the Mkata Valley. A modern TTC hotel, it provides reasonably comfortable accommodation. Just below the lodge, a spring-fed pool is a busy watering place for animals during the dry season. The dilapidated Mikumi Tented Camp is located just off the main highway and lacks charm. Several official campsites, none with any facilities, are found on hardpan ridges on the valley floor, close to park headquarters and the main entrance gate.

Direct travel between Mikumi and the Selous is possible on a very interesting route via the town of Morogoro. Skirting the Uluguru Mountains, you pass below granitic peaks that reach as high as 8,681 feet. The fast-disappearing forests of this ancient range are known for endemic bird species, some of which were only recently discovered—although you are unlikely to see them without time and effort. The road passes through lovely remnants of mountain forest and crosses the jungle-fringed Ruvu River before descending toward the Selous's Matambwe Gate.

TOURING THE PARK

Mikumi is well populated with game year round, although many tracks outside the headquarters area are closed during the flooded rainy seasons. The park is small enough to be explored in a single day. Morning and evening game drives are the general rule, but if you want to be sure to maximize your exposure to the park's habitats, you should plan a full day's outing with a picnic in the bush.

The principal game tracks fan out from the entrance gate on the north side of the Dar-Zambia highway. The exact direction to take may have to be determined by the weather and the state of the roads. Generally, after reconnoitering the black cotton grasslands near park headquarters, you should head northward past the hippo pool to the Chamgore Waterhole. The track parallels the Mkata River, passing through broken savanna country that is a good place to encounter kudu and elephant. Sable sometimes descend from the wooded hills on the western edge of the park, and there is a good chance to encounter Lichtenstein's hartebeest. Large herds of impala are found around Chamgore, so be alert there for Cape hunting dogs, which favor these small antelope as prey in Mikumi. Wild dogs are actually seen fairly often in the park, and have even been encountered sitting on the road in front of the lodge.

An interesting side track extends for 15 miles through the wooded Uluguru foothills at the southern end of the park. Large numbers of animals will not be seen there, but it is one of the better places for exploring *miombo* forest. Although dominant in so much of central Tanzania and Zambia, *miombo* is actually hard to penetrate in any of the national parks. Rhinos are now very rare in Mikumi, as everywhere, but the hill track was formerly the best place to see them, so it is still possible that you will encounter one of these forlorn beasts. More likely are sable antelope, which, along with Lichtenstein's hartebeest, are very typical *miombo* animals. The *angolensis* variety of black-and-white colobus monkey is also found in the hill forests. Birders will particularly enjoy the opportunity to search for endemic *miombo* species such as racquet-tailed roller, Arnott's chat, and Shelley's double-collared sunbird. The latter feeds on the red flowers of *Loranthus*, a conspicuous mistletoe-like plant that parasitizes the *Brachystegia* trees so typical of *miombo* forests. Sunset views from the hill track are spectacular, as the sun sinks into the western hills across the Mkata Valley.

Ruaha National Park

Far from the regular tourist routes, Ruaha may be Tanzania's best-kept secret. Second in size among the nation's parks and contiguous with the equally large Rungwa Game Reserve, Ruaha preserves yet another massive chunk of raw African wilderness. This unique park is as different from the Serengeti as from the Selous, harboring a truly distinctive collection of animals among landscapes of hauntingly savage beauty. Hot and tsetse-infested, but teeming with game and empty of tourists, Ruaha's rugged bush is the real Africa.

Ruaha is primarily a woodlands park. An 800-foot escarpment makes a neat ecological divide between the valley of the Great Ruaha River and the higher plateau country of the park's western reaches. Atop the 3,300-foot high plateau, unbroken *miombo* forest—the haunt of sable antelope—sweeps on into the vastness of the Rungwa Game Reserve. Beneath the escarpment, the climate is dryer but vegetation is more diverse. A light scrub of *Commiphora-Combretum* woodland dominates a gently undulating landscape that rolls down to the banks of the Ruaha River. In the stunted woods, high grass grows among wiry shrubs and small trees, providing good forage for both greater kudu and roan antelope. Grand isolated peaks, reaching as high as 6,234 feet, as well as smaller boulder-strewn outcrops, are scattered around the park. So too are patches of grass-covered plain, baobab woodland, and terminalia thicket that break the monopoly of the combretum bush. Sand rivers descend from the escarpment to the Ruaha. Their courses through the woody scrub are clearly traced by lines of lusher sausage, fig, and tamarind trees. The Great Ruaha itself is a scenic delight as well as a magnet for wildlife. The river first tumbles through rocky gorges before spreading into a wide and shallow stream, its sandy bed fringed with lovely groves of tall *Acacia albida*.

Although game densities are low compared to those of some grass-country parks, Ruaha can scarcely be equaled for variety of species. In addition to the aquatic fauna living along its main river, the park's woodlands mosaic is ideal habitat for a wide spectrum of browsing animals. Elephant are numerous: their effect on the landscape is very evident when comparing the park's ravaged scrub with the dense forest beyond its boundaries. Other browsers such as kudu, eland, impala, giraffe, and dikdik also thrive. Grazers, like grasslands, are less abundant. Wildebeest are altogether absent, but small bands of zebra and good herds of buffalo are found. Grant's gazelle are also present; in fact, Ruaha is the southernmost point in their range. The park's real specialty is its collection of spectacular antelopes. It is the only major East African reserve where both roan and sable occur, or where greater kudu are common and widespread. Their diminutive but no less beautiful cousin, the lesser kudu, is also resident.

ACCESS AND ACCOMMODATION

By any standards, Ruaha is remote. The park is a very long day's drive from Mikumi, which is a distance of 203 miles. The paved Dar-Zambia road passes though the scenic Ruaha Gorge before reaching Iringa. This sleepy town, perched atop bluffs overlooking the winding Little Ruaha River, is quite attractive when its purple-flowering jacaranda trees are in full bloom. Wonderful basketwork is on sale in the market, but you will have little time to do more than fill up with gas (take plenty extra because none is available in the park) if you expect to make it to Ruaha the same day. Beyond Iringa, the pavement soon ends as you continue past the farms and villages of the local Hehe tribe. These gradually give way to tracts of uninhabited forest. Spared the attentions of elephants, the woods are considerably taller and denser than those inside the park. After a 75 mile journey on a sandy, lonely, and almost unmarked track, you reach the Great Ruaha River, where a hand-pulled cableferry waits to carry your vehicle across. From the ferry, it is another 5 miles to the park headquarters at Msembe, or about 8 (in the opposite direction) to the lodge.

The journey may feel like an expedition into unknown country; it is. Almost the sole visitors to Ruaha are expatriates working in southern Tanzania: by avoiding the weekend, you are more than likely to have the entire park to yourself. Even in a worst-case crowd scenario, you would not see many other parties—but you might not be able to find unreserved accommodation at the hotel. The tiny Ruaha River Lodge is tastefully built into a riverside *kopje*. Its bungalows are rustic but comfortable, and the food is good by Tanzanian standards. It is beautifully situated above a rock pool where animals, especially elephants, are frequent visitors both by day and night. If you are in one of the outlying cabins on the riverbank, you must be very alert for the presence of buffalo as you walk to the lodge or toilet at night. The park also has a self-catering tented camp near the Msembe headquarters, but it is not in good shape. It would be infinitely preferable to make your own camp. Idyllic sites are to be found along the river, under shady *Acacia albida* trees.

Elephants, impala, and baboons are all very fond of albida seed pods, so you can expect a lot of animal activity in camp when the trees are in fruit.

TOURING THE PARK

Ruaha is open all year and game is always present. The rains fall in one extended period between December and April. The Ruaha Valley gets about 20 inches per year; the higher *miombo* country receives about 32. The rains make it more difficult to get around, but the park is then very green and bursting with both bird and animal life. Animals naturally tend to concentrate near the river more during the dryer months, although water is also available at numerous springs and sand rivers. In any event, game viewing is easier in the dry season, when the bush is leafless, especially after fires have burnt off the high grass. Ruaha's tsetses are always superabundant in bushy areas. They are an annoyance that comes with the territory— just be prepared for them and you will enjoy the park.

Only a relatively small part of Ruaha's total area has been developed for the public. No roads scale the escarpment to the *miombo* country, but a good network of game tracks facilitates exploration between the Ruaha River and the base of the plateau. This is the most scenic part of the park and has the best variety of habitats. A stay of three nights, with two full days, is the minimum time recommended for game viewing. An additional day could well be spent just watching animal life at the river. You may even wish to devote some time trying to catch the feisty tiger fish that live in the Ruaha gorges. Foot safaris are allowed in Ruaha; you can arrange for the necessary armed rangers with the park authorities.

Keep in mind that animals in Ruaha are generally shy because they see relatively few vehicles and must contend with quite a bit of poaching. Viewing is also made difficult by the density of the bush. But part of Ruaha's charm is the sense of constant expectation for what may be discovered suddenly and at close quarters: you round a bend in the track and are abruptly face to face with a giant kudu bull, standing stock-still in a mantle of camouflaging bush. In order to maximize your chances, you must proceed slowly and take lots of time for observation at waterholes and other vista points.

Drives along the Ruaha River are spectacularly scenic and provide the easiest and most comfortable game viewing in the park. Waterbuck, impala, elephant, and baboon are always to be seen on the wide, shallow riverbed between Msembe and the mouth of the

Mwagusi Sand River, and there is always a fair chance of spotting lion along the banks. Riverside birdlife inevitably includes yellow-billed stork, hammerkop, spurwing and Egyptian geese, Goliath heron, and several types of kingfishers, swifts, and swallows. Just upstream from the ferry is a remarkable pool in which large numbers of hippo spend their days during the dry season. As the river falls, fish also get packed into the pool, which becomes a madhouse of feeding activity by birds and crocodiles alike. For ultimate crocodile viewing, you'll have to walk a short way upstream into a stony gorge. If you are quiet, you will be able to watch leviathan crocs haul out on the rocks below you. A herd of roan antelope is often met in the scrub- and grass-covered hills above the river, between the ferry and Msembe.

The Mwagusi Sand River track is a favorite for explorations into the Ruaha hinterland. Where the Mwagusi joins the Ruaha, there is an impressive view of the sand river, its wide mouth choked with fallen trees carried down on the wet-season flood. Following the Mwagusi upstream, the track passes through thick riverine bush that is the best place to look for lesser kudu. Greater kudu and elephant are likely to be encountered there as well. Farther from the sandy streambed, there are impressive groves of gnarled baobab and areas of open grass plain where ostrich are usually seen. These plains are also the place to find Grant's gazelle and their principal enemy, cheetah. There are numerous side loops to explore off the Mwagusi track, which extends some 15 miles to a seepage area at the foot of the escarpment.

The other major game circuit follows the Mdonya Sand River to the gorge from which it exits the escarpment. This long track traverses some thick bush country, which is hot and tsetse-ridden. In spite of the discomforts, the Mdonya is worth exploring. It is a good place to watch elephants dig for water in the sand and you can expect to see greater kudu, eland, steinbok, zebra, and buffalo along the way. Be sure to take the return loop via the Makindi Spring, which is farther along the foot of the escarpment. Sable antelope and Lichtenstein's hartebeest are sometimes seen watering there, at the edge of the *miombo* woodlands. From Makindi, a track leads directly back to the upper Ruaha River, which is then followed downstream for some 8 miles to the lodge.

Lions are heard nightly in Ruaha, but seeing them in the dense bush is purely a matter of luck. The same is true of leopard, which are very common in the park. The chances are rather better to encounter wild dogs, which seem unafraid of human beings or vehicles.

In addition to the display of waterbirds along the river, Ruaha has a particularly good collection of woodland birds. Noisy flocks of green wood hoopoes and Von der Decken's hornbills vie with superb starlings (superb is their proper name) and brown parrots for your attention. Flocks of helmeted guinea fowl, which are a familiar sight in almost every African park, reach almost ridiculous proportions and almost refuse to yield the track to oncoming vehicles. The rarer crested guinea fowl is also resident in riverine bush.

Gombe Stream National Park

Chimpanzees are our closest relatives. Intensely social, with many human characteristics, they are particularly fascinating animals. Chimps have long been familiar to the public because of their performances in circuses and television, but not until Jane Goodall studied them was much known about their life in the wild. Her research area at Gombe Stream has now been made into a national park and opened to the public. There is no better place to observe free-living chimpanzees.

Gombe is located on the shores of Lake Tanganyika, one of the deepest of the Rift Valley lakes. Above the lakeshore, high closed-canopy forest fills a series of steep valleys that cut into an imposing escarpment. The forests thin to wooded savannas on more exposed slopes, and rise to grassy balds atop the plateau. Although they are more popularly thought of as animals of primary rainforest, chimps also thrive in such mixed habitat, where they can exploit a greater variety of food resources. Other animals found in the park include buffalo, bushbuck, and bushpig, as well as baboon and red colobus monkey.

Chimpanzees (*Pan troglodytes*) are not only close to humans biologically; they are also quite near in intelligence and live in highly complex social groups. They use a great vocabulary of sounds and body postures for communication with each other, and you will hear their "hoo-hoo" calls carrying far over Gombe's valleys. Fruits lead their list of food items. These are supplemented by a wide variety of other plants, as well as honey, termites, and insect larvae. Goodall discovered that the Gombe chimps are fond of meat: piglets, monkeys, and young baboons are preyed on during cooperative hunts. She also observed them engaged in startlingly violent behavior against their own kind, recording incidents of murder and even cannibalism. Tool use was revealed, too. Grass stems are used to "fish" termites from their nests, while sticks are brandished to intimidate rivals during aggressive displays. More such remarkable behaviors may be discovered as long-term research continues to document the lives of the Gombe apes.

ACCESS AND ACCOMMODATION

Because Gombe is so far from other major tourist destinations, it is more the territory of the independent traveler than the safari tour. It takes a lot of special effort to get there.

Gombe is accessible via Kigoma, Tanzania's major town on Lake Tanganyika. The lake is the longest in the African Rift and plunges to a staggering depth of 4,710 feet. Its frigid depths are virtually sterile, but the surface teems with fish, of which more than 125 species are found nowhere else. One of them, locally known as *dagaa*, forms huge schools that are important to the local economy. By night, lights flicker on the lake as boatmen try to attract shoals of fish to their nets. Kigoma is near Ujiji, the lakeside village where Stanley met Livingstone in 1871: a small plaque there commemorates the famous rendezvous.

Kigoma is reached from Dar on Air Tanzania or by a two-day train journey (take only first class). Travelers coming from Rwanda or Zaire can take a weekly steamer on an overnight lake voyage from Bujumbura in Burundi. There are no real tourist-class hotels in Kigoma; the Kigoma Railway Hotel is the best in town, but a new and nicer lakeshore hotel is under construction.

Once at Kigoma, you must get a boat to the park, which is about 16 miles up the lakeshore. Twice weekly, a lake steamer goes to a village beyond Gombe's northern boundary; from there you must walk about two hours, or take a small boat for the final leg. Alternatively, you can catch a motorized *jahazi* from Ujiji very cheaply; they depart daily, whenever they are full, and take three to four hours. To return from Gombe, you flag down a passing boat from shore. A private boat charter from Kigoma will cost $300–$400 for the return trip; a good vessel and reliable service are provided by Kirit Viatha and the Aqua Products tropical fish center. The services of Gombe Stream Tours are much shakier.

Gombe is only marginally developed for tourism. Currently, there is no lodge, only cabins within which "rooms" have been curtained off. The cabins are screened to keep primates out, not insects, and no mosquito nets are provided. Alternatively, you can set up your own tent. Either way, you must bring all your food supplies with you. You can stock up on fruits and vegetables in Kigoma, but should plan on purchasing any fancier dry or canned items in Dar, Bujumbura, or Nairobi. Kitchen facilities are available at the park. Considering all the effort needed to get to Gombe, a stay of three nights is recommended. The Park's special daily entry fee is $30. The cost of a cabin is expected to rise to $25 per night; standard national park fees apply to camping.

TOURING THE PARK

The introduction of tourism to Gombe has been somewhat controversial. Researchers fear that the chimps are suffering undue stress from increased human presence, and that they are liable to catch infectious diseases from travelers. The park administration is still experimenting with regulations that will both protect the animals and permit tourism to be developed as a source of income.

For a number of years, Goodall attracted chimps to feeding stations by doling out bananas. That practice is being gradually phased out, but the Gombe apes remain well habitutated to humans through years of daily monitoring by researchers. At present, no reservations are needed for visiting the park, but a trained guide must accompany you through the reserve. (Guide fee: $10 per person daily, in addition to regular park entrance costs.)

Chimp watching is not the same as gorilla viewing. Although considerably smaller than gorillas, chimps are more dangerous. A mature male can weigh up to 120 pounds and is much more powerful than a man. Because of their volatile and sometimes aggressive personalities, it is not always safe for tourists to sit among a group of chimpanzees, as is routinely done with gorillas.

Bananas are still distributed at one Gombe feeding station, where five people at a time are allowed to watch the proceedings. For their own security, visitors are confined to a tin hut that is screened to keep excited animals from molesting them. Unfortunately, it is oppressively hot inside the hut and views of the feeding area are partially obscured.

Tracking chimps is much more stimulating, but is not always easy. Hours of hard walking (and possibly climbing) on steep, forested slopes may be needed to find the animals, and there is no guarantee that they will ever be seen at all. Once found, however, there is no time limit to your viewing. Chimp watching is easiest when the apes are traveling and feeding on the ground in the grassier savannas. In the forest, you may see some spectacular acrobatics, for chimps can make 30-foot leaps from one branch to another. When the chimps are feeding in fruiting trees, observers can expect to face a rain of feces and urine from above, so don't wear your best safari clothes: some chimp researchers wear motorcycle helmets to protect themselves from falling debris.

Mahale Mountains National Park

This beautiful park also features fantastic chimpanzee viewing, but is completely undeveloped at this time. Although an excellent grid of forest trails has been cut by researchers, there are no guides available to show tourists around: you are left completely on your own and must be pretty bushwise to explore with confidence (avoid grassy areas where buffalo graze). The spartan guesthouse at the research station has no bedding or mosquito nets; you must bring all your own food and equipment.

Mahale is located on the shores of Lake Tanganyika, about a hundred miles south of Kigoma. It can be reached cheaply on a crowded fourteen hour journey by motorized *jahazi*. It is far more comfortable to take a lake steamer to the village of Mombo (six hours), then hire a small outboard to the park (about two hours). Because of the steamer schedule, you must plan on a stay of one week. You can also check on traveling directly to Mahale on the park's supply boat; inquire from the warden, Edeus Massawe, who lives opposite the electric power plant in Kigoma. Also ask about copying his map of the park. Standard national park fees are payable to the warden. Also keep in mind that the Japanese researchers at Mahale are pretty isolated, and greatly appreciate any special tidbits of food you can bring down.

Katavi National Park

Located about 160 air miles to the southeast of Kigoma (some 218 miles by road), the remote Katavi National Park is very seldom visited. Its seasonally flooded valley grasslands support good herds of buffalo, topi, and zebra, while areas of higher elevation host sable, roan, and other antelopes associated with *miombo* woodlands. Lions and elephants are both present, though the pachyderms have been much reduced in numbers by poaching. Extraordinary concentrations of water birds are found on lakes Chada and Katavi. Puku (an impala-sized antelope related to the waterbuck) and southern reedbuck may also be seen in the park. Both inhabit the grasslands of the shallow Rukwa Valley—an ancient and silted-up section of the Rift, just south of Katavi—that is also a little-known but very prolific wildlife area. Neither Katavi Park nor the Rukwa Valley is currently well developed for tourism (a four-wheel-drive vehicle is essential to negotiate their black cotton soil bottomlands), but one day they may become more accessible.

Rubondo Island National Park

Rubondo Island (approximately 175 square miles) is located in the southwest corner of Lake Victoria. A national park, it is notable for the sitatunga antelope that inhabit the papyrus marshes along its shores. Although most species of big game (such as elephant and lion) are absent, chimpanzee and black rhino have been introduced to the island sanctuary, and other rare animals may someday be brought in as well. Game watching is therefore potentially interesting, but few people are able to visit: tourist facilities are nonexistent, and the park is practically inaccessible except by charter aircraft. Rubondo does not easily fit into either Tanzania's northern or southern tour circuits; future access may be improved from the city of Mwanza (75 air miles distant), which is already linked to Dar by Air Tanzania.

6

At the Heart of the Continent: Rwanda, Eastern Zaire, Burundi, Uganda

In the very center of Africa, where the widening crack of the Rift Valley splits the continent, rise two great and mysterious mountain ranges: the snow-crowned, mist-shrouded Ruwenzori and the emerald-green Virunga Volcanos. Together they form the continental divide of Africa's watershed. The abundant rains falling on their slopes eventually flow either northward to the Nile or west to the mighty Zaire (Congo) River. The mountains form almost an exact ecological divide as well. Toward the rising sun lie the open plains of the East African savannas. To the west, the primeval rainforest stretches to the distant Atlantic.

Among the last reaches of the continent to be explored, this remote region long remained the darkest heart of Africa. Tales of the snow-topped Mountains of the Moon, of a race of dwarfs, and of savage ape-men persisted through the centuries. The stories were spawned by dim contacts gleaned by ancient emissaries of Egyptian pharoahs, then later kept alive by the reports of Arab slave caravans returning to their Indian Ocean strongholds. After centuries of ridicule and disbelief, the ancient tales were proved true when European explorers discovered a region as fascinating as its myths.

A twin reputation for remarkable scenery and bizarre savagery persists to this day. Although the lyric beauty of its mountain forest and savanna landscapes remain, the political history of the region since independence has been filled with disconcerting violence. The protracted civil war of the 1960s in the former Congo (now Zaire), the tribal massacres in Rwanda and Burundi, the orgy of bloodletting in Uganda in the wake of Idi Amin—all have advanced the reputation for violent instability. That and the difficulties of travel in primarily French-speaking countries have kept mass tourism out of the area.

But changes have come. Political calm reigns in Rwanda, and the Mobutu regime in Zaire, albeit scandalously corrupt, has brought enough stability to make travel safe. Only Uganda, once aptly described as "the pearl of Africa" and the sole English-speaking nation in the region, remains too risky for tourism.

With the dramatic surge of interest in the mountain gorilla, the once-dark heart of Africa has become a beacon for modern explorers.

RWANDA

Land of the Mountain Gorilla

Up until a few years ago, Rwanda was just another newly independent African nation, known outside Africa only to ardent crossword puzzle fans and the few Belgian colonials who had enjoyed the good fortune to live there. The praises of "the Land of a Thousand Hills" went unsung. A postage-stamp-size country at the very center of the continent, Rwanda was on no tour itinerary.

Not that the country lacked charm. The ubiquitous hills are extremely scenic: a patchwork of golden millet fields and green banana groves covers each one. The climate is delightful—a perpetual springtime typical of humid tropical highlands. Roads and hotels were missing, but more significantly, there was no perceived reason to go. The country was heavily settled, so better wildlife viewing could be had elsewhere at less expense.

All that changed with the opening of the world of the mountain gorilla. Today, Rwanda is very much on the tourist map of Africa. Good roads, excellent hotels, and new vehicles have brought a vast improvement in services, and the popularity of gorilla safaris has made tourism Rwanda's third biggest earner of foreign exchange. Still, most visitors come exclusively to see gorillas, and get only a by-the-way look at the rest of the country.

Rwanda seems a peaceful agricultural nation, moving forward with development. It is very well organized in comparison to its neighbors. Road construction, development projects, government administrative offices, and church missions are everywhere. If you

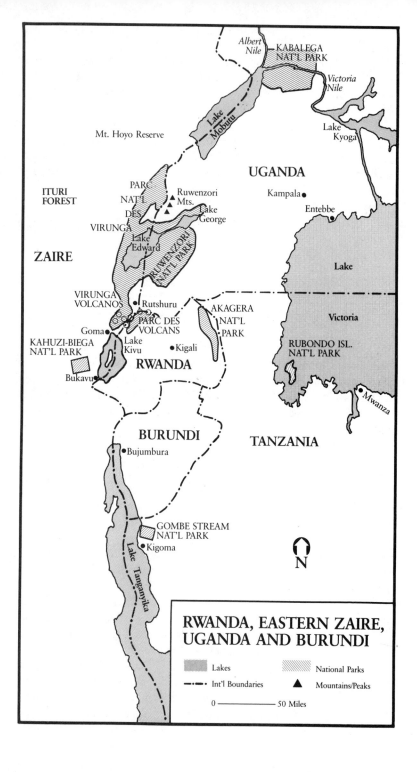

Albert
Nile

KABALEGA
NAT'L PARK

Victoria
Nile

Lake
Kyoga

Lake
Mobutu

Mt. Hoyo Reserve

UGANDA

ITURI
FOREST

PARC
NAT'L
DES

Ruwenzori
Mts.

Kampala

Entebbe

Lake
George

VIRUNGA

ZAIRE

Lake
Edward

RUWENZORI NAT'L PARK

Lake

VIRUNGA
VOLCANOS

Rutshuru

AKAGERA
NAT'L
PARK

Victoria

Goma

PARC DES
VOLCANS

RUBONDO ISL.
NAT'L PARK

KAHUZI-BIEGA
NAT'L PARK

Lake
Kivu

Kigali

RWANDA

Bukavu

BURUNDI

TANZANIA

Mwanza

Bujumbura

GOMBE STREAM
NAT'L PARK

Kigoma

N

Lake Tanganyika

RWANDA, EASTERN ZAIRE, UGANDA AND BURUNDI

Lakes

National Parks

–·–·– Int'l Boundaries

▲ Mountains/Peaks

0 ——————— 50 Miles

enter the country from Zaire or Tanzania, you are immediately struck by the relatively prosperous appearance of the people. They are well dressed. The men wear Western-style clothes (sports jackets are much favored); the women tend more toward colorful African-style prints. Everywhere are knots of people: gangs at work on the roads, tea pickers bent double among the neat rows of plantations, crowds thronging village markets, schools bursting with uniformed students. Children are everywhere.

It is obvious that Rwanda is overcrowded. The country occupies just over 10,000 square miles in total area. Its population is about six million, and growing at the African average of some 3 to 3.5 percent a year. The typical Rwandese woman gives birth to nine children. The traditional African reliance on large families and love of children, and the dominance of the Catholic Church, have left little room for population control.

A century ago, at the time of the first European explorations, Rwanda was ecologically a very different place. Forests covered a much greater part of the country and the population was a bare fraction of today's. The most numerous group were the Hutu, agriculturists eking out a living on shifting plots. They were dominated by the WaTutsi, the tall, thin-boned Nilotic pastoralists. The Tutsi ran the country as aristocratic feudal lords. Their main interest was their cattle, prized not only for sustenance but as the ultimate reckoning of wealth. Politics was a major preoccupation, for both the Tutsi of Rwanda and Burundi seemed forever involved in political intrigues to overthrow or succeed whoever was the current *mwami*, or Great Chief. A third group was the BaTwa, pygmoid hunter-gatherers who were the descendants of the aboriginal Pygmy race and the earliest Bantu immigrants. The BaTwa ranged the forests in small bands, living off the land and trading with the more culturally advanced newcomers for products such as iron. Over the centuries before the arrival of the Europeans, these three groups shared the country.

The colonial period began with the arrival of the Germans in 1894. They introduced European administration, the first public schools, and the cultivation of coffee, while allowing the Catholic Church to open its first missions and schools. The Germans did not last long: they were booted out by the British and Belgians during the First World War. At the end, Belgium was awarded the administration of Ruanda-Urundi as a mandated territory under the League of Nations. They ruled until independence in 1962.

As everywhere in Africa, colonialism had a revolutionary effect. The introduction of cash crops such as coffee and tea, the seeds of general education, and the upsetting of traditional values and political power led to rapid modernization. Most important was the creation of a system of rudimentary health care, notably widespread vaccinations, which reduced infant mortality. The result was a burgeoning population that grows to this day.

Rwanda is today an independent republic. Tribalism is no longer an important political issue, since the decisive victory of the Hutu in the civil wars at the time of independence. Almost 90 percent of the population are Hutu (or WaHutu), the rest Tutsi (or WaTutsi), except for a very small remnant of BaTwa (a mere 1 percent). The government of President (and Major General) Juvenal Habyarimana deserves credit for its sensible approach to development: it takes aid from all comers. Perhaps because of its perceived "strategic" position, it has many benefactors. China, Libya, France, the Soviet Union, and the United States all give aid. The Rwandese wisely take from all while promising nothing in return.

The national administration has some interesting features. The country is broken into provinces, which are in turn composed of communes (purely an administrative term—it has nothing to do with communism). The commune consists of the basic building block of Rwandese society—the *colline*, "the hill." Each of the thousand hills of the country is quite literally given a number and has its own hill leader who is responsible for the activities of the other inhabitants. The system is a holdover from precolonial times, when every hill was the domain of a Tutsi lord.

The government also has established a unique system for maintaining public works. Every person must give one day's labor per month to the local commune. This ensures a ready labor force for rebuilding dirt roads, harvesting crops on commune property, and a variety of other chores. Not even the president is exempt from this public service obligation.

By African standards, the government really does run an orderly society that seems to have brought about a decent measure of good for the ordinary citizen. It remains to be seen how it can cope with the looming population crisis. A family-planning program is under way: the government has called on each family to limit itself to four children. Stronger measures must come, for already every bit of arable land is under cultivation and the country must depend on imports to feed itself. The national parks and a few remnant forest reserves are the country's only remaining uncultivated lands. Although the government seems genuinely interested in preserving them, the pressure of a land-hungry populace may some day force them open for cultivation.

Safari Facts

Entry. Visas are required and can be collected at any Rwanda embassy. If entering at Kigali's Kayibanda International Airport without one, you *might* get in, but some people have been promptly deported. Proof of vaccination for yellow fever and cholera are also needed.

Currency. Rwanda francs (1989: approximately RF 74 = U.S. $1). It's advisable to exchange money on arrival at the airport. All major hotels also have official banks that exchange at the same rate but their hours are irregular. Exchange at hotel desks is at a 10 percent lower rate. It is no longer necessary to declare currency on entry, but do keep all your exchange receipts in case you have extra francs to exchange for dollars on departure. The black market pays about 10 percent higher than the official rate but is not worth tinkering with. Some U.S. cash is useful for emergencies.

Language. The official language is Kinyarwanda. All educated people, and a great many others, speak French. If you speak French, you will have no trouble getting around. English and Swahili are generally not useful.

Air Travel. International flights serving Kigali include Sabena from Brussels, Air France from Paris, Kenya Airlines from Nairobi, and Air Tanzania from Kilimanjaro. Air Rwanda serves Ruhengiri (near Parc des Volcans), Gisenyi on Lake Kivu (at the border of Goma, Zaire), and Kamembe (near Bukavu, Zaire). There is a $15 departure tax on international flights payable only in U.S. currency; RF 200 for domestic.

Transportation. Green public buses serve all the main towns, but do not run often. An extensive network of roads throughout the country is continuously plied by passenger-carrying minivans and trucks. They are cheap but amazingly crowded. No regular transport serves either national park. Suzuki four-wheel-drive cars can be rented, self-drive, from Rwanda Travel Service.

On Your Own. Rwanda is not a difficult country for the independent traveler to get around in, and there are hotels to fit every pocketbook. But a visit can be extremely frustrating if you have come to see gorillas or Akagera National Park and have little time or money. For Akagera, a car is a necessity. For gorillas, there is the permit problem. If you have unlimited time, or are prepared for camping, your chances of getting to see the gorillas are good. If you are budgeting time, better book a tour in advance.

Tours. Several local agencies in Kigali book gorilla tours. The main tour operator, Rwanda Travel Service, is located in the Hotel Diplomat. Urubano Tours is in the Meridien Hotel, near Kigali's airport. Either can provide a vehicle with driver (English-speaking not always assured) and make all hotel and permit reservations. If you are on your own or a couple, their services are expensive. Furthermore, if you arrive in Kigali without prebooking a tour, these agents probably will have no luck getting gorilla permits on short notice. They may have some influence in getting priority on the waiting list. It is extremely hard to make advance plans with them, as they are very slow to reply to correspondence.

If your time is limited and you can afford it, it is advisable to make arrangements through a knowledgeable U.S. tour operator long in advance of your departure for Africa. Most offer "optional" Rwanda extensions to their East African safaris. These are generally quite expensive, due both to the high costs charged in Rwanda and to the endless office time needed to organize a trip there. Although a satisfactory gorilla-viewing trip could be accomplished in as few as four days, ORTPN (Organization Rwandese de Tourisme et Parcs Nationaux) officials give priority for the purchase of gorilla permits to foreign tour operators who book their clients for a minimum stay in Rwanda of one week. These extra days add extra cost, a fact not lost on a government anxious to reap maximum revenue from the country's prime tourist attraction.

If you are thinking of booking a gorilla-viewing extension to a safari package, find out beforehand exactly what is included. Most extensions include all transport and accommodation as well as the gorilla permits. Ordinarily your driver doubles as guide while you are traveling; when tracking gorillas, you will have only the French-speaking park guides as escorts. Never book any gorilla program that does not offer at least two days of gorilla viewing. The best gorilla tours include several tracking sessions and visits to other areas of Rwanda; ideally, they continue into Zaire. When planning your trip, be sure to note that children under 15 years old are not allowed to visit gorillas.

Kigali

There is little to do in Rwanda's tiny capital. Although surrounded by green terraced hills, it has no parks or even a national museum. It's a place to get your business done and get out. The central business area is very compact: the main hotels, embassies, government offices, and market are all within blocks.

Hotels. The Diplomat and the Mille Collines are the best hotels in town. Foreign businessmen and expatriate Europeans can always be found around the pool at the Mille Collines, but it can be intolerably noisy. (Try for a room in the rear of the hotel, otherwise the shouts of taxi drivers and car engines will keep you up all night.) The Diplomat is quieter, but has no pool. Both are very central. The posh Meridien, although isolated from town, is near the airport and more relaxing. In the city center, the Kyovu is a comfortable African hotel. There are also many cheaper guesthouses.

Restaurants. If you are staying at one of the better hotels, that is where you should eat. All feature very good continental restaurants. If you are on a budget, many cheap restaurants serve local fare: *andazi* (white cornmeal mush—same as *ugali*) usually served with a meat sauce, eggs, rice, and beans. An excellent variety of fruits and vegetables can be found at the market.

Tourist Office. The Organization Rwandese de Tourisme et Parcs Nationaux (ORTPN) has its office near the Mille Collines Hotel. If you need gorilla permits, this is where you go. Don't expect a warm reception; it has a rather blasé bureaucratic atmosphere. Be polite and see what they have. If you are lucky and permits are available, pay for them there and make sure to be at the park early on the correct day. If not, you can still go up to the park and try your luck. The ORTPN office is the place to get information about the national parks: books, pamphlets on procedures for gorilla viewing, excellent maps of both Parc des Volcans and Akagera Park. Snap them up, because they may be unavailable elsewhere. The same goes for gorilla posters, postcards, and national park pins.

Outfitting. If you are going to be camping, you'll want to buy most of your foodstuffs in Kigali. The market has a great variety of fruits and vegetables. Perishables won't last long (you won't have refrigeration). You can restock food like bananas anywhere, but other items are not so easy to come by. If you are going directly to a park and have room, buy your supplies in Kigali and be done with it. Tinned goods (try Russian tinned mackerel) and excellent local cheese (it's wax sealed and keeps quite well) are found in the Kigali market. The Allirwanda supermarket is packed with all sorts of useful camping foods, as well as French delicacies such as wine and paté. You could outfit your entire expedition from this shop. It's convenient but, of course, expensive. Don't expect to get any standard camping equipment in Rwanda. Come prepared. You can buy kerosene (locally called *pétrol),* lanterns, and plastic jerry cans (essential for water if you want to camp inside either of the parks).

Shopping. Several small crafts shops are located around the market. Most items are not high quality, but good pieces can be found. Wood carvings predominate. Many are carved at church missions and have typical village activities as motifs. An excellent line of ceramic sculpture has the same themes: families cooking, drinking banana beer, even funerals. Basket work is good, especially the series of shrinking conical baskets that nestle one into the other. "Antique" carvings from Zaire may be presented to you. They are probably not very old, though they may have spent several months buried in an ashheap to make them look aged. They are nonetheless fascinating pieces, and will look great in your house if you can manage to get them home. Crafts are also sold by wandering vendors. Wherever you find a good piece, bargain hard, except in mission shops throughout the country. They sell at reasonable fixed prices.

Warning. Beware of pickpockets. They work in gangs in Kigali.

Parc National Des Volcans

The Virunga Volcanos occupy that corner of Africa where the boundaries of Rwanda, Uganda, and Zaire meet. Three volcanos stand in line on the border between Rwanda and Uganda: the perfect cone of Muhabura (13,540 ft.), flat-topped Gahinga (11,397 ft.), and jagged Sabinyo (11,923 ft.). Some 6 miles to the southwest, another cluster of extinct volcanos straddles the Rwanda-Zaire boundary: green Visoke (12,175 ft.) and the giant Karisimbi (14,787 ft.), with the spirelike plug of Mikeno (14,557 ft.) behind. A few miles deeper into Zaire, two active volcanos, Nyiragongo and Nyamulagira, complete the range. A moist climate and rich volcanic soils have made the Virunga region one of the most densely populated in Africa. Its once mighty forests have now shrunk right to the bases of the great volcanos. These forests are the focus of intense international interest because they are the home of the mountain gorilla.

Rwanda's portion of the Virunga range is protected in the Parc des Volcans (in English, Volcanos National Park) a narrow crescent of land pushed against the frontiers of Uganda and Zaire. The park encompasses three major life zones: bamboo, hagenia-hypericum forest, and subalpine moorlands. A fourth zone, that of mixed highland forest, formerly covered vast tracts of country around the volcanos. It has been completely destroyed and converted to farmland.

Bamboo dominates extensive areas at elevations between 7,500 and 9,500 feet. Bamboo (*Arundinaria alpina*) is a tree-size grass, often growing in dense stands. Where it dominates, it may grow almost to the exclusion of other plants, creating veritable forests of delicate cane. Bamboo forests are pleasant and easy to walk through on game paths. With the notable exceptions of the gorilla and the golden monkey, few animals feed on bamboo.

Along the park boundary on Visoke Volcano, no bamboo zone is left, and you immediately enter hagenia-hypericum forest, which grows between 8,500 feet and 11,500 feet. A hagenia forest is a rather magical place. The gnarled trunks and broad, spreading limbs of hagenia trees are massively draped with thick carpets of green moss, orchids, and ferns, while their green foliage is delicately bearded with lichens. Flowers grow in the forest understory, and the air seems alive with the scent of damp vegetation. Tree-sized St. John's worts (*Hypericum lanceolatum*) are also characteristic of these upland woods. They are recognized by their delicate leaves and masses of bright yellow flowers.

At about 11,000 feet, the forest gives way to the bogs and weird plants of the subalpine zone. Drenching rains, a year-round growing season, and intense ultraviolet radiation have resulted in vegetative giantism. Most conspicuous are the giant groundsels or senecios. Elsewhere in the world, senecios are undistinguished members of the sunflower family. In African mountains, however, these plants attain huge size, growing up to 20 feet tall over a life span of more than a hundred years. They develop thick corky stems, with huge leaves clustering on branches that look like grotesque arms. Their yellow flowers grow on long spikes. They are complemented by the graceful vertical flower spikes of the lobelias, another Afro-alpine giant. Only in the Virungas and the equally rain-swept Ruwenzori do groundsels and lobelias grow so profusely as to form forests. Among the giants are an abundance of normal-sized "everlasting

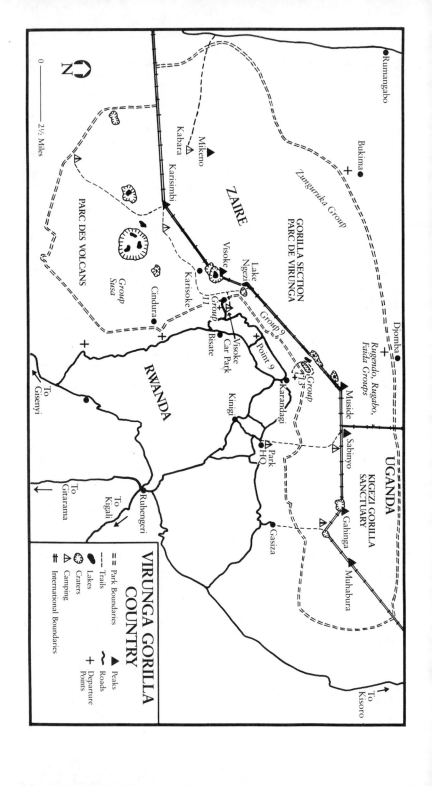

flowers" (*Helichrysum spp.*) and delicate ground-dwelling orchids.

The subalpine zone is a moody environment, in which sunlit vistas are closed off in minutes by swirling mists. You'll have to climb the volcanos to reach these unworldly moors. Buffalo go that high to graze the tussock grasses of the bogs, and gorillas sometimes wander there, too.

The wildlife of the Virungas is extremely difficult to observe. Animals tend to be secretive, and many are nocturnal. Unless you camp in the park, you are more likely to find animal spoor than have actual sightings. Your chances are better when camping, because you have the opportunity to stake out or patrol the edges of clearings at dawn and dusk.

Elephant are much reduced in numbers but still live in the Virungas. You are not likely to meet them, but if you do, be careful. Few experiences are as unnerving as hearing elephants trumpet while you are walking through a bamboo tunnel. These are created when the elephants make regular paths through the bamboo. Inside, your visibility is limited to the length of the tunnel; the green wall of bamboo closes down within a few yards of the trail's edge. You do not want to walk into an elephant! Buffalo feed in grassy openings at all elevations. You don't want to meet them at close quarters either, so watch for fresh droppings. Neither buffalo nor elephant is ordinarily seen when tracking the habituated gorilla groups.

Duiker and bushbuck are common, but shy. Both are reddish-brown antelopes that can be found throughout the park. Bushbuck (*Tragelaphus scriptus*) are very deerlike in appearance. The male is a richer dark brown and has thick, spiraled horns. The black-fronted duiker (*Cephalofus nigrifrons*) is smaller and more rounded in shape, with its forelegs shorter than the hind. This gives them an almost piglike appearance, a resemblance that is carried over to their feeding habits. Like pigs, they are fairly omnivorous, digging for roots and even eating carrion and small animals in addition to more antelope-like fare (leaves and grasses). The black giant forest hog also occurs but is mostly nocturnal.

One nocturnal animal that you are likely to encounter if you camp in the park is the tree hyrax (*Dendrohyrax arboreus*). Hyrax look like large rodents, but are actually more closely related to elephants. These animals are occasionally seen at dusk browsing in bushes and small trees. They are much more likely to be heard. Their eerie, screeching cries, rather terrifying, fill the night with a chorus of disembodied sound.

Giant groundsels growing above the lake-filled crater of Visoke Volcano. *Photo by Allen Bechky.*

The rare golden monkey (*Circopithecus mitis kandti*) is a park specialty, restricted to the Virunga range. This beautiful monkey has a distinctive color scheme: its golden-red body contrasts sharply with black crown, legs, and shoulders. It is an animal of the bamboo zone.

The largest predators in the park are spotted hyena and leopard. Neither is likely to be seen or to bother you. Only one species of snake has been found in the park, and that one is not poisonous.

Virunga birdlife is interesting, but difficult to see. Most impressive are the gemlike sunbirds, of which there are several species, all brilliantly colored. You'll see them feeding on the nectar of flowers, even high among the lobelias of the subalpine zone. In hagenia forests, keep alert for the fantastic Ruwenzori turaco. It is large but inconspicuous until it flies away with a flash of bright crimson wings. They live in pairs, so if you see one fly off, a little patience could reward you with a good view of the multicolored bird.

One unusual animal deserves mention, although it is hardly appealing. On wet forest trails, you may come across the giant earthworm. This invertebrate looks exactly like its pinkish cousins everywhere, except that it is about a foot long and proportionately thick! Some specimens are blue in color.

NATURAL HISTORY OF THE GORILLA

The shape and face of the gorilla are as unmistakable as its scientific name, *Gorilla gorilla*. There are three subspecies. The most common is the western lowland gorilla found in the equatorial forests of Africa's Atlantic coast. Although threatened by increasing habitat destruction, it is the most numerous of the gorilla types, with an estimated population of about 40,000. This is the variety most familiar to zoo-goers, for virtually all animals in captivity are western lowland. Separated by hundreds of miles from the western animals is the range of the eastern lowland gorilla *(Gorilla gorilla graueri)*. Between 2,500 and 4,500 of these live in the forests of eastern Zaire. Rarest of all is the mountain gorilla *(G. g. beringei)*. Their stronghold is the Virunga Volcanos, where only 280–310 animals remain. Another small population of mountain gorillas lives in Uganda's Impenetrable Forest Reserve, just north of the Virungas.

The differences between the mountain and eastern lowland subspecies are not easily recognizable. Both have long blackish fur, which at least distinguishes them from the western types, whose fur is shorter and browner. The mountain gorilla has a higher-crowned head, which makes it seem larger than the eastern lowland variety. There are slight differences in the life histories of the various types, but here I'll concentrate on that of the mountain gorilla.

Gorillas are the largest anthropoid (human-like) apes. Considerable differences exist between the sexes. Females reach a maximum size of about 5 feet in height. They weigh from 155 to 240 pounds. Males reach just under 6 feet in height, and may weigh up to 440 pounds. Males of this imposing size are called *silverbacks* because of the distinguishing gray mantle they develop at maturity.

Gorillas live in family groups. These consist of a dominant silverback male, his females with their dependent offspring, and juveniles of both sexes. Lowland gorilla groups tend to be small, while bands of mountain gorilla may number up to thirty animals. Such large groups may contain several fully mature silverbacks.

Life in the group is a peaceful one. Gorillas wake early and begin snacking off the foliage around their nests, generally not getting into serious foraging before about 8 A.M. It then takes a couple of hours of determined eating to fill their large bellies, after which they rest for several hours. They resume activity in mid-afternoon, feeding and roaming until settling down before dusk. Each individual makes its own simple nest, folding underneath itself any leaves and branches that are conveniently within reach. Young up to about

A silverback mountain gorilla in Parcs des Volcans, Rwanda. *Photo by Allen Bechky.*

three years old sleep in the mother's nest. The Virunga gorillas make their nests on the ground, with only the odd juvenile bedding down in the lower branches of trees. New nesting sites are used each night.

Gorillas are vegetarians. They eat a wide variety of plants including leaves, shoots, bark, roots, and fruit. In the Virungas, they are especially fond of wild celery (it looks just like the stuff you buy in the market), purple-flowering vernonia shrubs, nettles, and tender bamboo shoots. Gorillas do not have to drink water. They get all they need from the enormous quantities of juicy plants they consume.

Females give birth at intervals of about four years. Infants are quite helpless; the females have to carry their clutching charges everywhere. By six months, the young can scramble around on their own while the group is feeding or resting. They remain dependent on their mothers up till about age four.

A dominant silverback is the leader and protector of his group. He will share females sexually with other mature males in his own group, but if strange males try to steal them, there may be serious fighting. Young females frequently transfer out to new groups in that way. If a dominant silverback weakens through age or disease and becomes unable to defend his family, the females will be taken over by neighboring males. When a silverback dies, all females are taken by rivals, unless there is another fully mature silverback already in the group who can defend it. Once the females are gone, all that remains of the group will be the juvenile males who stay together. One day they will try to abduct females for themselves. When a silverback succeeds in taking a new female, he kills her newborn offspring. This infanticide causes the female to come into estrus again as soon as possible, thus giving the silverback an early chance to reproduce.

Most days gorillas do not move great distances, often no more than a kilometer or two. They travel single file, walking on all fours. In the Virungas, they sometimes climb as high as the zone of the giant senecios, but mostly remain lower down in the hagenia forest. When new shoots are plentiful, gorillas spend a lot of time feeding in the bamboo groves.

Gorillas rarely walk bipedally. Walking on two feet is reserved for short distances only, and is often associated with threat displays. Chest beating is practiced by males from a very young age. Among silverbacks, chest beating is a means of communicating to rival groups. The popping sounds can be heard at a distance, so direct confrontations can be diplomatically avoided. The chest beat is also a dramatic part of the silverback's threat charge.

The great apes have few enemies, although leopards may occasionally take them. The chief natural causes of death among mountain gorillas are respiratory diseases such as pneumonia.

Humans are the major threat to gorillas. Poaching is the most publicized problem because it produces grisly photographs of animals with severed heads and missing hands. This activity gets a lot of press attention, and is usually blamed on the tourists' insatiable demand for souvenirs. In fact, most gorillas killed in profit-hunting schemes die because the poachers are seeking young animals for sale to zoos and private collectors. To get to the young, poachers must kill both silverbacks and mothers. Whole groups can be destroyed to obtain infants, which usually die before they reach their place of ultimate captivity. This type of poaching cannot take place without the collusion of government officials somewhere along the line. Fortunately, there does not seem to be any current activity of this sort in Rwanda.

Some heads and hands reportedly do wind up being surreptitiously offered to tourists. Needless to say, do not buy them; try instead to report the vendor to police!

Incidental poaching is a serious threat. The BaTwa people often set snare traps in the park, hoping to catch small antelope for the pot. Snares do not discriminate. If a gorilla catches its hand in the wire, it may suffer terrible lacerations struggling to free itself. The wounds often infect and lead to crippling disfigurement or death.

Although poaching is the most visible threat to the gorilla, it actually runs a poor second to habitat destruction. As long as the ape's available living space continues to shrink, its numbers will decline. Hopefully, that process has been arrested in the Virungas, where the success of the Mountain Gorilla Project has led the Rwanda government to protect Parc des Volcans from further human encroachment. That in turn has opened the eyes of the authorities in Zaire to the economic benefits of gorilla-based tourism, and stimulated the creation of a parallel conservation program in Zaire. The development of tourism on the Zaire side of the volcanos can only lead to better protection of that vital portion of the mountain gorilla's limited range.

Ironically, the very success of conservation through tourism has raised new concern about the welfare of the Virunga gorillas: some fear that the great apes may succumb to infectious diseases (such as the common cold or measles) that could be transmitted by human visitors. Park regulations have lately been tightened to reduce that risk, (see the sections on permits, procedures, tracking, and gorilla viewing in the Parc des Volcans, later), but nothing can be done to eliminate it completely.

ACCESS AND ACCOMMODATION

Access to the park is through the town of Ruhengeri. An excellent paved road connects Ruhengeri with Kigali (a drive of less than three hours) and there is plenty of public transport. Getting to the park itself is trickier. It's a 40-minute drive (though only 9 miles) from town to the park headquarters at Kinigi. No public transport from Ruhengeri to the park is available, so if you do not have your own vehicle you must walk or hitch. That's not a problem if you are going to be camping at Kinigi, but if you stay in town you will be hard pressed to make it to headquarters by 8 A.M. It's best in that case to try to connect with someone driving up to the park. Check at the Muhabura Hotel the previous evening for shared rides. If you have no luck, you can hire a car in town to take you up for the day (it's expensive: $80–$100). Remember, from Kinigi you still have to cover up to 9 miles to reach the staging areas for gorilla tracking, and you are expected to be at your rendezvous by about 9 A.M. Numerous rough dirt roads crisscross the area between Ruhengeri and Kinigi. If you are driving up on your own or walking, give yourself plenty of time.

Most tour groups accommodate at the Meridien Hotel IZUBA in Gisenyi, on Lake Kivu. It's a top-standard hotel, but requires an extra hour's travel time *each way* in commuting to the park. Some gorilla watchers stay at the Muhabura Hotel in Ruhengeri. It is moderately expensive, run down, and rather gloomy, but it does have hot water and clean rooms. Rumor has it that it will soon be spruced up. For now, it's the only real hotel in town. For clean budget accommodation, ask for the Centre d'Accueil, located near the Prefecture building in Ruhengeri.

Those without transport or gorilla permits will want to stay at Kinigi in order to be on hand at park headquarters for the early morning permit muster. Camping is allowed there (RF 500), but the site is in well-populated country and thieves are a problem. It's better to stay in the national park's guesthouse, in which separate bungalows each accommodate up to five people (at RF 800 per person). Shared toilet and washing facilities are clean and have hot water. Drinks and some local food dishes are available at the hostel's bar, but it's advised to bring your own food supplies. If you already have your permit, you can camp at the Visoke Ranger Post and car parking place, which is the starting point for tracking gorilla Group 11. Since it's located on the park boundary, you can at least spend time exploring in the forest around camp. Water and latrines are there, and a rough canvas tent is available for rent.

Several other interesting campsites are located inside the park. A tin hut near the Cindura Ranger Post, the principal start-off point for tracking Group Susa, provides good shelter. It is an excellent place to experience the magic of night within the hagenia forest. (If you are visiting Group Susa, see more about this hut below.) The hut at Lake Ndezi is a total ruin. It is supposed to be one of the better places for observing park wildlife, because antelope and buffalo may be observed around the marshy lakeshore at dawn and dusk. Camping is not ordinarily permitted there, but *if* you can get permission, bring a tent. Various huts are available as campsites for volcano climbers: one each on Karisimbi and Sabinyo, another (in poor condition) on the saddle between Muhabura and Gahinga. It's a good idea to have a tent along, just in case the huts prove uninhabitable.

Keep in mind that if you will be camping, your tent had better be good. When it rains in the Virungas, it *pours*. Your gear will be severely tested. Also note that you should avoid sleeping on the bare floors of huts in this part of Africa. An endemic typhuslike disease is contracted through the bites of insects that live in the soil of human habitations.

GORILLA VIEWING IN PARC DES VOLCANS

Park Fees: There is no getting around it, gorilla watching is expensive. Because of the limited number of places available and the huge demand, the cost of permits skyrockets year by year. Current charges (1989; including 6 percent tax) for a gorilla-viewing permit are RF 10,070 (U.S. $138) each (per day) plus a RF 2,120 (U.S. $29) entrance fee to Parc des Volcans (good for four days). Anyone prebooking a gorilla permit from abroad must buy an "excursion ticket" that includes the cost of entry to Akagera Park, an additional RF 1,590 (U.S. $22), as well as the gorilla permit, for a total of RF 11,660 (U.S. $160). Camping fees in the park are RF 530 (U.S. $7) per night inclusive of tax.

Permits: Many groups of gorillas live in Parc des Volcans, but only four are open to public viewing. A maximum of eight permits per day are issued for each group. Since demand far outstrips the supply, even high-priced tour operators find it difficult to secure permits for their clients. Permits are only firmly reserved on cash payment to the ORTPN for a specific date and no refunds whatsoever are given for no-shows. Permits are transferable, however, and those of canceled tour members are often up for resale at Kinigi Park Headquarters. In order to protect the gorillas from contact with infectious diseases, *no one* showing any signs of illness (or a cold) will be allowed on tracking sessions (in such cases, the permit fee is refundable). Children under age 15 are strictly prohibited from taking part in gorilla viewing (proof of birth date may be required if authorities have any doubts about age).

Groups 11 and 13 are by far the most visited. Because permits for them can be bought in advance, these groups are heavily reserved by overseas tour operators. Group 9 ranges back and forth across the border between Rwanda and Zaire, but is only accessible to visitors when it is on the Rwanda side. Permits for Group 9 are therefore sold exclusively at Kinigi. When the gorillas are in the country, permits are issued daily on a first-come, first-served basis. People are often camped at Kinigi, waiting for the opportunity to visit Group 9 or the possibility to buy the permits of no-shows reserved for Groups 11 and 13. A considerable crowd of hopefuls is sometimes in attendance.

Permits to visit Group Susa can also be booked in advance. Since access to this group requires a steep approach march or an overnight of camping in the park, it is less often prereserved by tour groups. Independent travelers therefore have their best chance to get an advanced reservation if they request a Susa viewing.

Procedures: Permit holders must be at the Kinigi park office no later than 8 A.M. When tour groups arrive, their leaders and drivers join the throng at the desk, where permits are carefully checked by park officials. It usually takes some time before all available permits are parceled out and the lucky holders are dispatched to the various starting points for gorilla tracking.

All permit holders are supposed to arrive at their staging areas to meet their official guides by 9 A.M. If you are late, the party may start without you.

Before leaving the staging area, you will have the opportunity to hire porters. The fee is RF 300 (about U.S. $4) per porter. You probably won't have much gear with you, but even a day pack stuffed with rain gear, water bottle, lunch, and extra camera equipment will start to weigh you down if it turns out to be a difficult tracking session. Porters can also lend a helpful hand on steep spots. If you are on a prebooked tour, porter costs will be included.

Every day, whether there are tourists or not, the park guides track the gorillas. Guides are well trained and know much gorilla lore, but cannot be relied on for detailed natural history information. They know where they left their gorilla groups the previous day, and they lead you to the most convenient point for entering the forest and beginning the actual tracking. At the forest's edge, the guide addresses your party in French, detailing the regulations for gorilla viewing. The rules are simple, sensible, and important:

- While tracking gorillas, you may talk and have access to your porters. After the apes are actually found, the porters will be left behind with whatever gear you do not need. If you have brought a bamboo walking stick, you must leave it with the porters.

- Once in the presence of the gorillas, talking, pointing, and sudden movements are forbidden.

- Flash photography is forbidden; autoflash cameras that do not have manual override will not be permitted near the gorillas.

- Visitors are to stay together, the guide remaining between you and the gorillas. Do not move in advance of the guide.

- Stay low; that is, crouch or crawl rather than move around in the erect posture of a human being. If the silverback stares directly at you, look down or away. Direct stares are regarded as threats among gorillas.

- All physical contact with gorillas is to be avoided. To reduce risk of spreading disease, park rules now call for visitors to remain at least 15 feet from the animals, but that distance is really impractical to maintain in the field because both apes and humans move around. In any event, do not touch the gorillas; if an animal touches you, move away. This directive is partly for your own protection, for physical contact could spark an aggressive reaction from the silverback.

- If a silverback charges, stay put. DO NOT RUN! Running may only provoke more aggression.

The rules have been worked out in the interest of minimizing disturbance to the animals and maximizing your safety. It takes up to two years to habituate a group of gorillas to the point where they will calmly accept a number of unfamiliar humans. Without this gradual process of habituation, no real gorilla watching would be possible. Unhabituated gorillas react quite differently to contact with people: they run away at the first hint of human proximity. Silverbacks will attempt to defend their group if severely provoked. When they do attack, they use their teeth, which would be the envy of any German shepherd dog.

It must be said that although injuries to tourists are very rare, they are possible. For example, one woman's arm was broken when a silverback accidently ran into her. Several researchers and photographers have been bitten in the course of gorilla studies.

The Groups. Visitors are always concerned about which group of gorillas is the "best" to see; an unnecessary worry because all offer excellent viewing. Gorilla bands are forever changing in size and makeup as new births, deaths, and transfers keep group composition fluid.

Group 11 is a small family group led by a silverback who lost one of his hands to a poacher's snare. The group has a home range on the northeast flank of Visoke Volcano. Steep, thickly forested slopes can make for difficult tracking sessions, but offer splendid mountain scenery. You might even get up to Lake Ngezi, a lovely crater pool. The starting point for tracking Group 11 is the ranger post at the Visoke car park, 9 miles from Kinigi.

Group 9 is the "migratory" group whose range extends into Zaire. This family includes a magnificent silverback, several females, and many babies. They inhabit the broken hill country between Visoke and Sabinyo volcanos. The park boundary comes to within a mile of the border there, so the group is very confined in its wandering on the Rwanda side. Most of their territory consists of bamboo forest. Walking is generally easy, unless the gorillas are hugging the top of the hills. Often, little time is required to locate the group. If they cross over into Zaire, you are not allowed to follow. The meeting place for tracking is "Point 9," 6 miles from Kinigi.

Group 13 is another family group with a large silverback. These gorillas range around the Muside cone, close to Sabinyo. Their country is largely bamboo, with forest in the higher areas. The starting point is the village of Karandagi, 4 miles from Kinigi.

Group Susa is an extraordinary band of gorillas. It is composed of more than twenty animals, including two fully grown silverbacks. Their territory is on the eastern slopes of Karisimbi Volcano. In this luscious country, mountain forest covers the decayed lava ridges that run down the volcano's flanks. The starting point for Group Susa visits is often the Cindura ranger post. Originally, it was required to spend the night there, before tracking the following morning. That is no longer the case, and those *with transport* can visit Susa on a one-day trip: visitors must check in at Kinigi (before 5 P.M.) the previous day to confirm their reservations. In the morning, the permit holders assemble at Kinigi by 5:30 A.M. sharp, and leave for one of three possible starting points. (Visitors staying at the Meridien in Gisenyi often arrange to meet the group at the proper roadhead, but even so, they have to get off to an extremely early start to arrive on time—no later than 7 A.M.—for the rendezvous.) Anyone contemplating a one-day Susa visit should be forewarned: the climb from the roadhead to the park boundary is steep, and may only be the beginning of a very long day.

Camping at Cindura makes an exciting expedition. After getting your permits at park headquarters, you proceed to the Visoke roadhead, where you present your credentials at the ranger hut. There you can pick up porters if you want them. You can also buy charcoal, which will be useful at Cindura hut, where there is a brazier. It comes in handy for heating the place as well as cooking. You can also inquire about renting a plastic jerry can for water, if you did not bring one.

It is about a two-hour walk to Cindura. Essentially you proceed right along the park boundary. There is quite a bit of up and down as you skirt the flanks of Visoke and Karisimbi volcanos. Eventually, you climb to the top of an old lava ridge to a large army tent that is the gorilla guides' quarters. The guides will tell you when to be ready in the morning. They can give you a good idea of where the gorillas are and how difficult it will be to find them. If they say the group is far, believe them—you are in for a long day. They will direct you to a trail leading straight up the ridge and into the forest. After five minutes, you come to the hut—a small metal rondaval with a packed dirt floor. Inside are six beds made of lashed wooden poles. The *zuma* (hut watchman) will appear to unlock the hut for you. He is a very important person, as he will guard your possessions while you are off gorilla tracking. He will also start your charcoal fire for you, and possibly fill your jerry cans with water. You should remember to tip him if he is helpful.

If you have brought many porters with you, you can have most of them return to Visoke immediately after dropping your gear at the hut. It costs an additional RF 500 (U.S. $7) per porter for an overnight stay. Arrange for them to return to help you on the day you will be walking out. It's a good idea to have at least a few porters remain overnight so they can help on the gorilla tracking, too. The really tough walking may still be ahead.

A night in the hut can be a great adventure in sound. If you don't have the wonderfully weird chorus of the hyraxes, you may hear the dramatic effects of torrential rains beating down on the metal roof, and the sharp close claps of mountain thunder. After a hard day's gorilla tracking, you'll be glad to be in the hut warming up by the charcoal brazier.

Tracking. For many visitors, the tracking portion of the experience is just as exciting as the actual gorilla viewing. For others it is sheer torture. How it goes will depend very much on your physical condition, the weather, and the amount of time you spend hiking. Sometimes the gorillas are found within fifteen minutes of entering the forest—a real stroll in the park. On other occasions, gorilla watchers must slog up and down densely vegetated, slippery slopes for more than four hours before making contact, then spend the same amount of time walking out—an utterly exhausting experience. The actual conditions of your gorilla tracking session will depend on the luck of the day. All you can do is be prepared for the worst.

Keep in mind that almost every tracking session is successful in finding the gorillas. Generally, only those people who give up will miss their viewing.

Mountain gorilla habitat is wet country. Frequent heavy rains produce the luxuriant vegetation that gorillas thrive on but that makes walking so difficult for humans. There are times when you find yourself treading atop thick foliage, without even touching the ground. Vines alternately trip you up, or hold you back. Virulent stinging nettles are abundant, especially in sunny areas where a broken forest canopy lets in light. You'll really appreciate gloves to protect your hands.

Climbing on steep slopes through thick bush is difficult, and possibly hazardous. Slips and falls are common. The bamboo poles that the guides cut for you are helpful, especially when balancing on thick brush, where it is easy to put a foot through into thin air.

Things get even rougher when it rains. Trails turn to slippery mud, making progress difficult and falls more likely. (Walking sticks help a lot on muddy trails, too.) Rainy seasons also bring out the safari ants. These carnivorous insects move across the forest floor in relentless columns. When you step on a column, the ants immediately swarm onto your shoes and clothing. Both soldiers (half an inch long, with jaws to match) and tiny workers bite hard and hang on till individually plucked off.

Tracking usually begins on regular trails that have been hacked out over time by guides on their daily forays to meet the gorillas. You proceed toward the place where the animals were seen the previous day, the tracker going ahead to look for fresh spoor. When he finds it, your guide may lead you off the trail and into the greenery. You follow close, struggling behind as he cuts a path with his *panga* (the African equivalent of a machete). You may see quite a lot of cutting in the course of the day. The apparent environmental damage distresses many conservation-minded visitors: not to worry, most of what is chopped are rapid-growing herbaceous plants such as nettles, which regenerate very quickly.

Excitement mounts as you start to find evidence of recent gorilla presence. The most obvious is gorilla dung, which has a characteristic three-lobed shape. Its smell is not at all offensive, but rather sweet and herby, like everything else in the forest. Often you come on the nests used by the gorillas the previous night. Once the nests are found, you are hot on the trail. Gorillas usually do not travel far or fast, so you can expect to come on them at any time. Sometimes that expectation is disappointed, and a long tracking session ensues.

Viewing. The guide will indicate when you are near the gorillas. This is the time to check your camera equipment: make sure cameras are loaded, that you have the lenses you need, and plenty of spare film. When your party is ready, the guide leads the advance, making curious gorilla vocalizations to signal friendly intent to the apes. Typically, the foliage is very thick, and you are crawling on your hands and knees. You may not be able to see anything until the guide silently points out a gorilla only a few feet away.

The gorillas seem almost oblivious to human presence. You may sit down while a whole group feeds all around you. Females go on munching wild celery stalks, or chew noisily on stinging nettles, while young ones roll over in play, or climb in the bamboo above you. Sometimes infants or juveniles approach with curious intent, studying you closely with clear brown eyes for a few moments before scampering back to their more familiar brethren. The great silverback stares intently at you from time to time, or softly grunts from within a screen of thick foliage: he lets you know that he is aware of your presence.

Most often, you find the gorillas during their mid-morning rest period or while feeding, and they do not move around much. The guide will move your party if necessary to give you better views and to point out the *chef* (or "chief"), as he calls the silverback, or young babies. The guides make every effort to ensure that you will have a satisfactory viewing. Few visitors are not thrilled by the experience. Each viewing session lasts about one hour. Under extraordinary circumstances, such as extended movement by the gorilla group, it might go on somewhat longer.

Tips. Depending on the size of your party, tips should run the equivalent of $16–$24 for the guide, the same or slightly less for the tracker or assistant, and about RF 100 each for porters (more for those who carry exceptional loads such as lunch coolers filled with pop and beer). To some travelers, this may seem high. Remember that tangible cash benefits are important in building local support for park conservation.

Photography. It is not easy to get good photos of gorillas. The most common problem is lack of light: the weather is often cloudy or the animals found in deep forest shade. The solution is fast film, 400 ASA or better. Of course, such film will make for bleached-out pictures if the gorillas move to an open sunlit area. Then you will have severe problems with contrast: dark animals against a bright background. There is no solution for that, but you'll want slower film (64 or 100 ASA) for sunlit situations. It's best to have both fast- and slow-speed films on hand, with two camera bodies. Otherwise, be willing to change film as the situation requires.

At least you won't have difficulties getting close to your subjects. The largest lens needed would be 200 mm (for full face portraits), but you can often do just as well with an ordinary 50-mm lens. The viewing sessions are ideal for video: nothing better captures the immediacy of the experience.

Equipment: Bring along a day pack to carry rain gear, a sweater, and water bottle. Wear long pants and long-sleeved shirt, or preferably a light jacket, to protect against nettles. Gloves are essential. Hiking boots are recommended, though running shoes with lug soles will do.

A HISTORY OF GORILLA WATCHING

Gorilla mania is not as recent a phenomena as you might think. A long succession of fascinating people have been caught in the spell of the mountain gorilla.

The first scientist to study gorillas in the wild was Carl Akeley of the American Museum of Natural History. He journeyed to the Virungas, where he "collected" (shot) the family group that now appears stuffed in the excellent habitat display in New York. Akeley became intrigued with gorillas and fell in love with their mountain habitat. In 1926, he returned to the Virungas, but died shortly after he began his work. He was buried just underneath the spire of Mikeno Volcano, in what was then the Belgian Congo.

After the Second World War, Walter Baumgartel settled in the village of Kisoro, Uganda. He opened a lodge in the shadow of the volcanos Sabinyo, Muhabura, and Gahinga. In the late 1950s, his Travellers Rest House became well known as the place to go to see gorillas in the wild. His guide, Reuben, was a celebrated gorilla tracker who took many clients on the trail of the apes. Those gorillas were not habituated, and it was a fortunate visitor who got more than a glimpse of fleeing animals. When pursued, the silverback would charge: witnessing that hair-raising display was one of the chief attractions of the visit. It became known that the charge was a scary bluff, and that if the pursuers stood their ground, the huge male would run off.

One of the visitors to Baumgartel's was George Schaller, a young American biologist. He spent a year in the Virungas, living at Carl Akeley's old campsite underneath Mikeno. He was of a new breed of biologist, a student of ethology, the study of animals in the wild. His pioneering research demonstrated that gorillas were actually gentle animals, and that they would tolerate human observation if habituated to undisturbed contact.

Schaller was followed by Dian Fossey, an amateur naturalist who volunteered (at the request of anthropologist Louis Leakey) to undertake a study of gorilla behavior. She began her work on the Zaire side of the volcanos, but switched to Rwanda shortly after her arrival. For close to fifteen years, she lived at the Karisoke Research Station, which she founded, in the rain-soaked hagenia forest between the Karisimbi and Visoke volcanos. She perfected a method for observing gorillas. It was an active technique in which she came to affect many of the behavior patterns of gorillas so that the animals would accept her close presence and carry on normally. She gained complete acceptance by several groups. Her work revolutionized the popular view of the great apes. No longer are gorillas viewed as savage King Kong killers; instead, they have the image of persecuted Gentle Giants, which is closer to the truth.

Fossey's landmark research brought a lot of attention to the plight of the mountain gorilla. In the mid-1960s *one-half* the Parc des Volcans had been opened up to human settlement and the cultivation of pyrethrum (a white, daisy-like flower that is the source of a natural pesticide, and a valuable export crop). By 1978 all that land, so recently covered with forest and bamboo in which gorillas had ranged, was planted in pyrethrum and potatos. When the government was on the point of ordering a new excision of park land, a coalition of international wildlife organizations created the Mountain Gorilla Project. The plan was to save the park by convincing the government of its economic value as gorilla habitat, through the development of tourism.

Several gorilla groups were then deliberately habituated to humans, in order to make them accessible to tourists. The strict rules governing permits and viewing procedures were carefully worked out. Training of park guards and gorilla guides was intensified, and a strong program of public education was initiated to teach the local populace that the animals could be a source of pride and income to Rwanda.

Since the opening of gorilla viewing to tourism, the situation for both the animals and the park has changed dramatically. Thousands of people have come to enjoy the gorilla experience, which is carefully controlled to maintain the dignity of both gorillas and tourists. The park more than pays for itself, its ranger staff is much enlarged and improved.

Ironically, Dian Fossey remained fiercely opposed to the development of tourism in the park. She feared disturbance to the animals, and basically believed that gorillas should be valued and protected for themselves, not turned into curiosities. Some say that she thought of the gorillas as her own, or that she preferred gorillas to people. It's certain that she could be an abrasive person, not given to the social skills required in the urban jungle. There is a story that she refused to allow the president of Rwanda to visit one of her study groups: she did not want the gorillas to get used to the scent of black people, because all the poachers are local Africans. This tale may be apocryphal or even malicious, but there is no doubt that she gave many local people reason to dislike her. She often confiscated cattle she found in the park and destroyed snares set for small antelopes. Her special ire was raised against poachers who specifically went after gorillas, whether for profit from the sale of infants, or for the fun of it. Such poachers had killed her favorite gorilla, the celebrated Digit. They may have killed her too: one night in the last days of 1985 she was hacked to death in her cabin. She is buried near Digit among the hagenias of Karisoke.

Although highly dramatized, the popular film, *Gorillas in the Mist* (Universal Studios and Warner Brothers, 1988) did a good job of capturing Fossey's character and dealt fairly with the broader issue surrounding her great passion—the continued survival of the mountain gorilla.

HIKING THE VOLCANOS

Challenging hikes to the summits of the volcanic peaks offer the chance to study the weird plants of the Virungas' alpine environment and to experience a part of mountain gorilla habitat that most visitors never see.

Five volcanos can be climbed in Parc des Volcans. Permits must first be obtained at the Kinigi headquarters. An official guide must accompany all hiking parties. His services are included in the park entry fee. The guide will assist in hiring porters if you want them.

Visoke (12,175 ft.) is the most accessible volcano; it makes a wonderful day's outing. The climb starts at the same Visoke ranger post where gorilla tracking for Group 11 commences. From the roadhead (roughly 8,500 ft.) the trail leads steeply up the southeast slope of the mountain, passing through hagenia forest most of the way. About five hundred feet short of the top, the zone of giant vegetation is entered. At the crater rim, you look down through groves of senecios and lobelia spikes onto the glassy green surface of the lake that fills Visoke's crater. It's a beautiful walk around the crater rim. If the mountain mists do not close in tightly, you will have wonderful closeup views of neighboring Karisimbi and Mikeno to the west and the more distant Muhabura group to the northeast. As you circle the western rim, you are actually standing in Zaire and you look down on the heartland of gorilla country. You may complete the circuit of the crater rim and return on the same trail, or descend the northeast slope on an even steeper path that overlooks Lake Ngezi. The whole trip could take as little as seven hours, though you should allow more time. If it's cloudy when you reach the top, explore and have patience while hoping for the mists to break—the views of the entire chain of volcanos are well worth the wait.

An overnight journey is needed for the ascent of Karisimbi (14,787 ft.). The trail starts at the Visoke ranger post and proceeds through the saddle between the two volcanos. This deep hagenia forest is excellent gorilla habitat. You will pass Fossey's Karisoke Research Station. Researchers do not like uninvited guests, however, so don't stop in. But you may have good luck spotting bushbuck or duiker in that area, because the animals have grown accustomed to people. There is the possibility that you will bump into gorillas while walking this trail, or those on Visoke. Probably you will hear their barking alarm calls before you see them. Do not attempt to make close contact with the animals, as they are probably study groups closed to public observation. A walk of about six hours brings you into the zone of giant senecios, in which a metal rest hut is located at about 12,000 feet. The next morning, a strenuous four-hour walk through open alpine meadows brings you to the rocky summit. This high country is often covered in snow—hence the name Karisimbi, "white shell." From the summit, you will have impressive views of the volcano's large crater.

Sabinyo (11,923 ft.) is the oldest of the Rwandan volcanos. The soft outer layers of ash have eroded away, leaving the serrated ridges of the hard volcanic core. *Sabinyo* means "the old man with large teeth," and the mountain's profile reflects his jagged mouth. The trail starts at Kinigi. After 2 miles you enter the park and proceed gradually upward through bamboo and giant subalpine vegetation until you reach a hut. From there, the trail is not for the timid: it climbs along a knife-edged ridge with sharp dropoffs on either side. On the rocky summit, you are standing on the boundary where three countries meet. The round-trip hike may take as little as six hours, though you can overnight at the hut.

The tall cone of Muhabura, "the guide," served as a beacon for native travelers and was considered a sacred mountain. At 13,540 feet, it is an impressive landmark. Its drier eastern lava slopes are extensively covered with tree heaths, oversized members of the heather family. A climb requires two days with an overnight in a hut on the saddle between Muhabura and Gahinga. Access is from the village of Gasiza, about 5 miles east of park headquarters. The hut, which is in very poor condition, is less than 3 miles from the roadhead, but it is another four- or five-hour climb to Muhabura's summit. The two small craters atop Gahinga (11,398 ft.) can be reached in about two hours from the hut, so an overnight expedition could bag both volcanic peaks.

The scenic crater Lake Ngezi nestles underneath the north slope of Visoke Volcano. A round-trip hike on a relatively easy trail (a steep ridge must be ascended), can be accomplished in as little as three or four hours from the Visoke ranger post. Buffalo and antelope drink there, but are unlikely to be seen unless you are there during the twilight hours.

Akagera National Park

Given the density of human population and its small size, it is a wonder that Rwanda has a game reserve encompassing nearly 10 percent of the country's landmass. Yet the Akagera National Park covers an area of about 1,500 square miles along the northeastern border with Tanzania. Established by the Belgians in 1934, Akagera is another African park that undoubtedly owes its existence to the tsetse fly (see the section on insects in Chapter 3). Its tsetse-infested bush was reserved for wild animals, with the object of maintaining its game population for the hunt. Later, Akagera was proclaimed a national park.

Akagera is exceptionally pretty country. Here the hills of Rwanda come rolling down to meet an extensive zone of lakes and papyrus-choked marshes on the floodplain of the Akagera River.

The papyrus marshes are one of the most interesting features of the park, because they shelter several remarkable animals that are rare or impossible to see anywhere else. These include the sitatunga and the whale-headed stork. The sitatunga (*Tragelaphus spekii*) is a highly aquatic antelope that has adapted perfectly to life in swamps. A strong swimmer, it readily takes to water when threatened, often diving and remaining submerged with only its nose breaking the surface. Its unique splayed hooves enable it to walk on rafts of floating vegetation, where it feeds on marsh grasses and water plants. Hidden by day in the reedbeds, sitatunga are rarely seen, and then only at dusk when they emerge to graze on the fringe of the swamps. The whale-headed stork (*Balaeniceps rex*) is an altogether extraordinary bird. A rather thick-bodied creature, it stands almost 5 feet tall, stationing itself in dense papyrus where it can scoop up frogs and other aquatic life. As its name implies, it has a very peculiarly shaped head, notable for its gigantic thick bill (for which it is sometimes called "the shoebill"). This avian oddity is one of the great prizes for any birder's life list.

Both these unusual animals are better seen at Akagera than any other African game park. That's still not to say they are easy to spot, because most of the papyrus swamps are totally inaccessible. But the marshes on Lake Hago can be explored by boat, and the park authorities have built the *Mirador*, an observation platform, overlooking a large papyrus swamp. When you have climbed the 30-foot-high ladder, you have a splendid view down into the papyrus. Sitatunga are commonly seen grazing or lying down among the reeds, and patient observers have been able to sight the weird shoebill. Akagera's marshes and lakes are also the haunts of hippos, crocodiles, and a tremendous variety of wetland birds.

Among the animals of the dry-land savannas are two species of antelope not often seen in East African game parks. The roan antelope (*Hippotragus equinus*) is a magnificent animal, its powerful horselike body crowned with backsweeping horns. These sharp-tipped protuberances are really meant to do business: the roan has a reputation for pugnacity, and aggressively defends itself even against lions. Males have been known to kill each other in furious fights for dominance. Roan antelope are found in small groups. They favor the small plains and grassy hillsides of the northern section of the park. The oribi (*Ourebia ourebi*) is a small, slender antelope found living in pairs on grassy plains. The males are distinguished by their slender horns. Oribi have the habit of crouching down quietly into cover when danger approaches. If the predator comes too near, the oribi springs up explosively, making a whistling alarm call as it runs swiftly to safety. After about a hundred yards, it stops for a backward look at its startled enemy.

The tsetse fly is still an abundant animal in Akagera, especially in the acacia woodlands of the south. As you drive through the park you, will notice car tires hanging from the branches of trees. These are poison traps for the fly: you will wonder about their effectiveness every time a buzzing cloud of tsetses pursues your vehicle. Although the flies can carry sleeping sickness, it is rare to contract the disease in Akagera.

Akagera is home to a good variety of other animals more familiar to visitors who have already been to the East African parks. Impala, waterbuck, zebra, and topi are common, as are vervet monkey and baboon. The local buffalo are noted for the spread and weight of their horns, and they are still prized trophies in the neighboring Gabiro Hunting Reserve. The rest of the Big Five, though present, are difficult to see. There are few elephants, and those are very shy. Lions are common, but hard to spot because of high grass and thick bush. This relative paucity of big game, and the annoyance of tsetse flies, can make a trip to Akagera disappointing for casual visitors. It really is a park for the ardent naturalist who wants to see new and beautiful country, and takes pleasure in the search for the unusual.

The park is open year round, although heavy rains in April, May, and November limit movement. December through March are more or less rainy months. Birdlife is particularly good then because of the presence of European migrants. During the drier months, uncontrolled fires rage through the park. These are set by poachers, who have seriously reduced the numbers of animals.

ACCESS AND ACCOMMODATION

A good paved road runs to the park from Kigali, a drive of only about two and a half hours. There are two main entrances: Gabiro, the park headquarters, in the north, and another near the Akagera Hotel in the south. There is bus service to Gabiro, but a car is essential for touring the park. Fees are RF 1,590 (U.S. $22) entry; RF 740 (U.S. $10) per vehicle; RF 1,060 (U.S. $15) for camping.

Each gate has a signboard that is well worth examining. Featured is a series of photo frames cut from a film. The first shows a tourist descending from his car with camera in hand. Next he is jumped by a lioness from behind. Then a closeup of his wife screaming. In the final shot, the lioness has been joined by a male and together they are devouring the hapless victim. This was a real event, incredibly filmed by onlookers—who could probably have used their vehicle to chase the lions off! The pictures are posted to discourage visitors from getting out of their cars. They are effective!

The Akagera Hotel is a very elegant resort, complete with swimming pool and superb French cuisine. From its hilltop location, you have wonderful views of Lac Ihema. The Gabiro Guest House is simpler, but no less comfortable. Its grounds include a group of caged chimpanzees that the park confiscated from illegal traders. They love attention. Both hotels have excellent, though pricey, gift shops. The Akagera's features masks from Zaire. At Gabiro you can acquire a useful treasure: a Black Stone from the White Fathers of the Congo. These chunks of superabsorbent charcoal are specially manufactured at a Catholic mission in Zaire. They are supposed to remove the poisons of scorpions, bees, and snakes when applied to the site of a bite. There is no guarantee that they work, but some experienced safari guides swear by them. Better pick one up unless you are going to Zaire, where they are much cheaper.

Camping is allowed in the park, though the supposed sites are impossible to find and are completely undeveloped. You must bring your own water. Camping by the big lakes is great fun. It gives you a real chance to become acquainted with hippos, which only come onto land to feed at night. Do not place your tent on one of their regular paths. They won't touch it, but the sound of a hippo nibbling outside your door while you are lying on the ground is not conducive to sleep.

TOURING THE PARK

You do not need a guide to tour the park, especially if you have one of the excellent maps put out by the ORTPN. For one-day tours, groups take the lakeside route between the Akagera Hotel and Gabiro. It is a full day's outing, especially if you want to stop for a picnic on the way and spend some time at the Mirador or take a boat ride into the papyrus swamps on Lake Hago.

If you start at Akagera, keep a sharp eye for klipspringer as you descend the hills. You soon arrive at Lake Ihema and the Pecherie, a small fishing village. A motor launch is available there for rental (about $20 an hour). If you are overnighting at Akagera, a boat trip is very worthwhile at dawn or sunset. It's especially rewarding for birders, because a small nearby island is the roosting place for a fantastic collection of herons, egrets, cormorants, and darters.

Beyond the Pecherie, the main track skirts the edge of the Akagera wetlands, passing through heavy bush, acacia woodlands, and riparian forest. This is the area to spot vervet and blue monkeys, and troupes of olive baboon, as well as waterbuck, warthog, and herds of impala.

At Lake Hago, boats are available to explore channels through the interior of the papyrus marshes. A two to three hour excursion can be fit into a one-day Akagera–Gabiro park tour. Longer journeys—of a half or full day—can also be chartered. All such boat tours should be arranged in advance.

The usual lunch place is the Plage des Hippos on Lake Mahindi. It is a pleasant spot overlooking a hippo-filled pool and a papyrus marsh. When the water is low, it is one of the best places in the park for a good look at crocodiles. If you are there on a weekend, however, it is always crowded with noisy local tourists. A good alternative would then be the Mirador, which is just a few miles beyond, on Lake Rwanyakizinga.

To the north of the Mirador, you enter grassy plains frequented by good herds of topi and zebra. This is the best country for roan antelope. Lion are most frequently spotted there, too. As the road proceeds west toward Gabiro, game gets sparser, but it is good for buffalo, bush duiker, and eland.

If you have more than a day at Akagera, charter a boat to probe the papyrus marshes, or explore the park's north, where the biggest buffalo herds are found. Then check out the Kamakaba and Kirara plains near Lake Rwanyakazinga. Both are good areas for roan antelope. Drives on the hilly tracks in the west of the park are usually less productive.

Lake Kivu

At 4,790 feet, Lake Kivu is the highest in the 1,300-mile chain of lakes in the Western Rift Valley. It is also one of the most beautiful. With its island-studded bays and fjords, set against the green of forest-covered hills, and a delightful temperate climate, it was a favorite resort for both Belgian and German colonists.

Located on the north shore, Gisenyi is Rwanda's principal lakeside town. It is a good place to rest up from the rigors of safari. It has a variety of accommodation, from the luxurious Meridien Hotel downward in price to the Palm Beach and Edelweiss hotels. Cheaper still is the Presbyterian Hostel. The lake's waters are reputed to be bilharzia free. Just outside town, the Nyondo Catholic Mission's crafts shop is worth looking into.

One way to appreciate Kivu's beauty is to take the lake steamer to Kibuye or to Cyangugu, on its southern end, opposite Bukavu, Zaire. A boat runs down the lake one day, returning northward the next. Kibuye's rocky bays make it a particularly attractive village. The Kibuye Guest House is comfortable, moderate in price, and offers swimming and rental of water sports equipment. Budget travelers will seek out the Home St. Jean, next to the Catholic Church.

A scenic mountain road connects Gisenyi to Kibuye. It passes through the Gishwati Forest Reserve. If you have your own vehicle and an interest in monkeys and birds, it's worth a visit. A larger reserve, the Nyungwe Forest, is located in the southern part of the country. Chimpanzees are among its resident animals, and the ORTPN hopes to develop the reserve for tourism. Guides are already available to track habituated colobus monkeys near the village of Pindaru, where a small hostel may be built.

EASTERN ZAIRE

A Different Face

Zaire is one of the largest countries in Africa. Although its heartland rests in the equatorial forests of the Congo basin, the eastern provinces are a continental transition zone in which the savannas of East Africa merge with the forests of the West. Renowned for its natural beauty, eastern Zaire is one of the most fascinating regions in Africa. At one time, it was a popular safari destination. The temperate highlands of Kivu Province were a favorite vacation enclave for whites during the colonial era. The Parc National Albert (now called the Parc National des Virunga, or Virunga National Park), set within sight of the snow-capped Ruwenzori, was then one of the most famous African wildlife enclaves. The years of political and economic chaos that followed independence virtually swept the region from international tour itineraries. Now interest is again building. Zaire is rapidly developing as a major center for gorilla viewing and, as travelers arrive for primate safaris, the Parc des Virunga is being rediscovered. The more adventurous are trekking into the mountains and exploring into the green world of the Ituri Forest. Every visitor discovers the face of an Africa completely unlike that seen in Kenya and Tanzania.

Zaire's history has not fostered a bright international image. Ever since Henry Morton Stanley emerged from the Congo jungles to report on his expedition "through darkest Africa"—as described in the book that chronicled his first harrowing journey down the Congo River (1874–1877)—the region has had a reputation for savagery and bloodshed. Stanley had to contend with native cannibals and Arab slavers. Then followed the region's appalling brutalization under the aegis of the Congo Free State, a private fiefdom of King Leopold II of Belgium, proclaimed in 1885. That unhappy period of ruthless exploitation witnessed the wholesale enslavement and deaths of millions of Africans for the enrichment of one man. (Leopold's Congo was the setting of Joseph Conrad's damning novel, *Heart of Darkness,* published in 1902). The Free State's excesses saddled the later colonial administration of the Belgian Congo with an unsavory reputation it did not deserve. From 1908 (when the government of Belgium took over administration from Leopold), the Belgians ran a fairly progressive colony, but cynically failed to prepare the Congo for self-governance. Five years of bloody civil war immediately followed independence in 1960. At the end of the conflict, General Joseph Mobutu emerged as unqualified ruler. He Africanized the name of the country: the Congo was originally named after the powerful Kongo tribe; the name *Zaire* derives from their word for "the river that swallows all rivers." He himself is now called President Mobutu Sese Seko, and went on to establish a cult of personality that has made him one of the richest men in the world. Mobutu's regime has been marked by endemic corruption and inefficiency, but has been successful in creating a centralized and peaceful nation. (Another literary classic, V. S. Naipaul's *A Bend in the River,* [1979], describes the reign of the "Big Man.") Although it is hard to say how the ordinary people of the country are faring, economic conditions have improved enough to encourage tourism.

Zaire is an extremely tough country in which to travel, whether independently or in groups. Abysmal roads are made all but impassable by heavy rains. In places, holes in its roadways are literally big enough to swallow a truck. At such spots, you wait in line for your turn to chance the crevasse, while a crowd attempts to dig and push each vehicle through. There are always people willing to help claw vehicles free, or perform any other services requested. In fact, this seems to be a major source of local employment. Naturally, assistants expect tourists to pay higher wages than local drivers.

Although paying for helpful services is fair enough, unceasing demands for *cadeaux* (gifts), whether deserved or not, quickly become tiresome to foreign travelers. Zaire does not have much tradition of public service. From the top down, society has a predatory cast, with the more powerful exploiting those below. Officials and ordinary folk have really had to learn to take the most advantage for themselves in every situation. This is not to say that you will not meet good and charming people, but that you will often be treated in a decidedly mercenary way. You will just have to get used to the constant refrain *"Donnez-moi un cadeau,"* "give me a gift."

Zaire is the kind of place where things can and will go wrong, or at least not proceed in the fast and logical way you may expect. If you can't bring patience and a sense of humor, Zaire is not the country for you.

Safari Facts

Entry. Visas are required. In the United States, they are far more difficult to obtain than those of East African countries. You must furnish proof of yellow fever vaccination, an ongoing air ticket, and a letter from your tour operator (if you have one) that details the exact time and place of entry and exit. Visas are also rather costly: in 1988, $20 for one month. Long-term travelers should apply for multiple entry (just in case) and should note that visas are only valid within six months of the date issued. On arrival, immigration officials routinely search documents for errors in order to solicit bribes, so keep your papers in order.

Currency. Currency is counted in Zaires (1989: approximately Z 385 = U.S. $1). Devaluations have reduced the black market value to a virtual par with the official rate of exchange, but transactions are much faster outside of banks. Travelers' checks can be extremely difficult to exchange in Zaire, even at banks and lodges: bring U.S. currency.

Language. French is official. The country has many native tongues, but Swahili is widely spoken, especially in the east.

Air Travel. This is one of the greatest obstacles to tourism! The capital, Kinshasa, is served by many carriers but there is no international service to Goma or Bukavu, the major towns of the eastern

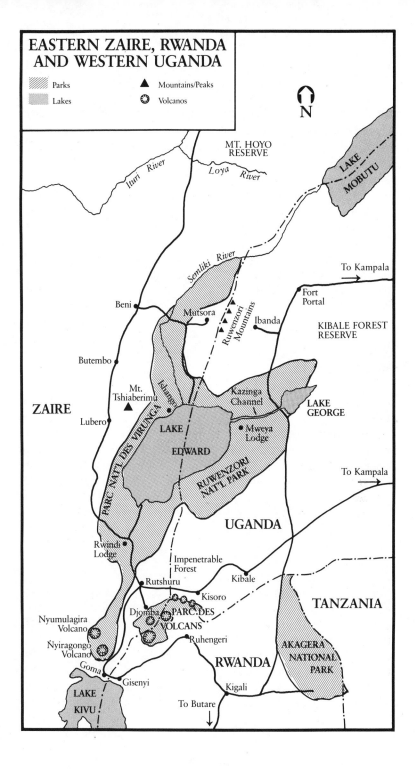

EASTERN ZAIRE, RWANDA
AND WESTERN UGANDA

Parks

Lakes

▲ Mountains/Peaks

✸ Volcanos

N

MT. HOYO
RESERVE

Ituri River

Loya River

Semliki River

To Kampala

Fort
Portal

Beni

Mutsora

Ruwenzori Mountains

Ibanda

KIBALE FOREST
RESERVE

Butembo

Mt.
Tshiaberimu ▲

Ishango

Kazinga
Channel

LAKE
GEORGE

ZAIRE

Lubero

LAKE

EDWARD

Mweya
Lodge

PARC NAT'L DES VIRUNGA

RUWENZORI
NAT'L PARK

To Kampala

UGANDA

Rwindi
Lodge

Impenetrable
Forest

Kibale

Rutshuru

Kisoro

TANZANIA

Nyumulagira
Volcano

Djomba

PARC DES
VOLCANS

Nyiragongo
Volcano

Goma

Ruhengeri

AKAGERA
NATIONAL
PARK

Gisenyi

RWANDA

Kigali

LAKE
KIVU

To Butare

region. Air Zaire connects them with Kinshasa, but it is a notoriously chaotic airline and is best avoided. Travelers, even those on tours,
most often fly to Kigali, then cross overland from Rwanda. Some
groups charter planes from Nairobi direct to Goma. Two private
airlines, VAC and Broussair, fly light aircraft daily between Goma
and Bukavu, and to other towns in eastern Zaire. The international
airport departure tax of $16 *must* be paid in U.S. dollars.

Transportation. Public transport almost does not exist. Travelers
pay for rides on trucks. Self-drive rentals are out of the question.
Minibuses with drivers are available from AMIZA (Agence Maritime Internationale du Zaire) in Goma and Bukavu, and from Zaire
Safari in Goma.

Tours. AMIZA arranges tours from Goma to Parc des Virunga
for game viewing or gorilla tracking. They can also send you to
Mont Hoyo to meet Pygmies. Their Bukavu office books gorilla trips
to Kahuzi-Biega. Zaire Safaris organizes the same excursions and
operates the deluxe Djomba Camp as a base for gorilla watchers.
(Many of the tour groups that use Djomba Camp are flown by
charter from Nairobi to Goma, after which all arrangements are
handled by Zaire Safaris).

National Park Fees. Fees for entry and services vary somewhat
at each park (and at each section of the Parc des Virunga), and are
subject to change. Current entry fees are Rwindi, $50; Nyiragongo-
Nyamulagira, $30; Mont Hoyo, $20; Ruwenzori, $40. Park entry
fees are payable *only* in U.S. dollars, and are generally good for
seven days. They include the services of guides, but there are extra
charges for camera (Z 50), video (Z 400), camping (Z 40–200 per
tent), and mountain huts (Z 40–100). Gorilla permits are currently
$120 per day, including the services of guides and trackers; an ad-
ditional $20 per day is charged for shooting gorilla videos.

NOTE ON GORILLA VIEWING IN ZAIRE

Zaire was actually the first country to feature tracking of habituated
gorillas in its national parks. That the program never caught the
public imagination, the way Rwanda's later did, was due partly to
the absence of a "star" of the stature of Dian Fossey. It was also
because of the poorer quality of the experience: when viewing was
initiated at Kahuzi-Biega National Park, any number of people were
allowed to visit the gorillas at the same time, creating a circus atmosphere that greatly disturbed the sensitive primates.

With the success of the Mountain Gorilla Project in Rwanda, the Frankfurt Zoological Society sponsored the development of a similar program on the Zaire side of the Virunga Volcanos. Several groups of gorillas have now been habituated and are available to public viewing. The same basic procedures are being used as in Rwanda (only six visitors per day are allowed to visit each gorilla group), so the integrity of the closeup experience is kept intact without distressing the animals. There are even some advantages to viewing on the Zaire side of the Virungas. At U.S. $120 each, fees for gorilla permits are currently cheaper than those in Rwanda (that could change soon: rumor has it that fees will soon be raised to $150 each, par with Parc des Volcans). More importantly, visits last up to two hours. These longer sessions are qualitatively superior because they allow you to enjoy relaxed observations rather than worry about watching the clock. Procedures at Kahuzi-Biega are also being reformed to improve the experience for both gorillas and humans.

Parc National Des Virunga

Stretching some two hundred miles along Zaire's border with Uganda, the Parc des Virunga marshals an extraordinarily diverse variety of habitats and attractions. Because of its size, each section of the park will be treated separately.

ACCESS

Goma is the gateway to the park. Located on the shores of Lake Kivu, it was, like neighboring Gisenyi across the Rwanda frontier, a favorite vacation retreat for Europeans in colonial days. Today, well-to-do Zairois, including President Mobutu, keep private villas along the lake. The dusty commercial section of the town is ramshackle and without much interest. The National Parks (*Institute Zairois pour la Conservation de la Nature* or IZCN) has its office there, located off the main street, next door to the Banque Commercial Zairoise, near the Post Office. It is the best place to purchase permits for gorilla viewing in the Virungas and for treks on the volcanos. The tour operator AMIZA has its office on Goma's main street. Zaire Safari is reached through the Masques Hotel, which is the best in town. The only other facility in its class is the nearby Hotel des Grands Lacs. There are many cheaper local guesthouses.

The trunk road that threads northward from Goma passes beneath the Virunga Volcanos on route to the town of Rutshuru (45 miles). From there, a track turns off toward the Uganda border and the village of Djomba, the principal center for gorilla tracking. The main road continues to Rwindi, which is is the most developed section of the park and offers the best game viewing. Beyond Rwindi, the road (locally dubbed *La Route de la Beauté*) climbs the spectacular Kabasha Escarpment. From its wooded summit, there are wonderful views of the Mitumba Mountains, the Rwindi plains, and Lake Edward (also called Lake Idi Amin).* If you are lucky, the skies over the Ruwenzori will clear long enough for you to glimpse the fabled Mountains of the Moon. Atop the escarpment, the 6,000-foot highlands are intensely cultivated and there is almost constant human habitation at roadside. You pass through innumerable villages and three major towns—Lubero, Butembo, and Beni. From Beni (137 miles from Rwindi), the Mutwanga road turns off for the Ishango and Ruwenzori sections of the park. The main "highway" continues northward into the equatorial forests of Haut Zaire Province and the Pygmy country around Mont Hoyo. For most tour groups and travelers, this long route must be repeated for the return to Goma, unless you fly back from either Beni or Bunia.

THE VIRUNGA VOLCANOS

The Virunga Volcanos occupy the southernmost section of the park. They are divided into two distinct clusters. Mountain gorillas live among the more ancient peaks that straddle the Rwanda and Uganda frontiers. A 6-mile-wide band of cultivated savanna separates them from the active volcanos Nyiragongo and Nyamulagira. These fiery mountains are the loci for interesting hiking activities.

GORILLA VIEWING IN PARC DES VIRUNGA

Dian Fossey originally began her gorilla research on the Zaire side of the Virungas, but had to abandon her camp when political turmoil flared. Although poaching and human encroachment on parklands are still problems there, the outlook for protection of Zaire's mountain gorilla population is now improving. Of an estimated

---

*The Ugandan dictator (now in exile in Saudi Arabia) rechristened the lake with his own name, but that appellation is bound to prove temporary. It is referred to here by its old title, which will undoubtedly also pass.

twenty-nine gorilla groups resident in Zaire's volcanos, four have been habituated and opened to the public. Each is named after its silverback leader.

The main center for gorilla tracking is near the village of Djomba, which is 62 miles from Goma. The final 17 miles of track from Rutshuru are very rough; it takes about five hours to cover the total distance. Above the village, at the forest's edge, a comfortable tourist-class lodge (Djomba Camp) has been built to accommodate guests on gorilla-viewing safaris. Clients are driven from Goma to Djomba village from which they have a half hour walk up to the lodge. Another hostel above Djomba is maintained by the Frankfurt Zoo project team. It is a far more simple affair, consisting of two large rooms with six beds in each ($4 each per night). Bedding and kitchen facilities are provided, but you should bring your own food.

Djomba is the starting point for tracking three different family groups of gorillas. The Rugabo and Rugendo groups are the most accessible. They inhabit the brushy plateau to the north of sawtoothed Sabinyo Volcano, quite near the Uganda border. Because the terrain in this part of the Virungas is relatively level, the physical effort needed to track these groups is often not as great as that required for gorillas living on the higher volcanos. Vegetation in the area consists of dense tangles of *Mimulopsis* thicket, with *Neoboutonia* trees towering above the undergrowth. The going would be very tough if a series of paths had not been cut in the forest to ease the early stages of tracking. Both elephant and buffalo inhabit the scrubby forest, which is a favorite habitat for giant three-horned chameleons as well as gorillas. Each of the silverbacks has an unofficial nickname. Rugabo, or Marcel, is the more habituated male. Rugendo, also called Oscar, is feistier and more prone to threatening displays. Both groups are large and make for fine viewing. The more recently habituated Faida group (which includes three silverback males) lives higher on Sabinyo Volcano, where tracking is more difficult. It also spends part of its time in Uganda, where visitors are unable to follow.

Visits to the Bukima (or Zunguruka, after its silverback) group require an overnight trek. The starting point is the park headquarters at Rumangabo (25 miles north of Goma on the Goma-Rutshuru road). From there, you have an easy three-or four-hour walk through cultivated sorghum fields to the village of Bukima. Just beyond, a primitive camp has been established on the park boundary. It consists of rough canvas tents and a cook shelter. You must bring your own sleeping bag and food for the overnight stay. The next day you track Zunguruka and his family group on the lower slopes of Mikeno Volcano.

Permits for visiting the Djomba and Bukima gorillas should be booked in advance at the IZCN office in Goma. Because the Faida group is partially migratory, permits are not sold in advance for it. In any event, Faida should be easier to book on short notice, because of the more rugged nature of its territory.

There is some question as to how the permit system for the Djomba gorillas is working. Zaire Safaris claims a monopoly on permits for the Rugabo and Rugendo groups, which would put all other visitors there on a standby basis. The Frankfurt Zoo project directors favor a quota system among various tour companies. The matter is somewhat fuzzy at the moment: apparently the Rugabo and Rugendo groups are reserved solidly by Zaire Safaris on Tuesdays, Wednesdays, Fridays, and Saturdays; the rest of the week, and during the months of April, May, and June, all permits are up for grabs. This arrangement could be changed at any time.

CHIMPANZEE VIEWING

Chimpanzees have now been habituated to humans in the Parc des Virunga. The chimps live at Tongo, near Nyamulagira Volcano. Exact procedures and fees are still undetermined, but these smaller apes should be opened to tourist viewing in 1989.

TREKKING THE LIVE VOLCANOS

The Virungas are one of Africa's geological hot-spots. Their two youngest volcanos are among the most active in the world. Although they have quiet periods, they regularly flicker with activity, either building new subsidiary cones on their flanks or merely grumbling with threat. In 1977, Nyiragongo suddenly sent a column of molten lava streaming toward Goma, forcing the entire population to flee in panic. At least sixty people were killed, and the town was only spared when the flow stopped near the airport, about 2 miles from Goma's center.

For many years, Nyiragongo (11,385 ft.) was famous for the liquid lava lake within its crater. Trekkers would climb for overnight views of the scarlet cauldron, and the eerie glow of its reflection was a regular feature of Goma's nighttime sky. Although recent eruptions have drained the lava pool, perhaps never to return, climbs to the volcano's summit are still a popular activity. The trek begins at the Camp des Guides at Kibati (about 8 miles from Goma, on the main north road), where you pick up your guide and porters. From Kibati (6,398 ft.), it is a steep four- to-five-hour walk to a hut located just beneath the summit cone, with another half-hour's climb to the crater rim. Although the ascent can be done in a day, it is better to plan for an overnight in order to take advantage of the clearest views at dusk and dawn, when the Virunga's cloud veil is most likely to be lifted. You'll look down on the crater's crusted-over lava floor. At night, you may have views of the glowing firepit and, if the lake refills, you will certainly witness an awesome pyro-technic display. Although the hut is not in very good shape, porters, guides, and charcoal are available at Kibati. Take warm clothing and a flashlight.

A fascinating three-day trek can also be made to neighboring Nyamulagira Volcano (10,026 ft.). This is a real jungle expedition requiring the presence of an armed game scout to guard against the forest elephant or buffalo that may be encountered on the way. Onyour trek through the highland forest, you may see duiker, bushbuck, and chimpanzee as well. You'll cross both old and re-cent lava flows, pocked with inviting rain-fed pools, and pass through all stages of vegetation regenerating in the wake of volcanic destruction.

Arrangements for the trek should be made at the IZCN office in Goma or at the Kibati ranger camp. The actual starting point for the hike is Kakomero (5,906 ft.), on the main road, 16 miles north of Kibati. The first day's walk takes you through forest cut by lava flows of all ages. After hiking about six hours, you reach a large but ramshackle hut at 8,202 feet. The next day, it takes about two hours to reach the crater rim. Vegetation gets scarce as you proceed through a zone of recent volcanic activity. The crater wall has itself been breached by a half-mile-wide gap from which lava periodically pours. You will probably want to spend several hours exploring the steaming crater, which is a mile and half wide. On its floor is a spectacular volcanic blowhole 1,300 feet in diameter. A second hut is located right inside the crater, but it is recommended to return to the forest hut for the night, and descend to Kakomero the follow-ing day.

Another fabulous trek can be undertaken among the older, ex-tinct volcanos: it is possible to hike to Kanyamagufa ("the place of bones"), a precipitous canyon that cuts into Mikeno's slopes. Deep in the hagenia forest, it is one of the most scenic spots in the whole of the Virunga range. A hut (in good condition) is located at 10,500 feet on the saddle between Mikeno and Karisimbi. Rock climbers can also attempt Mikeno's summit. Check at the IZCN office in Goma for permits and guides.

Guide costs for all these treks are supposed to be included in the park entry fee (U.S. $30), and porters cost only Z 100 per day. But additional gratuities are welcomed, and handing out cigarettes is almost mandatory.

RWINDI

The best game viewing in Parc des Virunga takes place on the Rwindi plains to the south of Lake Edward. This section of the park abuts Uganda's Ruwenzori National Park. At one time, the region was celebrated for the incredible mass of animal life that its rich grasslands and riverine bush could support. Huge numbers of buffaloes, elephants, and hippos created the heaviest biomass of any wildlife area in the world. The Zaire elephants suffered terribly during the Congo civil war, while Uganda's animals were largely exterminated during its long years of near anarchy. Poaching continues to take a steady toll, and elephants are now relatively scarce on both sides of the border. But the number of hippos is simply unbelievable. The Parc des Virunga population is conservatively estimated to be 25,000 animals. They choke the rivers so much beyond capacity that hippos have even made permanent wallows in mud puddles on the Rwindi plains. Those lush grasslands support good numbers of antelope, of which topi and especially Uganda kob are the most common. The kob (*Kobus kob thomasi*) looks somewhat like an impala, but is strictly a grazer and thrives on moist grasslands. Males are extremely territorial: each adult bull has his domain staked out on the plain. The hornless females and their offsping wander from one male's acreage to the next, following their appetites more than the lure of the various males' sex appeal. Lions are common and easily seen in the game-rich open country around Rwindi.

Access and Accommodation. A journey of three to four hours is needed to cover the 75 miles between Goma and Rwindi. Near the town of Rutshuru, a slight detour from the main road brings you to the attractive Rutshuru Falls. From town, it's another dozen miles through cultivated country to the national park boundary, marked by the Rutshuru River. At that point the Rutshuru is a lovely jungle stream, lined with palms and dotted with tiny islands. Dense, but stunted, forest closes in as you skirt Kasali Mountain—a good place to watch for colobus monkeys and baboons. The country opens up as you follow the Rutshuru River, passing a streamside hot spring, until you reach the wide grasslands of Rwindi.

Rwindi Lodge is the only hotel in the park. It is a very charming old-style camp, with accommodation in white-washed rondavals. The cabins are very comfortable, food is generous and well prepared. Nightly buffets inevitably include grilled meat and tilapia, as well as delicious Belgian-style fried potatoes, and a variety of salads. The lodge also has a swimming pool.

Unfortunately, camping is not currently permitted in the Rwindi area. Campers must therefore set up along the Rutshuru River, just beyond the park boundary. Although very scenic, this site is rather far from the prime game-viewing areas.

Touring the Park. The open plains surrounding Rwindi Lodge are ideal for prebreakfast game drives. They are crowded with topi and Uganda kob, and support smaller groups of waterbuck and reedbuck. Lions are almost invariably found there. Hyenas and side-striped jackals are often seen in the early morning. Several fantastic hippo pools are located in the heart of the grassland. You could literally walk across these foul-smelling muck puddles on the backs of wallowing hippopotamuses!

Mind-boggling numbers of hippos are seen from the track that follows the Rutshuru River. You proceed along cliffs above the winding stream, in every bend of which there are huge herds. You will see literally thousands. The country is bushier along the riverbanks, and it is a good area to spot Defassa waterbuck, buffalo, and bushbuck. Giant forest hog, which are usually associated with deep forests, are also to be seen, even in lightly bushed grassland. Another popular track follows the Rwindi River, also clogged with hippos, to its junction with the lake at Mwiga Bay, where there are masses of aquatic birds.

The dung produced by the thousands of hippos living in Lake Edward provides food for teeming shoals of fish. This rich source of protein is exploited by humans. The fishing village at Vitshumbi is a popular rest stop for visitors from Rwindi and makes a good place to enjoy a taste of spicy native-style (*pili pili*) grilled tilapia. The lakeshore village is redolent of drying fish, which attract hordes of marabou storks and pelicans. Bull elephants apparently feel secure in the neighborhood, too. Several of the big tuskers that frequent the nearby marshes make a habit of strolling through the village at will.

Although local tour operators and drivers are used to a relaxed routine of short morning and evening drives, there are many tracks to explore and it may be worth taking a picnic into the bush for a full day's tour. One interesting route is the Ishasa track, which runs along the Ugandan border in an area that is famous for tree-climbing lions. The Ishasa sector has plenty of antelope and a notable forest of cactuslike giant euphorbia trees, although poaching activity makes it an unlikely place to look for elephant. Other less traveled routes include the Kibirizi track, which leads to the foothills of the Mitumba Mountains and the Kibasha Escarpment. The Muhaha River track flows beneath them.

ISHANGO

More fine game viewing is to be found in the park's Ishango sector to the north of Lake Edward. Its savanna grasslands support large numbers of topi and kob, while the lakeshore teems with hippos and aquatic birds. The decayed Ishango Lodge is beautifully set atop a bluff where the Semliki River exits the lake. It is known for panoramic vistas. These are particularly glorious on cloudless mornings, when the snowy peaks of the Ruwenzori, some 40 miles distant, are clearly visible.

Ishango is only accessible by road through Beni, which is about 137 miles from Rwindi. Road conditions make this an even longer trip than the distance would indicate: tour groups proceeding from Rwindi count on spending a night at Butembo (35 miles south of Beni) on the way. From Beni, another 65 miles must be covered on the Mutwanga road before you return to the lake. This isolation, plus the fact that the lodge at Ishango has been defunct for many years, ensure that the area sees few visitors. Plans to restore the lodge are now rumored to be in the works. Once that is done, visitors will be able to reach Ishango by boat from the village of Vitshumbi in a matter of hours. That will make a nice game-viewing excursion. In the meanwhile, Ishango is really only a practical destination for self-sufficient camping parties.

Currently, there are very few game tracks to explore in the Ishango area. Because of the abundance of antelope, lion are fairly common there, but elephants are very scarce. The Semliki River harbors crocodile, which are not found in Lake Edward. As the Semliki flows northward toward Lake Mobutu and the Nile, it passes through equatorial forest in the northernmost region of the park, but there is absolutely no access to it at this time. Eastern lowland gorillas inhabit the forests of Mount Tshiaberimu, an isolated peak close to the shore of Lake Edward and the Ishango camp. If they are properly protected and habituated, Ishango could eventually become another center for gorilla watching.

The Ruwenzori

The Ruwenzori are one of Africa's great mountain ranges. Seventy miles long and 30 wide, they include six snow and glacier-clad peaks, the tallest of which, Mount Stanley (16,763 ft.), is the third highest mountain in Africa. From ancient times, tales of the existence of these "Mountains of the Moon" had tantalized geographers searching for the sources of the Nile. Henry M. Stanley was the first European to see the peaks, and he christened them with a local name, Ruwenzori, "the hill of rain." The mountains live up to this title: while only 30 inches of rain per year fall on the plains at their feet, more than 100 inches drench their middle and upper slopes. This excessive moisture has produced the moss-covered bogs and luxuriant giant vegetation for which the Ruwenzori are so famed. Scarcely less renowned are the clouds and mists that almost perpetually enshroud the peaks. That misty veil inspires a constant aura of mystery, for even when you are passing very close to the range the Ruwenzori are most often hidden from view. You never know when the clouds will break and the dazzling white mountains will appear suddenly in the African sky.

Unlike the other giant East African peaks, the Ruwenzori are not volcanic in origin. They were pushed upward by massive block faulting associated with the creation of the Western Rift Valley. Elephants and chimpanzees inhabit their forest zone, but you are unlikely to encounter either species while trekking. Tree hyrax are common among the weird vegetation of the mist-bound subalpine zone between 10,000 and 14,500 feet. In that eerie world, thick beards of moss drape both hagenia and heather trees, and form deep, spongy carpets underfoot. Giant groundsels (senecios) and lobelias thrive in the soaking mists, as do the *Carex* sedges that grow in the infamous tussock bogs. Ruwenzori turaco and mountain buzzard are among the more noticeable birds. The alpine zone contains the largest glaciers on the continent, and is famous for the beauty of its rime cornices, phantasmagoric outcrops of wind-sculptured ice.

Trekking in the Ruwenzori is a fascinating experience, but should not be undertaken lightly. The usual difficulties of mountain hiking—altitude sickness and nighttime cold—are compounded by perpetual damp and the extra exertion needed to go through sucking bogs. Trekkers should be in good physical condition and keep a positive state of mind.

Access and Accommodation. There are a number of trekking routes on the Uganda side of the mountains, but only one established trail in Zaire. Although steeper and requiring a return journey along the same path, the Zaire route has one cardinal advantage over those in Uganda: the trail keeps to rocky ridges, mostly avoiding the dreadful bogs that are such an obstacle to progress. The Zaire side also receives somewhat less rain, especially at the higher elevations. Closeup views of the peaks are therefore often quite good. The Zaire route leads directly toward Mount Stanley and takes five days to complete.

The trek begins near Mutwanga, which is about 30 miles from Beni. Permits, porters, and guides are arranged at the nearby Mutsora Park Station. In addition to the normal park entrance fee (U.S. $40, good for seven days), a guide costs Z 1600, each porter (carrying a maximum of 18 kg or 40 pounds) is Z 800, and huts or camping cost Z 100 per night. You may also have to purchase food for the porters and guides, and must be sure to bring enough cigarettes to keep your staff happy. Buy your provisions in Beni, where there are plenty of shops.

The Hotel Ruwenzori in Mutwanga is a large and potentially charming lodge, but has been quasi-abandoned for years. There are rumors of plans to refurbish and reopen it. You can camp there or at the Camp des Guides, just inside the park boundary. The huts in the mountains are solidly built, but poorly maintained. You may want to bring along sheets of plastic to seal broken windows.

The best times for trekking in the Ruwenzori are the driest months: late December to late February and mid-June to mid-August. Even during those periods, you must be prepared for rain. You will need good equipment to protect yourself against wet and cold, as well as a warm sleeping bag and foam pad.

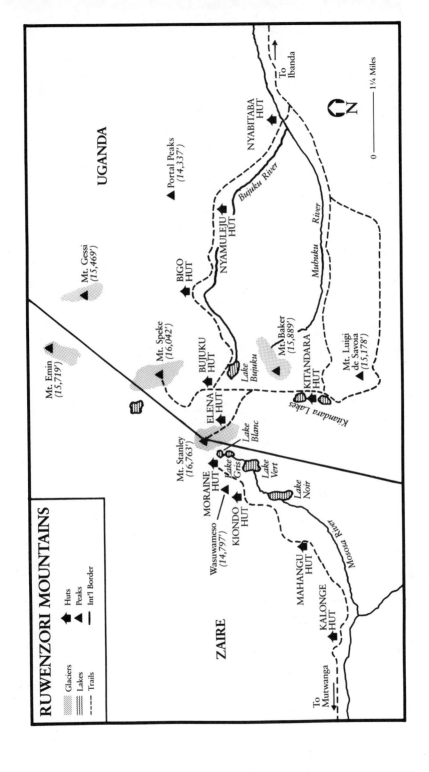

THE TREK

Starting from the Camp des Guides (5,577 ft.),* the first day's march proceeds gently up the valley of the Butawu River. A wide trail goes through dense but scrubby montane forest. Bracken ferns are ubiquitous, and you will notice begonias and wild banana trees as you walk for about five hours to Kalonge Hut (7,005 ft.).

The next day's walk is considerably harder as you climb to Mahangu Hut (10,936 ft.). You pass through a zone of nettle and bamboo, then enter the misty country of the giant heaths in which everything—the ground, hidden roots, and heather trees—is blanketed with thick carpets of moss. It takes at least five and a half hours to reach Mahangu.

The trail deteriorates as you climb toward the third hut, but the scenery gets progressively better. You go through mossy hagenia forest, then emerge into the zone of the giant senecios, in which everlasting helichrysum flowers are scattered among the tall spikes of lobelias and the weirder-shaped groundsels. It takes about four and a half hours to reach the stone Kiondo Hut (14,119 ft.), below which is the beautiful lake, Lac Noire. Another hour on a side trail takes you to the top of a ridge, Wasuwameso, from which there are fantastic closeup views of Mount Stanley. Because of the intense cold at Kiondo, some trekkers prefer to return to Mahangu for the overnight. If you plan to do that, make sure to get a good early start for a very long day.

The next day, the trek route continues for another mile to Moraine Hut at 14,749 feet. Although the elevation gain on the way is negligible, you must cross an area of steep rocks on which a fixed cable has been placed as a handhold. Beyond, there are fine views of a chain of alpine lakes, each named for its particular color: Lac Vert (Green), Lac Gris (gray), and Lac Blanc (white). You then pass near the snout of the West Stanley Glacier before arriving at the hut. Trekkers can either stay at the small wooden cabin or return to Kiondo or even Mahangu for overnight. The usual descent from Moraine Hut to Mutwanga takes a day and a half.

Climbers use the Moraine Hut as a base from which to scale Peak Margherita, Mount Stanley's highest point. The climb is not technically difficult, but should be attempted only by experienced

---

*All Ruwenzori elevations given are approximate. Sources disagree on everything: even the height of Mount Stanley is alternatively quoted at both 16,763 and 16,795 feet.

and fully equipped mountaineers. It is advisable to plan for an extra night on the mountain at the top hut, in case bad weather delays the summit ascent.

Mont Hoyo and the Pygmies

Mont Hoyo is a protected reserve on the eastern edge of Zaire's famous Ituri Forest. It is the most convenient place to experience Africa's tropical rainforest and meet the people who live in it, the legendary Pygmies.

Although the equatorial rainforest is one of nature's most complex biological communities, it is a difficult environment to fully appreciate. The jungle presents us mostly with confined views of plants—especially on its fringes, where vegetation runs riot in the bright sunlight. Its virgin interior is celebrated for exotic wildlife, but animals are uncommon and hard to see in the perpetual twilight of the forest understory. Even birds, whose presence is advertised by the tantalizing variety of squawks and whistles that emanate from the treetops, are not always easy to locate. Probably no habitat in Africa is as foreign to our sensibilities. The tall trees, dim light, and hot, humid climate make us uncomfortable and feed our preconditioned fears of crawling insects and venomous snakes. To us, the rainforest remains mysterious, even ominous.

Most Zairois are also disconcerted by the deep forest. To them, it is the domain of restless spirits and hostile ghosts. As agriculturalists, they stay near the plantations they have cleared along jungle roads. Only the Pygmies truly call the forest home. The BaMbuti, as the Pygmies of eastern Zaire are called, are one of the oldest peoples in Africa. Racially and linguistically distinct, their roots are lost in time, though it is certain that they were the first humans to inhabit the great African forest.

Pygmies have an odd symbiotic relationship with the other African peoples who later moved into their forest realm. Attracted by the lure of tasty foods and Iron Age technology, the Pygmies fell under the domination of the newcomers. Over time, the materially more advanced blacks, or Negroes, came to believe that they owned the Pygmies in the manner of serfs. Through the control of introduced rituals such as circumcision and marriage, they bound the hunters to their servitude. The Pygmies provided their "masters" with the most valuable forest products—meat and ivory. In return, they received such delectables as bananas and beer, plus desirable commodities such as tobacco and metal spear blades. Although the situation has been complicated by the introduction of money, for the most part, the old economic roles and social attitudes persist to this day. Few Pygmies have adopted farming as a way of life. Most prefer to divide their time between the world of the forest and that of the village. Although the conventional view holds that the Pygmies are exploited, some modern researchers suggest that the hunters merely play along with their neighbors in order to freeload when they want to take a break from life in the forest. Whatever the merits of that argument, the Pygmies, like hunting peoples everywhere, are politically powerless against their more sophisticated and numerous neighbors. Yet they are the utter masters of the forest realm, while the negroid blacks remain alien to it.

Pygmy men are experts in the use of bow and arrow, and know the secrets of making deadly poisons. Mushrooms, honey, and edible plants are gathered by both men and women, then carried in bags that are woven from leaves on the spot. Leaves are also used as the walls and roofs of Pygmy houses. These very simple rounded structures are built by the women in a matter of hours. When hunting, Pygmy bands go deep into the forest and construct temporary encampments, where they remain as long as game is abundant. Singing and dancing are a very prominent part of nighttime life in such camps. Most Pygmies eventually return to the neigborhood of "their" villages, which being along the roads, is where they are seen by tourists.

ACCESS AND ACCOMMODATION

Mont Hoyo is 70 miles north of Beni. The road is barely passable after heavy rains, so the time required to reach the reserve is impossible to predict. A two-night stay is the minimum needed to see the usual sights; three nights are far better if you want to really explore the forest or get acquainted with the Pygmies. If time or weather conspires against a Mont Hoyo expedition, you can probably encounter Pygmies at the Oicha Mission, which is only about 20 miles outside of Beni.

Two decades ago, the Beni road passed through almost continuous rainforest. Now villages and habitations line most of its length. You still pass through some short stretches of undisturbed forest, but the evidence of cutting and burning for the creation of new plantations is everywhere. Because cattle do not thrive in the jungle environment, game is highly valued as a source of meat, and it is common to see Africans offering animals they have killed for sale along the road. Although not the optimal wildlife-viewing situation, it is really worth stopping to investigate. This is probably the only way that you will see most of the forest mammals: you might view such oddities as brush-tailed porcupine, tree pangolin, potto, and dwarf antelope.

Just beyond the Loya River, some 70 miles north of Beni, a rough 6-mile-long track turns off toward the reserve. You pass-through forest broken by the small cultivated plots of the BaLese, the dominant negroid tribe in the eastern Ituri. At road's end is the Auberge de Mont Hoyo. At the ramshackle lodge, amenities like hot water are not guaranteed, but food can be surprisingly well prepared. Camping is permitted on the grounds.

TOURING

The Mont Hoyo reserve is eventually supposed to be incorporated into the Parc des Virunga, but separate park entrance and camera fees must be paid. Entrance is U.S.$20. The main sights are the beautiful Venus Staircase waterfall and several grottos complete with toothy stalagmitic formations. These are interesting, but the real attraction is the forest itself and the Pygmies who live in the area. The climate at Mont Hoyo is actually quite pleasant, rather than oppressively hot. Walks in the forest are well shaded, but the midday sun is murder if you are trekking along the open road. Afternoon thunder showers with impressive lightning displays are common.

The lodge is located on the edge of the reserve, so access to the forest is immediate. Since it is a national park, the Pygmies are not allowed to hunt there and you may see large troops of red-tailed guenons (also called white-nosed monkey or *Cercopithecus ascanius*) or blue monkeys close to the hotel grounds. The forest hosts several varieties of duiker, as well as Bate's dwarf antelope (*Neotragus batesi*), which is smaller than a dikdik. Red forest buffalo live in the reserve, but do not frequent the area around the lodge. They might be encountered if you spend a day hiking to Mont Hoyo's summit (4,757 ft.), an activity of which very few visitors avail themselves. Forest, or dwarf, buffalo are very distinct from the better-known Cape variety: they are reddish in color, are smaller in size, and have shorter crescent-shaped horns. Their pugnacious reputation is equal to or worse than that of their larger cousins, so an armed game scout should accompany you on any extensive forest explorations. Chimpanzees live in the Mont Hoyo area, too. They are actually more likely to be seen along the approach road than in the reserve, because they often come to native farms to steal bananas. These animals are not habituated and are often hunted, so you will be lucky to get even a long-distance view. Promise the Pygmies an extra reward *if* they show you chimps, and they will give it a good try. But be sure to tell your guides that you want to *see* chimps, not kill or capture them. Birding is also somewhat easier along the approach road, where you are likely to see huge wattled hornbills, flocks of great blue turacos, and pairs of gray parrots feeding in fruiting jungle trees.

A national park guide will take you to the waterfalls and grottos. It is only a short walk, but it is worthwhile to hire Pygmies to carry day packs or camera gear. Porters are not really needed; it is just a good opportunity to start to form personal relationships with the forest people.

Some visitors are disappointed by their encounters with the Pygmies. They are put off by the usual tourist routine, which is limited to purchasing souvenirs, listening to unceasing requests for *cadeaux*, and visiting the Pygmy "village" to watch a dance performance. As usual, the quality of the experience varies, and it is largely what *you* make of it. It helps to go prepared with a good assortment of desirable gifts: bring tobacco, salt, sugar, and cornmeal (all of which can be easily purchased in Beni). It is highly recommended to hire the Pygmies to take you into the forest. They will simulate hunts (be forewarned that if outside the park, they may actually kill animals they encounter) and gather any edibles they find on the way. If you do any real forest walking, you will quickly understand the adaptive advantage of Pygmy stature to the environment: they proceed silently through the forest understory with a rapid pace, while you struggle to keep up amid a succession of leafy barriers.

Although clearly staged for tourists, the dance show is a unique experience. The dancing is pretty good, though not sophisticated. Pygmies are excellent mimics of the animals celebrated in the various pieces, and you will readily appreciate their renditions of elephants and chimpanzees. But perhaps more fascinating than the dancing itself is the sociology of the scene that surrounds the performance, when the symbiotic relationship between the tribes is amply revealed. The local BaLese chief arranges the show early in the day. In the late afternoon, a huge procession of BaLese join you in the walk to the Pygmy "village" (few actually live there). On their heads, the BaLese carry souvenirs for sale to tourists and staple items to sell to the Pygmies, so it is actually a sort of portable market. Then follow negotiations with the Pygmies, who clearly don't entirely buy the authority of the BaLese chief. Finally, a BaLese must be paid for rental of the drum, which the Pygmies play but do not own. Following the dancing, the Pygmies use the cash they earn to buy goods from the villagers.

While at Mont Hoyo, you should take the opportunity to explore the Loya River by dugout canoe, or pirogue. While BaLese boatmen pole you along the jungle-fringed river, you will pass elaborate wicker fish traps and tiny Pygmy encampments, dwarfed by giant forest trees. On the way, you will probably spot several types of exotic jungle birds—notably hornbills, turacos, and kingfishers. Pirogues are always available at the bridge where the Beni road crosses the river.

Beyond Mont Hoyo

Two fascinating places in Eastern Zaire are currently beyond the range of normal tourism. Epulu, in the heart of the Ituri Forest, is the site of research on the okapi (*Okapia johnstoni*), a unique forest-dwelling giraffe-like animal endemic to the Ituri region. Even scientists rarely encounter wild okapis, but several specimens can be seen at the government capture station. The Pygmies at Epulu will take you into the forest to show you how they hunt. Unlike those at Mont Hoyo, they hunt in large communal groups. A line of nets is strung across the forest floor, after which game is driven into the mesh and dispatched with spears or bows. Epulu is about 110 torturous miles west of Mont Hoyo, and is really only visited by transcontinental overland groups.

The Garamba National Park is the last refuge of the northern white rhino. Once common in the savannas of Uganda, Sudan, and Haut-Zaire, the subspecies has been reduced to a mere fifteen or twenty individuals, and these probably will not long survive in the face of continued poaching. The nearby research station at Gangala na Bodio was the site of a historic wildlife project: African elephants were successfully trained there as work animals, proving that the species could be domesticated. The enterprise was started by the Belgians, but was pretty much wrecked during the civil war. A decade ago, only nine trained elephants were left and it is doubtful if the program will ever be truly revived. Garamba is currently only accessible to those with their own vehicles or using charter aircraft.

Kahuzi-Biega National Park

Kahuzi-Biega is a major center for gorilla viewing. The animals there are eastern lowland gorillas (*G. g. graueri*) which, though marginally smaller, are very similar in appearance to the mountain variety. In Kahuzi-Biega's hilly terrain, vegetation varies from equatorial rainforests at lower elevations, especially in the remote western reaches of the park, to bamboo thickets and tree heaths on the heights of Mount Kahuzi (10,853 ft.). This blend of habitats supports a wide range of fauna that includes chimpanzees, forest elephants, and the gamut of jungle birdlife.

The Kahuzi-Biega gorillas were habituated to humans by warden Adrien Deschriever, whose methods were far more passive than those of Dian Fossey. He never tried to imitate gorilla behavior or interact with his subject animals. He was nonetheless successful in winning their confidence, and several groups were opened to public viewing long before any were available in Rwanda. Unfortunately, the program was very poorly managed. Crowds of up to forty people at a time could track one gorilla family, and there was an unbelievable amount of chopping of underbrush to improve photo opportunities. It was not always a great experience for either humans or apes. That situation has been cleaned up, and you can now view these lowland gorillas without feeling that you are doing them harm. Currently, no more than eight tourists can visit a gorilla group at one time, though several clusters of tourists may visit consecutively in the same day. Further regulations may limit visitors to a total of eight per day.

ACCESS AND ACCOMMODATION

The park is near Bukavu, Zaire's major city on the south end of Lake Kivu. Bukavu can best be reached by air or lake steamer from Goma (rather than negotiate 125 miles of bumpy road). The quickest way to or from Kigali is to fly to Cyangugu (Kamembe Airport), the town just across the border from Bukavu. Bukavu itself is an attractive city with a good range of hotels. The best is the Hotel Résidence, which has an excellent restaurant.

The park entrance is only some 22 paved miles from Bukavu, making it easy to find accommodations in town and do gorilla viewing as a day trip. It is a pleasant ride along the lake, then upward through coffee farms and plantations of cinchona trees, from the bark of which quinine is extracted. You can arrange transport with AMIZA or hire a taxi. Budget travelers can take local buses or hitch along the main lakeshore road, but often have to walk the final 5 uphill miles to the park. No lodging is available there, but camping is permitted at the entry gate at Tshivanga.

TOURING THE PARK

In the past, gorilla watchers would simply turn up at the Tshivanga Station by 8 A.M. to arrange a tracking session. Now that the number of permits is more restricted, it is wise to prebook at the IZCN office in Bukavu (185 Ave de Président Mobutu). Permits are U.S. $120. This includes the cost of park entrance, guides and BaTwa trackers, but additional tips should be given. Originally, a permit *guaranteed* a gorilla sighting or you would be allowed to return for another free tracking session the following day. With the more limited permit system, this may no longer be the case.

Two gorilla family groups are habituated for viewing. Both live in the hilly eastern section of the park. Although these are technically *lowland* gorillas, do not be deceived by the name into thinking that tracking is any easier than it is in the Virunga Volcanos. You can expect to tramp through thick jungle, climbing steep foliage-covered hillsides and crossing swampy valleys in which spiny tree ferns grow. You will probably see the spoor of forest elephants and may even hear them trumpet, but your guides will try to keep you from coming into close contact with these aggressive beasts. As always, gorilla tracking can prove to be a five-minute walk or a ten-hour expedition.

Aside from gorilla viewing, it is possible to hire guides for day hikes to the summit of Mount Kahuzi or walks in the lower rainforest. Extended treks can supposedly be arranged, but would be logistically very difficult.

BURUNDI

The Elephants' Graveyard

Tiny Burundi is Rwanda's twin in size, tribal mix, and colonial history. It differs principally from its neighbor in that the aristocratic Tutsi continue to rule over the Hutu majority. The country is scenically located on the eastern shore of Lake Tanganyika, but lacks any major wildlife attractions. Several small parks have been recently established, however. These include the Parc National de la Kibira, notable for chimps and forest monkeys, and the Lake Rwihinda Nature Reserve, which is a paradise for aquatic birds. Neither they nor the Parc National de la Ruvubu, a savanna reserve bordering one of the country's largest rivers, are currently well developed for touring. Most travelers merely use Burundi as a conduit for transport between Zaire, Rwanda, and Tanzania.

Burundi was once notorious in conservation circles. Though not a single elephant lived there, the country was one of Africa's biggest ivory exporters. The tusks of animals poached in neighboring Tanzania and Zaire were smuggled in, laundered with official papers, and then flown to Belgium for re-export. Things improved in 1988 when Burundi became party to the Convention on International Trade in Endangered Species.

Safari Facts

Entry. Visas are required. If you arrive by air without one, you may well be deported!

Currency. Burundi francs (1989: BF 85 = U.S. $1)

Language. French is official. KiRundi and Swahili are also used.

Transportation. Bujumbura is served by Sabena, Air France, Air Tanzania, and Kenya Airways. Local minibuses and shared taxis can be used to travel overland from Rwanda and Zaire. A weekly ferry connects Bujumbura with Kigoma, Tanzania. It officially departs on Mondays, but is often considerably delayed.

Bujumbura. The modern lakeside capital has several modern hotels, the best of which are the Meridien "Source du Nil," the Novotel, and the Golden Tulip. Somewhat cheaper are the Burundi-Palace and the Hotel Résidence. Budget accommodation is hard to find. The Musée Vivant is a replica of a traditional village, featuring daily concerts of African drumming. Troupes of Tutsi *ntore* dancers may occasionally perform at hotels and public ceremonies.

UGANDA

The Tainted Pearl

Uganda is renowned for its physical beauty. Strung like a necklace around its borders are some of the continent's greatest geographical landmarks. A full circuit would take you from the shores of Victoria, queen of African lakes, to the Virunga and Ruwenzori mountains, the Western Rift Valley lakes Edward and Albert, the Nile, and Mount Elgon. The country encompasses golden savannas, semi-desert thirstlands, equatorial rainforests, and farmlands said to be so fertile that a seed dropped on the ground will sprout and bear fruit without benefit of care. Often described as the "Pearl of Africa," this lush tropical land is the true birthplace of the Nile, where the great river spills out of Lake Victoria and starts its long journey to the Mediterranean Sea. At one time, Uganda's national parks were counted among the best in Africa. Celebrated as much for fine scenery as for wildlife, which was superabundant, they were despoiled in the madness of the post-Amin era, when successive armies invaded them, shooting everything they could for fun or profit. Uganda's massive elephant herds all but disappeared in the slaughter, and many other species suffered terrible losses.

Nor was pain and death confined to the wildlife community. At independence in 1962, Uganda was a prosperous nation with an economy that thrived on exports of cotton, coffee, and tea, as well as a vigorous tourist industry. Its superb Makerere University produced first-rate professionals who were to be the technical and intellectual leaders of the future. Everything was spoiled in the chaos that came in the wake of the mad dictator Idi Amin. During his regime, and those of Milton Obote and Tito Okello, which followed, the country dissolved in an orgy of political terror. Estimates of the number of people massacred between 1971–1986, when the current government of Yoweri Museveni took power, range from a half to one and a half million victims. The exact number will never be known, but bones still line the roads of the infamous Luwero Triangle, grisly monuments to the hundreds of thousands who were systematically murdered or starved there.

Although Uganda seems to be in the process of recovery from its years of horror and civil strife, the situation is still too uncertain for commercial tourism. But oddly enough, bold independent travelers have been passing through for years. In fact, even during very troubled times, Uganda has been something of a Mecca for budget travelers because the black market value of the dollar has made living exceedingly cheap. Visitors almost universally report that they like the country and find its people extremely friendly. Although it is doubtful that Uganda's parks will ever be what they once were, they are still wonderfully scenic and, with protection, the smaller animals—especially antelope and the predators that depend on them—can come back in numbers very quickly. Also, in addition to the classic big game viewing of its parks, Uganda can offer opportunities for trekking and primate watching to rival those of Rwanda and Zaire. Someday the country may once again become a prime tourist destination.

That time has not yet come, however. Rebellions and banditry still plague some regions, and a struggling economy does not support any normal tour services. Therefore, rather than present a detailed account of safari travel in Uganda, I will briefly summarize the country's unique attractions. When the situation there calms down sufficiently, these will be the places of major interest. In the meantime, independent travelers will no doubt continue to visit.

Safari Facts

Entry. Visas are required.

Security. The U.S. State Department routinely issues warnings against travel in the northern and eastern districts. If you are planning to go, it is best to check their latest bulletins, stay abreast of current events, and keep your ear tuned to the travelers' grapevine.

Language. English is official. Swahili is widely used, as is Luganda, the mother tongue of the populous Buganda tribe.

Currency. Uganda shillings. (1989: USh 200 = U.S. $1). The black market rate was once computed in huge multiples of the official figure. Successive revaluations may now have stabilized it at about twice the official rate.

Transportation. International air service to Kampala is still very limited. Uganda Airlines, Sabena, Ethiopian Airlines, and Kenya Airways are the main carriers. Road and rail connections to Kenya exist, but security is still sometimes touchy. Roads inside the country are neglected and public transport is typically poor.

Hotels. The Uganda Hotels Corporation operates lodges in the larger towns and national parks. As for all Uganda hotels, payment must be made in U.S. dollars or other hard currency.

Kampala. The capital suffered tremendous damage in the years of strife and still shows it. Aside from the newly opened Sheraton, most of its hotels are in bad shape: the Fairway, Imperial, and Speke Hotels are serviceable. The Hotel Diplomat, outside town, is comfortable. The government's Ministry of Parks and Wildlife is located near the U.S. Embassy. The tourist office there can give you the latest information regarding what facilities are available at the various parks and reserves. The most important cultural site in town is the Kabaka's Palace and Kasubi Tombs, where the royal chiefs of the Buganda were interred.

National Parks And Game Reserves

Kabalega National Park (formerly called Murchison Falls) occupies more than 1,500 square miles of grassy savanna on the banks of the Victoria Nile. There, the fast-moving young river is funneled through a 20-foot fissure in the African bedrock, to plunge 150 vertical feet in the celebrated Murchison (Kabalega) Falls. After its awesome drop, the river continues to its junction with Lake Albert (Lake Mobutu), from which it immediately exits northward and is rechristened the Albert Nile. Kabalega was once one of Africa's premier wildlife paradises. Its plains were well stocked with elephant, white rhino, Uganda kob, oribi, Rothschild's giraffe, and Jackson's hartebeest. But the glory of the park was the animal life on the Nile itself. Boats carried visitors on a 7-mile journey to the foot of the falls, passing hundreds of hippos and monster crocodiles on route. Today elephants are rare and rhinos are gone, but the aquatic animals and small game are recouping their numbers. The Nile boats still operate when there is fuel, and the ride is as thrilling as ever. Although Paraa and Chobe lodges are open (albeit no longer luxurious), park infrastructure remains badly damaged. The security situation in the region is still poor, so there is little hope of early recovery.

Things are much more settled in the region of the Ruwenzori National Park. Formerly named after Queen Elizabeth, it now honors the mountain range that soars upward within a dozen miles of its northern boundary. The park is spread along the eastern shore of the Rift Valley's Lake Edward (Lake Amin). Due to the incredible numbers of heavy-weight animals—elephants, hippos, and buffalo—that lived there, it once had the distinction of carrying the largest wildlife biomass in the world. Elephants were very hard hit in the war years, but the herds of topi, kob, and hippo are now in good shape. The park's northern section is particularly scenic. When the weather permits, there are tremendous views of the Ruwenzori peaks from its plains, which are decorated with giant candelabra euphorbia trees. In the Kikorondo area, plains give way to the sensuous cones of extinct volcanos, some of which are filled with beautiful crater lakes. The most spectacular game viewing takes place by boat on the Kazinga Channel, which connects Lake Edward with its smaller brother, Lake George. The channel is packed with thousands of hippos and multitudes of fish-eating birds. On the south end of Lake Edward, the rolling Ishasa plains are contiguous with those of Zaire's Parc des Virunga. Ishasa is one of the few places known for tree-climbing lions. Chimps inhabit the Maramagambo Forest, between the northern and Ishasa sectors. The Mweya Safari Lodge is still operating. It has a wonderful location on a promontory above Lake Edward, just at the mouth of the Kazinga Channel. Boats are available for the channel cruise.

Two reserves in Uganda have tremendous potential to be developed for gorilla viewing. The Kigezi Gorilla Reserve, on the northern rim of the Virunga Volcanos, was once a prime area for gorilla tracking. Because of human encroachment, it has been substantially abandoned by the apes in recent years. But some intact habitat still exists there and, with protection, it is possible that gorillas will recolonize the slopes of Sabinyo and Muhabura volcanos. No such resuscitation is necessary in the Impenetrable Forest. An estimated 100–130 mountain gorillas inhabit this remote reserve near the Zaire border, some 20 miles north of the Virungas. This is the only population of mountain gorillas existing outside the volcanos. Researchers currently studying the animals there are habituating several family groups and it is possible that they will be opened to the public. Tracking is difficult in the hilly terrain because the forest's vegetation is as dense as its name would imply. It is hoped that the Impenetrable (also called Bwindi) Forest will soon be declared a national park because human population pressure is already intense. The park would harbor many creatures typical of both lowland and highland rainforests.

The Kibale Forest is another area of great interest to primatologists. The reserve is inhabited by a wonderfully diverse community of animals, which includes red colobus, red-tailed guenon (white-nosed monkey), gray-cheeked mangabey (*Cercocebus albigena*), blue monkey, L'Hoest's monkey (*Cercopithecus l'hoesti*), and black-and-white colobus. Along with these are olive baboon, bushbaby, the nocturnal potto, and chimpanzee. These animals have been the subjects of long-term research projects, so they are now tame and easy to observe. A trail grid has been cut in the forest to facilitate walking. Kibale is located just east of the Ruwenzori, near the town of Fort Portal. Perhaps one day, it will have an important place on Uganda tour itineraries.

Other faunal reserves in Uganda include the newly created Lake Mburo National Park, which features both aquatic and acacia bush habitats. It is the only park in the country in which impala are found. The Toro Game Reserve is located on the Semliki River flats to the south of Lake Albert. Its plains are known for big numbers of Uganda kob. The beautiful Kidepo Valley National Park was once a well-known haven for the wildlife of Uganda's northern Karamoja District. Karamoja is rugged semidesert country. No government has ever been able to wield complete authority over its nomadic inhabitants. Certainly, no one has been looking after Kidepo Valley's animals in the last few years. Since Karamoja remains the least secure part of Uganda, the park is likely to remain *terra incognita* for some time to come.

Uganda's Ruwenzori

Uganda offers the greatest number of trek and climbing routes in the Ruwenzori. In more peaceful times, the Mountain Club of Uganda developed an extensive system of huts and trails. The huts have since fallen into disrepair and many of the trails have now disappeared, but treks can still be organized from the village of Ibanda, which is reached through the town of Fort Portal. John Matte, the former agent of the Mountain Club, is still there to help with the hire and outfitting of porters. You are expected to provide their rations, cooking gear, blankets, carry bags, and cigarettes. Barefoot porters will not go into snowy areas, so you may have to buy some shoes as well. All these items can apparently be procured locally.

The favored route begins at 5,300 feet and follows the Mubuku and Bujuku rivers deep into the central Ruwenzori. It affords a relatively gentle ascent to Bujuku Lake (13,000 ft.), which is surrounded by a cluster of giant peaks—Mounts Stanley (16,763 ft.), Speke (16,042 ft.), and Baker (15,889 ft.). That trek takes a minimum of five days. Seven or eight days are needed if you want to do a loop return via Scott Elliot Pass (14,350 ft.) and the beautiful

Kitandara Lakes (13,200 ft.) and have time to visit the top huts at the bases of the great peaks.

Anyone planning an expedition, especially for climbing, is well advised to get hold of the Uganda Mountain Club's *Guide to the Ruwenzori* by H. A. Osmaston and D. Pasteur (Goring, Readings, Berks, U.K.: West Col, 1972).

Appendices

Appendix A:
Safari Tour Operators

UNITED STATES

Abercrombie & Kent International, 1420 Kensington Rd., No. 103, Oakbrook, IL 60521. Tel.: (800)323-7308; (312)954-2944. Lodge tours, both quality and deluxe camping tours, custom safaris.

Adventure Center, 5540 College Ave., Oakland, CA 94618. Tel.: (800)227-8747; (415)654-1879. Specialists in overland expeditions; books Encounter Overland and Guerba Expeditions.

African Holidays, P.O. Box 36959, Tucson, AZ 85740. Tel.: (800)528-0168; (602)742-1161. Lodge safaris; includes West Africa.

African Safari Trails, 50 Water St., South Norwalk, CT 06854. Tel.: (800)233-2585; (203)866-7137. Holiday safaris.

African Travel, 1000 East Broadway, Glendale, CA 91205. Tel.: (800)421-8907; (818)507-7893. Lodge safaris; southern Africa.

Bicycle Africa, 4247 135th Place S.E., Bellevue, WA 98006. Tel.: (206)746-1028. Bike tours in Kenya and West Africa.

Born Free Safaris, 12511 Oxnard St., North Hollywood, CA 91606. Tel.: (800)372-3274; (213)877-3553. Lodge, camping, and specialty tours; custom safaris.

Cheeseman's Ecology Safaris, 20800 Kittredge Rd., Saratoga, CA 95070. Tel.: (408)741-5330. Nature tours for nonsmokers.

Classical Tours International, One East Wacker Dr., Chicago, IL 60610. Tel.: (800)828-8222; (312)644-7878. Lodge safaris.

East Africa Safari Company Ltd., 250 West 57th St., New York, NY 10017. Tel.: (800)7-SAFARI; (212)757-0722. Custom safaris.

Fun Safaris, P.O. Box 178, Bloomingdale, IL 60108. Tel.: (800)323-8020; (312)893-2545. Lodge safaris; zoo groups.

Geo Expeditions, Box 3656, Sonora, CA 95370. Tel.: (800)351-5041; (800)826-9063 (in CA). Camping tours; custom safaris.

Harmsafari, 418 3rd Ave., San Diego, CA 92101. Tel.: (619)233-5849. Lodge safaris.

Hemphill Harris, 16000 Ventura Blvd., Suite 200, Encino, CA 91436. Tel.: (800)421-0454; (818)906-8086. Luxury holiday safaris.

Henderson Tours, 931 Martin Luther King, Jr., Drive N.W., Atlanta, GA 30314. Tel.: (800)241-4644; (404)522-6881. Specializes in black heritage tours in West Africa.

International Expeditions, 1776 Independence Ct., Birmingham, AL 35216. Tel.: (800)633-4734; (205)633-4734. Lodge safaris.

Joseph Van Os Nature Tours, P.O. Box 655, Vashon Island, WA 98070. Tel.: (206)463-5383. Specialty photography tours.

Ker Downey Selby, 7701 Wilshire Place Drive, Suite 504, Houston, TX 77040. Tel.: (713)744-3434; (800)392-4159. Deluxe custom safaris in Botswana and Tanzania.

KLR International, 1560 Broadway, New York, NY 10036. Tel.: (800)221-4876; (212)869-2850. Lodge and camping safaris.

Lindblad Travel, P.O. Box 912, Westport, CT 06681. Tel.: (203)226-8531; (800)243-5657. Lodge and deluxe camping tours.

Magical Holidays, 501 Madison Ave., New York, NY 10022. Tel.: (212)486-9600. African heritage and cultural tours in West Africa.

Micato Safaris, 57 East 11th St., New York, NY 10003. Tel.: (212)777-9292. Holiday lodge safaris.

Mountain Madness, 7103 California Ave. S.W., Seattle, WA 98136. Tel.: (206)937-8389; (800)523-4576. East African climbs and treks.

Mountain Travel, 6420 Fairmount Ave., El Cerrito, CA 94530. Tel.: (800)227-2384; (415)527-8100. Quality and luxury camping safaris; specialize in walking safaris and climbing tours; also custom safaris.

Nature Company, P.O. Box 2310, Berkeley, CA 94702. Tel.: (800)227-1114. Small selection of quality camping safaris.

Overseas Adventure Travel, 349 Broadway, Cambridge, MA 02139. Tel.: (800)221-0814; (617)876-0533. High-quality overland truck camping safaris in Tanzania; also custom safaris.

Park East Tours, 1841 Broadway, Suite 900, New York, NY 10023. Tel.: (800)223-6078; (212)765-4870. Holiday lodge safaris.

Questers, 257 Park Ave., New York, NY 10010. (212)673-3120. Bird and nature tours; lodge safaris.

REI Adventures, P.O. Box 8090, Berkeley, CA 94707. Tel.: (800)622-2236; (800)624-2236 (in CA). Camping and walking safaris.

Safaricentre, 3201 N. Sepulveda Blvd., Manhattan Beach, CA 90266. Tel.: (800)223-6046; (800)624-5342 (in CA). Booking agent for a wide variety of African safari tour operators.

Safari Consultants of London, 3535 Ridgelake Dr., Suite B, Metaire, LA 70002. Tel.: (800)648-6541. Custom safaris.

Safariworld, 40 East 49th St., New York, NY 10017. Tel.: (800)221-4737; (212)486-0505. Holiday lodge safaris.

Sobek Expeditions, Box 1089, Angels Camp, CA 95222. Tel.: (209)736-4524. River-rafting and camping safaris on the Rufiji (Selous Reserve) and Zambesi Rivers.

Special Expeditions, 720 Fifth Ave., New York, NY 10019. Tel.: (800)762-0003; (212)765-7740. Luxury camping tours.

United Touring International, 1315 Walnut St., No. 800, Philadelphia, PA 19107. Tel.: (800)223-6486. Holiday lodge safaris.

Victor Emanuel Nature Tours, P.O. Box 33008, Austin, TX 78764. Tel.: (512)477-5091. Birding safari specialists.

Voyagers, P.O. Box 915, Ithaca, NY 14851. Tel.: (607)257-3091. Holiday lodge and luxury camping safaris.

Wilderness Travel, 801 Allston Way, Berkeley, CA 94710. Tel.: (800)247-6700; (415)548-0420. Quality camping tours.

Wildlife Safari, 23 Orinda Way, Orinda, CA 94563. Tel.: (800)221-8118; (800)526-3637 (in CA). Holiday lodge safaris.

KENYA

Aardvark Safaris, P.O. Box 69496, Nairobi. Tel.: 334863. Telex: 25039 AARDVARK. Lodge and camping safaris.

Across Africa Safaris, P.O. Box 49420, Nairobi. Tel.: 33274. Telex: 22501. Lodge safaris.

Adventure Associates, P.O. Box 24959, Nairobi. Tel.: 882594, Cable: SANDRIVERS. Luxury safaris.

Bantu Lodge, P.O. Box 333, Nanyuki. Tel.: Burguret 1. Mount Kenya treks. (Booked through Kenya Wildlife Trails, see below.)

Best Camping Tours, P.O. Box 40223, Nairobi. Tel.: 28091. Telex: 23025. Budget safaris.

Bruce Safaris, P.O. Box 40662, Nairobi. Tel.: 27311. Telex: 25440 BRUSAFARIS. Custom outfitters and diving specialists.

Bushbuck Adventures, P.O. Box 67449, Nairobi. Tel.: 728737/60437. Telex: 25517 DIVADVICE. Unusual low-cost camping tours; custom safaris.

Cheli & Peacock, P.O. Box 39806 Nairobi. Tel.: (0311)20241. Telex: 39051 SAFARICLUB. Custom camping tours.

Flamingo Tours, P.O. Box 44899, Nairobi. Tel.: 28961. Telex: 22314. FAX: 333262. Holiday lodge tours; camel safaris.

Gametrackers, P.O. Box 62042, Nairobi. Tel.: 338927; 22703. Telex: 22258 TRACKER. Budget camping.

John Alexander Safaris, P.O. Box 20127, Nairobi. Tel.: 891447. Telex: 25116 DYNAMICJBA. Luxury camping safaris.

Kenya Wildlife Trails Ltd., P.O. Box 44687, Nairobi. Tel.: 28960. Telex: 25711 WILDTRAIL. Lodge safaris and hotel bookings.

Ker & Downey Safaris, P.O. Box 41822, Nairobi. Tel.: 556466. Telex: 24223 KERDOW. FAX: 552378. Oldest operator of custom luxury camping safaris.

Let's Go Travel, P.O. Box 60432, Nairobi. Tel.: 29540. Telex: 25440. Holiday lodge safaris and customized bookings.

Michaelides Safaris, P.O. Box 48010, Nairobi. Tel.: 520358. Telex: 22958. Luxury safaris.

Mount Kenya and East Africa Guides, P.O. Box 44827, Nairobi. Guided technical climbs on Mount Kenya and other African peaks.

Naro Moru River Lodge, P.O. Box 18, Naro Moru. Tel.: Naro Moru 17 or Nairobi 337501. Telex: 22591 ALLIANCE. Treks on Mount Kenya.

Nilestar Safaris, P.O. Box 42291, Nairobi. Tel.: 337392. Telex: 22292. Holiday lodge safaris; books other safari services.

Prestige Safaris, P.O. Box 43987, Nairobi. Tel.: 27977. Telex: 22043. FAX: 333669. Holiday safaris and hotel bookings.

Rhino Safaris, P.O. Box 48023, Nairobi. Tel.: 28102. Telex: 22081. Holiday lodge safaris and hotel bookings.

Richard Bonham Safaris, P.O. Box 24133, Nairobi. Tel.: 882521. Telex: 25547 BONHAM. Custom camping safaris. Walking safaris in Tanzania's Selous Game Reserve.

Safari Camp Services, P.O. Box 44801, Nairobi. Tel.: 28936; 330130. Telex: 25108. Camping tours; from budget (they operate the Turkana Bus) to luxury styles.

Safaris Unlimited, P.O. Box 20138. Tel.: 332132. Telex: 22380 ENLITEN. Camping safaris; specializes in horseback safaris.

Special Camping Safaris Ltd., P.O. Box 51512, Nairobi. Tel.: 338325. Telex: 25260 CLOGGY. Budget safaris.

Star Travel and Tours, P.O. Box 48225, Nairobi. Tel.: 26995. Telex: 25598. Lodge and budget camping safaris.

Sunny Safaris, P.O. Box 74495, Nairobi. Tel.: 26587. Telex: 28871 SUNNY. Budget camping tours.

Tana Delta Limited, P.O. Box 24988, Nairobi. Tel.: 882826. Boat and camping safaris in the Tana River Delta.

Thorn Tree Safaris, P.O. Box 42475, Nairobi. Tel.: 254641. Telex: 22025. Lodge safaris and bookings.

Tropical Ice Safaris, P.O. Box 57341, Nairobi. Tel.: 740811. Telex: 22108 TROICE. FAX: 740826. Quality and luxury camping safaris. Specializes in walking safaris and Mount Kenya treks.

United Touring Company (UTC), P.O. Box 42196, Nairobi. Tel.: 331960. Telex: 22228. FAX: 331422. Lodge safaris.

Universal Safari Tours, P.O. Box 49312, Nairobi. Tel.: 21446. Telex: 22054 UST. FAX: 254-2-728440. Lodge tours.

Yare Safaris, P.O. Box 63006, Nairobi. Tel.: 725610. Telex: 25788. Budget camel safaris.

TANZANIA

Bushtrekker Safaris, P.O. Box 3173, Arusha. Tel.: 3727. Telex: 42125. Holiday lodge safaris.

Coopers & Kearsley Travel, P.O. Box 142, Arusha. Tel.: 3421. Telex: 42126. Holiday lodge safaris.

Dorobo Safaris, P.O. Box 2534, Arusha. Tel.: 3255. Telex: 42018 AVESA. Quality camping safaris and unusual walking safaris.

Foxtreks, P.O. Box 84, Mufindi. Operates Ruaha River Camp.

Gibb's Farm Touring, c/o Wildlife Explorer, "Manyara," Riverside, Nanpean, St. Austell, Cornwall, U.K. PL26 7YJ. Tel.: (0726)824132. Telex: 8951182 GECOMS G. Deluxe camping safaris.

Gorge Tours and Safaris, P.O. Box 348, Dar es Salaam. Tel.: 29551. Telex: 41495. Safaris in the Selous from Stiegler's Gorge Camp.

Himat Tours, P.O. Box 7008, Arusha. Telex: 42075 MAUA. Budget camping safaris.

Hotel Tours and Management Ltd., P.O. Box 5350, Dar es Salaam. Tel.: 31957. Telex: 41178. Safaris to the Selous' Mbuyu Camp.

Isles Touristers, P.O. Box 7365, Dar es Salaam. Tel.: (255)061-32902. Telex: 41207. Holiday tours on coast and Zanzibar.

Kibo Hotel, P.O. Box 102, Marangu. Tel.: (Moshi)Marangu 4. Telex: 42095 S.S. Cable: KIBOTEL, Moshi. Outfits Kilimanjaro treks.

Mountain Madness. P.O. Box 6125, Arusha. Telex: 42103 AFTA. Kilimanjaro climbs.

Ngare Sero Safaris, P.O. Box 425, Arusha. Tel.: 3629. Telex: 42047 MM. Deluxe camping safaris.

Ranger Safaris, P.O. Box 9, Arusha. Tel.: 3074/3023. Telex: 42017. Lodge and quality camping safaris.

Sengo Safaris, P.O. Box 207, Arusha. Tel.: 3181 Ext. 1518/1519. Telex: 42006 SENGO TZ. Camping safaris.

Star Tours, P.O. Box 1099, Arusha. Tel: 3181 Ext. 2202/2281. Budget safaris.

Tanventures, P.O. Box 20058, Dar es Salaam. Tel.: 63546. Operates Rufiji River Camp in the Selous Game Reserve.

Tanzania Guides, P.O. Box 1182, Arusha. Tel.: 3625. Telex: 42038. Quality camping safaris and Land Rover (with driver) hire.

Tanzanite Wildlife Tours, P.O. Box 1277, Arusha. Tel.: 2038. Telex: 42094 MOMELLA. Cheap holiday safaris; budget camping.

Tracks, c/o Coopers & Kearsley Travel, P.O. Box 142, Arusha. Tel.: 3421. Telex: 42126. Budget truck camping safaris.

Valji and Alibhai Ltd., P.O. Box 786, Dar es Salaam. Tel.: 20522. Telex: 41334. Vehicle hire (chauffeured) in southern Tanzania.

Wildersun Safaris, P.O. Box 390, Arusha. Tel.: 3880. Telex: 42126. Holiday safaris.

RWANDA

Mimosas Travelcar, B.P. 954, Kigali. Tel.: 73729. Telex: 575 RW.

Rwanda Exploration, B.P. 1545, Kigali. Tel.: 73284. FAX: 250-7-3525.

Rwanda Travel Service, P.O. Box 140, Kigali. Tel.: 72210. Telex: 22507 or RWATRAVEL 42 SITA KGLRTSN. FAX 250-72734. Holds a near-monopoly on gorilla tours and permits.

Umubano Travel, P.O. Box 1160, Kigali. Tel.: 2176.

ZAIRE

AMIZA, B.P. 372, Goma. Tel.: 514. Also reached at: B.P. 7597, Kinshasa. Tel.: 24602. Telex: 21019 AMIZA ZR. Lodge safaris and gorilla bookings.

Equatoria, 7 Oak Street, Lechlade, Glos. GL7 3AX, England. Tel.: (0367)52830. Telex: 445787 MANTA G. Lodge trips; budget truck camping and walking trips; gorilla safaris.

Zaire Safari, c/o Masques Hotel, B.P. 350, Goma. Telex: 22601 PUB GSY RW. Lodge safaris and gorilla bookings. Operates luxury Djomba Camp.

NOTES ON TELEPHONING AFRICA

To direct-dial Africa, use the international access number (011), then the country code, followed by the city code and local phone number. The most useful codes for East Africa follow:

Kenya: country (254); Nairobi (2); Mombasa (11).

Rwanda and Burundi: cannot be dialed directly; tell the operator to use routing 1260257.

Tanzania: country (255); Arusha (57); Dar es Salaam (51).

Uganda: country (256); Kampala (41).

Zaire: country (243); Kinshasa (12).

Appendix B:
East African Embassies, Consulates, and Tour Offices: for visas and information.

Embassy of Kenya
2249 R Street N.W.
Washington, DC 20008
Tel.: (202) 387-6101

Kenya Consulate
Kenya Tourist Office
424 Madison Avenue
New York, NY 10017
Tel.: (212) 486-1300

Kenya Consulate
Kenya Tourist Office
9100 Wilshire Boulevard
Los Angeles, CA 90212
Tel.: (213) 274-6635

Embassy of Tanzania
2139 R Street N.W.
Washington, DC 20008
Tel.: (202) 939-6125

Tanzania Mission to the
United Nations
205 East 42nd Street
New York, NY 10017
Tel.: (212) 972-9160

Tanzania Tourist Corporation
P.O. Box 2485
Dar es Salaam
Tel.: (255) (51) 27671 through
27674
Telex: 41061

Embassy of Rwanda
1714 New Hampshire Avenue
Washington, DC 20007
Tel.: (202) 232-2882

Embassy of Burundi
2233 Wisconsin Avenue N.W.
Washington, DC 20011
Tel.: (202) 726-7100

Embassy of Uganda
5909 16th Street N.W.
Washington, DC 20001
Tel.: (202) 726-7100

Embassy of the Republic of Zaire
1800 New Hampshire Avenue N.W.
Washington, DC 20009
Tel.: (202) 234-7690

Appendix C:
U.S. Embassies and Consulates in East Africa

Kenya
U.S. Embassy
Moi and Haile Selassie Avenues
P.O. Box 30137 (or APO
NY09675)
Nairobi
Tel.: (254) (2) 334141
Telex: 22964

U.S. Consulate
Palli House, Nyerere Avenue
P.O. Box 88079
Mombasa
Tel.: (254) (11) 315101
Telex: 21063 AMCONS

Tanzania
U.S. Embassy
36 Laibon Road
P.O. Box 9123
Dar es Salaam
Tel.: (255) (51) 37501 through
37504
Telex: 41250 AMEMB DAR

Uganda
U.S. Embassy
British High Commission Building
Obote Avenue
P.O. Box 7007
Kampala
Tel.: (256) (41) 259791 through
259795

Rwanda
U.S. Embassy
Boulevard de la Revolution
B.P. 28
Kigali
Tel.: (205) 75601 through 75603/
72126 through 72128

Burundi
U.S. Embassy
Avenue du Zaire
Bujumbura
B.P. 1720
Tel.: 234-54 through 234-56

Zaire
U.S. Embassy
310 Avenue des Aviateurs
Kinshasa
Mail to: APO NY09662
Tel.: (243) (12) 25881 through
25886
Telex: 21405 US EMB ZR

Appendix D:
Swahili Glossary

GREETINGS, PLEASANTRIES, AND TITLES

hello	*jambo*	Have a good trip!	*Safari njema!*
how are you?	*habari?*		
(very) good	*mzuri (sana)*	Mr. (sir)	*bwana*
goodbye	*kwaheri*	Mrs.	*mama*
please	*tafadhali*	Miss	*bibi*
thank you	*asante*	friend	*rafiki*
welcome	*karibu*	elder male	*mzee*
Sorry!	*Pole!*	boy	*kijana*
		child	*toto*

GENERAL

yes	*ndio*	slowly	*pole pole*
no	*hapana*	later (yet)	*bado*
I want to . . .	*nataka*	good	*mzuri*
I don't want . . .	*sitaki*	bad	*mbaya*
I like . . .	*napenda . . .*	okay	*sawasawa*
where?	*wapi*	big	*mkubwa*
where is . . .?	*iko wapi . . .*	small	*kidogo*
hurry	*haraka*	how many (shillings)?	*(shilingi) ngapi?*

NUMBERS

one	*moja*	twenty	*ishirini*
two	*mbili*	thirty	*thelathini*
three	*tatu*	forty	*arobaini*
four	*nne*	fifty	*hamsini*
five	*tano*	sixty	*sitini*
six	*sita*	seventy	*sabini*
seven	*saba*	eighty	*themanini*
eight	*nane*	ninety	*tisini*
nine	*tisa*	one hundred	*mia*
ten	*kumi*	one hundred and one, etc.	*mia na moja, etc.*
eleven	*kumi na moja*		
twelve, etc.	*kumi na mbili, etc.*	two hundred	*mia mbili*
		one thousand	*elfu*

LANDMARKS, OBSTACLES, DIRECTIONS

farm	*shamba*	dust	*fumbi*
hill	*mlima*	rain	*mvua*
hole	*shimo*	near	*karibu*
river	*mto*	far	*mbale*
rock	*mawe*	danger	*haraka*
tree	*mti*	watch out	*angalia*
road	*barabara*	left	*kushoto*
gully, ravine	*korongo*	right	*kulia*
stones	*mawe*	direct, straight ahead	*moja kwa moja*
thorns	*mwimi*	above (high)	*juu*
ocean	*bahari*	below (low)	*chini*

FOR CAMP AND CAR

camp	*kambi*	bath water	*maji ya kuoga*
tent	*hema*	hot (also fire)	*moto*
park bungalow (sparsely furnished)	*banda*	cold	*baridi*
		journey	*safari*
		car	*gari*
chair	*kiti*	gas or oil	*mafuta*
toilet	*choo*	tire	*mpira*
water	*maji*	puncture (flat tire)	*puncha*
drinking water	*maji ya kunywa*		
washing water (hands)	*maji ya kunawa*		

FOOD, DRINK, AND MEDICINE

food	*chakula*	fish	*samaki*
fruit	*matunda*	coffee	*kahawa*
vegetables	*mboga*	tea	*chai*
rice	*mchele*	shop (noun)	*duka*
potatoes	*viazi*	medicine	*dawa*
bread	*mkate*	sick	*mgonjwa*
milk	*maziwa*	doctor	*daktari*
meat	*nyama*		

ANIMALS

antelope	*paa*	giraffe	*twiga*
baboon	*nyani*	hippo	*kiboko*
bird	*ndege*	hyena	*fisi*
buffalo	*mbogo* or *nyati*	gazelle	*swala*
cheetah	*duma*	leopard	*chui*
cow, cattle	*ng'ombe*	lion	*simba*
crocodile	*mamba*	mosquito	*mbu*
donkey	*punda milia*	rhino	*kifaru*
elephant	*ndovu* or *tembo*	snake	*nyoka*
game (meat)	*nyama*	tsetse fly	*dorobo*
goat	*mbuzi*	wildebeest	*nyumbu*

RECOMMENDED FOR FURTHER LANGUAGE
INFORMATION

Berlitz Swahili for Travelers. Lausanne: Editions Berlitz, 1974. A
phrasebook.

Swahili, Phrase Dictionary and Study Guide. New York: Dun Donnelly,
1974.

Perrott, D. V. *Teach Yourself, Swahili.* London: Hodder & Stoughton,
1980. A lesson book.

Perrott, D. V. *Teach Yourself, Swahili Dictionary.* London: Hodder &
Stoughton, 1984.

Appendix E:
Conservation Organizations
Involved in East Africa

African Fund for Endangered Wildlife, P.O. Box 15004, Langata, Nairobi,
Kenya.

African Wildlife Foundation, 1717 Massachusetts Ave NW, Washington,
D.C. 20036.

East African Wildlife Society, P.O. Box 20110, Nairobi, Kenya. Telex:
22153 FUNGA. FAX: 254-2-729612.

Frankfurt Zoological Society, Alfred-Brehm-Platz 16, D-6000, Frankfurt/
Main, West Germany

Flora and Fauna Preservation Society, c/o London Zoological Society,
Regents Park, London NW1 4R4, England.

Tanzania Wildlife Protection Fund, P.O. Box 1994, Dar es Salaam,
Tanzania.

The Digit Fund, c/o Morris Animal Foundation, 45 Inverness Drive East,
Englewood, CO 80112.

Wildlife Conservation International, New York Zoological Society, Bronx,
NY 10460.

World Wildlife Fund, 1250 Twenty-Fourth Street NW, Washington, D.C.
20037.

Bibliography

GENERAL, HISTORY, EXPLORATION, AND ANTHROPOLOGY:

Hemingway, Ernest. *Green Hills of Africa*. New York: Scribner's, 1935. Brilliantly captures the feel of a hunting safari.

Heminway, John. *No Man's Land: The Last of White Africa*. New York: Harcourt Brace Jovanovich, 1983. Fascinating portraits of white hold-overs living in postcolonial Africa.

Hibbert, Christopher. *Africa Explored: Europeans in the Dark Continent, 1769–1889*. New York: Norton, 1982. The journeys of the famous explorers, based on their own records.

Huxley, Elspeth. *Livingston and His African Journeys*. New York: Saturday Review Press, 1974.

Johanson, Donald, and Maitland, Edey. *Lucy: The Beginning of Humankind*. New York: Simon & Schuster, 1981. Human evolution.

Lamb, David. *The Africans*. New York: Random House, 1983. An American journalist looks at contemporary Africa.

Leakey, Richard. *The Making of Mankind*. London: Michael Joseph, 1981. Human evolution from the celebrated anthropologist's point of view.

Marnham, Patrick. *Fantastic Invasion*. New York: Harcourt Brace Jovanovich, 1979. An unsettling view of foreign meddling in Africa: touches conservation, aid, economics, and politics.

Mazrui, Ali. *The Africans: A Triple Heritage*. Boston: Little, Brown, 1986. History and contemporary affairs from an African point of view; stimulating and controversial.

Miller, Charles. *Battle for the Bundu*. New York: Macmillan, 1974. The First World War in Africa.

Moorehead, Alan. *The Blue Nile*. New York: Harper & Row, 1962. History and exploration in Ethiopia and the Sudan.

Moorehead, Alan. *The White Nile*. New York: Harper & Row, 1960. Classic story of the search for the sources of the Nile.

Naipaul, Shiva. *North of South*. New York: Simon & Schuster, 1979. A critical portrait of Kenya, Tanzania, and Zambia; an incisive discussion of the Asian community in Africa.

Reader, John. *Missing Links: The Hunt for Earliest Man*. Boston: Little, Brown, 1981. Reviews the fossil evidence and sorts out the politics, egos, and controversies involved.

Roosevelt, Theodore. *African Game Trails*. New York: Scribner's, 1910. Describes his celebrated hunting expedition.

Severin, Timothy. *The African Adeventure: Four Hundred Years of Exploration in the "Dangerous Continent."* New York: Dutton, 1973. Illustrated history of exploration from the search for Prester John to the Boer's Great Trek.

Shoumatoff, Alex. *African Madness*. New York: Knopf, 1988. A traveler investigates the dark riddles posed by Dian Fossey, Madagascar, the Emperor Bokassa, and the AIDS crisis.

Stanley, Henry Morton. *In Darkest Africa*. New York: Scribner's, 1890. Describes his weird expedition to the Sudan to "save" Emin Pasha.

Stanley, Henry Morton. *Through the Dark Continent*. New York: Harper & Brothers, 1878. Describes his epic journey down the Congo River.

Sterling, Thomas. *Stanley's Way*. New York: Atheneum, 1960. A journey through colonial Tanganyika and the Belgian Congo, following in the footprints of the famous explorer.

Swift, Jeremy. *The Sahara*. Amsterdam: Time-Life Books, 1975. An excellent geographical overview of Africa's great desert.

Turnbull, Colin. *The Lonely African*. New York: Simon & Schuster, 1962. Powerfully documents the West's cultural assault on native African beliefs and values, and its sad consequences.

Turnbull, Colin. *The Mountain People*. New York: Simon & Schuster, 1972. A thought-provoking account of the social disintegration of the Ik, a tribe of hunter-gatherers in Uganda.

NATURAL HISTORY AND WILDLIFE

Adamson, Joy. *Born Free*. New York: Harcourt, Brace & World, 1960. The story of Elsa the lioness.

Adamson, Joy. *Living Free*. New York: Harcourt, Brace & World, 1975. Further Elsa stories.

Beard, Peter. *The End of the Game*. San Francisco: Chronicle Books, 1988. Chronicles the destruction of wildlife; vintage photos and drawings from the heyday of big game hunting, plus disturbing pictures documenting the mass starvation of Tsavo's elephants in the drought of 1971–72. Grisly, yet fascinating.

Britton, J. L., ed. *Birds of East Africa: Their Habitat, Status and Distribution.* Nairobi: East Africa Natural History Society, 1980. For the dedicated lister or specialist.

Brown, Leslie. *East African Coasts and Reefs.* Nairobi: East African Publishing House, 1975. Informative; with photos.

Brown, Leslie. *East African Mountains and Lakes.* Nairobi: East African Publishing House, 1971. Geology and ecology.

Burton, Jane. *Animals of the African Year.* New York: Holt, Rinehart & Winston, 1972. Great ecology primer; color photos.

Douglas-Hamilton, Iain and Oria. *Among the Elephants.* New York: Viking, 1975. Fascinating elephant research at Lake Manyara.

Fossey, Dian. *Gorillas in the Mist.* Boston: Houghton Mifflin, 1983. Her own account of her research among mountain gorillas.

Goodall, Jane. *In the Shadow of Man.* Boston: Houghton Mifflin, 1983. Her bestseller about the early years of her field study of wild chimpanzees.

Goodall, Jane. *The Chimpanzees of Gombe, Patterns of Behavior.* Cambridge, Mass.: Harvard University Press, 1986. A scholarly work.

Jackman, Brian, and Scott, Johnathan. *The Marsh Lions, The Story of an African Lion Pride.* London: Elm Tree Books, 1982.

Karmali, John. *Birds of Africa.* New York: Viking, 1980. An informative survey, with photos in color and black and white.

Karmali, John. *The Beautiful Plants of Kenya.* Nairobi: Westlands Sundries, 1988. Color photos identify native and exotic plants.

Kruuk, Hans. *Hyaena.* London: Oxford University Press, 1975. A highly informative text; with great black and white photos.

Mackworth-Praed, C. W., and Grant, C. H. B. *Birds of Eastern and Northeastern Africa.* London: Longman, reissued 1981. Definitive two-volume set covers identification, distribution, nesting, etc.; a reference work for serious birders.

Martin, Esmond, and Bradley, Chrissee. *Run Rhino Run.* London: Chatto and Windus, 1982. On conservation and the poaching trade.

McLachlan, G. R., and Liversidge, R. *Roberts Birds of South Africa.* Cape Town: Voecker Bird Book Fund, 1980. A reference work.

Moss, Cynthia. *Elephant Memories: Thirteen Years In the Life of an Elephant Family.* New York: Morrow, 1988. Fascinating study.

Moss, Cynthia. *Portraits in the Wild.* Chicago: University of Chicago Press, 1982. A readable compendium of research projects documenting the life histories of a variety of African species.

Myers, Norman. *The Long African Day.* New York: Macmillan, 1972. A wide-ranging look at animals, ecology, and conservation. Photos in color and black and white.

Nichols, Michael. *Gorilla: Struggle for Survival in the Virungas*. With essay by George Schaller. New York: Aperture Press, 1989. A color pictorial on the mountain gorilla.

Reader, John, and Croze, Harvey. *Pyramids of Life*. Philadelphia: Lippincott, 1977. African ecology; black-and-white photos.

Schaller, George. *Golden Shadows, Flying Hooves*. New York: Knopf, 1973. A popular account of his lion research.

Schaller, George. *Serengeti, A Kingdom of Predators*. New York: Knopf, 1972. Records the lives of the carnivores, with color photos.

Schaller, George. *The Serengeti Lion*. Chicago: University of Chicago Press, 1972. Scholarly life study with supporting data.

Schaller, George. *The Year of the Gorilla*. Chicago: University of Chicago Press, 1964. An informative and readable account of his ground-breaking research on the mountain gorilla.

Strum, Shirley C. *Almost Human: A Journey into the World of Baboons*. London: Elm Tree Books, 1987. Baboon behavior.

Van Lawick, Hugo, and Goodall, Jane. *Innocent Killers*. London: 1970. A sympathetic treatment of wild dogs and other predators.

Vesey-Fitzgerald, Desmond. *East African Grasslands*. Nairobi: East African Publishing House, 1973. A good discussion of woodland-grassland succession ecology; for the lay person.

Willock, Collin. *Africa's Rift Valley*. Amsterdam: Time-Life Books, 1974. Geology and natural history of the Rift.

Ziesler, Gunter, and Hofer, Angelika. *Safari: The East African Diaries of a Wildlife Photographer*. New York: Facts on File, 1984. Anecdotal text with excellent color photos.

FIELD GUIDES

Blundell, Michael. *The Wildflowers of Kenya*. London: Collins, 1982. With color-keyed photos and identifying text.

Blundell, Michael. *Collins Guide to the Wildflowers of East Africa*. London: Collins, 1987. See preceding entry—here expanded to include the flora of Tanzania and Uganda.

Carcasson, R. H. *Collins Handguide to the Butterflies of Africa*. London: Collins, 1981. Compact; with color plates.

Dorst, Jean. *A Field Guide to the Larger Mammals of Africa*. Boston: Houghton Mifflin, 1969. Good text and color plates.

FitzSimons, V. F. M. *Field Guide to the Snakes of Southern Africa*. London: Collins, 1970. Also useful for East Africa.

Haltenorth, Theodor, and Diller, Helmut. *A Field Guide to the Mammals of Africa including Madagascar*. Excellent and complete.

Hedges, Norman. *Reptiles and Amphibians of East Africa*. Nairobi: Kenya Literature Bureau, 1983. Not thorough, but useful.

Heinzel, Hermann. *The Birds of Britain and Europe*. London: Collins, 1979. Useful for identifying migrants in Africa.

Mack, Peter. *Night Skies*. Cape Town: Struik Pocket Guides for Southern Africa, 1987. Sky charts and astronomical objects of the southern sky. Also useful for East Africa.

Newlands, Gerry. *Spiders*. Cape Town: Struik Pocket Guides for Southern Africa, 1986. Also useful for East Africa.

Newman, Kenneth. *Newman's Birds of Southern Africa*. Johannesburg, 1983. Useful in southern Tanzania; essential further south. Excellent layout and text; with color illustrations.

Palgrave, Keith Coates. *Trees of Southern Africa*. Cape Town: Struik, 1977. An authoritative, keyed, identification guide.

Patterson, Rod. *Snakes*. Cape Town: Struik Pocket Guides for Southern Africa, 1986. Also useful for East Africa. Compact; excellent text and color illustrations.

Williams, J. G. *Field Guide to the Birds of East Africa*. London: Collins, 1980. The standard field reference; color plates.

Williams, J. G. *Field Guide to the National Parks of East Africa*. London: Collins, 1967. Includes color plates and basic descriptions of the common mammals and birds.

FICTION

Achebe, Chinua, ed. *African Short Stories*. London: Heinemann, 1985. An interesting collection from around the continent.

Achebe, Chinua. *Things Fall Apart*. New York: Astor-Honor, 1959. A great novel about the collision of cultures with the arrival of colonial administration in Africa. Set in Nigeria, the story and themes apply equally to other parts of Africa.

Conrad, Joseph. *Heart of Darkness*. Originally published in 1902. Reprint. Cambridge, Mass.: Bentley, 1981. Horror and madness in King Leopold's Congo.

Hemingway, Ernest. *The Snows of Kilimanjaro and Other Stories*. New York: Scribner's, 1961. Evocative hunting tales.

Kamante. *Longing for Darkness, Kamante's Tales from Out of Africa, with Original Photographs and Quotations from Isak Dinesen*. Collected by Peter Beard. New York: Harcourt Brace Jovanovich, 1975. Richly illustrated Kikuyu stories.

Mwange, Meja. *Going Down River Road*. Nairobi and London: Heinemann, 1976. A portrait of the lives of working class Africans in modern Nairobi.

Naipaul, V. S. *A Bend in the River.* New York: Knopf, 1979. A great novel about modern Africa, set in Mobutu's Zaire.

Ruark, Robert. *Something of Value.* New York: Doubleday, 1955. A novel set during the Mau Mau Emergency in Kenya.

Ruark, Robert. *Uhuru.* New York: McGraw-Hill, 1962. A story of Kenya during the first years of independence.

Soyinka, Wole. *Collected Plays.* Oxford: Oxford University Press, 1974. The works of Africa's first Nobel Laureate for literature.

Soyinka, Wole, ed. *Poems of Black Africa.* New York: Hill & Wang, 1975. A collection of African voices.

Wa Thiong'o, Ngugi. *Petals of Blood.* New York: Dutton, 1978. A novel that probes the political and economic inequities of post-independence Kenya, by Kenya's best-known black writer.

MASAI

Saibull, Solomon Ole, and Carr, Rachel. *Herd and Spear: the Masai of East Africa.* London: Collins, 1981. An interesting portrait by the conservator of the Ngorongoro Conservation Area.

Saitoti, Tepilit Ole. *Masai.* New York: Abrams, 1980. A superlative book, with color photography by Carol Beckwith.

Sankan, S. S. Ole. *The Masai.* Nairobi: East African Literature Bureau, 1971. Not very readable, but crammed with information on Masai customs and legends; includes riddles and proverbs.

KENYA

Adamson, Joy. *The Peoples of Kenya.* New York: Harcourt Brace Jovanovich, 1967. A readable account of vanishing tribal customs, with beautifully detailed paintings and photographs.

Amin, Mohamed. *Cradle of Mankind.* London: Chatto & Windus, 1981. Safari in northern Kenya. Great color photos of tribespeople.

Amin, Mohamed. *Journey Through Kenya.* London: Bodley Head, 1982. An overview of the country, with color plates.

Dinesen, Isak. *Isak Dinesen's Africa: Images of the Wild Continent from the Writer's Life and Words.* Introduction by Judith Thurman. San Francisco: Sierra Club Books, 1985. Color photos.

Dinesen, Isak. *Out of Africa.* New York: Random House, 1938. The author's acclaimed account of her life in the Kenya colony between the world wars. Brilliantly written.

Ghaidan, Usam. *Lamu: A Study of the Swahili Town.* Nairobi: East African Literature Bureau, 1975. In depth; illustrated.

Graham, Alistair. *Eyelids of Morning.* Greenwich, Conn.: New York Graphic Society, 1973. Fascinating story of the crocodiles and peoples of Lake Turkana. Richly illustrated; photos by Peter Beard in color and black and white.

Hillaby, John. *Journey to the Jade Sea*. New York: Simon & Schuster, 1964. A camel safari through northern Kenya.

Huxley, Elspeth. *On the Edge of the Rift*. New York: Morrow, 1962. More memoirs of life in Kenya.

Huxley, Elspeth. *The Flame Trees of Thika*. New York: Morrow, 1959. Immensely popular story of her girlhood on a settler farm in Kenya during the First World War.

Huxley, Elspeth. *The Mottled Lizard*. Leicester: Ulverscroft, 1983. Further stories of her youth.

Johnson, Osa. *Four Years in Paradise*. Philadelphia: Lippincott, 1941. The Johnsons' life at Marsabit in the 1920s.

Jones, David Keith. *Shepherds of the Desert*. London: Elm Tree Books, 1984. A good primer on the tribes of northern Kenya, with excellent photos in both color and black and white.

Kenyatta, Jomo. *Facing Mount Kenya*. London: Secker & Narburg, 1938. A celebrated ethnological treatise on the Kikuyu people, by the man who was to become Kenya's first president.

Markham, Beryl. *West with the Night*. San Francisco: North Point Press, 1983. A beautifully written autobiography covering an extraordinary woman's youth in the Kenya colony and the pioneering days of aviation.

Miller, Charles. *The Lunatic Express*. New York: Macmillan, 1971. The strange history of the building of the Uganda railroad.

Mollison, Simon. *Kenya's Coast*. Nairobi: East African Publishing House, 1971. Excellent for historical, ethnological, and natural history information, though dated on hotels.

Patterson, Col. J. H. *The Man-Eaters of Tsavo*. New York: Macmillan, 1927. The hunt for Kenya's most infamous lions.

Spencer, Paul. *The Samburu*. Berkeley: University of California Press, 1965. Scholarly anthropological study.

Trzebinski, Errol. *The Kenya Pioneers*. New York: Norton, 1986. The early history of a colony filled with colorful characters.

TANZANIA

Amin, Mohamed; Willets, Duncan; and Marshall, Peter. *Journey Through Tanzania*. London: Bodley Head, 1984. A survey of the country with color photographs.

Grzimek, Bernard. *Serengeti Shall Not Die*. New York: Dutton, 1960. An influential book, though somewhat out of date.

Huxley, Elspeth, and Van Lawick, Hugo. *Last Days of Eden.* New York: Morrow, 1977. The parks and wilderness places of northern Tanzania, with color photos.

Iliffe, John. *Tanganyika Under German Rule.* Nairobi: East African Publishing House, 1972. History.

Iwago, Mitsuaki. *Serengeti: Natural Order on the African Plain.* San Francisco: Chronicle Books, 1987. A superb photo pictorial.

Kaplan, Irving, ed. *Tanzania: A Country Study.* Washington: American University, 1978. Geographical and political portrait.

Kimambo, I. N., and Temu, A. J. *A History of Tanzania.* Nairobi: East African Publishing House, 1969.

Matthiessen, Peter. *Sand Rivers.* New York: Viking, 1981. A personal account of a foot safari in the Selous Game Reserve. Photos by Hugo van Lawick.

Matthiessen, Peter. *The Tree Where Man Was Born.* New York: Crescent Books, 1972. Great descriptions of safaris in northern Tanzania and Kenya, with photos by Eliot Porter.

Van Lawick, Hugo. *Savage Paradise.* New York: Morrow, 1977. Superb color photos of the Serengeti.

KILIMANJARO

Hutchinson, J. A., ed. *Tanzania Notes and Records: Kilimanjaro.* Dar es Salaam: The Tanzania Society, 1974. Geology, fauna, flora, climbing history, Chagga legends and culture.

Lange, Harold. *Kilimanjaro: The White Roof of Africa.* Seattle: The Mountaineers, 1985. Illustrated history of the mountain.

Reader, John. *Kilimanjaro.* New York: Universe Books, 1982. Excellent text, with photos by author.

RWANDA, ZAIRE, AND UGANDA

Forbath, Peter. *The River Congo.* New York: Harper & Row, 1977. History from the Kingdom of the Kongo to the birth of Zaire.

Hallet, Jean-Pierre. *Congo Kitabu.* New York: Random House, 1964. The author's amazing adventures; interesting information on the Pygmies.

Hallet, Jean-Pierre. *Pygmy Kitabu.* New York: Random House, 1973. Further adventures.

Mowat, Farley. *Woman in the Mists.* New York: Warner Books, 1987. An intimate biography of gorilla researcher Dian Fossey.

Synge, Patrick. *Mountains of the Moon.* New York: Hippocrene Books, 1986. A reprint of a naturalist's 1934 trip to Uganda.

Turnbull, Colin. *The Forest People.* New York: Doubleday, 1962. A wonderful account of the author's anthropological research among the BaMbuti Pygmies in the Ituri Forest.

MOUNTAINEERING AND TREKKING

Allan, Iain, ed. *Guide to Mount Kenya and Kilimanjaro.* Nairobi: Mountain Club of Kenya, 1981. Covers geology, natural history, glaciers, and climate, as well as descriptions of climbing and trekking routes.

Boy, Gordon, and Allan, Iain. *Snowcaps on the Equator.* London: Bodley Head, 1989. Excellent treatment of all the great African mountains, plus many lesser-known ranges. Includes history, ethnology, flora and fauna, and climbing lore. Color photos by Clive Ward.

Benuzzi, Felice. *No Picnic on Mount Kenya.* London: Kinder, 1952. Amazing story of Italian prisoners of war who escaped just to attempt an ascent of Mount Kenya.

Osmaston, H. A., and Pasteur, D. *Guide to the Ruwenzori.* Goring, Reading, Berkshire, U.K.: West Col, 1972. Essential for both trekkers and climbers.

Robson, Peter. *Mountains of Kenya.* Nairobi: East African Publishing House, 1969. A brief trekking and climbing guide.

Taylor, Rob. *The Breach.* New York: Coward, McCann & Geoghegan, 1981. Account of a disastrous ice-climbing adventure on Kili.

Wielochowski, Andrew. *East Africa International Mountain Guide.* Goring, Reading, Berkshire, U.K.: West Col, 1986. Describes Kenya's best rock climbing sites, as well as technical routes on Mount Kenya and Kilimanjaro. Also covers trekking those mountains, the Ruwenzori, and spelunking sites in Kenya.

TRAVEL GUIDES

Amin, Mohamed, ed. *Insight Guides: Kenya.* Hong Kong: APA Productions (Prentice-Hall), 1985. Thorough and informative.

Bradt, Hilary. *Backpacker's Africa.* Cambridge, Mass.: Bradt Enterprises, 1983. Selected treks in East, Central, and Southern Africa.

Crowther, Geoff. *Africa on a Shoestring.* Berkeley, Calif.: Lonely Planet, 1985. The entire continent for the budget traveler.

Crowther, Geoff. *East Africa: A Travel Survival Guide.* Berkeley, Calif.: Lonely Planet, 1987. Indispensable for the budget traveler.

Glen, Simon and Jan. *Sahara Handbook.* London: Lascelles, 1981. A goldmine of information for outfitting a vehicular expedition.

Hewat, Johnathan and Theresa. *Overland and Beyond.* London: Lascelles, 1981. Material useful for driving across Africa.

Jewell, J. H. A. *Mombasa and the Kenya Coast: A Visitor's Guide*. Nairobi: Evans Brothers, 1987. Restaurants, hotels, activities.

Macintyre, Kate. *The Nairobi Guide*. London: Macmillan, 1986.

Nolting, Mark. *African Safari: The Complete Travel Guide to Ten Top Game Viewing Countries*. Pompano Beach: Global Travel Publications, 1987. A summary of parks and attractions.

Taylor, Jane and Leah. *Fielding's Literary Africa*. New York: Morrow, 1987. Safari routes keyed to classics of African literature.

Tomkinson, Michael. *Kenya: A Holiday Guide*. London: London & Hammamet, 1981. Compact and informative; especially useful to self-drive motorists.

SOME USEFUL SOURCES FOR HARD-TO-FIND BOOKS

Buteo Books/Safari Museum Books, P.O. Box 481, Vermillion, SD 57069. Tel.: (605) 624-4343. Birds, natural history, Africana.

Phileas Fogg's, #87 Stanford Shopping Center, Palo Alto, CA 94304. Tel.: (415) 327-1754; (800) 533-FOGG; (800) 233-FOGG (in CA). Books and maps for the traveler.

Russel Friedman Books, 23 Paisley Place, London, Ontario N5X 3J3, Canada. Tel.: (519) 667-1434. FAX: (519) 667-1314. For nature books published in South Africa.

West Col Productions, Goring, Reading, Berkshire RG8 9AA, England. Tel.: (0491) 681284. Mountaineering books and maps.

Index

Key: B = Burundi; R = Rwanda; T = Tanzania;
U = Uganda; Z = Eastern Zaire